The Handmade Paper Industry in Western Fujian: A Social History Study

By Chen Yao

Translated by Cai Ruizhen & Wu Ai

CHICAGO ACADEMIC PRESS

The Handmade Paper Industry in Western Fujian: A Social History Study
Author: Chen Yao
Translator: Cai Ruizhen & Wu Ai
Language: English
Word Count (for space of all pages): Approximately 400 Thousand words
Publisher: Chicago Academic Press
Number of Pages: 488
ISBN: 979-8-901-86004-5

Publishing   Chicago Academic Press

5923 N Artesian Ave

Chicago IL 60659

Email   contact@chicagoacademicpress.com

Website   http://chicagoacademicpress.com/

Book Size   6X9 inches

First Edition   November, 2025

Translator Profile

Cai Ruizhen is a Professor and Editor-in-chief of the Journal of Sanming University, and serves as a Master's supervisor in Fujian Normal University and Fujian University of Technology. She is a council member of the Social Translatology Committee,China Association for Comparative Studies of English and Chinese. Her academic focus encompasses social translatology, translation pedagogy, and pragmatic translation. She has completed 14 teaching and research projects including one funded by the National Social Science Fund, published 5 monographs and textbooks on translation and more than 40 academic papers.

Wu Ai is an associate professor with a Master's degree, who serves as a Master's supervisor at Sanming University. She spent four months as a visiting scholar at the University of Delaware, USA. Her research interests lie in foreign linguistics and applied linguistics. She has presided over three provincial-level projects and four municipal-level projects, published 11 papers and contributed to editing 3 textbooks.

About the Author

Chen Yao is an Associate Professor at the School of History and Cultural Heritage, Xiamen University. She received her B.A. and M.A. in History from Xiamen University and her Ph.D. in History from The Chinese University of Hong Kong. She has been a Visiting Scholar under the Hong Kong SAR University Grants Committee's Areas of Excellence (AoE) project "Historical Anthropology of Chinese Society" funded by the University Grants Committee of the Hong Kong Special Administrative Region, Chinese University of Hong Kong, as well as at the Institute for Research in Humanities, Kyoto University, Japan. Her research has long focused on the socio-economic history of regional societies from the Ming and Qing dynasties onward. She is the author of *The Dynamics of Grain Purchase and Sale: Rice Trade and Local Society in Xiangtan during the Qing Dynasty* (Xiamen University Press, 2017) and *Rivers and Voyages: Boatmen and Wooden Sailboat Shipping in the Middle Reaches of the Yangtze River in Modern Times* (The Commercial Press, 2023).

Foreword I

Having carefully read Professor Chen Yao's manuscript *Yukou Paper*, I was moved in more ways than I had expected. This response, as I gradually came to realize, stemmed not only from the depth of Chen Yao's meticulous fieldwork and the scholarly weight of the book itself, but also from resonances with my own nearly two decades of field research on traditional Chinese papermaking. Her work stirred reflections long lingered in my mind and prompted associations that arose naturally in the course of reading.

My first response, of course, was directed toward Yukou Paper as an object of study in its own right. Yukou paper was, in modern and contemporary China, one of the largest categories of handmade paper in terms of production scale and workforce, with a distribution network that extended widely and deeply, all while embodying distinct cultural and traditional traits. For instance, it is the most representative variety within China's bamboo-based raw material papermaking tradition. What makes it representative is not only the authenticity of its materials and techniques, but also the rare synthesis it achieved: combining a mass-market industry serving everyday needs with the preservation of high-level artisanal skill. Furthermore, the production of Yukou paper was concentrated in the Hakka regions of western Fujian—including both the southern and northern subregions, as well as adjacent counties in southern Jiangxi—and extended into smaller She communities as well. Historically, its principal markets included regions of Chaozhou, Meizhou, and Guangzhou, from where it was further exported to overseas Chinese communities in Southeast Asia, particularly those of Hakka descent. Producers, traders, and consumers of Yukou paper were all closely tied to Hakka cultural life, woven seamlessly into the rhythms of Hakka society.

Such realizations inevitably draw attention to the striking absence of sustained scholarly inquiry into Yukou paper, despite its historical significance as a cultural heritage with wide influence across southeastern China and the Chinese communities in Southeast Asia. Since 2018, my own research team, under the project the *Chinese Handmade Paper Archive*, has undertaken systematic investigations into the survival of papermaking traditions in Fujian. Because the handmade bamboo paper industry that once thrived in northern and eastern Fujian has all but vanished, our field research has necessarily concentrated on the only remaining "living" tradition of Yukou paper in western Fujian (including the variant known as Xishan paper in Jiangle county, which has been inscribed in the first batch of China's National Intangible Cultural Heritage list). Over the course of nearly four years and about twenty field trips, supplemented by extensive archival work, despite Yukou paper being a classic, comprehensive case study of modern Hakka papermaking techniques and ethnic community culture, we have been struck by the paucity of scholarship devoted to this subject. Apart from a handful of memoirs published in local historical journals and a few scattered academic articles, the existing literature is thin: Lin Cunhe's 1941 survey *Papers of Fujian*; *A History of Papermaking in Changting*, a compilation led by Huang Majin; the 1955 local government report on papermaking in Zhiping, Ninghua County; and the works of Gui Shuzhong, including his documentary *Yukou Paper* and *Visual Records of Local Customs in Western Fujian: From Yukou Paper to Old Clan Genealogies*. Yet a holistic study of the broader Yukou paper system and the papermaking industry in Hakka regions—encompassing craftsmanship, culture, ethnicity, consumption, and evolutionary dynamics—remains a glaring gap.

It is precisely in this context that the significance of Chen Yao's *Yukou Paper* becomes clear. The book represents, to my mind, a contribution of scholarly value in at least three respects.

First, it is the very first monograph devoted to the broader Yukou paper system. It constructs a comprehensive framework for analysis and thereby offers a foundational model for subsequent studies in a field long lacking holistic inquiry. The book encompasses conceptual clarification, integration of academic and local sources, mapping of production regions and networks of papermaking sheds and depots, accounts of raw materials and technologies, genealogies of clans and cultural lineages in the Hakka heartland of western Fujian, historical economic data on production and consumption, and the trade routes by which Yukou paper circulated both domestically and abroad. While the study naturally gives greater depth to the core area of Zhiping in Ninghua—due to commission requirements and the author's emphasis on Zhiping itself—the work nonetheless surveys all major production areas with varying breadth and depth.

Second, the study demonstrates the methodological rigor and scholarly discipline of a historian. Unlike memoirs or descriptive accounts that confine themselves to recording techniques or cultural phenomena, or papers that merely verify a single claim through literature, Chen Yao and her team conducted their research through a rigorous combination of historical philology, cultural anthropology, and oral ethnography. The first research trajectory took the form of comprehensive field investigations and village residencies among the Hakka and She papermaking communities linked to the broader Yukou paper system. With crucial guidance from local experts, including Gui Shuzhong, the team assembled detailed first-hand evidence on production villages, paper markets, depots, significant craftsmen, and paper workshops. These findings are anchored in clearly defined temporal and spatial settings and involve concrete social actors. The study's engagement with a large number of field participants also produced oral narratives and observational records that are both substantial and strikingly vivid. The second trajectory of inquiry is embodied in a meticulous effort to retrieve and synthesize a wide spectrum of textual sources bearing upon Yukou paper, its artisanal communities, and the broader history of its circulation across China and beyond. The materials brought together include published monographs, references in historical records to papermaking villages, local histories and memoirs, government archives, statistical reports compiled by trade organizations across eras, and genealogical manuscripts handed down by prominent lineages in the core producing areas. While this endeavor may not be wholly pioneering in its discoveries, its systematic compilation and thoughtful organization provide a critical foundation for subsequent scholarship.

Third, I was especially drawn to several features that align closely with my own interests on Fujian Yukou paper in the *Chinese Handmade Paper Archive*. Notable among these are: the multi-perspectival analysis of the concept and naming of "Yukou paper," an issue long debated without consensus around the origin of its name and its connotations, where Chen Yao's team has made meaningful progress; the compilation of documents and oral testimonies with key figures from that era relating to papermaking in the Central Soviet Region, which sheds light on an under-explored historical episode; and the detailed reconstruction of trade routes by which Yukou paper moved from Zhiping's Neishan core through Changting to Hakka areas in Guangdong and on to Southeast Asia. This provides a crucial, yet understudied, perspective on the relationship between Yukou paper and the Hakka ethnic group.

As someone who has long dedicated to field research on Chinese papermaking traditions and the cultural lineages of multi-ethnic craft communities, I cannot but feel a profound resonance upon encountering this first systematic and integrative study of Yukou paper, undertaken by Chen Yao and her team. It is both a work that stirs personal associations and affinities, and one whose scholarly merits I am glad to commend with sincerity.

Tang Shukun

Institute for Handmade Paper Studies at University of Science and Technology of China

September 5, 2023

Forward II

Much of Antiquity Has Faded Away—In Lieu of a Foreword

How many traces of antiquity have already faded into the past? How often has the decline of Yukou paper been lamented in the melancholy tones of autumn birds? More than a decade ago, when I first conceived the idea of filming *Yukou Paper* as my debut documentary, it was, as a close friend observed, less a matter of historical consciousness than the pastoral nostalgia of a poet's temperament.

Afterwards, the documentary *Yukou Paper* began to circulate through film festivals and screenings, drawing attention beyond my expectations. Audiences would press me with the question: what motivated you to make this film? The truth is, there was no lofty mission, no youthful sense of cultural responsibility. If the work gained a wider resonance, I suspect it was because the very name "Yukou paper" captured people's imagination. The distinguished curator Zuo Jing, in particular, championed the film in various venues, and through his recommendations I found myself unexpectedly bound up with the destiny of Yukou paper. Enthusiasts seeking to buy Yukou paper, journalists, and researchers began to seek me out, until I became, almost unwittingly, a "contract person" for this paper hidden deep in the mountains.

The original film was made by a small, makeshift circle of close friends—Kong Delin, Li Jingqing, Hu Guilin, among others. Without these kindred spirits brought together by chance, the project could never have materialized. Yet, the film has its shortcomings—shortcomings that have been questioned and criticized. These range from the "amateur" status of its creators to gaps in recording Yukou paper's production processes, and even limitations in its value as visual documentation of Yukou paper.

For that reason, I once rashly promised that a second film, *Yukou Paper II*, would one day be made in the style of a scientific or educational record. That casual vow, uttered half in jest, became the quiet force that carried me through more than ten years of revisiting Yukou paper—sometimes with joy, often with frustration. I would return again and again to Hu Lanshan, the master papermaker featured in the film, coaxing him with words of encouragement—"hold on, just hold on!" I once described this years-long perseverance with Yukou paper as "holding on by a thread." Whether filming missing stages of production, revisiting sites for my *Visual Records of Local Customs in Western Fujian: From Yukou Paper to Old Clan Genealogies*, or accompanying visitors from afar, I lost count of the journeys made into the mountains. "I've eaten half your family's rice bowls empty," I joked with Hu. And yet, time after time, he revealed himself as a living encyclopedia of Yukou paper, each encounter yielding new knowledge, new discoveries.

After 1949, genealogy compilation ceased (to date, I have found no genealogies in Ninghua from 1949 to the early 1980s), and the "Destroy the Four Olds" campaign severed many traditional practices. With reform and opening-up, however, a wave of traditional cultural revival emerged naturally. Genealogy compilation and ancestral hall construction gradually resumed, even becoming widespread—and this in turn sparked surge in the demand for Yukou paper. By the 1980s and early 1990s, workers and paper merchants from other regions flocked to Zhiping, drawing huge crowds to Kaizi Mountain in Gaofeng Village (at an altitude of 700–800 meters). Back then, the village even had hotels, restaurants, karaoke bars, video parlors, and hair salons. In my view, this prosperity stemmed from two factors: first, the revival of genealogy compilation; second, the massive demand for ritual paper in Southern Fujian, Guangdong, and Southeast Asia. Yet this "golden age" was, in truth, little more than the mass production of ritual paper for superstitious use. Once machine-made paper entered the market, traditional methods collapsed almost overnight, leaving only a few like Hu Lanshan and Lei Yusheng struggling to hold on.

In the summer of 2021, Professor Chen Yao of Xiamen University brought her students to Ninghua to conduct research on handmade paper. I told her how, in my own village of Shuiqian, it had taken me four years to traverse nearly every settlement—15 administrative villages, 239 natural villages, and 68 historic sites—merely to complete a rudimentary survey. Such work far exceeds the strength of any individual. So I proposed: if we could secure funding, or if the government would take the lead in collaborating with universities, we could arrange for students to come to Ninghua for summer social practice—sending a group to each township, and spending one or two years to document every village in the county. Villages are collapsing, documents are vanishing, elders are passing away—in terms of preserving local cultural information, this is a task of urgent importance. At just such a moment, the local government of Zhiping She Ethnic Township, in preparing to establish the Yukou Paper Museum, sought urgently to collect and systematize relevant materials. Coincidentally, I had been assigned to work in Zhiping—the once "Paper Capital"—as a village resident, and was tasked with deciding who could take on this responsibility. So I found myself both persuading Professor Chen to undertake the task and recommending her to the local authorities.

She accepted, and since then has led her students repeatedly into Ninghua and the surrounding papermaking regions of Changting, Liancheng, and Shicheng. They have gathered archival records and folk documents, visited production sites and ruins, and conducted extensive oral history interviews, thus grounding their research in first-hand empirical investigation. Acting as a local guide and occasional porter, I witnessed firsthand the diligence and methodological rigor of a young scholar in the field, and gained much from the experience myself.

If one's aim was merely to slap together a project by cutting and pasting existing materials, repeating hearsay and perpetuating errors, there would be no difference from local cultural enthusiasts who are content with superficial understanding. The myth that Yukou paper once printed the *Selected Works of Mao Zedong*, for instance, still circulates uncritically in people in Ninghua, appearing even in the 30th volume of *Ninghua Historical and Cultural Materials* (published this year, p. 168). Similarly, facile explanations of the term "kou" as a mere unit of measure persist without scrutiny.

Professor Chen, however, brings a spirit of critical inquiry: always asking why claims are made, on what grounds, and with what evidence. Her work clarifies and corrects long-standing misconceptions in the history of Chinese papermaking and resolves many puzzles that had troubled me in my own *Visual Records of Local Customs in Western Fujian: From Yukou Paper to Old Clan Genealogies*.

In the two years of her investigations, I have also taken the opportunity to fulfill my long-cherished goals: the filming of *Yukou Paper II*[1] and the creation of a cultural map of Ninghua Zhiping Papermaking Cultural Heritage Site Group.[2]

The present volume, *Yukou Paper*, grew out of that collective effort to gather and organize materials for the township government. Yet Professor Chen, approaching the subject as a historian, has gone far beyond the mere

---

1 Documentary *Yukou Paper II* (41 minutes), produced by Zuo Jing and Wang Yanzhi, filmed and directed by Gui Shuzhong; presented in the first season of the "New Culture Producers" project, *Revival of Handicrafts*, jointly initiated by the Power Station of Art (Shanghai) and the CHANEL Culture Fund in 2022.
2 "Ninghua Zhiping Papermaking Cultural Heritage Site Group" website: https://yukoupaper.com/

compilation of local records. From the objective stance of a cultural outsider, she traces Yukou paper through the academic lenses of economic, social, and cultural history, situates Yukou paper within broader contexts, and provides both interpretation and narration. This is, to date, the only serious academic monograph devoted to Yukou paper, and it stands as a work of scholarly integrity and devotion.

If, in the future, humankind truly enters an age "without paper," then we may yet be grateful that this dispassionate record endures—preserving the story of Yukou paper, and with it, the memory of a world and a craft now passing into history.

Ning Yuanguai (Gui Shuzhong)

July 31, 2023

Contents

1. The Story of Yukou Paper

For millennia, paper has been so thoroughly integrated into everyday life that few recall a time before its invention and widespread use. In China, the birthplace of paper, hemp paper took root in cultural life as early as the 3rd century. Yet paper did not enter the households of the general populace until the Song dynasty (960-1279 CE), when papermaking had become a technically advanced and economically efficient process. Prior to the 4th century, China's official documentation and the intellectual labors of the literati relied on primitive meterials—oracle bones, bronze vessels, bamboo and wood slips, as well as silk fabrics—many of which were later preserved underground or passed down through generations. For the vast multitude, however, paper remained a rare commodity in daily life, and even more rarely used. Their lives unfolded in what can only be termed a "pre-paper" epoch.

Now, in the 21st century, people around the world have gradually been distancing themselves from paper and paper-based products. Activities such as reading, writing, creating, and information dissemination—once grounded in paper—now have migrated in mass to electronic devices and online platforms. Traditional paper formats—from newspapers and station-ery to physical currency—have undergone digital transformation. Paradox-ically, paper packaging resurfaces as a retro trend with its packaging framed as an eco-friendly choice. Only paper for calligraphy and the sanitary needs remain relatively irreplaceable. And these have sparked renewed obsession in paper quality standards. Some have noticed, almost with dread: a paper-less world is no longer a fantasy, but a looming return. We may ask: Will the age-old legacy of papermaking and paper use fade into history? How have we made and used paper over the past thousands of years? In what ways has paper fundamentally reshaped human civilization? Which specific domains will still necessitate paper usage, and what specialized qualities does this demand? These questions signal a growing awareness: it may be time to revisit and reflect on a "paper-based mode of life."

As the anxiety increases with the uncertain fate of paper and printed materials[3], Fujian's traditional handmade Yukou paper and its techniques, have come under the spotlight and entered the national register of intangible cultural heritage alongside with other time-honored papermaking traditions.[4]

---

3 Alexander Monro, *The Paper Trail: An Unexpected History of a Revolutionary Invention*, translated by Liao Yanbo, Lianjing Publishing Co., Ltd., 2017;
Oodaira Kazue, *The God of Paper* (紙さまの話), photographed by Kobayashi Kiyu, translated by Yang Ling, the Shanghai People's Press, 2020;
The Multigraph Collective, *Interacting with Print: Elements of Reading in the Era of Print Saturation,* translated by Fu Li, Beijing United Publishing Co., 2021;
Lothar Muller, *White Magic: The Age of Paper*, translated by He Xiaoyi and Song Qiong, Guangdong People Publishing House, 2022.
4 In addition to the bamboo paper-making techniques of places such as Fuyang and Wenzhou in Zhejiang, Jiajiang in Sichuan, Jianyang in Fujian, and Leiyang and Longhui in Hunan, techniques for producing Xuan paper in Jing County, Anhui; Liansi paper in Yanshan County, Jiangxi; as well as various local methods of making paper from mulberry bark, hemp, and sandalwood bark, and even the handmade papermaking techniques of ethnic minorities such as the Uyghur, Tibetan, Dai, and Naxi peoples, have all been included in the national list of representative items of intangible cultural heritage. The Yukou paper-making technique was included in the representative list of intangible cultural heritage at the provincial level in Fujian in 2019.

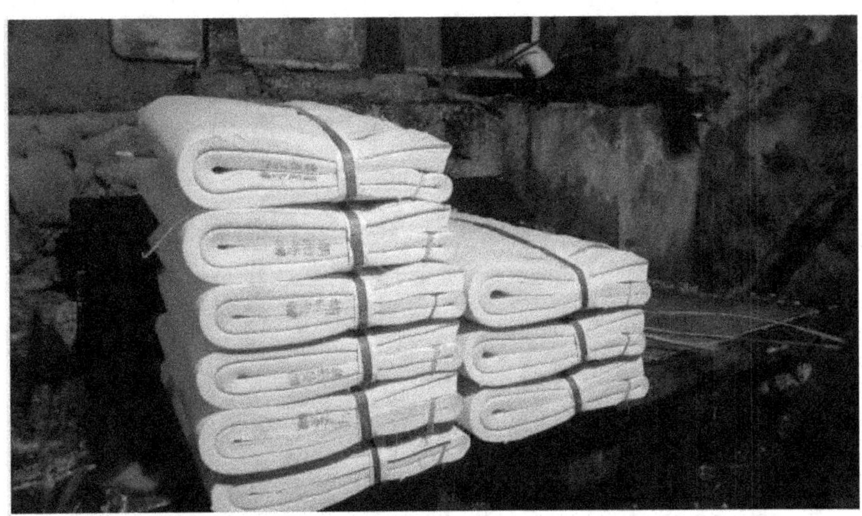

(Pic1 Yukou Paper Preserved in the Home of Hu Lanshan in September, 2021)

In 2006, CCTV-7's *Searching the World* dispatched its crew to the bamboo-covered hills of Zhiping Township in Ninghua County. The resulting program, *Paper Workshops in the Bamboo Township*, bore witness to the craft. A few years later, in 2009, independent director Gui Shuzhong (real name: Ning Yuanguai) released his documentary *Yukou Paper*, a detailed chronicle of the final manual workshop and the intricate production processes.[5] By 2017, the CCTV-4 team behind *Chinese World* returned to Zhiping and produced another episode—*Yukou Paper in Ninghua*—further preserving the visual memory of this regional art. Meanwhile, scholars like Tang Shukun advanced the study of papermaking through a dual approach: field investigation and laboratory science. Their surveys extended across provinces—Yunnan, Guizhou, Guangxi, Anhui, Zhejiang—documenting not only the practices of the Han majority but also those of minority groups such as Xizang, Dai, Bai, Naxi, and Miao. Recently, the arc of research and preservation has curved back toward Fujian, focusing anew on the heritage and continuation of Yukou papermaking.[6]

Guided by both dominant media channels and independent outlets, the broader public has gradually come to recognize a painful contradiction: on one hand, the ingenuity of China's traditional handmade papermaking dazzles the imagination; on the other, its actual survival hangs by a thread. As late as the 1980s and 1990s, the last generation of artisans in the mountainous west of Fujian were still engaged in the mass production of Yukou paper. Today, as they reflect on those years of labor, their hearts may swell with emotion, but the memories feel so distant, as if from another lifetime. It is precisely for this reason that there is no better time than now to write a chronicle of Yukou paper. To narrate the story of Yukou paper, to revisit the craft and the memory it bears, and to document the lived experiences of those who shaped their existence around paper—this, too, is a vital act of historical preservation.

---

5 Gui Shuzhong, *Filmic Ethnography of Local Customs in Western Fujian: from The Yukou Paper to Old Genealogy*, Chinese National Publishing House, 2019
6 Tang Shukun et al., *Library of Chinese Handmade Paper*, University of Science and Technology of China Publishing House, 2020;
Tang Shukun and Zhu Yun, "Handmade Paper Production in Southern China and Its Industrial Ecosystem Building: A Field Research," *Southeast Culture*, No. 4, 2017.

What, then, is Yukou paper? What technological characteristics define its making? How should we assess its quality? When did the Yukou paper industry take shape, what locality served as its core, where did its products circulate, and how much value did it generate? What historical singularities marked the society of its production region, and what kind of legacy did it leave behind? Faced with all these questions, those who once toiled in Yukou paper production could respond with pride. Yet despite their living memory, systematic historical verification, archival collation, and coherent scholarly narration have all remained absent. This book undertakes the task of addressing that absence. It gathers and organizes a diverse array of materials—from local government records and investigative reports to newspapers, magazines, genealogies, contracts, ritual observations, and oral interviews—to compose a specialized historical account of "Yukou Paper and Its Craftsmanship", a tradition officially recognized as intangible cultural heritage of Fujian Province.

The study begins by probing the meaning of the name "Yukou" and its place in the history of papermaking technology, the technical procedures for producing Yukou paper, and the tools and sites required. With Zhiping She Ethnic Township in Ninghua County—honored as the "Paper Capital of Western Fujian" and renowned for its superior Neishan Yukou paper—as its geographic focal point, the book traces the industry's spread into nearby regions, including Anjie and Tiechang Townships in Changting County, as well as Hengjiang Town in Shicheng County, Jiangxi Province. This regional case study further investigates the natural conditions of these mountainous locales, the interethnic relations between the She and Hakka peoples, the structure of village clans and ritual alliances, and the rise and influence of papermaking in Zhiping. It analyzes the commodity chains of production, distribution, and sales amid the upheavals of modern history, and examines the history of paper, the papermaking industry, and the socio-economic developments surrounding the transformation of the Yukou paper industry—from a system of unified state purchasing and selling to market-based operations in contemporary times. In doing so, the book endeavors to embed Yukou paper and its traditional craftsmanship within broader contexts: the cultural logic of rural society, the institutional mechanisms of the national economy, and the scope of the global paper market. Through this lens, it recounts the rise, decline and reform of its industry and communities over time.

The present volume sets out from the advances made in the technological history of paper, tracing the evolution of China's traditional papermaking methods while illuminating the specific technical traits of Yukou paper. It also provides a critical interpretation of the term "Yukou paper" itself. From there, the inquiry turns to the studies in the economic and cultural histories of paper, mapping scholarly efforts to understand the traditional handmade paper industry and its accompanying cultural constructs. This work further calls for a social-historical approach that situates the Yukou paper enterprise within the broader spatiotemporal matrix of Chinese artisanal papermaking, so as to reconstruct the development of this distinctive paper tradition.

1.1. Yukou in Paper

China, the birthplace of paper, boasts a verifiable history of papermaking spanning over two millennia. As the practice and experimentation of papermaking evolved into a conscious endeavor, its techniques entered the field of vision of court historians and literati. Since the Han dynasty onwards, methods of papermaking gained written documentation and achieved ever-widening dissemination. In more recent centuries, the study of paper history has become an integral part of the study of the history of science and technology. Scholars from China and abroad have delved into academic discussions. They started detailed academic study of the history of paper from multiple perspectives: textual research, historical evolution, artifact authentication, technological reconstruction, and technological transmission. Yet debates have long simmered over issues such as the origins of ancient Chinese papermaking, the identity of its inventor, and even the very definition of "paper"—disagreements that persist to this day.[7] Researchers have attempted to define paper based on raw materials, production processes, quality, functionality, and usage. Drawing on definitions from modern encyclopedias and specialist works, scholar Pan Jixing proposed the following: "Paper, in the traditional sense, refers to a material used for writing, printing, or packaging. It is made from plant fibers. These fibers undergo mechanical and chemical treatments to become relatively

---

7 Lao Kan, "The Invention of Paper in China", *Bulletin of the Institute of History and Philology*, Academia Sinica, Vol. 19, 1948;

Chen Pan, "On Papermaking as Inferred from the Ancient Practice of Bleaching Raw Cotton—Also a Rebuttal of the Claim that Pre-Cai Lun 'Paper' Was Actually Silk or Hemp Fabric", *Bulletin of the Academia Sinica*, No. 1, 1954;

Tsuen-Hsuin Tsien, translated by Liu Zuwei, *The History of Chinese Science and Technology: Paper and Printing*, Shanghai Guji Press, 1990;

Tsien Tsuen-Hsuin, "New Evidence on the Origin of Paper: A Tentative Study of the Character 'Zhi' (Paper) in Qin Bamboo Slips from the Warring States Period", *Wenxian*, No. 1, 2002;

Fu Kui, "References to 'Zhi' (纸) and 'Zhi' (帋) in Eastern Han Bamboo Slips Unearthed in Changsha and Related Issues", *Journal of Chinese Historical Studies*, No. 2, 2019.

pure and dispersed. Mixed with water to form a pulp, the mixture is then passed through a porous mold (a screen) that drains the water, leaving a thin, wet layer of fibers on the screen's surface. Once dried, this layer becomes a sheet-like material with a certain strength, its cellulose fibers bound together by hydrogen bonds to create a substance of structural integrity."[8] Given this definition, one might ask: What, then, is Yukou paper? What place does it occupy in the temporal and spatial landscape of ancient Chinese papermaking's overall development? And what significance does it hold in the history of technology? To answer these questions, we must delve deeper into the broader trends of evolution in ancient Chinese papermaking, as well as examine specific properties of Yukou paper: the nature of its raw materials, its manufacturing procedures, its technological sophistication, modes of applications, historical references to its name, and its regions of primary production. Only then can we piece together its story.

Regarding the history of Chinese papermaking technology, since the mid-20th century, leading scholars in the history of Chinese papermaking, including Pan Jixing, Hong Guang, Huang Tianyou, Liu Renqing, Xu Mingqi, Dai Jiazhang, Wang Juhua, Zhu Xia, and Li Xiaochen, have conducted comprehensive and in-depth researches. Their work covers the evolutionary history of ancient Chinese papermaking techniques, raw materials, manufacturing methods, production processes, and the the spread of papermaking skills across regions.[9] These distinguished scholars generally

---

8 Pan Jixing, *History of Science and Technology in China: Volume on Papermaking and Printing*, Science Press, 1998, p. 3.
9 Pan Jixing, *A Draft History of Chinese Papermaking Technology*, Cultural Relics Press, 1979;
Pan Jixing, *History of Science and Technology in China: Volume on Papermaking and Printing*, Science Press, 1998.
Hong Guang & Huang Tianyou, *A Brief History of the Development of Papermaking in China*, Light Industry Press, 1957.
Liu Renqing, *A Historical Narrative of Ancient Chinese Papermaking*, Light Industry Press, 1978.
Xu Mingqi, *A Study on the Origins of Ancient Chinese Papermaking Technology*,

agree that by the 3rd century CE, hemp paper had completely supplanted bamboo and wooden slips, becoming the primary material for Chinese books. The art of bamboo papermaking, recognized as another monumental Chinese invention, is debated to have originated during the Jin dynasty or as late as the late Tang dynasty. The most renowned bamboo paper came from Guangdong and Zhejiang provinces, with the technique achieving widespread adoption by the Northern Song dynasty.[10] Evidence from Song-era historical records, combined with modern material analysis of surviving documents, suggests that the technology of bamboo papermaking reached maturity during the Northern Song period. The abundance and affordability of bamboo raw materials enabled this innovation to rapidly eclipse the hemp and rattan papers that had flourished during the dynasties of Sui (581-618 CE), Tang (618-907 CE), and Five dynasties (618-907 CE) periods. Bamboo paper, alongside bast paper, came to dominate the papermaking industry—a supremacy that endured well into the modern era. Beyond the traditional bamboo paper strongholds of Guangdong and Zhejiang, Fujian emerged as a significant new production center during the Song dynasty. The province's paper manufacturing clustered in bamboo-rich regions including Jianyang, Chong'an, and the Wuyi Mountain regions in western Fujian. The numerous block-printed editions from the dynasties of Song and Yuan (1271-1368 CE) that survive today—particularly those published

Shanghai Jiao Tong University Press, 1991.
Edited by Dai Jiazhang, *A Concise History of Chinese Papermaking Technology*, China Light Industry Press, 1994.
Wang Juhua, *A Technological History of Ancient Chinese Papermaking Engineering*, Shanxi Education Press, 2006.
Liu Renqing, *The Traditional Craft of Chinese Handmade Paper*, Intellectual Property Publishing House, 2019.
Zhu Xia & Li Xiaocen, "A Survey and Study of Papermaking Techniques among Ethnic Minorities in Yunnan", *Ethno-National Studies*, No. 1, 1999.
Li Xiaocen, "Pouring and Spreading: Two Distinct Papermaking Systems Preserved in Mainland China", *Journal of Dialectics of Nature*, No. 5, 2011.
10 Compiled by Su Yijian (Song dynasty), edited, collated and punctuated by Zhu Xuebo, *Book of Four Treasures of the Study*, Vol. 3 "Treasures on Paper", Shanghai Bookstore Publishing House, 2015, p. 59.

in Fujian—were printed on bamboo paper.[11] By the Ming (1368-1644 CE) and Qing (1636-1912 CE) dynasties, bamboo paper production led in production volume. Song Yingxing, in his seminal work *Tiangong Kaiwu* (天工开物, *The Exploitation of the Works of Nature*), proclaimed: "All bamboo paper is made in the southern provinces, with Fujian Province monopolizing its excellence."[12] During this period, the most prevalent varieties were the *lianshi paper* and *maobian paper* produced in Jiangxi and Fujian provinces. Notably, the renowned Ji'guge editions published by the Mao family in Changzhou, Jiangsu province, at the end of the Ming dynasty, were printed on bamboo paper made in these very regions.[13]

Papermaking from bamboo was, in itself, a major technological breakthrough in the history of papermaking. The production of high-quality bamboo paper remains a skill that drew the attention of the world. The earliest known modern scientific investigation into China's traditional hand-

---

11 Pan Jixing, *History of Science and Technology in China: Volume on Papermaking and Printing*, Science Press, 1998, pp. 148, 185, 188;
Wang Juhua, *A Technological History of Ancient Chinese Papermaking Engineering*, Shanxi Education Press, 2006, pp. 260–261.
See also: *Huai Hai Ji* (淮海集, *Collected Works of Qin Guan*), the first block-printed edition by the Gaoyoujun School in 1173 (the ninth year of Qiandao era, Song dynasty), and the revised and reprinted edition in 1192 (the third year of Shaoxi era, Song dynasty), were both printed on bamboo paper.
Lin Ting Zhi (临汀志, *The Chorography of Linting*) from the Song dynasty records paper as a local commodity, reflecting the boom in book printing in Jianyang, Fujian, which stimulated papermaking and trade in the region.
See Qin Guan (Song dynasty), *Huai Hai Ji*, National Library of China Publishing House, 2018;
Hu Taichu (Song dynasty), compiled by Zhao Yumu (Song dynasty), *Lin Ting Zhi*, section "Local Products: Goods and Commodities", Fujian People's Publishing House, 1990, p. 35.
The papermaking tradition in Fujian can be traced back at least to the early Song period. For instance, Quanzhou was known for its *Juanfu paper* (蠲符纸) and Tingzhou for its *Juan paper* (蠲纸).
See *Taiping Huanyu Ji* (太平寰宇记, *Universal Geography of the Taiping Era*), Vol. 102 "Jiangnan East Circuit No. 14", Zhonghua Book Company, 2007, pp. 2031, 2036.
12 Song Yingxing (Ming dynasty), annotated and translated by Pan Jixing, *Annotated Translation of Tiangong Kaiwu,* Shanghai Guji Press, 2008, pp. 225–230.
13 Pan Jixing, *History of Science and Technology in China: Volume on Papermaking and Printing*, Science Press, 1998, p. 227.

made papermaking methods dates back to the 1880s. In 1882, Inoue Nobumasa (井上陳政, real name: Narahara Nobumasa 楢原陳政) was dispatched by Japan's Ministry of Finance Printing Bureau to study printing and papermaking techniques in China. From 1885 onward, he conducted a relatively systematic and covert survey of traditional papermaking techniques across provinces such as Jiangxi, Anhui, Zhejiang, Jiangsu, and Fujian, marking the first modern scientific survey of China's hand papermaking techniques. His report, "The Papermaking Methods of the Qing Empire," documented his findings on the raw materials, additives, tools, and procedures involved in producing various types of Chinese paper—such as *xuan paper* (rice paper), *lianshi paper*, and *maobian paper*. Driven by Japan's paper industry's eagerness to gain insights into China's bamboo papermaking techniques at the time, Inoue recorded in detail the manufacturing processes of *lianshi paper* and *maobian paper* as they were practiced in the late Qing dynasty. Around 1905, another Japanese investigator, Masamuro Yukinori (真室幸教), conducted further research into bamboo papermaking in Liancheng and Longyan in Fujian. His findings were compiled into a report titled "Inspection Record of the Papermaking Industry in the Qing Empire". This work, along with Inoue's "Diary of a Tour Investigating Papermaking in the Qing Empire", was compiled by Seki Takeshi (関彪) and then published in 1934 under the title *Papermaking Industry in China*. Also included in that volume was an essay by Shigematsu Yoshinori (重松義則), "The Bamboo Paper Industry in China," further underscoring Japan's keen interest in China's bamboo papermaking—particularly that of Fujian. One aspect that merits deeper scholarly attention is the distinction between different regional techniques. Inoue Nobumasa claimed that his account of maobian paper production came from Changting in western Fujian. However, what he recorded actually describes the process for *shuliao maobian*—a "cooked pulp" method involving the boiling of raw materials. This notably differs from the local *shengliao maobian* method practiced in the same region, which does not require boiling.[14] A similar observation can be made regarding Masamuro Yukinori's records from his investigations in Liancheng, Shanghang, Linting, Longyan, and Yong'an in Fujian province. His focus was likewise limited to papermaking techniques based on the cooked pulp method.[15] In recent years, researchers of paper history have increasingly turned their attention to the craft and history of bamboo papermaking, with studies on *lianshi paper* (a type of *maobian paper*) growing increasingly rich and in-depth.[16] Yet Yukou paper remains a largely overlooked subject, still awaiting the focused study it deserves.

Yukou paper from Changting County, Fujian—once a famed variety of bamboo paper that enjoyed distinguished reputation both at home and abroad—only began to receive scholarly attention from major research institutions and comprehensive scholarly works on ancient Chinese papermaking in the 1980s and 1990s. Following China's reform and opening-up, the growing demand for exports prompted Changting County to revitalize its traditional handmade paper production. Local authorities

---

14 Compiled by Seki Takeshi, *Papermaking Industry in China*, Tokyo: Seishindō, 1934. Chen Gang, "Inoue Nobumasa and *The Papermaking Methods of the Qing Empire*," *Historical Review*,No. 3 (2012).

15 Masamuro Yukinori, Inspection Record of the Papermaking Industry in the Qing Empire, Civil Affairs Department of the Governor-General of Taiwan, *Investigative Report on the Papermaking Industry of Taiwan*, with the "Inspection Record of the Papermaking Industry in the Qing Empire", 1909, pp. 6–8.

16 Wang Shiwen, "A Historical Review of Traditional Chinese Bamboo Paper and a Discussion of Its Production-Technology Characteristics," *Research on the History of Paper*, No. 15 (1996).
Deng Jinkun, *Liancheng Xuan Paper*, Economic Science Press, 2008.
Su Junjie, "A Study on the Preservation of the Craft of Lianshi Paper Production," master's thesis, Fudan University, 2008.
Chen Gang, "Inoue Nobumasa and *The Papermaking Methods of the Qing Empire*," *Historical Review*, No. 3 (2012).
Liu Renqing, "On *Lianshi Paper*," *Paper and Papermaking*, No. 4 (2012).
Zou Chunwen, "A Study of *Lianshi Paper* from Liancheng," master's thesis, Fujian Normal University, 2016.
Chen Ling, "The Craft of *Lianshi Paper* and Its Scientific Significance," *Journal of Dialectics of Nature*, No. 3 (2021).

launched dedicated field investigations to document the historical develop-ment and current state of local handmade paper. These efforts yielded not only valuable samples of papers used in rural communities for writing con-tracts, IOUs, and printing genealogies, but also led to the recovery of the techniques and craftsmanship for producing Yukou paper. In 1988, Huang Majin of the Changting County Economic Committee brought 13 samples of traditional handmade bamboo papers collected from local communi-ties—including Yukou and Maobian papers—to the Paper Industry Re-search Institute under the Ministry of Light Industry for testing and analysis. These samples spanned multiple historical periods, from the Qing dynasty (1 from the Yongzheng era, 2 from Qianlong, 2 from Daoguang, 1 from Xianfeng, 1 from Tongzhi, 3 from Guangxu, and 1 from Xuantong) and 2 from the early Republican period. After examining the samples, senior en-gineers Wang Juhua and Li Yuhua prepared a detailed experimental report and published an article titled "An Analytical Study of Several Handmade Bamboo Paper Samples from Changting, Fujian (Qing and Early Republi-can Periods)". The full text, together with the test report and photocopies of the samples, was published in *Research on the History of Paper*, (Issue 8, 1990), a journal jointly sponsored by the Paper History Committee of the China Paper Society and the Fujian Paper Association. Scientific analysis of the paper samples focused on physical properties, fiber composition, pulp-ing and beating processes, surface appearance, and the impression of screen marks. The findings revealed that the Yukou paper from Qing dynasty was distinguished by its fine, soft, lightweight texture and smooth, delicate sur-face. It showed no signs of filler or coating, and was generally bore a pale beige hue. A few samples appeared bright white, likely due to lime-soaking and sun-bleaching processes. The paper exhibited slight water resistance, making it well-suited for calligraphy and traditional Chinese painting. The study also noted that the exceptional fineness of Yukou paper was closely tied to the region's unique bamboo resources. The local unbranched young bamboo used in papermaking offered natural advantages: its fibers were relatively long and bound together with notable strength, contributing to the paper's exceptional quality.[17]

This comprehensive analysis and testing of maobian paper and Yukou paper from the Qing dynasty and Republican periods in Changting County, Fujian, sparked renewed interest among scholars in the technological development and applications of Fujian bamboo paper in the post-Ming and Qing eras. Scholars of paper history have observed that, following the Qing dynasty, bamboo paper varieties in Fujian and other provinces proliferated to no fewer than forty to fifty distinct types, including *lianshi paper*, *Gongchuan paper*, and *maobian paper*. Among these varieties, maobian paper emerged as particularly significant due to its high production volume and affordable pricing, establishing itself as the paper of choice for everyday writing and book printing among the general populace. The Changting region of Fujian achieved the highest maobian paper production, offering diverse varieties such as *maobian, zhongbian, guandui, shanbei,* and *kou papers*. The reinforced maobian paper represented the finest quality among these varieties and was specifically designated for imperial memorial submissions during the Ming dynasty. Within Fujian's renowned *kou paper* family, the *qingsi kou* from Jiangle, Fujian, and the *xizhuang kou* from Yong'an stood as premium local examples. From a technological perspective, researchers have identified that the pulping techniques employed in Jianyang, Shaowu, Tingzhou[18], Putian, and Shunchang regions—utilizing the "cooked material method" and natural bleaching processes for bamboo

---

17 Wang Juhua, *A Technological History of Ancient Chinese Papermaking Engineering* Shanxi Education Press, 2006, pp. 356–359.

18 Located in western Fujian Province, Tingzhou was established as a prefecture in the twenty-first year of Kaiyuan era, Tang dynasty (733 CE), with its administrative seat in present-day Changting County. During the Ming and Qing dynasties, it remained a prefectural-level administrative unit under the jurisdiction of the Fujian Provincial Administration Commission (Buzheng Shisi), governing eight counties: Changting, Ninghua, Qingliu, Guihua, Liancheng, Shanghang, Wuping, and Yongding.

paper production—represented a major breakthrough in ancient bamboo papermaking technology. These innovative techniques substantially enhanced paper quality. Subsequently, Fujian craftsmen disseminated these advanced methods to Jiangxi, Anhui, Hunan, Guangxi, and other provinces, thereby expanding the geographical reach of superior bamboo papermaking practices across southern China.

Scholars also turned their attention to the raw material method used in the production of maobian paper in the provinces of Zhejiang, Jiangxi, and Fujian. They outlined the essential steps of this technique: tender *mao zhu* (*Phyllostachys edulis*) is cut into thin strips, with the inner bamboo membrane and nodes carefully removed. The strips are then placed in a soaking pond, where they undergo fermentation for several months with the aid of lime, eventually breaking down into bamboo pulp. This pulp is repeatedly washed and beaten into a fibrous slurry, to which sizing agents are added and stirred thoroughly. Sheets are then formed using bamboo moulds, pasted onto heated walls for drying, and emerge as finished maobian paper. The raw material method is characterized by its gentler chemical action, and its duration varies depending on ambient temperature and humidity. Because it omits a bleaching process, any residual impurities in the bamboo may cause the pulp—and thus the paper—to take on a yellowish or pale beige hue. Conventional wisdom among researchers in paper history holds that paper produced using the raw material method tends to be coarser in texture, contains more impurities, and displays a duller color when compared to paper made using the cooked material method.[19] However, the high-quality Yukou paper traditionally produced in Ninghua and Changting in Fu-

19 Edited by Dai Jiazhang, *A Concise History of Chinese Papermaking Technology*, China Light Industry Press, 1994, pp. 149–152, 220–221, 228;
Wang Juhua, *A Technological History of Ancient Chinese Papermaking Engineering*, Shanxi Education Press, 2006, pp. 319–320;
Liu Renqing, *A Manual of Ancient Chinese Paper*, Intellectual Property Publishing House, 2009, pp. 142–143.

jian—despite being made via the raw material method—challenges this perception. Its unexpected refinement has opened up broader possibilities for reimagining the technical sophistication, the quality of its products, and the range of its applications.

Before Huang Majin submitted the paper samples to the Paper Industry Research Institute of the Ministry of Light Industry for scientific analysis, a local initiative was already underway in Changting County. In 1987, the county established a compilation committee for the *A History of Papermaking in Changting*. This team began by collecting and verifying historical records related to paper across local institutions, including the county archives, museum, exhibition hall, Party History Office, economic commission, statistics bureau, and Second Light Industry Bureau. To supplement documentary research, the committee dispatched survey teams to 15 townships across Changting County. These field investigations examined local bamboo resources, the state of handmade paper industry, and the history of papermaking in over 40 key paper-producing villages. These teams conducted interviews with veteran papermakers, paper workshop owners, paper traders, and other knowledgeable locals. Topics ranged from the evolution of papermaking techniques to production scales and commercial networks. Building on this groundwork, the team collaborated collectively, with Huang Majin serving as chief editor, and completed the collective writing of *A History of Papermaking in Changting*, published in 1992.[20] A

---

20 *A History of Papermaking in Changting* (China Light Industry Press, 1992) is a compilation-style volume on the papermaking history of Changting and holds the distinction of being the first regional monograph on papermaking history in China. Despite its significance, the book is marred by critical limitations: the majority of its historical material is cited secondhand without specifying original sources, and the text is plagued by typographical errors and omissions, ambiguous phrasing, and misreading. Similar issues are found in other authoritative works on the history of papermaking, such as Pan Jixing's *A History of Papermaking in China* and Wang Juhua's aforementioned *A Technological History of Ancient Chinese Papermaking Engineering*. See Chen Zhiping and Zhuang Linlin, "An Analysis of Errors in the Use of Historical Sources in Chinese Papermaking History Research," *Research in Chinese Economic History,* No. 3 (2021).

subsequent article, "Preliminary Study of the History of Papermaking Technology in Changting, Fujian," drew heavily on this monograph. It discussed the regional significance of Changting's paper industry, the unique qualities and production techniques of Tingzhou's Yukou paper, and key historical issues surrounding Changting's modern paper industry.[21] This wave of local research invigorated the broader study of paper history. It forged stronger connections between the history of technology and regional socioeconomic history. By incorporating local archives and folk historical texts, it greatly expanded both the sources and perspectives available to scholars of Chinese papermaking. Moreover, it marked an important shift toward integrating paper history with the study of regional development and rural industries.

A History of Papermaking in Changting stands as the first monographic compilation and study focused specifically on Yukou paper and Maobian paper produced in Changting, Fujian. It argues that the primary varieties of handmade paper in Changting—Yukou and Maobian—were traditionally produced using the raw material pulping method. This technique demands exceptional craftsmanship and strictly adheres to seasonal rhythms, involving a complex sequence of procedures and rigorous technical standards. As early as the late Ming dynasty, the prevalence of bamboo papermaking in the Tingzhou region had already been documented. In *Min Shu* (闽书, Book of Fujian), He Qiaoyuan wrote explicitly that "Yanping, Jianyang, Shaowu, and Tingzhou make paper from bamboo,"

Ironically, this very article contains its own inaccuracies—for instance, misdating the publication of *A Draft History of Chinese Papermaking Technology* as 1997 instead of 1979, and mistaking the 2006 publication of *A Technological History of Ancient Chinese Papermaking Engineering* as 2005.

21 Guan Ming, "A Preliminary Study on the Papermaking Techniques of Changting, Fujian," in Zhou Ji (ed.), *Research on the History of Science and Technology in Fujian*, Xiamen University Press, 1990.

offering clear evidence of the practice's status at that time.[22] According to *A History of Papermaking in Changting*, historical papermaking regions were categorized into "upper mountain" and "lower mountain" zones, with the former further divided into "inner" and "outer" mountain areas. The inner mountain zone included places such as Anjie, Tiechang, and Sibeiling (modern-day Zhiping) in neighboring Ninghua. The outer mountain zone encompassed Guanqian, Tongfang, Xinqiao, and Sibao (the latter was incorporated into Liancheng County in 1951). The lower mountain zone covered areas like Gucheng in the west and Hetian, Cewu, Nanshan, Tufang, Xuancheng, and Sidu in the south. Towns such as Tufang and Xuancheng—especially villages like Yanggu and Fuyao—and Meixi in Zhuotian were known for producing coarse straw paper. Among all these, paper from the upper mountain regions was regarded as the highest in quality, benefiting from favorable soil conditions, thicker bamboo stalks, finer fibers, and cleaner water sources. Inner mountain paper, particularly, enjoyed great renown under the name "Inner Mountain Yukou." By contrast, paper from the lower mountain areas tended to be of inferior quality due to poor soil, thinner bamboo stalks, coarser fibers, and more impure water. Drawing on the 1946 "Survey of Papermaking in Changting, Fujian," published by the Southeast Office of the Chinese Industrial Cooperatives Association, *A History of Papermaking in Changting* notes that, out of more than 60 counties in Fujian Province at the time, 43 engaged in paper production. Among them, only 2 specialized exclusively in cooked material paper, 31 specialized in raw material paper, and 10 counties produced both. Liancheng's Gutian town was recognized as the top producer of cooked material paper, while Changting was considered the finest origin of raw material paper. Between 1956 and 1957, papermakers in Sidu Township, Changting

---

22 He Qiaoyuan (Ming dynasty), *Min Shu* (Book of Fujian), collated and punctuated by the *Min Shu* Collation Group of Xiamen University, Fujian People's Publishing House, 1994.

County, produced 80 *dao* (a traditional Chinese unit of paper quantity, equal to 100 sheets per *dao*) of Grade 1 and Grade 2 Yukou paper. Tiechang Township also achieved a record in producing Grade 1 Yukou paper.[23]

According to *A History of Papermaking in Changting*, the production of Yukou paper in the region was blessed with a number of natural advantages. First and foremost is the abundance of local bamboo forests—supplying thick, supple, and smooth bamboo fibers ideal for papermaking. Second, the mountainous terrain and dense woodlands provide a constant supply of pristine spring water, renowned for its clarity and purity—perfect for producing fine paper. Together, these natural endowments and the refined craftsmanship of local papermakers have long defined the superior quality of Changting's Yukou paper. Yukou paper is made exclusively from young bamboo, giving it a remarkable set of characteristics: long and fine fibers, a smooth yet resilient texture, strong tensile strength and resistance to pilling from friction. Its sheets were uniformly formed, with a jade-like white luster. Its color is bright and clean, free from chemical additives, safe for everyday use, with excellent ink absorption, quick drying, and durability that resists fading and insect damage over time. This paper is not only favored for traditional uses such as calligraphy and ritual ceremonies but is also a fine choice for cigarette rolling.[24]

Outside of *A History of Papermaking in Changting*, the renowned paper historian Liu Renqing also took note of Yukou paper. However, his description is not entirely accurate. He identifies *Yukou paper* as a Qing dynasty variety, also known as *sichi maobian* (four Chinese foot maobian paper), originally produced in several counties of Fujian—including Nanping, Ninghua, Changting, Liancheng, Shanghang, Qingliu, and Longyan. Ac-

---

23 Huang Majin (chief ed.), *A History of Papermaking in Changting*, China Light Industry Press, 1992, pp. 8, 9, 17, 23, 24, 27, 28, 72.
24 Huang Majin (chief ed.), *A History of Papermaking in Changting*, China Light Industry Press, 1992, p. 36.

cording to his account, it is made from young bamboo, has a soft and smooth texture, a beige tone, and strong absorbency. Thicker than most maobian papers, it is mainly used for printing ancient classical texts and Buddhist scriptures, and for writing letters, as well as for making rubbings of stone inscriptions. Liu further suggests that the name *Yukou* derives from two elements: *yu* (jade), referring to the paper's jade-like purity and texture, and *kou*, allegedly a historical unit of measurement meaning 100 sheets of paper. He also notes that the paper later became widely distributed and well-loved for its quality—finding even unusual applications, such as being used in cooking the famous Wuzhou dish paper-wrapped chicken in Guangxi.[25] However, many of Liu's claims regarding the number of sheets per unit, the definition of the term *kou*, and the geographic distribution of Yukou paper are inaccurate. His misreadings underscore how even leading paper historians still lack a full understanding of this highly localized and culturally significant variety of handmade Chinese paper.

In sum, Yukou paper is a renowned regional variety of handmade paper native to Changting in western Fujian. It belongs to the category of bamboo paper that came to dominate Chinese papermaking after the Song dynasty, primarily produced with the raw material method. It was not until the 1980s and 1990s that Yukou paper entered broader historical narratives of traditional Chinese papermaking and handmade paper industries. To date, academic research has yet to fully capture the history and current status of Yukou paper and its craftsmanship. Much remains to be explored in detail—including the origin of the paper's name, the intricacies of its production techniques, the transmission of related technologies within and beyond China[26], as well as the networks of production, distribution, and consump-

---

25 Liu Renqing, *A Manual of Ancient Chinese Paper*, Intellectual Property Publishing House, 2009, p. 159.
26 The questions of when, by whom, and through what channels the techniques for producing Yukou paper and other varieties of bamboo paper were introduced into the

tion. In particular, the roles played by the various actors in the papermaking ecosystem—papermakers, paper workshop owners (known as 槽户), paper merchants, and paper trading houses—along with the social structure of the production regions, offer rich terrain for further historical investigation.

1.2.   The Meaning of Yukou

Throughout China's long history, the number of distinct names for paper runs into the hundreds. Even within Fujian province alone, more than two hundred distinct varieties have been recorded. In the premodern era, these names functioned as a form of localized knowledge, with clear meaning and utility within regional markets and among those involved in the paper trade. Despite their abundance and apparent complexity, such naming conventions rarely caused confusion for producers, distributors, or consumers of handmade paper.[27] It was not until the modern era that these traditional names began to draw criticism. People started to question the inconsistency in naming, vagueness in definitions, and lack of systematic classi-

---

mountainous regions of Fujian merit further investigation. Moreover, Chinese handmade paper continued to be exported in significant quantities well into the modern era. This raises the important question of whether the regions that consumed Chinese paper also adopted its papermaking technologies. For example, Yukou paper was widely distributed across provinces during the Qing dynasty and was praised for being "sold throughout half the empire." Following the opening of five treaty ports for foreign trade, its export to overseas markets increased significantly. Whether the craftsmanship of Yukou paper was transmitted beyond China remains an open and intriguing subject. For discussions on related issues, see:

Ji Xianlin, "On the Time and Place of the Introduction of Chinese Paper and Chinese Papermaking Techniques into India," *Historical Research*, No. 4, 1954;

Li Shuhua, "The Spread of Papermaking and the Discovery of Ancient Papers," in *Collected Essays on Historical Artifacts*, vol. 1, Taipei National Museum of History, reprinted by the Compilation and Translation Bureau, 1985;

Huang Shengzhang, "On the Time and Route of the Introduction of Chinese Paper and Chinese Papermaking Techniques into the Indian Subcontinent," *Historical Research*, No. 1, 1980;

Li Xiaocen, "The Route of Chinese Paper and Chinese Papermaking Techniques into the Indian Subcontinent," *Historical Research*, No. 2, 1992.

27 Lin Renchuan. "Paper Production and Distribution in Fujian during the Republican Era." *Research on Chinese Socio-Economic History*, No. 1, 1989.

Xu Jianqing. "Papermaking Industry in the Qing Dynasty." *Journal of Chinese Historical Studies*, No. 3, 1997.

fication in the terminology used for materials such as paper. Relying solely on craft-based intuition and experiential judgment came to be viewed as unscientific. As a result, debates emerged over seemingly simple questions: What exactly is Yukou paper? How should we define lianshi paper or maobian paper? These inquiries reflected a broader shift toward standardizing, categorizing, and rationalizing handmade paper within a modern scientific framework.

The origins of the name Yukou paper remain somewhat obscure. Among local communities in what is now Zhiping She Ethnic Township, Ninghua County, Sanming City, Fujian province—widely recognized as the heartland of Yukou paper production—all handmade paper produced in and around this region bears the name Yukou paper. However, historical records indicate that paper labeled Yukou was not exclusive to Fujian. Other provinces, such as Hunan, also documented papers with similar names, including *Chang Yukou*, *Ping Yukou*, and *Roukou paper* from places like Shaoyang and Rucheng.[28] The earliest known textual reference to Yukou paper appears in the *Chorography of Renhua County*, compiled during the Tongzhi era of the Qing dynasty. It lists local paper varieties with names such as *Gongkou, Yukou, Shanbei, Youtong, Qingtong, Zhongtong, Gaofang, Huozhi*, and *Biaoxin*, all produced in the Changjiang and Fuxi areas of the county.[29] In the Qing dynasty, Renhua County was part of Shaozhou Prefecture in Guangdong province. Changjiang Town and Fuxi Town were the representative production hubs for Renhua's Yukou paper. Local oral tradition holds that Renhua's papermaking techniques were introduced from

---

28 Zhang Renjia. "The Paper of Hunan." In *Selected Historical Materials on the Economy of Republican-Era Hunan (Vol. 3)*, edited by Zeng Saifeng and Cao Youpeng,Hunan People's Publishing House, 2009, pp. 625, 627.
29 *Chorography of Renhua County* vol. 5, "Customs and Products." In *Complete Collection of Guangdong Historical Chorography: Shaozhou Prefecture Vol. 6*, compiled by Guangdong Provincial Office of Local Chronicles, Lingnan Fine Arts Publishing House, 2007, p. 429.

Fujian, with production skills gradually maturing during the Qianlong era and flourishing after the first year of Daoguang era (1821). A stone stele erected in the eleventh year of Guangxu era (1885) at the Guangzhou Guild Hall in Changjiang town proudly proclaims: "Changjiang paper is more prized than even the renowned paper of Luoyang."[30] Given the scarcity of references to Yukou paper in late Qing sources, it is likely that the name did not emerge widely until the mid-Qing period, and even then only in scattered locales across eastern Guangdong and western Fujian.[31]

Another widely accepted explanation—echoing the view of paper historian Liu Renqing—is that the term *yu* (jade) refers to the paper's smooth, lustrous texture, while *kou* (unit) originally denoted a measure of quantity. Together, they form the name yukou paper. However, the meaning of the word *kou* is far from settled. At least three interpretations exist: in addition to being a unit of measurement, *kou* has also been used to designate a type of paper or to refer to the width of a paper sheet. This raises important questions: where and when did the name yukou first emerge? What specific kind of paper qualified as yukou paper? In what follows, we explore the issue through an examination of terminology, paper texture, and surviving physical specimens.

---

30 "Traditional Papermaking Techniques: 'Changjiang Paper is More Prized than Luoyang'." *Shaoguan Daily*, June 6, 2020. Accessed October 23, 2023. https://m.thepaper.cn/baijiahao/7743711.

31 For example, the earliest reference to *liansi paper* (连四纸, also called "lianshi paper") can be traced back to the Yuan dynasty. It was frequently mentioned in Ming dynasty chorographies and literary collections, and later cited in *Tiangong Kaiwu* (The Exploitation of the Works of Nature). During the Qing dynasty, "liansi paper" appeared regularly in official archives and documents. The Qing-era variety of this paper, now known as *Kaihua paper* (开化纸), represented the pinnacle of thin "liansi paper" used for printing, characterized by its fine, white, and durable texture. In the late Qing, "liansi paper" came to be made exclusively from bamboo pulp, evolving into the white bamboo paper still in use today. See Ai Junchuan, "A Philological Note on Liansi Paper," originally published in *Wenjin Xuezhi*, No. 11, 2018, reprinted in *New Studies on the History of Chinese Printing*, Zhonghua Book Company, 2022, pp. 289–296.

The earliest known reference to the term yukou paper appears in the *Chorography of Renhua County* of Tongzhi era, as noted above. This suggests that the name *yukou* was already in widespread use among local communities by that time. The meaning of *yu* (jade) is relatively straightforward—it evokes the paper's fine, smooth quality. The term *kou*, however, remains more ambiguous. Even in the paper's primary production areas—such as Ninghua and Changting—local Hakka speakers today cannot offer a definitive explanation based on regional dialect. Interestingly, the *Imperial Revised Manchu–Chinese Lexicon* includes entries for both *yi dao zhi* (a knife of paper) and *yi kou zhi* (a kou of paper), suggesting that *kou* and *dao* were not interchangeable. While dao (刀, knife) is a well-known traditional unit of measurement for paper, the pairing of these two terms in the lexicon implies that *kou* might also have functioned as a distinct unit for quantifying paper—though its exact usage remains uncertain.[32]

Beyond serving as a unit of measurement, the term *kou* also came to signify a broader category of paper. The earliest known textual references to such *kou paper* or papers with names ending in *kou* appear in Ming dynasty sources such as the *Wanshu Zaji* (宛署杂记, Miscellaneous Records of the Wanping County) and *Taichang Xukao* (太常续考, Further Studies of the Court of Ceremonies), both of which mention *bangkou paper*—a type of paper used in imperial rituals.[33] By the late Qing, the term had extended to describe high-end artistic paper as well. For example, Ye Changchi's *Yuandulu Riji Chao* (缘督庐日记钞, Excerpts from the Diary of the Yuandu Studio) notes on the 24th day of the twelfth lunar month in the year of

---

32 *Yuzhi Zengding Qingwenjian* (Imperial Revised Manchu–Chinese Lexicon), vol. 7, *Wenyuange Siku Quanshu* (文渊阁四库全书, Wenyuange edition of Complete Library of the Four Treasuries), vol. 233, Shanghai Ancient Books Press, 2003, p. 61.
33 Shen Bang, *Wanshu Zaji* (Miscellaneous Records of the Wanping County), vol. 14, Beijing Publishing House, 1962, pp. 107–125;
Taichang Xukao (Further Studies of the Court of Ceremonies), vol. 1, *Facsimile Edition of Wenyuange Siku Quanshu*, vol. 599, Commercial Press, 1986, p. 26.

Dingyou (1897) that *huang kou zhi* (yellow kou paper) was worth ten taels of silver[34]—a strikingly high price, likely reflecting its use in calligraphy or painting. One of the most detailed and regionally relevant accounts comes from Guo Bocang's mid-Qing treatise *Min Chan Lu Yi* (闽产录异, Record on Specialties of Natural Products of Fujian Province), which not only describes the names and qualities of papers produced across Fujian, but also documents local papermaking techniques. For this reason, this valuable record is cited in full below:

In Fujian, the counties of Yanping, Jianyang, Shaowu, and Tingzhou were all known for their papermaking traditions. Various species of bamboo—Huang Zhu, Ma Zhu, Mian Zhu, and Chijian Zhu—were widely used. These bamboos have thick stalks, and the youngest, most tender ones were selected to produce superior- and medium-grade papers. For inferior-grade papers, materials such as hemp fiber, mulberry bark, paper mulberry (in Fujian, the catalpa tree is called *gu*; records mentioning "paper made from *gu* bark" refer to catalpa bark), rattan (thin and thick), kudzu bark, and the pliable parts of rice straw were utilized. Papers made from bamboo tend to be light, delicate, and lustrous, whereas those from hemp, rattan, mulberry, and similar fibers tend to be coarse and rough.

In Fujian workshops, bamboo stalks were gathered in spring, mixed with lime, and either pressed under boulders into pits or stored in wooden vats. By the Summer Solstice, the pulp was taken out, sorted into coarse and fine grades, pounded and washed in stream water, then sun-dried and stored as raw paper material. When ready for production, rice starch was added to the

---

34 Ye Changchi, *Yuandulu Riji Chao* (Excerpts from the Diary of the Yuandu Studio), vol. 7, National Library of China Press, 2007, p. 389.

pulp, which was then poured into vats and scooped out with fine bamboo screens. The first skimmings produced the finest sheets, called *pi liao* (皮料, bark stock), while subsequent ones formed *ci pi* (次皮, second grade bark). The denser sheets were called *juan zhi* (卷纸, paper for exam), used in the imperial civil service exams. (That said, Fujian's *juan zhi* was not considered as fine as that from Guangdong, which was made from cotton and known as "Ming Cotton"—ming mian—said to resist insects for over 500 years, as attested by surviving examples in the Tianyige Library.) One grade below *juan zhi* was known as *zhi zhong* (致中, fine medium). All four grades—*pi liao, ci pi, juan zhi,* and *zhi zhong*—were collectively referred to as *bai liao* (白料), or "white stock." These sheets bore various names, often specific to each papermaking vat. If not properly dried, they were prone to insect damage.

Papers made without rice starch were called *zhu zhi* (bamboo paper). These sheets, width close to but less refined than *pi liao*, were also known as *kou zhi* (kou paper). Its name varied with each vat's production. A grade called *lou kou* (篓扣, basket kou) was deemed superior—being both thin and firmly bound, thin enough to resist insects, firm enough to avoid tearing. Those not packed in baskets tended to be loose and thick—qualities that made them fragile and easily infested.

In printing houses, an extremely thin grade called *mao tai* (毛泰) was used. It was so delicate that turning pages without damage was difficult.

Among the most prized varieties were *qingsi kou* (青丝扣, black silk kou) from Jiangle and *xizhuang kou* (西庄扣, West

Village kou) from Yong'an—papers noted for their smooth, lustrous, fine and firm texture. Slightly inferior was *jianyang kou* (建阳扣, Jianyang County kou), which locals simply referred to as "book paper." During the Song and Yuan dynasties, for two hundred years, the famous *Mashaban shu* block-printed books were all produced using this paper. In later times, printing houses in Suzhou would pay a premium to secure exclusive use during the pressing season, thus preventing others in Fujian from obtaining jianyang kou.

Shaxian produced the largest volume of paper, including a type called *da kou* (大扣, large kou), though it was often too thick and therefore prone to insect damage. It became commonly used for printing reference books in later periods.

A type from Songxi was known as *songkou* (松扣, Songxi County kou paper), but its texture was soft and loose.

Paper from Ningyang, a grade just below *pi liao*, was known as *Ningyang zhi*. It was light, thin, and inexpensive—so ideal for calligraphy and painting restorers that it earned the nickname "divine paper."

For village schools, a smaller format measuring six to seven inches in width and eight to nine inches in length was called *jingzhi* (京纸, capital paper). The thickest variant was known as *dingbiao* (顶标, top mark), followed by *gechang* (割长, cut length), and then *bojing* (薄京, thin capital paper), the thinnest grade.

A particular variety made in Yangjiashan, Yifeng Town, Jiangle County, was also called *jing zhi*. It was thin, tough, and insect-resistant, widely circulated in Hubei, Hunan and Jiangxi. Zhu Yizun's poem, "The vats of Jiangle are bitterly small," refers to this very paper. From Longxishan came the broadest sheets, known as *qiebian* (切边, cut edge), while a slightly narrower version was called *gulian* (鼓连, drum link)—both snowy white in color and colloquially referred to as *xishan zhi* (西山纸, West Mountain paper). When I was nine, accompanying my father in Jiangle, I used it for copying texts; the manuscripts remain intact to this day.

In Fuzhou, 30 to 40 paper workshops used kou zhi as the base to create *huajian* (花笺, decorative letter paper) by dyeing and *lajian* (蜡笺, wax paper) by waxing. Xinghua, known for its red flowers, used *wu mei* (乌梅, smoked plum) to dye paper—a cheap and efficient process, though lacking the deep crimson hue achieved by repeated dyed paper from Beijing workshops.

Another variety, a rice-colored paper called *jiumu* (九牧), was adorned with fine gold powder for decorated for title slips and margin frames. It was sturdy and tear-resistant. Though counties produced tens of thousands of taels' worth of such paper annually for painting and calligraphy, it still fell short of the quality from Xuancheng and Jingxian.

Then there was *zhi bei* (纸被, paper quilt), made from paper mulberry bark and produced in five counties: Ou'ning, Jianyang, Songxi, Chong'an, and Nanping. Lu You once wrote,

"A paper quilt wraps the body through snowy nights,

Whiter than fox fur, softer than cotton."

Zhi xiao (纸箫, paper flute) was once made in the Kaiyuan Temple of Fuzhou, crafted from fan paper mixed with oil.

In Yuexi, Nanping, a special kind of *ge zhi* (葛纸, kudzu paper) known as *Yue Ge* (岳葛) was widely circulated and put to extensive use.

Meanwhile, Shanyang in Gutian made *qian zhi* (钱纸, money paper), the ritual paper money used for offerings to deities and ancestors.

Finally, in Nanya Pass of Jian'an, *cu zhi* (粗纸, rough paper) was made—used in Yanping and Jian'an both for sacrificial purposes and also as toilet paper.[35]

According to *Min Chan Lu Yi* (Record on Specialties of Natural Products of Fujian Province), kou paper was one among many varieties of bamboo paper, notable for several distinguishing features. First, it was smaller in both length and width than *pi liao*, as the term "kou" referred specifically to a set width of the sheet.[36] Secondly, it was prized for being

---

35 Guo Bocang (Qing dynasty), collated and punctuated by Hu Fengze, *Min Chan Lu Yi* (Record on Specialties of Natural Products of Fujian Province), vol. 1, Yuelu Publishing House, 1986, pp. 20–23.
Guo Bocang (1815–1890), a native of Houguan County, Fujian (now part of Minhou County), was a juren (recommended man) by degree. He served in various official posts including county instructor, Neige Zhongshu (Secretary in the Grand Secretariat), and zhushi (Section Chief). He was also a prolific author.
36 According to *A History of Papermaking in Changting*, maobian paper is a general term for raw material paper among hand-made papers across China. In Changting, maobian paper is categorized into heavy and light varieties. The heavy paper is thicker, with a larger sheet size, and is known as yukou paper; the light paper is thinner and smaller in size, and is called *changxing paper* (长行纸). Later, in order to meet market demand, the width (kou, a local term for the width of paper) and height (计, *ji*) of changxing paper were increased, resulting in a type resembling yukou paper, known as *daguang paper* (大广纸), which remains a thin paper. During the Republican period, paper size standards and quality inspections were implemented: heavy paper was 139.5 cm long and 62 cm wide; yukou paper was 118.5 cm long and 62 cm wide; changxing paper was 131 cm long and 58 cm wide. See Huang Majin (chief ed.), *A History of Pa-*

thin—resistant to insect damage—and firmly woven, meaning it was not easily torn. A third hallmark was its smooth, lustrous, fine and firm texture (光润幼结). Though many paper types across Fujian were labeled as "kou," few truly met the true standard of kou paper. Of all its qualities, firmness or tightness—expressed as *jie* (结)—was considered most essential, and its antonym was looseness (松). The editor of the modern annotated edition notes that the character *you* (幼), often translated as "young," in the local dialect actually connotes fineness or delicacy.[37] This reinforces the notion that authentic kou paper was expected to be thin, lustrous, smooth, and above all, finely textured and tightly composed—attributes that marked it as a high-quality paper. The "yu" (jade) in yukou paper may have served to further emphasize its lustrous, smooth appearance.

The name Yukou paper first appeared in the *Renhua Xianzhi* (Chorography of Renhua County), compiled during the Tongzhi era of the Qing dynasty. However, this earliest mention offers little more than the name itself, with no further detail about the paper's quality or characteristics. A more substantial and accurate description comes from the *Comprehensive Chorography of Chinese Provinces*, compiled by the Japanese organization East Asia Common Culture Society (東亜同文会) based on field investigations. Its volume on Fujian Province, published in 1917, stands as one of the earliest records to provide a clear account of Yukou paper. In the second chapter, which details the papermaking industry of Fujian, the text begins by identifying the most renowned paper-producing regions: Liancheng, Qingliu, Ninghua, and Changting in Tingzhou Prefecture; Yong'an, Youxi, Jiangle, and Shunchang in Yanping Prefecture; as well as counties under Shaowu Prefecture, Jianning Prefecture, and Longyan Subprefecture. Con-

---

permaking in Changting, China Light Industry Press, 1992, p. 83.

37 Hu Fengze, "Note from the Collator," in *Min Chan Lu Yi* (Record on Specialties of Natural Products of Fujian Province) by Guo Bocang (Qing dynasty), collated and punctuated by Hu Fengze, Yuelu Publishing House, 1986, p. 10.

trary to the cooked material method described by Inoue Nobumasa and Masamuro Yukinori, the Chorography notes that papermaking in these areas employed the raw material technique. Regarding paper produced in Changting County, the volume classifies it by weight into two types: heavy and light. The heavier variety, known as Yukou, weighs between ten and eleven *jin* (斤, 500 grams) per *dao* of 200 sheets. Each sheet measures approximately 4 *chi* (尺, one third of a meter) 4 *cun* (寸, one thirty of a meter) in length and 2 *chi* 0.5 *cun* in width (around 145 cm × 67 cm).[38] This precise description of weight and dimensions captures the very criteria that distinguish Yukou paper from other types of maobian paper.

In 1941, Lin Cunhe compiled and published *Papers of Fujian*, building on existing sources to offer a systematic overview of the region's papermaking traditions. He noted that the great variety of paper types in Fujian stemmed from differences in quality, intended use, place of origin, and market demand. These variations had given rise to a multitude of names and categories. To bring order to this complexity, Lin proposed a classification system based on both manufacturing techniques and functional purposes. In terms of manufacturing techniques, Fujian's papers fell broadly into two categories: *shuliao* (熟料, cooked material) and *shengliao* (生料, raw material). The former involves a bleaching and boiling process for the raw materials, while the latter omits this step. Yukou paper, according to Lin, is generally a refined product within the *shengliao* category. Only in Liancheng was a version of Yukou paper made using the *shuliao* method; elsewhere, it was predominantly a *shengliao* paper. The main production areas for *shengliao* Yukou were Ninghua, Changting, and Yong'an. Functionally, Lin divided Fujian's papers into three major groups. The first was *bailiao zhi* (白料纸, white stock paper), high-quality writing paper used for documents

---

38 East Asian Common Culture Society (ed.), *Comprehensive Chorography of Chinese Provinces*, Vol. 14: Fujian Province, 1917, pp. 751, 771–772.

and correspondence. This type was characterized by fine texture, carefully selected materials, labor-intensive production, and a clean, bright white appearance. While typically made using the *shuliao* method, it also included some premium *shengliao* paper. The second type, known as *jia zhi* (甲纸, grade 1 paper), was coarse, unrefined paper used mainly for wrapping. Its fibers were rough, its thickness uneven, and its color murky—nearly all examples fell under the *shengliao* category. The third type, called *hai zhi* (海纸), was produced specifically for ritual use, such as the making of spirit money and paper foils, and other superstitious items. Within this taxonomy, Yukou paper stood out as a top-grade *shengliao* paper within the *bailiao* class.[39]

In a 1946 investigation conducted by the Southeast Office of the Chinese Industrial Cooperatives, researchers noted that Yukou paper was a heavier variety compared to another locally produced paper known as *Changxing paper* (长行纸). Specifically, Yukou paper was packed seven *dao* to a *dan* (a traditional unit of weight), whereas Changxing paper required ten *dao* for the same measure—a *dan* of Yukou paper weighed roughly seventy *jin* on the old Chinese scale. Yukou paper was generally graded into five levels: Grade 1 (*zhenghao*), Grade 2 (*fuhao*), and 3, 4, and 5 respectively. The highest quality, *zhenghao* paper, demanded superior raw materials and workmanship: young bamboo and hemp fibers, sufficient lime treatment, a clean white color, evenly cut and sized sheets, adequate weight, and no root membrane residue—essentially, no visible flaws across any part of the paper. Lower grades, however, allowed for certain imperfections. *Fuhao* Yukou paper, for example, might use slightly older fibers, ample lime, retain a slightly bluish-white tone, adequate weight, evenly cut and sized sheets, and contain minor traces of root membrane—but these flaws

---

39 Lin Cunhe (ed.), *Papers of Fujian* (Fujian Survey and Statistics Series No. 4), issued by the Statistical Office of the Fujian Provincial Government, 1941, pp. 13–20.

were not enough to detract from the paper's overall quality. By contrast, Grade 5 paper displayed the most significant deficiencies: coarse texture, uneven sizing, insufficient lime, yellowish hue, lack of weight, and a high presence of root membranes—all hallmarks of inferior processing. Yet these classifications were more descriptive than prescriptive. There was no rigid standard system enforced. The grading of paper relied entirely on the judgment of *kan zhi xiansheng* (看纸先生, paper inspectors), whose expertise was earned through years of experience and whose authority came from industry-wide recognition by paper shops, merchants, and paper workshop owners alike.[40]

After the founding of the People's Republic of China, to maintain the reputation of Fujian's handmade paper products, expand its domestic and international markets and promote the recovery and development of marketable varieties, the provincial authorities introduced measures to standardize the grading and quality inspection standards for Yukou paper and maobian paper. In December 1964, the Fujian Provincial Handicraft Industry Administration, the Fujian Provincial Supply and Marketing Cooperative, and the Fujian Provincial Bureau of Foreign Trade jointly issued the Specifications and Quality Standards for Fujian Handmade Paper. This regulation laid the groundwork for unifying the names, specifications, and quality standards of traditional paper types used for similar purposes. In accordance with the release of the standard, in 1965, local supply cooperatives and handmade paper stations across the province began displaying paper samples. These samples were graded publicly and democratically, with corresponding prices and incentives for higher-quality products. Purchases were made by comparing submitted paper against these public samples. Yukou paper was divided into twelve grades: Grades 1 through 10,

---

40 Southeast Changting Office of the Chinese Industrial Cooperatives Association (comp.), *Survey of Papermaking in Changting, Fujian*, held at the Changting County Archives, 1946, pp. 19, 22–23.

plus Upper Coarse and Lower Coarse. Grades 1 to 3 were considered top-quality Yukou paper. Grade 1 Yukou paper was required to weigh at least 12 *jin* and 4 *liang* (两, 6.2 kg in total) per *dao*, and to conform precisely to the standard length and width. The paper was expected to exhibit a pale bluish-white hue, a smooth and glossy texture, consistent thickness, and strong durability, without any tears, stains, or visible defects.[41] As late as 1976, the *Handbook for Export Handmade Paper* still stipulated that Yukou and Maobian papers falling short of the required weight must be supplemented. Any *dao* of Yukou paper weighing less than 10 *jin* was to be purchased as Maobian paper instead, according to official procurement rules.[42]

According to *A History of Papermaking in Changting*, the types of paper produced in Changting prior to the Ming dynasty are not clearly recorded in historical texts. By the Qing dynasty, however, several distinct varieties had emerged, including *guanbian* (official-edged paper), *huajian* (decorative letter paper), *maizi* (麦子, wheat paper), and *huangdu* (黄独, yellow tuber paper). Since the Republic of China, the local paper industry have diversified further, introducing over a dozen varieties such as Yukou, Changxing (also known as Daguang), reformed paper, cooked maobian, heavy Yukou, native newsprint, *dabao* (大包, large package), *shuanghe* (双合, double-layered), and doufang (斗方, square-cut).[43] What *Linting Huikao* (临汀汇考, General Survey of Linting) refers to as *guanbian* and *huajian* correspond to Yukou and maobian paper, while *maizi* and *huangdu* were names for what came to be called *shuanghe* and *caozhi* (草纸, grass

---

41 *Standards for the Specifications and Quality of Handmade Paper in Fujian Province* (December 1964), archived at the Ninghua County Archives, collected and provided by Lei Shaoqiu.

42 Foreign Trade Station of Longyan, Fujian Province (comp.). *Handbook of Export Handmade Paper*. July 1976, p. 60.

43 Huang Majin (chief ed.). *A History of Papermaking in Changting*. China Light Industry Press, 1992, p. 82.

paper).[44] Mao Xing, former chairman of the Changting Industrial Cooperative Federation and a scholar of western Fujian's paper industry, offered further classification. He noted that raw material paper—made through the soaking and retting method—was generally called *maobian*, while cooked material paper, produced by steaming and boiling the pulp, was referred to as *lianshi paper*. Among *maobian* types, the heavier grades were known as *zhongzhi* (重纸, heavy paper), with the finest quality specifically called Yukou. By contrast, lighter variants were called *Changxing*, which had smaller sheet dimensions and weighed as little as 3.25 kilograms per *dao*. Around the time of the War of Resistance against Japanese Aggression, manufacturers enlarged the dimensions of *Changxing paper* to match those of Yukou, creating a new thin paper variety called *Daguang*. After the founding of the People's Republic of China, the term Yukou paper came to serve as a standard designation for all heavier papers, while Daguang was incorporated under the broader category of maobian. The original Changxing paper gradually ceased production.[45] This evolution reveals that in the Changting region, the name Yukou paper was a modern development, gaining prominence in the Republican era and solidifying after 1949 as naming and quality standards became more formalized. It ultimately became the regional representative name for high-grade bamboo-based heavy paper, encompassing older categories such as *guanbian* and *huajian* under one unified designation.

---

44 Huang Majin (chief ed.). *A History of Papermaking in Changting*. China Light Industry Press, 1992, p. 35.
45 Mao Xing, "The Historical Origins of the Paper Industry in Ninghua and Tingzhou," in *Ninghua Historical and Cultural Materials (Special Volume on Industry and Commerce)*, compiled by the Committee for the Study of Historical Materials, CPPCC Ninghua County, 1990, p. 72.

Producing Area	Name	Level	Unit	Weight (*jin*)	Number of Sheets Per *Dao*	Length (*chi*)		Quality Standards
... County, Ning ...	Yukou Paper	Grade 1	*dao*	More than 12 and 4/16	200	4.14	1.85	Whitish with a bluish tint. Made from fine *zhuma* pulp that is tender, smooth, and lustrous. Free from dark roots,
... Lian-cheng								limp roots, red roots, yellow joints, sand grains, bamboo dregs, insect shells, lan leave dust, and
Yong'an County								stains. Sheets are uniform, the surface smooth and glossy, strong and crisp. Free from signs of
								scorching, clay residues, nut shells, oil soot, and other firing defects. Screen lines are delicate, without broken screen marks
								or pulp clots, free from water-stained spots, streaks, crab-foot marks, or dry hard spots, and without uneven
								or ragged edges. All four trimmed edges are neat and well-shaped.
	Yukou Paper	Grade 2	*dao*	More than 12 and 4/16	200	4.14	1.85	Whitish with a bluish tint. Made from fine zhuma pulp that is tender, smooth, and lustrous. Free from miscellaneous roots,
								yellow joints, sand grains, bamboo dregs, insect shells, lan leave dust, and stains. Sheets are uniform,
								with a smooth surface, strong and crisp. Free from clay residues, nut shells,
								oil soot, and other firing defects. Screen lines are delicate, without broken screen marks or pulp clots, free from water-stained spots,
								streaks, crab-foot marks, or dry hard spots, and without uneven or ragged edges. All four trimmed edges are neat and well-shaped.

Specifications and Quality Standards for Major Types of Handmade Paper in Fujian Province (Provisional Draft)

(Pic2 Excerpt from the 1964 Provisional Draft of Specification and Quality Standards for Major Handmade Paper in Fujian Province)

As early as the Qing dynasty, *Min Chan Lu Yi* (Record on Specialties of Natural Products of Fujian Province) already reveals a bewildering variety of paper names. By the Republican era, surveys recorded that Fujian boasted hundreds of distinct paper types.[46] In addition to gleaning information about Yukou paper from these textual resources, we can still encounter tangible examples of it today. Small sheets of Yukou paper can be found in standardized paper sample albums compiled after the founding of the People's Republic of China, in publications printed on Yukou paper, and in Japanese paper catalogues. These samples allow us to feel the texture of the paper. Even more directly, authentic specimens of traditionally crafted Yukou paper—along with books, letter papers, genealogies, and contracts made from it—are still preserved in the hands of intangible cultural heritage inheritors and private collectors. In terms of physical characteristics, Yukou paper is distinguishable from ordinary maobian paper. Though made by similar processes, Yukou paper is denser and more compact—giving it noticeably more weight than comparable sheets.[47]

Due to the absence of direct historical records explaining the precise meaning of terms such as kou, kou paper, or Yukou paper, this book draws upon scattered references—such as those to "such-and-such kou," "kou paper," and "Yukou paper"—to offer a concise synthesis of the paper's characteristics. Yukou paper is identified as a locally named handmade paper produced in Changting, Fujian. It represents the finest quality of raw material bamboo paper among heavy maobian papers once known in the Qing dynasty as *Guanbian* and *Huajian*. During the Republican era, it rose to become a regionally recognized and distinguished paper. Folk usage in that

---

46 Lin Cunhe (ed.), *Papers of Fujian* (Fujian Survey and Statistics Series No. 4), issued by the Statistics Office of the Fujian Provincial Government, 1941, pp. 13–24.

47 Based on an interview with Hu Lanshan conducted on September 3, 2022. According to Hu, Yukou paper, known as "heavy paper," is made with the same raw materials and techniques as Maobian paper and Changxing paper, which are considered lighter papers. However, one *dao* of Yukou paper must weigh at least 10.5 *jin* (approx. 5.25 kg) in order to be suitable for writing and printing. To reach around 11 *jin* per *dao*, papermakers must rely on their judgment and experience to control the concentration of bamboo and hemp fiberin the vat. If the concentration is too high, the paper becomes overly heavy and wastes material; if too low, the final product is too light and classified as Maobian paper. This suggests that the character *kou* connotes that the bamboo fibers in the paper are densely packed—thin, yet heavy.

period classified Yukou paper into ten numbered grades. After the founding of the People's Republic of China in 1949, the grading system was revised to twelve tiers. In terms of craftsmanship, Yukou paper is primarily produced using raw material techniques. High-grade Yukou paper, known for its jade-like appearance, smoothness, brightness and fine texture, was prized for cultural uses—such as calligraphy, painting, and book printing. Lower-grade Yukou paper, however, was virtually indistinguishable from ordinary *jia zhi* or even *hai zhi*, and was relegated to more utilitarian roles like packaging or ritual burning as spirit money. Field research conducted in Zhiping She Ethnic Township, Ninghua County—once dubbed the "Capital of Yukou Paper"—reveals the paper's deep integration into local customs. In popular use, Yukou paper served as material for printing genealogies and scriptures in temples. Since the Song dynasty, court officials often used such paper for writing memorials to the emperor. Among the people, therefore, it earned the nickname: "paper worthy of Heaven's gaze."[48]

1.3. Historical Reflections on the Paper Industry

Since the opening of the five treaty ports for foreign trade in the Qing dynasty, foreign industrialists and merchants, eager to break into the Chinese market, began to take a keen interest in surveying the country's regional resources, commercial products, advanced technologies, and social and cultural landscape. This led to extensive investigations into local industries and techniques, many of which left behind invaluable records—particularly regarding traditional handmade papermaking. By the Republican era, the Nationalist government and private industrialists also carried out numerous surveys on China's papermaking techniques and the development of the paper industry across different regions. These surveys

---

48 Communist Party Committee of Zhiping She Ethnic Township & People's Government of Zhiping She Ethnic Township. *Research Report on the Development of the Yukou Paper Industry in Zhiping She Ethnic Township,* Ninghua County. December 2021.

have since become foundational sources for modern historical research on China's paper industry.

As previously discussed, Inoue Nobumasa's late 19th-century report on traditional Chinese papermaking objectively stands as the first scientifically framed modern record of regional hand-papermaking techniques across China during the Qing dynasty. Entering the 20th century, Masamuro Yukinori's fieldwork in Liancheng and Longyan in western Fujian offers a more industry-focused perspective. In just 24 pages, his report covers a remarkable breadth: the origins and conditions of high-grade *Tang paper* (唐纸, a term used by Japanese referring to traditional Chinese paper), an overview of papermaking sites in Liancheng and Longyan, bamboo varieties and bamboo forest revenues, *Tang paper* production techniques and categories, market prices in mountainous areas, transport costs to seaports including taxes and levies, production volumes, export figures, and even the broader economic landscape—agriculture, commodity prices, units of measure, and currency. Together, these insights form a rich portrait of the paper industry and papermaking regions in western Fujian.[49]

In the decades that followed, particularly throughout the 1930s and 1940s, papermaking surveys flourished across China. Provinces such as Zhejiang, Jiangsu, Anhui, Jiangxi, Hunan, and Fujian became hubs of documentation and investigation. Numerous reports were published in trade-focused newspapers and journals, and even more comprehensive provincial compilations and research emerged—such as *The Paper Industry of Zhejiang*, *The Paper Industry of Fujian*, and *The Paper Industry of Hunan*. These works offered detailed accounts of the handmade paper trade, span-

---

49 Masamuro Yukinori, Inspection Record of the Papermaking Industry in the Qing Empire, Civil Affairs Department of the Governor-General of Taiwan, *Investigative Report on the Papermaking Industry of Taiwan*, with the "Inspection Record of the Papermaking Industry in the Qing Empire", 1909, pp. 6–8.

ning production, transportation, sales, and markets from the late Qing dynasty through the Republican era.[50]

During this time, the Fujian provincial government placed particular emphasis on the paper industry. Papermaking was formally included in the province's comprehensive surveys of regional specialties, culminating in the publication of *The Paper Industry of Fujian*. In addition to this official volume, researchers such as Lin Jingliang, Zhang Yonghui, and Xie Shenchu conducted their own field studies in regions like Changting, Shaxian, and Liancheng, producing valuable reports on local paper economies.[51] In 1941, Lin Cunhe expanded and revised the earlier work *The Paper Industry of Fujian* to produce *Papers of Fujian*, a more detailed and structured publication. This book covered an impressive range of topics: types of paper, changes in production and distribution, regional centers of production, output values, production organizations, raw materials and techniques, packaging and transport, market structures, pricing and costs, taxation and government oversight, as well as technical innovations. Today, it remains a key resource for understanding the paper industry in Republican era Fujian.[52] In 1946, the Southeast Office of the Chinese Industrial Cooperatives, based

---

50 Mo Guli, *The Native Papermaking Industry in Guangdong*, Lingnan Journal Press, Lingnan University, 1929; *The Paper Industry in Zhejiang*, Zhejiang Provincial Planning Council, 1930; *The Paper Industry of Fujian* (Statistical Bulletin on the Fujian Investigation, No. 1), compiled and mimeographed by the Statistical Office of the Secretariat of the Fujian Provincial Government, 1939; *Paper*, Jiangxi Provincial Department of Construction, 1939; Zhang Renjia et al., *The Paper Industry of Hunan*, 1942, reprinted in: Zeng Saifeng and Cao Youpeng (eds.), *Selected Historical Materials on Hunan's Economy during the Republican Period (Vol. 3)*, Hunan People's Publishing House, 2009, pp. 620–793.
51 Lin Jingliang, "An Investigation of the Papermaking Industry in Changting, Fujian," *China Construction (Shanghai)*, Vol. 14, No. 5, 1936;
Zhang Yonghui, "An Investigation of Handmade Papermaking in Shaxian and Liancheng, Fujian (No. 1 in the Industrial Survey Reports of the Central Industrial Research Institute)," *Industrial Center*, June 1937;
Xie Shenchu, "A Study on the Papermaking Industry in Changting," *Journal of Economic and Commercial Studies* (Xiamen), No. 1, 1941.
52 Lin Cunhe (ed.), *Papers of Fujian* (Fujian Survey and Statistics Series No. 4), issued by the Statistical Office of the Fujian Provincial Government, 1941.

in Changting, published a focused study on the local paper trade. It investigated the region's production and sales figures, paper merchants and high-interest lending, quality standards and the role of the *kan zhi xiansheng* (paper inspectors), as well as the economic conditions of papermakers and paper workshop owners. The report also detailed the production process, costs, innovations, and the development of the industry under the guidance of the the Industrial Cooperatives organization in Changting.[53]

Since the founding of the People's Republic of China—especially from the 1980s onward—historical research on papermaking has taken on a new direction, often framed within economic history. Scholars began to study papermaking not merely as a craft, but as a sector of the national economy, situating it within general economic history and the broader history of Chinese handicraft industries. These economic-historical studies tend to focus on two major periods: papermaking during the Qing dynasty and its transformation in modern times. Spatially, many studies address the paper industry across China as a whole, while others examine specific regional cases, such as those of Fujian[54] and Jiangxi[55]. Adopting frameworks such as

---

53 Southeast Changting Office of the Chinese Industrial Cooperatives (comp.), *Survey of Papermaking in Changting, Fujian*, 1946.

54 Lin Renchuan, "Production and Distribution of Paper in Republican Fujian," *Studies in Chinese Socioeconomic History*, No. 1, 1989;

Huang Majin (chief ed.). *A History of Papermaking in Changting*. China Light Industry Press, 1992;

Zhou Xuexiang, *Socioeconomic Changes in Hakka Border Areas of Fujian and Guangdong during the Ming and Qing Dynasties*, Fujian People's Publishing House, 2007, pp. 205–213;

Yu Ruxian, *A Study of Rural Informal Lending in Western Fujian from the Qing to the Republican Era*, Tianjin Ancient Books Publishing House, 2010, pp. 159–174;

Xu Xiaowang, *Socioeconomic Transformation in the Southeastern Mountain Regions during the Ming and Qing—Focusing on the Fujian-Zhejiang-Jiangxi Border*, China Literature and History Press, 2014, pp. 151–158.

55 Wang Anchun, "Papermaking in Guangxin Prefecture, Jiangxi during the Ming Dynasty," *Journal of Shangrao Normal University*, No. 4, 2001;

Liao Han, "Small Commodity Economy in the Papermaking Industry of the Qing Dynasty—A Case Study of Yanshan County, Jiangxi," *Anhui Historical Studies*, No. 6, 2020;

Liao Han, "Social Mobility of the Shed People in Qing Dynasty Jiangxi—A Case Study of Huangbi Village in Yanshan," *Qing History Journal*, No. 3, 2021;

"mountain are economies," "small commodity economies," "rural industries," and "rural handicrafts," scholars have used the development of traditional papermaking to explore larger theoretical questions. These include the rise of capitalist elements in premodern China, the economic development of China's southern mountain areas, and the commodity economy in traditional Chinese society.

In recent years, influenced by growing environmental concerns, digitalization, and other shifting cultural paradigms, as well as technological advancements, people have developed increasingly complex anxieties and feelings of estrangement toward paper, printed materials, and paper products. In this context, studies of the history of the paper industry from a cultural-historical perspective have drawn renewed attention from scholars in both historical and literary fields around the world. Researchers such as Chen Xiejun, Wu Jialing, Alexander Munro, and Lothar Müller have examined paper through the lens of history of paper itself and cultural history, tracing its deep-rooted significance in the shaping of human civilization. Their works revisit and document the profound value and significance of paper to human culture. Voices from various corners of the world now ask: What would the world be like without paper? Does paper still have a future? These questions reflect a collective unease about whether the traditional, paper-bound way of life can endure in the digital age. At the same time, they inspire new conversations about how to preserve both the material and intangible cultural heritage associated with paper.[56]

Yang Yong, "A Review of the Papermaking Industry in Republican Jiangxi," *Journal of Jiangxi Normal University (Philosophy and Social Sciences Edition)*, No. 3, 2001.
56 Chen Xiejun (Ed.), *Zhi* [Paper], Peking University Press, 2012.
Wu Jialing, *The Cultural Industry and Experiencing Aesthetics of Paper: Taking Chih-liao-wo, Guang Shin Jr Lyau, and the Suho Memorial Paper Culture Foundation As Examples*, Liwen Culture, 2015.
Wen Xiaoxing, " 'Sacred Consumption' and the Productive Protection of Intangible Cultural Heritage in Traditional Crafts: A Case Study of 'Hengjiang Heavy Paper' Production in Shicheng County, Jiangxi." *Journal of Northwest Minzu University (Philoso-*

The history of papermaking has long captured the attention of scholars in both economic and cultural history. In recent years, however, a growing body of research from a social history perspective has begun to shed new light on the field. These emerging studies explore the social dynamics within key papermaking regions of China—examining the people, organizations, and structures that sustained the industry. A pioneering work in this regard is *A History of Papermaking in Changting*, the first local monograph dedicated to the subject. The book offers valuable insights into various participants along the papermaking supply chain, including workers, workshop owners, merchants, and trade associations—making it a rich resource for social historians.[57] Building on this foundation, researcher Lai Yang'en investigated the relationship between the handmade paper industry in Tiechang township, Changting County and the role of clan organizations in rural society.[58] In other regions—such as Sichuan, Guizhou, and Zhejiang—recent studies have also begun to consider the social dimensions of papermaking, including individual actions, decision-making, and broader community impacts. Among these, Jacob Eyferth's social history research on the paper industry in Jiajiang, Sichuan, stands as the only monograph to date examining China's paper industry history from a social history perspective. Based on extensive fieldwork and archival research conducted between 1995 and 2004 in Jiajiang, Sichuan, Eyferth's book traces the transformation of handmade papermaking villages through the 20th century. He explores how family life, social organization, and commercial networks

phy and Social Sciences Edition), No. 4, 2017.

Alexander Monroe, *The Paper Trail: An Unexpected History of a Revolutionary Invention,* translated by Shi Xiantao, Sanlian Publishing House, 2018.

The Multigraph Collective, *Interacting with Print: Elements of Reading in the Era of Print Saturation*, translated by Fu Li, Beijing United Publishing Company, 2021.

Lothar Muller, *White Magic: The Age of Paper*, translated by He Xiaoyi and Song Qiong, Guangdong People Publishing House, 2022.

57 Huang Majin (chief ed.). *A History of Papermaking in Changting*. China Light Industry Press, 1992, pp. 54–62.

58 Lai Yang'en. *Research on the Structure and Driving Forces of Rural Chinese Society*, Huazhong University of Science and Technology Press, 2014.

weathered waves of disruption and reform, while also examining how papermaking skills interacted with and helped shape local social structures. His work offers a compelling model for writing the social history of traditional industries in modern China.[59]

This book takes Yukou paper—a celebrated regional handmade paper—as a lens, seeking to uncover scattered traces of its production, transport, sale, and use across various types of historical sources from the handmade paper era, extending into modern times. It draws not only from official records and trade documents, but also from local histories and fieldwork in papermaking communities, where the artistry of traditional techniques and the bittersweet lives of papermakers still echo today. Through this social-historical lens, the book aspires to preserve the memories of a paper-bound way of life—a world where life accompanied by fine paper—in anticipation of a future that may one day be entirely paperless.

---

59 Jacob Eyferth, *Eating Rice from Bamboo Roots:The Social History of a Community of Handicraft Papermakers in Rural Sichuan, 1920-2000,* translated by Han Wei, Jiangsu People's Publishing House, 2016.

2. The Craftsmanship of Yukou Paper

In earlier times, wise predecessors who recognized the precious value of papermaking meticulously recorded their observations and insights into the process, offering future generations a rare window into this ancient craft. Beginning in the Song dynasty, the technique of making paper from bamboo became widespread across southern China. Yet it wasn't until the late Ming dynasty that the bamboo papermaking techniques of Fujian were formally documented, preserving their legacy to this day. This chapter gathers and examines a range of historical texts—from the late Ming, mid-Qing, Republican era, and the period following the founding of the People's Republic of China—that describe the bamboo papermaking procedures in Fujian, including the production of Yukou paper. These records are brought into conversation with the author's recent fieldwork in the paper workshops of Hulan Mountain and Leiyusheng in Zhiping She Ethnic Township, Ninghua County, Sanming City, where traditional Yukou paper is still handmade alongside veteran papermakers. By comparing historical texts with practical contemporary experiences, this chapter aims to illuminate the transmission and transformation of Yukou papermaking—a regional treasure and a living example of China's intangible cultural heritage—across centuries of change.

(Pic 35   Testing Water Retention in the Soaking Pond, If the Pond Leaks, the Fibers Will Rot Quickly, Photographs by Gui Shuzhong)

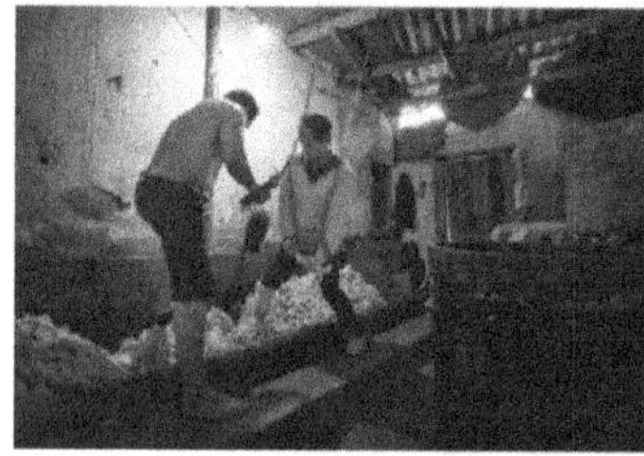

(Pic3   Main Production Processes of Yukou Paper, Photographs by Gui Shuzhong)

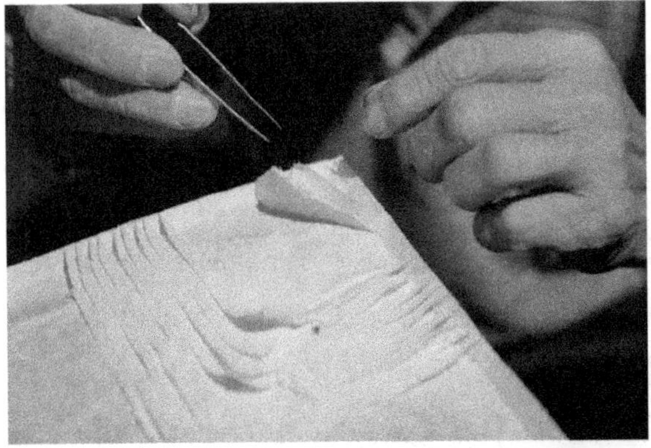

(Pic3   Main Production Processes of Yukou Paper, Photographs by Gui Shuzhong)

2.1.   Papermaking Process

2.1.1.   The Process of Making Cooked Material Bamboo Paper in Fujian as Recorded in Tiangong Kaiwu

Often hailed as "the technological encyclopedia of 17th-century China," *Tiangong Kaiwu* offers a vivid and detailed portrayal of bamboo paper production in Fujian. The text includes five woodblock illustrations and an extensive written account, carefully documenting the primary   aw materials, intricate procedures, underlying principles, and critical precautions involved in the craft. This highly professional record allows for comparisons with later techniques of handmade bamboo paper, facilitating an examination of how bamboo papermaking skills have been inherited and developed since the Ming dynasty. While most historical studies on the history of paper merely quote the text's opening line to highlight Fujian's prominence as a major center of bamboo paper production during the Ming period, the full passage holds far greater significance. It faithfully captures the essence of *shuliao* (cooked material) bamboo paper craftsmanship in Ming-era Fujian. For this reason, the entire excerpt is reproduced below:

All bamboo paper is made in the southern provinces, with Fujian Province monopolizing its excellence. The process began shortly after bamboo shoots had sprouted. Craftsmen would inspect the mountain valleys, evaluating the terrain and bamboo growth to find the ideal stalks for harvest. Young bamboo stalks that were just about to grow branches and leaves were considered the finest raw material. Harvesting took place around the time of the *Mangzhong* (Grain in Ear) solar term. The bamboo was cut into lengths of five to seven *chi* and soaked in water-filled pits dug on the mountainside. To prevent the water from drying out, bamboo pipes were installed to continuously divert fresh stream water into the pools, ensuring constant immersion. The bamboo would be left to soak for over a hundred days. After this prolonged soaking, the next step involved intensive pounding and washing to remove the rough husk and green outer skin—a step known as *sha qing* or "killing the green." The remaining bamboo stalk, now resembling ramie, was coated with a slurry of high-quality slaked lime and placed in a steaming wooden vat for cooking. This stage required intense heat over the course of eight days and nights. All bamboo boiling is done with a cauldron, typically four *chi* in diameter and sealed with a mixture of mud and lime. It resembled the sturdy basins used for salt boiling used in the Guangzhong region. The cauldron could hold more than ten *dan* (石, 100 Chinese litre) of water and was covered by a steaming vet that measures fifteen *chi* in circumference and over four *chi* in diameter. After the bamboo was fully steamed for eight days, the fire was extinguished for one day and the fibers were removed and rinsed in a clean water pond. The bottom and sides of the pond was carefully lined with fitted wooden planks to avoid contamination from mud—a precaution not taken when making coarse paper. Once thoroughly cleaned, the fibers were again treated, this time with lye made from wood ash. They were then returned to the vat, where a layer of rice straw ash about an *cun* thick was spread evenly over the top. The mixture was heated until boiling, removed to another vat, and doused repeatedly with the rice straw ash solution. If the solution cooled, it would be reheated and poured again. This process was repeated for over ten days until the bamboo fibers naturally decayed and fermented. The resulting pulp was then transferred to a mortar for pounding—often done with water-powered hammers, common in mountainous regions—until it reached the consistency of fine paste. The pulp was then poured into a paper vat. The vat, roughly the size of a square *dou* (斗, a traditional Chinese measuring implement), was scaled according to the size of the bamboo mould, which in turn is determined by the paper being produced. Once the bamboo pulp is ready, the *dou* is filled with clear water, covering the pulp by about three *cun*. A paper-sizing agent, derived from a plant resembling *taozhu* leaves (桃竹, its name varied by region), was added. This gave the paper a clean, white finish once dried. The paper mould itself was finely crafted from meticulously shaved bamboo strips. When unrolled and spread out, it is supported by a rectangular frame with crisscrossing braces underneath. To form a sheet, the two papermakers would hold the mould with both hands, dip it into the vat, and gently agitate it to catch the pulp on the surface. The thickness of each sheet was determined by the makers' technique—a light agitation produced thinner paper, while a heavier agitation yielded thicker sheets. As the bamboo pulp settled on the mould, excess water drained away. The mould was then inverted to lay the wet sheet onto a board, and sheets were stacked in layers. Once a sufficient number were piled, a board is placed on top, and ropes and wooden poles are used to press it—much like the method used in wine pressing—to squeeze out all excess water. After pressing, each sheet was carefully lifted using fine copper tweezers and dried on heated walls. The heated walls were built from bricks to form narrow drying alleyways. The ground of this alley is covered with bricks, with every few bricks leaving a gap. Firewood is lit at one end, and the heat permeates through the brick gaps to warm the entire alley. Once the bricks are hot, the wet paper sheets are pasted onto them to dry, then peeled off and stacked into bundles.[60]

Although The Excerpt from *Tiangong Kaiwu* does not specify the precise location of the cooked material bamboo paper-making process it describes, the methods it outlines can be regarded as representative of widely practiced or commonly recognized techniques across various parts of Fujian at the time. The text offers a remarkably concise yet comprehensive overview of the entire production process—from selecting and soaking the bamboo to boiling, washing, and pounding it into pulp, followed by sheet

---

60 Song Yingxing (Ming Dynasty), *Annotated Translation of Tiangong Kaiwu*, annotated and translated by Pan Jixing, Shanghai Ancient Books Publishing House, 2008, pp. 225–230.
Song Yingxing (1587–ca. 1666), a native of Fengxin (modern-day Yichun) in Jiangxi province, passed the provincial-level imperial examination in the 43rd year of the Wanli era, Ming dynasty (1615). In the seventh year of the Chongzhen era, Ming dynasty (1634), he was appointed as an education officer in Fenyi. His renowned work *Tiangong Kaiwu* (The Exploitation of the Works of Nature) was published in the tenth year of the Chongzhen era, Ming dynasty (1637), and the following year, in 1638, he was appointed as a judicial officer (推官, tuiguan) in Tingzhou Prefecture, Fujian.

formation, the application of sizing agents, and drying the paper over heat. Each stage is detailed with notable clarity, specifying the required standards, tools, additives, duration, site requirements, frequency, and techniques involved in each step. Of particular significance is the mention of two separate rounds of bamboo boiling, along with the specific vessels, additives, and timing involved. This step is a hallmark of Fujian's cooked material bamboo papermaking technique and constitutes the most fundamental distinction between the raw and cooked methods. The full production process as portrayed in *Tiangong Kaiwu* can be summarized in the following steps:

Harvesting Bamboo (young bamboo of the current year's growth)—Trimming and Slicing—Soaking and Fermentation (immersed in a pond added with agents for fermentation)—Washing and Softening (the hard outer green rind and coarse outer layers are washed and crushed to remove tough tissues around the vascular bundles as well as the inner bamboo membrane, allowing the vascular bundles to separate into filaments)—Half-Processed Bamboo Fiber—Mixing the Half-Processed Bamboo Fiber with Lime Paste—Boiling the Material in a Wooden Vat (First Boil)—Placing It in a Material Pond for Rinsing—Preparing the Pulp by Adding Alkali Liquid Made from Firewood and Straw Ash—Boiling the Material in a Wooden Vat (Second Boil)—Steeping and Rotting into Pulp by Pouring Ash Alkali Liquid over it—Final Rinse—Pounding into Fine Pulp—Putting it into a Paper Vat, Adding Paper Sizing Agents and Stirring Evenly—Forming Paper with a Screen—Pressing—Drying

The production process described above represents the achievement of centuries of accumulated expertise in making high-quality unbleached bamboo pulp paper using the cooked material method, dating from the Song dynasty to the Ming dynasty. In the bamboo papermaking regions of Fujian, this traditional method has been largely preserved to the present day. While some steps and techniques have undergone minor adjustments or improvements, the core process remains unchanged. This continuity not only reflects the technical maturity of Fujian's papermaking craft during the Ming dynasty, but also suggests that it had reached a level of refinement capable of representing the most advanced bamboo papermaking techniques of its time.

2.1.2.   The Process of Making Cooked Material Bamboo Paper in Tingzhou, Fujian as Recorded in Linting Huikao

The *Min Chan Lu Yi* (Record on Specialties of Natural Products of Fujian Province) cited previously outlines the general papermaking procedures used in Fujian workshops, yet omits crucial steps such as bamboo boiling and pulp preparation. As such, it likely reflects one of the earliest accounts of raw material bamboo pulp papermaking techniques. Slightly predating that publication is the *Linting Huikao* (General Survey of Linting), another frequently cited source in the study of Fujian's papermaking history. While most scholars have focused solely on its opening line—which identifies paper as the most widely sold local product—the text in fact provides a detailed and technically informed description of the bamboo paper production process in Tingzhou. This account complements that of the *Min Chan Lu Yi* (Record on Specialties of Natural Products of Fujian Province), and together, they form a valuable record of mid-Qing dynasty bamboo papermaking practices in Fujian. By comparing these historical techniques with those of the Ming dynasty before and with those of the Republic era and contemporary times after, one gains a fuller picture of the craft's evolution. For this reason, the full passage is reproduced below:

> Among all the goods produced in the Tingzhou Prefecture,
> paper was the most widely traded, reaching distant markets

across the empire. Each county had its own distinctive styles and names for paper. In Changting, for instance, varieties included *guanbian*, *huajian*, *maizi*, and *huangdu*, while colored papers came in shades such as *huangdan* (黄丹, red lead) and *muhong* (木红, wood red). However, the bamboo and tribute papers sold in local markets were not made in Changting but originated from the counties of Guihua and Liancheng. The red paper of Guihua County was considered the finest. Its gold and silver papers were created by brushing tin foil onto the surface or by dyeing the paper yellow to serve as spiritual money for funerary use. In Liancheng County, paper types included *lianshi*, *guanbian*, *yanzhi* (烟纸, smoke paper), *gaolian* (高帘, tall screen paper), and *jiaban* (夹板, splint paper), all made from bamboo stalk.

The process began with splitting fresh bamboo and *sha qing* (killing the green), preserving only the pale inner layer. This material was then soaked in underground pits filled with alkaline ash water. After a long fermentation period, the fibers were removed and spread out to dry in the sun. The longer it basks under the sun, the whiter and finer the resulting paper becomes; if dried too quickly, the result was coarse and porous. This intermediate product was known colloquially as *zhuma* (竹麻, bamboo hemp) To begin actual papermaking, workers constructed large rectangular stone vats, about one *zhang* (丈, approximately more than three meters) in length and width, to hold cooking woks. The bamboo hemp was boiled with lime to soften its texture. Nearby streams were diverted to power waterwheels and pestles, which pounded the fibers until they broke down into a soft pulp. The pulp was then transferred to water vats, stirred constantly to keep it evenly suspended. A bamboo screen was dipped into the vat and gently pulled upward; with a single smooth motion, a sheet of paper would take shape. The wet sheet was then laid onto a wooden board, with one corner folded to make it easier to lift later. For drying, the sheets were pressed onto a specially constructed wall above a ground oven. The wall had a hollow interior to channel hot air, allowing the paper to dry more quickly than in direct sunlight. Within the papermaking community, there was an old saying: "A single sheet of paper is no easy feat—seventy-two steps to shape it." This proverb captured the complexity and labor-intensive nature of the entire craft.[61]

In addition to listing the types and origins of paper traded in Changting, *Linting Huikao* (General Survey of Linting) provides a concise yet telling glimpse into the complicated and labor-intensive papermaking practices of the Tingzhou region. Compared with the more systematic descriptions found in the Ming dynasty's *Tiangong Kaiwu* (The Exploitation of the Works of Nature), this account is notably sparse in technical detail. Nevertheless, it pays particular attention to one revealing step: sun-drying the bamboo pulp—"the longer it basks under the sun, the whiter and finer the resulting paper becomes." This indicates that as early as the mid-Qing period, sun-bleaching had already become a widely adopted technique in Tingzhou region, where the cooked material method dominated production. Remarkably, this very process can still be observed today in the traditional

---

61 Yang Lan (Qing Dynasty), *Linting Huikao* (General Survey of Linting), vol. 4, *Wuchan Kao* (Treatise on Local Products), the fourth year of Guangxu era, Qing dynasty edition (1878), pp. 14–15. Held in the Library of Fujian Normal University.
Yang Lan, whose exact birth and death years are unknown, was a native of Changting, Fujian. He passed the provincial level imperial examination in the 54th year of the Qianlong era, Qing dynasty (1789) and later served as magistrate of Zhaohua County in Sichuan during the first year of the Daoguang era, Qing dynasty (1821).

lianshi paper-making practices preserved in Gutian Town in Liancheng County.

2.1.3. The Raw Material Method in Surveys of Papermaking in Changting, Fujian During the Republican Era

By the 1930s, field investigations carried out by multiple researchers in Changting revealed a shift in papermaking techniques. The cooked material method, once dominant, was no longer the only widely practiced approach. Increasingly, attention turned to the raw material method, which began to emerge as a prevalent alternative. These investigative reports left behind a wealth of detailed, first-hand descriptions of the raw material papermaking process. Among the earliest and most comprehensive accounts can be found in *The Paper Industry of Fujian*, compiled and published in 1939. This work was based on the province-wide survey of local specialties organized by the Statistics Office of the Secretariat of the Fujian Provincial Government in 1935, and it offers a concise yet insightful summary of the raw material method.

1. Raw Material Processing

Bamboo Harvesting—

The bamboo selected for raw material papermaking was typically young bamboo. However, the harvest could be delayed slightly—usually until after the *Lixia* (立夏, Beginning of Summer) solar term, and often as late as *Xiaoman* (小满, Lesser Fullness of Grain). Beyond this period, usage declined, since bamboo grown past *Xiaoman* tended to become too coarse and fibrous for paper production. A local saying from Yongding goes, "*Zhuma* shouldn't drink the *Xiaoman* waters," referring precisely to this transformation. In Shanghang County, dietary customs also reflected this rhythm: eating bamboo shoots was prohibited before *Guyu* (谷雨, Grain Rain) to allow optimal growth for papermaking bamboo. Once past that date, the shoots could be freely harvested—timed so that they reached maturity just before *Xiaoman*. (That said, for lower-grade raw material paper, older bamboo was sometimes used.) The methods of cutting and gathering the bamboo mirrored those used in the cooked material method: after felling, the stalks were collected in one place to await splitting.

Bamboo Splitting—

Again, similar to the cooked material method. However, in counties known for producing finer-quality raw material paper—such as Shaxian, Shunchang, Youxi, and Jianle—the bamboo's outer skin was peeled off prior to splitting.

Lime Steeping—

This was where the raw method diverged sharply from its cooked counterpart. Split bamboo slats were layered in soaking ponds, alternating with layers of lime—one layer of bamboo followed by one layer of lime, and so on. The pile was then covered with wooden planks or old bamboo slats, weighed down with heavy stones to prevent floating when water was added. The pond was equipped with inlet and outlet pipes. Once the layering was complete, clean water was introduced to begin steeping. Typically, the lime-to-bamboo ratio was around 1:10 (e.g., 10 *dan* of lime for 100 *dan* of bamboo pulp). Under this ratio, the soaking lasted around 40 days, although in places like Ningyang, Nanping, Zhangping, and Pinghe, the process could extend beyond two months, depending on the quantity of lime used.

Rinsing and Washing—

After soaking, the bamboo was loosened with hoes or iron hooks to wash away residual lime. Wastewater was drained through the outlet, and the material was piled beside the pond. Fresh water was introduced to clean the pond. Then the bamboo was returned to the pond, and fresh water was introduced again to wash the bamboo.

Freshwater Soaking—

After washing, the bamboo pulp was stacked again in layers, covered with straw or bamboo peel, and weighted with stones. Clean water was added, and the pit was inspected daily. Once the water turned yellow, it was replaced with fresh water. Initially, water was changed every one to two days, and later every seven to eight days. This process continued for roughly 50 days, until the water no longer turned dark—indicating that impurities had been sufficiently removed. (In Shaowu, the makers of *doufang* paper skipped this step altogether, relying instead on 40 days of natural bleaching through sun and rain.)

Peeling the Bark—

Once the bamboo pulp had softened through soaking and sun-drying, the outer bark was removed. This was made easier due to the pulp's softened state. In cases where the bamboo bark had been stripped earlier, this step was unnecessary—only remaining scraps were picked off manually.

Pulp Pounding—

In the process of pulp pounding, some employed the method of pounding it in a mortar, while others made use of human or animal power to trample it—a process mentioned in the cooked material method. However, a key difference is that cooked material used only bamboo pith during pounding or trampling, while raw material varied. For high-grade raw pulp, only bamboo pith was used—its skin having been removed earlier. Mid-grade paper mixed the pith with softened bark, while the lowest-grade paper used mostly bark. The proportion of skin to pith greatly influenced the final paper quality. After this pounding, the pulp was ready for papermaking. (In some counties like Pucheng and Zhenghe, the pounded pulp was further steeped in alkaline water for about ten days.)

Main Steps in Sequence—

Bamboo Harvesting → Bamboo Splitting → Lime Steeping → Rinsing and Washing → Freshwater Soaking → Drying → Bark Removal → Pounding

2.   Papermaking Process

To make raw material paper, the softened pulp was first transferred to the papermaking vat. Clean water was added and mixed slowly with bamboo rakes until even. Coarser fibers and undigested fragments were filtered out using a bamboo strainer. A sticky plant-based glue was then added while the mixture was stirred continuously to ensure even distribution. Upon finishing, a bamboo comb was placed at the bottom of the vat to prevent thick pulp from floating upward and causing uneven paper thickness. The actual sheet-forming process using bamboo screens was essentially the same as in the cooked material method and is not elaborated here.

Papermaking Sequence—

Add water and mix thoroughly → Skim coarse fibers → Add glue → Stir → Sheet-forming → Sheet stacking → Pressing to drain water

3.　Finishing Process

The finishing process for raw material paper closely mirrored that of cooked material paper. However, for low-grade raw material paper, the sheets were simply sun-dried—skipping the heat wall drying step. They also omitted further surface treatments like polishing with stones and bricks, which were reserved for higher-end products.[62]

The book *The Paper Industry of Fujian* presents separate accounts of the methods used for cooked material paper and raw material paper. The process for raw material paper is divided into three main stages: raw material preparation, papermaking procedures, and finishing steps. It highlights key differences between the two techniques—especially in how the bamboo is soaked and how the fibers are pounded. Of particular note is the attention paid to regional variations across the province. The text mentions counties such as Yongding, Shanghang, Shaxian, Shunchang, Youxi, Jiangle, Ningyang, Nanping, Zhangping, Pinghe, Shaowu, Pucheng, and Zhenghe. However, it omits any reference to the two major production hubs for raw material paper: Changting and Ninghua. This omission suggests that the investigators may have had only limited familiarity with the key regions of raw material paper production.

---

62 *The Paper Industry of Fujian* (Statistical Bulletin on the Fujian Investigation, No. 1), compiled and mimeographed by the Statistical Office of the Secretariat of the Fujian Provincial Government, 1939, mimeographed edition, 1939, Central Volume, pp. 17–21.

A year later, in 1936, researcher Lin Jingliang[63] conducted a brief but focused investigation into the papermaking practices of the Changting area. His report included a concise outline of the basic production steps.

(A) In the second and third months of the lunar calendar, payments are made to secure laborers for bamboo cutting.

(B) By the fourth month, funds—often advanced through connections between paper merchants and paper producers—are used to purchase rice, which serves as provisions for the workers.

(C) In the fifth month, the bamboo cutting begins in earnest. Wages are paid out to the cutters, and once felled, the bamboo is soaked in limewater.

(D) During the sixth and seventh months, the lime-soaked bamboo is thoroughly washed and rinsed.

(E) In the eighth month, further payments are advanced to paper merchants to reserve skilled papermakers for the coming production cycle.

(F) From the ninth month through to the following first month, the papermaking season is in full swing, with wages distributed to workers engaged in the craft.[64]

---

63 Lin Jingliang (1912–1994), a native of Putian, Fujian. In 1929, he was admitted to the Agricultural College of the Shanghai Labor University. After the university was forced to close in 1931, he transferred to the Department of Soil and Agricultural Chemistry at Peking University's Agricultural College, graduating in 1933. From 1934 to 1936, he held technical positions in the Zhejiang Provincial Office for Chemical Fertilizer Management and at the Jiangxi Provincial Academy of Agriculture. In 1937, he became Senior Technical Officer and Section Chief at the Fujian Provincial Agricultural Improvement Bureau, where he conducted soil and fertilizer research at the province's main agricultural experiment station.

64 Lin Jingliang, "An Investigation of the Paper Industry in Changting, Fujian," *China Construction (Shanghai)*, Vol. 14, No. 5, 1936.

Lin Jingliang also provided a concise account of traditional papermaking methods in Changting:

In the third or fourth lunar month, freshly grown bamboo—still without leaves—is felled and chopped into small pieces. These are then soaked in limewater, using fifty *jin* of lime for every hundred *jin* of bamboo. Large stones are placed on top to ensure full submersion. After about forty days, the bamboo chips are removed and rinsed in ponds or running streams, then soaked again in clean water with a layer of reeds laid over them to prevent dust from settling. Another forty days later, the bamboo has softened sufficiently. It is then handed over to workers who remove bamboo nodes and other impurities. Next, foot-pulpers stomp the softened material until it becomes a tofu-like pulp. Papermakers then use bamboo screens to filter and spread the pulp evenly, removing excess water and forming sheets of uniform thickness. The wet sheets are stacked—sometimes one or two *chi* high—on a flat surface. Finally, the sheets are separated and dried individually by paper-drying workers. At this stage, the papermaking process is complete.[65]

This account reveals that the traditional method observed by Lin Jingliang in the Changting region lacks two essential steps typical of the cooked material method: boiling the raw material and bleaching it in sunlight. Instead, what he recorded aligns with the raw material technique. Unlike the process described in *Tiangong Kaiwu*, where bamboo was soaked in clear water for a hundred days before being lime-treated, Lin's account skips the water-soaking stage and uses limewater directly after *sha qing* (killing the green). Another innovation is the foot-pulping step, which re-

---

65 Lin Jingliang, "An Investigation of the Paper Industry in Changting, Fujian," *China Construction (Shanghai)*, Vol. 14, No. 5, 1936.

places the older method of boiling bamboo into pulp. In contrast to textual records from the Ming and Qing periods, Lin went a step further by illustrating the process in a sequential diagram (see pic4), offering readers a clearer grasp of the procedure.

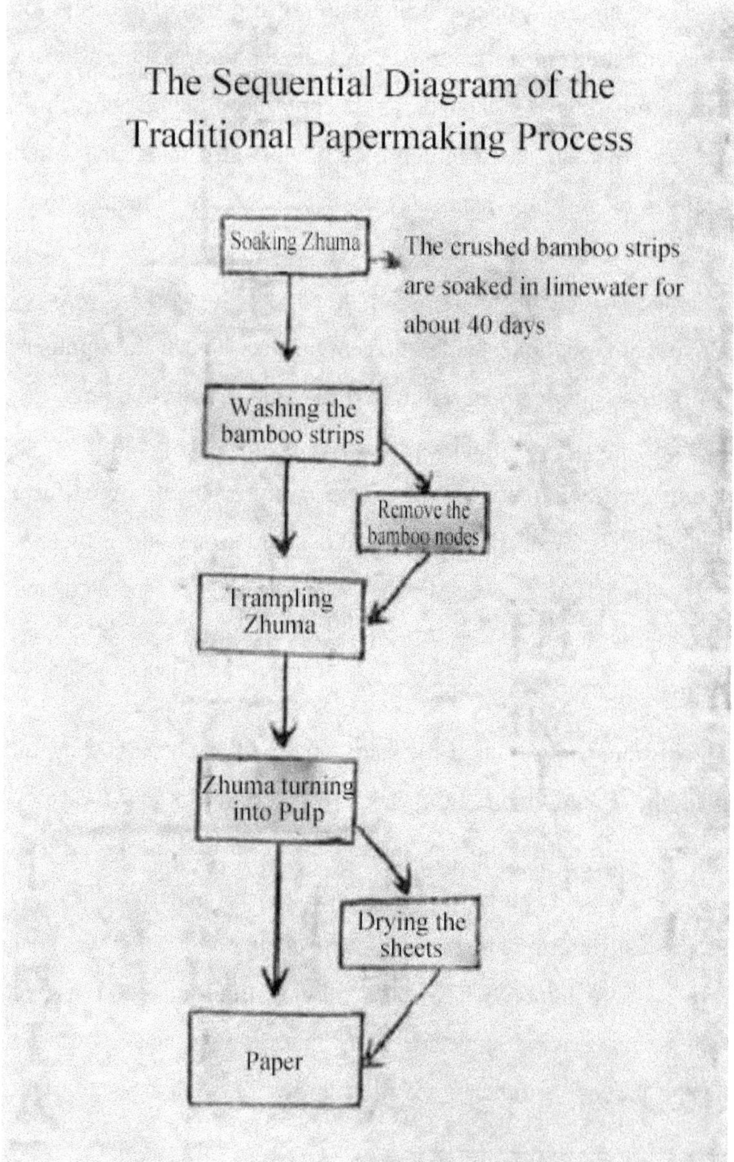

(Pic4   The Sequential Diagram of the Traditional Papermaking Process)

A few months after Lin Jingliang's investigation, Zhang Yonghui conducted his own survey of the hand-made paper industry in the counties of Shaxian and Liancheng. He observed that both cooked material paper and raw material paper were being produced simultaneously in these regions. In particular, he documented the method used to manufacture raw material *maobian* paper as follows:

Each year, during the latter part of the third lunar month (between *Qingming* and *Lixia*), when young bamboo shoots of *Ma Zhu* (Phyllostachys pubescens) have just emerged from the soil and their leaves have not yet sprouted, the bamboo is harvested. The culms are cut into sections of four to five *chi*, split into thin strips, and submerged layer by layer in a pond. The pond, typically measuring about 12 *chi* in length, 6 in width, and 4 in depth, is filled with alternating layers of bamboo and lime—about 14 *jin* of lime for every 100 *jin* of young bamboo. (At that time, lime cost roughly 0.4 *yuan* per 100 *jin*, and 60 *jin* of young bamboo could produce one *dao* of paper, or 196 sheets.) Once filled, the pond is topped off with water to submerge the bamboo entirely. Reed mats and heavy stones are placed on top to ensure full immersion. After about 30 days of soaking, the wastewater is drained. The bamboo is then rinsed with fresh water—once a day, for ten consecutive days. Afterward, the pond is again filled with clean water and the material is soaked for another month. By then, the raw material is considered ready.

At this stage, the softened bamboo is peeled by hand to remove the outer skin, inner bamboo membrane and nodes. The moisture is squeezed out, and the pulp is trampled underfoot into fine, cotton-like fibers. These fibers are then stored in wooden pulp tubs, awaiting further use. To make paper, the softened fibers are poured into a paper vat (typically 6 *chi* long, 5 *chi* wide, and 3 *chi* deep), mixed with water, and stirred with a wooden rake. Coarse fragments are skimmed off with a bamboo strainer. Then, a solution made from *langye* juice is added. After further stirring to achieve an even consistency, a papermaker uses a traditional bamboo screen to scoop and shape the pulp into individual sheets. The wet sheets are laid one atop another on bamboo frames until the stacked thickness reaches around three *chi*. At that point, the entire stack is transferred to a wooden press to squeeze out excess water, resulting in damp paper sheets. These are then carried to a drying chamber, where one corner of each sheet is clipped open, and each sheet is peeled apart and affixed individually onto a heated drying wall. The wall, which is hollow and heated from within by fire, is coated with a smooth mixture of tung oil and egg white to give it a glossy finish. The warm surface dries the paper evenly. Once dry, the sheets are removed, trimmed, inspected, and finally packed for sale.[66]

---

66 Zhang Yonghui, "A Survey of the Handmade Paper Industry in Shaxian County and Liancheng, Fujian (Industrial Investigation Report No. 1 by the Central Industrial Research Institute). *Industrial Center*, June 1937.

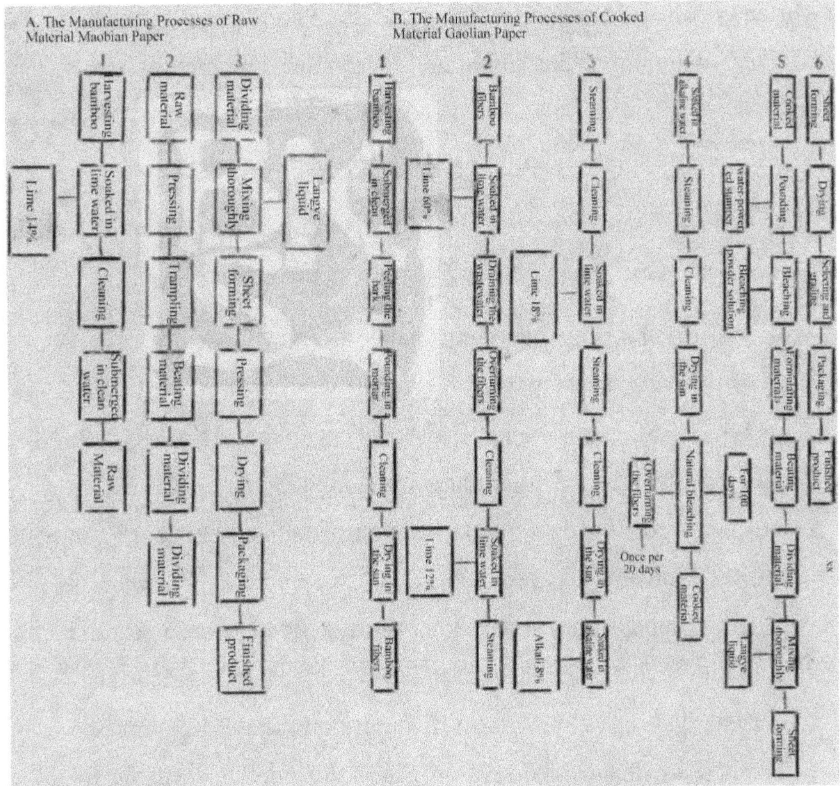

***(Pic5   The Manufacturing Processes of Raw Material Maobian Paper
and Cooked Material Gaolian Paper)***

Although Zhang Yonghui conducted his fieldwork in different locations from Lin Jingliang, his documentation of the raw material method aligns almost exactly with Lin's observations. He too emphasized the use of foot-treading to produce soft, fibrous pulp—a detail that suggests how widespread both the raw material technique and this specific method of pulp preparation were throughout western Fujian at the time. Compared to the cooked material method, the raw material process required a significantly greater amount of lime. While Lin and Zhang recorded slightly different proportions and immersion techniques, both agreed that lime-soaking alone was sufficient to break down the bamboo fibers—eliminating the need for boiling altogether. Zhang went a step further by producing schematic diagrams illustrating the procedures for both raw material Maobian paper and cooked material Gaolian paper (see Pic5). When viewed side by side, these diagrams make the contrast clear: the raw material method is simpler, faster, and involves fewer additives. Naturally, these differences also result in variations in product quality and market price.

Following Zhang's work, Lin Zhaohe conducted an even more technically detailed investigation into traditional papermaking in Fujian:

The harvesting of young bamboo—known locally as *zhu ma*—typically takes place around the end of the third lunar month, between the solar terms of *Qingming* and *Xiazhi* (the Summer Solstice). At this stage, the young bamboo shoots have just emerged from the ground, reaching lengths of 12 to 15 *chi*, but the branches and leaves have yet to sprout. The bamboo is felled, stripped of its outer skin, cut into five *chi* sections, and split into several slats. The inner nodes are removed, and the slats are bundled into 20 *jin* stacks for transportation. These bamboo bundles are then transferred to a soaking pond measuring approximately 12 *chi* in length, 6 in width, and 4 in depth. Lime is layered between each layer of bamboo at a ratio of 1:9—meaning 100 *jin* of lime is used for every 900 *jin* of bamboo. This amount is sufficient to produce one *dan* (担, 50 kilograms) of Maobian paper. The cost of one *dan* of lime, including transportation, was around one yuan in national currency at the time. Once the pond is fully packed, water is added until the bamboo is submerged, then the surface is covered with reed mats and weighted with stones. The bamboo remains submerged for 50 to 60 days. The process is temperature-dependent: warmer weather accelerates the fermentation, while colder weather prolongs it. Once properly steeped, the wastewater is drained, and the bamboo is repeatedly rinsed with fresh water in a process known colloquially as *piao liao* (漂料, bleaching). This washing occurs daily for about ten rounds, followed by an additional month-long soak in fresh water. Altogether, the bamboo fiber takes about two months to mature and become usable.

After fermentation, the softened bamboo is peeled by hand to remove both its outer bark and inner membrane. (The outer bark is reserved for coarse paper, while the inner membrane can be used for low-grade writing paper. The stripped bamboo is then squeezed to remove excess moisture—about 480 *jin* of bamboo can be pressed daily, enough to produce one full load of paper. With skilled hands, two experienced workers can manage this amount.) Next comes the treading stage. The bamboo pulp is transferred to a sunken platform and kneaded by foot until it becomes a soft, wool-like mass. This fine pulp is then stored in vats, ready for papermaking. To begin the papermaking process, pulp is poured into a paper vat—eight *chi* long, eight *chi* wide, and two *chi* deep. Water is added, and the mixture is stirred thoroughly with a wooden rake. Coarse fibers are skimmed off with a bamboo fork, and the remaining pulp is blended with juice from *langye* (榔叶). A wooden plank divides the vat in two; the narrower section in front is for paper forming, with a bamboo fence placed horizontally across it, and another bamboo fence hanging beneath the board. These help regulate the pulp's consistency and filter out clumps. Sheets of paper are formed using a bamboo screen, and each sheet is laid onto wooden boards. The boards and sheets are separated by layers of paper screens to prevent sticking. Once the pile reaches eight to nine *cun* in height, a board is inserted to separate layers. After stacking three such tiers, the pile stands roughly three *chi* tall and is ready for pressing. A wooden press is used to squeeze out water from the paper stack. When the thickness reduces to about one-quarter of its original height, the sheets are separated. 13 sheets are grouped together, their corners clipped open to help them part more easily. The separated sheets are then transferred to a drying chamber. In the drying chamber, each sheet is peeled apart and pressed onto the smooth, heated walls, a traditional paper dryer, colloquially called *beiliao* (焙樤), made of bamboo rods, bamboo strips, and yellow clay, forming a hollow gable-shaped wall. The wall surface is coated with a mixture of tung oil and egg white, making it smooth. A fire is lit inside to heat the wall, evaporating the moisture from the paper. Once dry, the sheets are peeled off, trimmed, sorted, and bundled—becoming the final product known as Maobian paper. In a typical paper workshop, nine workers would be assigned to one vat, each with specific roles as outlined above. On average, one team could produce seven *dao* of *zhongzhi* (heavy paper), *i.e.* Yukou paper, per day. Each *dao* contained 200 sheets weighing about ten and a half *jin* in total, with a market value of approximately two yuan in national currency at the time. As for the thinner Changxing paper, ten *dao* could be produced per day, with each weighing a little over seven *jin* and commanding a similar price. Though lighter in weight, the production cost was higher, making the unit price roughly equal or even slightly higher than that of heavy paper.

The production methods for *Jia zhi* and *Hai zhi* were largely similar to those for Maobian paper, though they utilized coarser bamboo pulp. This included leftover bark and inner membrane discarded from the Maobian process, or even whole, unpeeled bamboo fiber. These were processed into paper following the same steps of treading and sheet formation.[67]

Lin Zhaohe's account of traditional papermaking methods is noticeably more precise and detailed than those of Lin Jingliang and Zhang Yonghui, especially in its emphasis on quantifiable data and production standards at each stage. For example, he notes that a *dao* of Yukou paper weighs approximately 10.5 *jin*—a figure that closely aligns with Lin Jingliang's earlier estimate of 11 *jin* per *dao*. This slight difference not only reflects the meticulousness of Lin Zhaohe's investigation, but also underscores the importance of weight as a key quality indicator for Yukou paper, which was considered a "heavy grade" among the various types of maobian paper. Moreover, Lin Zhaohe translated the complex production process of raw material maobian into a clearly structured diagram (see Pic 6), offering readers a visual summary of the steps involved.

---

67 Lin Zhaohe, "An Overview of the Handmade Paper Industry in Fujian and Its Ongoing Improvements". *Construction Weekly*, Vol. 7, No. 6, 1938.

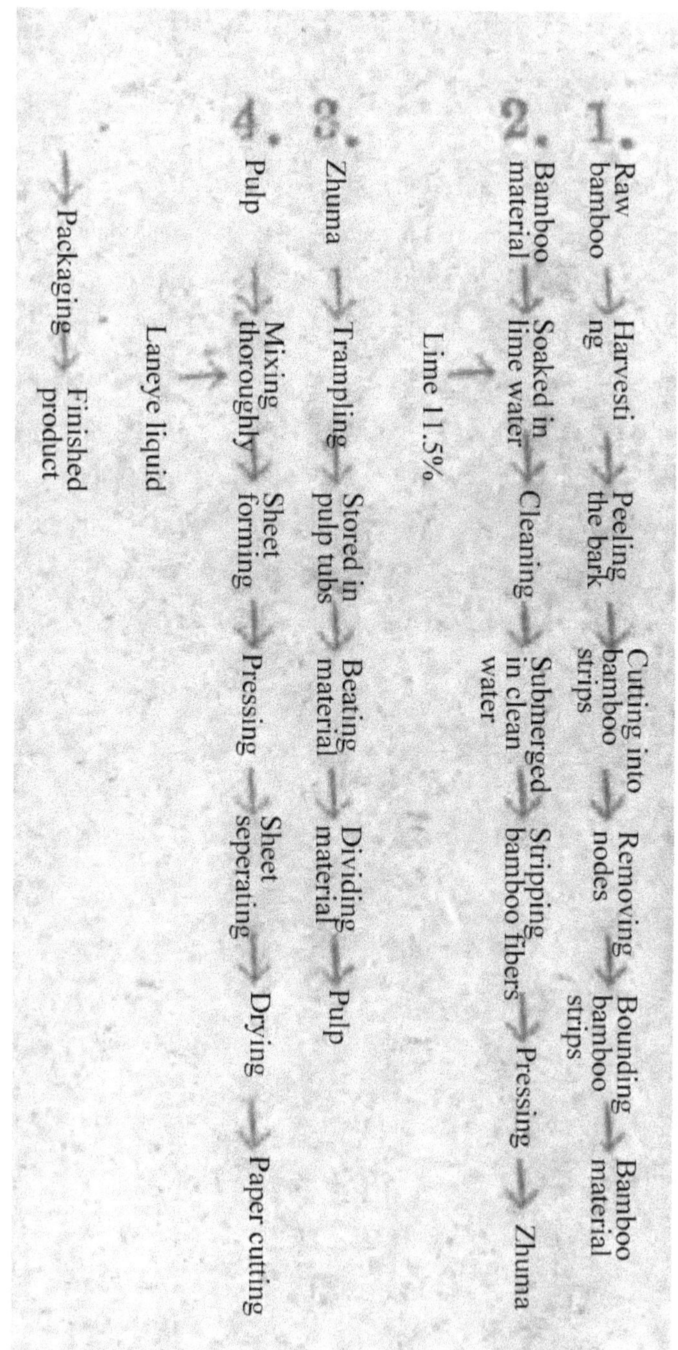

(Pic6   Production Process of Raw Material Maobian Paper)

The above mentioned four reports during the Republican era on papermaking techniques and the paper industry in Fujian were all conducted in the 1930s, particularly between 1934 and 1938, when numerous government bodies and professional organizations launched a series of field investigations. The frequency and depth of these surveys vividly reflect the level of attention the authorities and experts of the time gave to the paper industry in western Fujian. These survey reports provide abundant empirical material for understanding the papermaking techniques in Fujian, especially in the Tingzhou region, during the early 20th century.

2.1.4.   The June 1955 Survey on Yukou Paper in Neishan, Zhiping District, Ninghua County

After the founding of the People's Republic of China, the Ninghua County People's Government initiated a detailed investigation in June 1955 to assess the quality, specifications, and production costs of Yukou paper. The purpose was to support the export of Yukou and Maobian papers. This study focused on Neishan in Zhiping District, known for producing the finest Yukou paper, and resulted in an survey on the production techniques of Yukou paper and the paper industry in the Zhiping area. The report surpassed all Republican-era investigations in clarity, depth, and technical precision. Given that the craftsmanship of Neishan Yukou paper represented the pinnacle of Yukou paper production, the report was initially classified as "confidential." Now declassified, the document reveals that the investigation focused on several key aspects: papermaking techniques (including materials, production, and packaging), papermaking industry (including the role of papermaking in the local economy of Zhiping, production and sales figures, as well as existing problems in the industry) and the production costs of Yukou paper. Of particular note is the meticulous account of the Yukou paper manufacturing process. The following is a compilation of the section detailing the production procedures as recorded in the report:

1. Technical Survey on Traditional Papermaking

1.1. Raw Materials

Three essential materials are used in papermaking: *zhuma* (a kind of bamboo fiber), lime, and the leaves of the *lan* plant (茑叶). Each is indispensable, but *zhuma* is the most critical. It is neither mature bamboo nor a young shoot; rather, it is the transitional stage between the two—when a shoot is just about to become a bamboo stalk. The optimal time to harvest is when the shoot tip has grown sufficiently thick and the outer sheaths begin to level out at the top. If the tip has become woody or branched, it is already too old. Using such overmature *zhuma* results in coarse, yellowish paper that can even make other good materials yellow as well when soaked together in the pond. If harvested prematurely, the *zhuma* is underdeveloped and cannot be fully utilized; the resulting paper will be soft and lack crispness, producing a dull, soft sheet prone to tearing and retain white fibers. Bamboo that has been damaged by insects tends to grow poorly and therefore must be harvested at a younger stage than usual to be suitable for papermaking. The second ingredient is lime. For every *dan* of Yukou paper, about 75 *jin* (old weight unit) of lime are ideal. The third essential component is *lan* leaves—without them, the pulp will not bind; they are crucial for the fiber to form a proper sheet. Each *dan* of paper requires about 2–3 *jin* of *lan* leaves.

1.2. Papermaking Process

1.2.1. Preparatory Work

1.2.1.1. Mountain maintenance

This work is done in winter. Frost and snow help kill off weeds, preventing them from sprouting vigorously in spring. The decayed vegetation enriches the soil, encouraging the growth of bamboo shoots. A well-maintained mountain also facilitates bamboo harvesting, which coincides with the busy spring farming season. If the undergrowth is too thick and paths are blocked, harvesting becomes inefficient. Using winter's agricultural slack for mountain maintenance ensures both spring farming and forestry production proceed smoothly..

1.2.1.2. Purchasing Lime

Lime is usually purchased in late winter or early spring, during the agricultural off-season. Transport is easier during this dry period, and the lime is less likely to be ruined by rain.

1.2.1.3. Repairing the Soaking Ponds

The soaking ponds are crucial in traditional papermaking. Their quality directly affects the storage and preservation of raw materials. They serve both as a storage area and a "cooking pot" for processing the fibers, and thus must be completely sealed with no leaks. Over a month before harvesting *zhuma*, the ponds have to be thoroughly inspected as early as the second month of the lunar calendar. Any cracks or structural issues need to be patched with yellow clay and lime, and ponds must be dried properly to avoid collapse. Throughout the drying process, wooden boards are used regularly to press and smooth the pond surface to prevent cracking. Once repairs are done, ponds have to be tested by filling them with water to ensure they are watertight. The banks and walls are covered with branches and leaves to protect against frost and snow.

Before soaking bamboo, ponds must be thoroughly cleaned—removing any dirt or stagnant water to ensure the bamboo remains uncontaminated.

1.2.2. Processing the Raw Materials (Mostly Performed Outdoors)

1.2.2.1. Cutting, peeling, and splitting *Zhuma*

This involves felling zhuma, removing its outer skin, and splitting it into strips. "Peeling" refers to removing the outer skin; "splitting" refers to cutting the bamboo into strips. The process occurs within a few days after *Guyu* (Grain Rain) solar term to around *Lixia* (Beginning of Summer).

Young bamboo must be harvested at a consistent maturity to ensure quality; both overly young and overly mature fibers compromise the paper. After cutting, the *zhuma* is collected to streamline peeling and splitting—this stage is called *liu zhuma* (slide bamboo).

Next comes peeling and splitting. The bamboo is cut into 4–5 *chi* sections to make peeling easier, and then split into strips about 1.5 *cun* wide for soaking. Care must be taken during this process: the strips must be uniform in size and thickness. To achieve this, each bamboo stalk is divided into three parts—tip, middle, and base—and each section is peeled accordingly: the tip is pilled more thickly, the middle more thinly, and the base most thinly. Two peeling techniques are also required: deeper for the tips, shallower for the bases. Uniformity and thorough removal of nodes ensure lime water penetrates fully, yielding tender, clean raw material with no waste. This process should be completed by

Xiaoman (Grain Full) solar term; after that, the bamboo is more prone to spoilage.

1.2.2.2.   Transporting the Zhuma to the Ponds

The prepared bamboo strips are carried to the soaking ponds. They must be kept clean and cannot be left overnight, or they will become stained or develop blemishes.

1.2.2.3.   Soaking with Lime

Bamboo strips are layered in the pond, alternating with layers of lime. Care must be taken to lay the strips evenly—no overlapping or exposed ends—so the lime is distributed effectively. Extra lime is applied at the ends (the tips), as these are harder to penetrate, while lime was distributed evenly through the middle. About 75 *jin* of lime per *dan* is ideal; any less results in paper that is neither firm nor glossy.

1.2.2.4.   Washing and Rinsing

The bamboo strips are washed to remove lime residue and impurities. Soaking time varies by sun exposure: fully sunlit ponds require about 40 days; half-sun ponds need 50–60 days; and shaded ponds may take up to 70 days. For the first three or four days of rinsing, the water is changed daily; thereafter, every other day for three changes, then every three days for another two changes. Each time the water is changed, workers step barefoot onto the bamboo layers and jump, agitating them to release trapped lime. After this, comes a stage known as *jiwu* (积乌, accumulating the black), referring to the sedimentation method used to remove remaining impurities and to keep zhuma completely clean. During this process, the water could only be discharged once it turns dark. If rain threatens, the dirty water must be released immediately to prevent staining the entire pond of bamboo.

1.2.3.   Sheet Formation (Mostly Performed Indoors)

1.2.3.1. Sorting the Fiber

Washed and rinsed bamboo is picked over for papermaking. Debris—grit, bamboo dust, and reddish fibers must all be eliminated. Only meticulous sorting ensures the final paper is not stained or yellowed. Once sorted, the material must be used promptly—ideally the next day—since evening winds might blow yellow sand, soil, and other debris onto them. The freshly sorted fibers have to be used immediately for papermaking; they should not be stored, as this could cause them to turn yellow. Ideally, fibers collected today should be processed the same day.

1.2.3.2. Treading the Fiber

The sorted fiber is placed in a large wooden trough, and workers stomp heavily on it with their feet until it becomes soft, fine, and even. This step ensures that the pulp breaks down properly and doesn't clump during sheet formation.

1.2.3.3. Papermaking

Water and pulp are mixed in a vat and stirred continuously to keep the mixture even. *Lan* leaves are gradually added to help the pulp bind, producing a smooth, glossy sheet.

1.2.3.4. Drying the Sheets

Water must be sprayed evenly to avoid "mayfly marks" (spots from uneven drying). Sheets cannot be left damp on the baking surface; the drying process uses wood fuel rather than grass, to prevent ash and dust from settling on the paper.[68]

The investigators believe that beyond technical skill, the key to producing high-quality paper lies in the careful selection and harvesting of raw materials—and, above all, in keeping those materials clean and fresh. Compared to earlier accounts of papermaking, this report adds a crucial section on "preparatory work before production," highlighting tasks such as mountain maintenance, Purchasing lime, and repairing the soaking ponds. These seemingly peripheral activities—raw materials preparation conducted outside the main production site—are, in fact, foundational. Mountain maintenance encourages the healthy and rapid growth of new bamboo shoots. Keeping the ponds clean is directly tied to the quality of *zhuma* fibers they yield. Every step involving *zhuma*—from harvesting to soaking—demands meticulous attention to cleanliness and detail. This report is impressively thorough, breaking down each phase with tireless precision. It allows the reader appreciate that producing high-quality Yukou paper from Neishan—through such a complex and time-consuming set of procedures—requires carefulness, meticulousness, and patience. A single moment of negligence can compromise the fiber quality and, ultimately, the integrity of the finished paper. In this sense, technical knowledge alone is not enough. what elevates craft to excellence is the care and dedication poured into every step of the process.

2.1.5. The Yukou and Maobian Papermaking Process as Recorded in *A History of Papermaking in Changting*

By the 1980s and 1990s, the wave of reform and opening-up had reached the relatively isolated mountainous regions of western Fujian. As

---

68 *Survey Report on Neishan Yukou Paper in Zhiping District, Ninghua County* (June 8, 1955), archived at the Ninghua County Archives, collected and provided by Lei Shaoqiu.

the demand for Yukou and Maobian paper surged with the rise of foreign trade and the supply of them could not keep pase, Changting County began to revitalize its traditional handmade paper industry. In the course of investigating the local papermaking landscape, the editorial team of *A History of Papermaking in Changting* collected extensive oral accounts. They not only documented the intricate steps involved in crafting Yukou and Maobian paper, but also created a clear, diagrammed flowchart of the production process, comprising 28 distinct stages (see Pic 7).[69]

It can be said that the 1955 government report and the 1980s research conducted for *A History of Papermaking in Changting* represent a further advancement in the textual documentation of papermaking procedures and techniques bringing it to a higher and more comprehensive level. Not only the production procedures and its associated standards are described with greater precision than ever before, but the costs and profits of the papermaking industry were also calculated with accuracy. These detailed records reveal a compelling truth: even amid the harsh realities of life in the mountainous regions of western Fujian, where papermakers struggled to make ends meet, there remained an enduring commitment to excellence. Through sheer determination and painstaking craftsmanship, they elevated the once-overlooked raw material method to the level of producing Yukou paper—a celebrated regional specialty. The ability to make high-quality Yukou paper using the raw material method is a testament to human ingenuity and resilience. It shows that even in environments where resources are scarce and production costs must be kept low, extraordinary results can be achieved through intense labor, deep care, and refined skill.

---

69 Huang Majin (chief ed.). *A History of Papermaking in Changting*. China Light Industry Press, 1992, pp. 72–81.

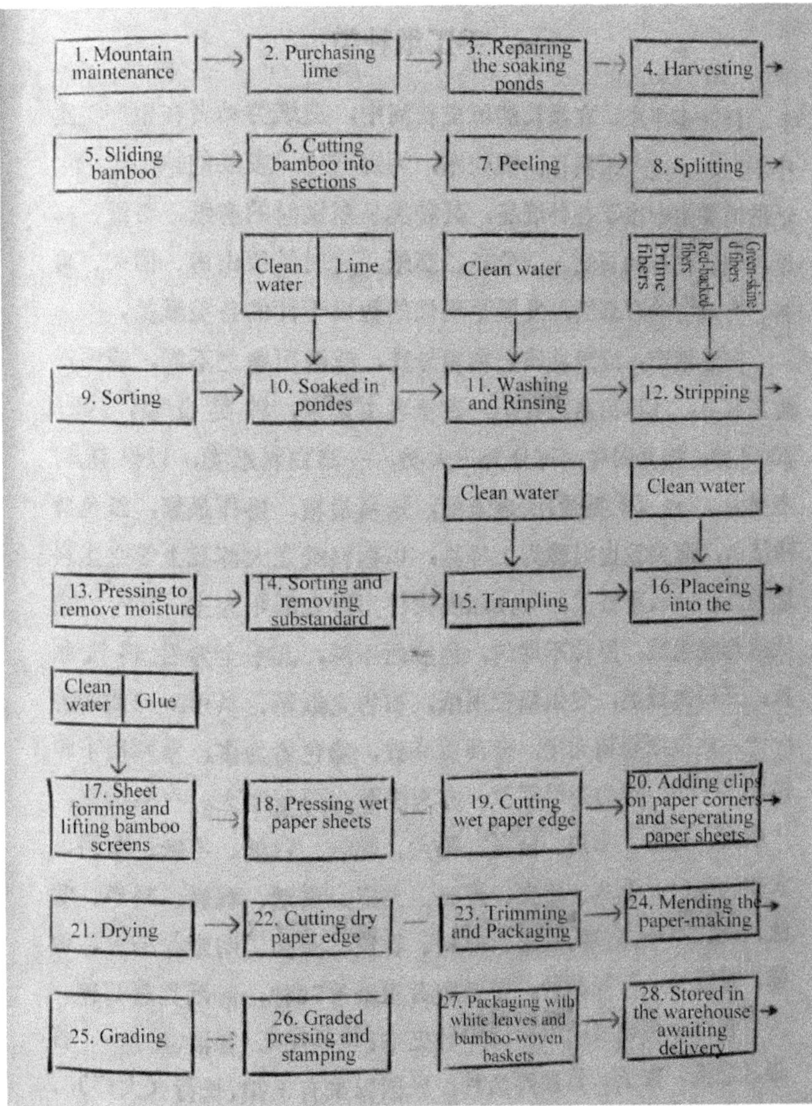

(Pic7　The flowchart of the production process of Yukou paper and Maobian paper)

2.2.　Craft Inheritance

During the Ming and Qing dynasties, Ninghua emerged as one of Fujian's key papermaking counties, with Yukou paper as its signature product. The primary production areas were concentrated in the southern mountainous regions of the county, where bamboo forests thrived. As described earlier, the handmade process of crafting Yukou paper is both intricate and labor-intensive. Locals refer to it as "one vat, ten roles"—a phrase that encapsulates the many essential procedures involved: peeling *zhuma*, treading the pulp, extracting the *lan* liquid (熬蓝), forming sheets, lifting bamboo screens, drying, hauling firewood, and managing the vat, among others. None of these steps can be skipped. The dozens of operations rely entirely on manual skill and physical endurance—a tradition that has endured to this day. To illustrate how this heritage continues in the present, we draw upon recent visual documentation by local historians and filmmakers such as Lei Shaoqiu and Gui Shuzhong. Their work captures the Yukou papermaking process in Zhiping She Ethnic Township, Ninghua County. We also incorporate firsthand accounts from 2021–2022 by experienced papermakers Hu Lanshan, Lei Yusheng, and Lei Changtian, who provide detailed insights into the production stages, tools, and workshop settings. Through this combination of text and imagery, we offer a vivid portrayal of how the craft of Yukou papermaking lives on in contemporary Fujian.

2.2.1.   Raw Material Preparation

1. Harvesting *Zhuma*:

The harvesting of *zhuma* follows a seasonal rhythm. It typically begins around *Guyu* (Grain Rain, late April) solar term when bamboo shoots mature and grow branches, and must be completed by the *Xiaoman* (Lesser Fullness of Grain, late May). A local saying goes, "*Zhuma* shouldn't drink the *Xiaoman* waters," warning that if bamboo is not harvested before this period, the rising temperatures and humidity may cause it to mildew or rot. Sustainable harvesting practices are essential: one must avoid overcutting nearby bamboo forests while neglecting those farther away. As the saying advises, "Protect the shoots, nurture the bamboo, and reserve suitable ones for propagation." Harvesting requires a special tool known as a *yuanyang axe* (鸳鸯斧). Craftsmen aim to cut deep into the bamboo *dou* (蔸, root-stock)—"an inch deep at the base is worth more than a *chi* off the stalk." After felling, the bamboo is placed with its root-end facing downhill to prevent damage during transportation. This avoids bruising the bamboo skin or darkening the flesh, which would compromise the quality of the finished paper.

2. Peeling and Splitting

Once the bamboo is gathered at the foot of the mountain, workers known as *xiao gong* (削工, peelers) clean the muddy root ends and classify the culms into four types. The outer green skin is then shaved off. Two of these types—*dou* culms and second culms—are fully peeled until no green remains, and are referred to as white culms. A third type, called *Guanyin culm* (观音筒, Avalokiteśvara culm), retains half green and half white, while the fourth, tail culm, is left unpeeled. After peeling, the bamboo is split lengthwise and the internal nodes are removed. Bundles of 40 to 50 thin bamboo slats are tied together and carried to the soaking ponds on the same day. Delays or exposure to rain may cause stains on the bamboo stalk. Bamboo that skips this peeling and splitting process can still be used for papermaking, but the resulting paper tends to be coarser in texture.

3. Soaking in the Lime Ponds:

The lime ponds used to soak bamboo are typically dug along small streams. Though variable in size, they usually hold between 600 and 800 *dan* (roughly 30,000 to 40,000 kilograms) of *zhuma*. Each papermaking workshop maintains several of these large soaking ponds, which are lined with stone on five sides. Before use, the ponds are sealed with tung oil and limewash to prevent leakage and are thoroughly cleaned. During soaking, bamboo slats are spread flat in the pond and submerged in water. A carefully measured amount of lime is evenly sprinkled over them. The use of lime is both an art and a science: uneven sprinkled lime can scorch the *zhuma*; insufficient lime leads to rotting fibers and fraying. On average, producing one *dan* of paper requires thirteen *dan* of bamboo and one hundred *jin* of lime. Once dissolved, the lime facilitates fermentation and softens the bamboo, breaking down non-cellulose components. The soaking period lasts about 40 days, but can vary depending on sunlight and water temperature. When the bamboo fibers snap cleanly and appear golden without a white core, the soaking is complete. The pulp is then rinsed to remove residual lime and impurities. The bamboo is re-submerged and spread evenly in the pond, and rinsed with clean water to remove the alkaline residue from the lime. After rinsing, this time it is covered with thatch or banana leaves to encourage controlled rotting. If rain is expected, water must be immediately drained; otherwise, the paper's color may be compromised. After this extensive lime-soaking and fermentation process, the bamboo fibers emerge purified and free from toxins—ready to be transformed into fine paper.

*(Pic 8&9   **Harvesting and Sliding Bamboo Downhill, Photographs by Gui Shuzhong)***

(Pic 10-12   Peeling Bamboo, Carrying Bamboo, Making Mazi, Photographs by Gui Shuzhong)

2.2.2.   Pulping Stage

1. Stripping the Bamboo Fiber:

The bamboo stalks are meticulously stripped to remove impurities and any residual nodes. What remains is clean, pure white bamboo fiber. Only the purest fibers are kept; anything with red roots, dark spots, yellow joints, sandy grains, or insect shells is discarded.

2. Pressing the Fiber:

Before entering the paper vat, the freshly stripped bamboo fibers are placed into a wooden press to squeeze out excess moisture. The press lever is operated by foot.

3. Trampling the Fiber:

The dried bamboo fiber is then poured into a circular wooden trough fitted with a woven bamboo base. Here, pairs of workers—barefoot and balancing on suspension ropes—trample repeatedly over the fiber. This rhythmic trampling, with constant turning and pressure, breaks the fibers down into a fine pulp. The process relies on friction between the fiber and the bamboo mesh. The pulp is considered ready when it is free of rough ends and knots. It is then transferred to the paper vat, where it can dissolve evenly in water. This ancient manual method is gentle on the bamboo fiber, preserving its long strands—resulting in paper of superior strength and flexibility. A common saying among papermakers reflects the importance of this stage: "A papermaker judges by the paper stack; the trampling master is known by the way his feet move; the drying master by the spread of the sheets" Skill in trampling the pulp lies in the subtle art of footwork—an intensely laborious task.

2.2.3. Papermaking Stage

1. Extracting the *lan* liquid (熬蓝):

Lan, also called *langye* (榔叶), refers to downy holly (Ilex pubescens). Specially designated workers are sent into the mountains to harvest the leaves. These are boiled in large pots, then rinsed in mountain streams, before being placed into bamboo baskets and stomped underfoot until they release a viscous, dark blue liquid. This thick extract is strained to remove residue and added to the pulp during paper formation. It serves a dual function: first, it imparts a soft luster and smoothness to the surface of the paper; second, it lubricates the wet paper, allowing for even thickness and easier separation. The extract must be properly filtered and free of grit.

(Pic 13&14　Soaking Bamboo Strips in the Pond and Spreading Lime, Photographs by Gui Shuzhong)

(Pic 15&16 Steeping Bamboo in the Pond and Rinsing Bamboo Fibers, Photographs by Gui Shuzhong)

(Pic 17-19 Rinsing Bamboo, Stripping Bamboo, Finished Bamboo Fibers,
Photographs by Gui Shuzhong)

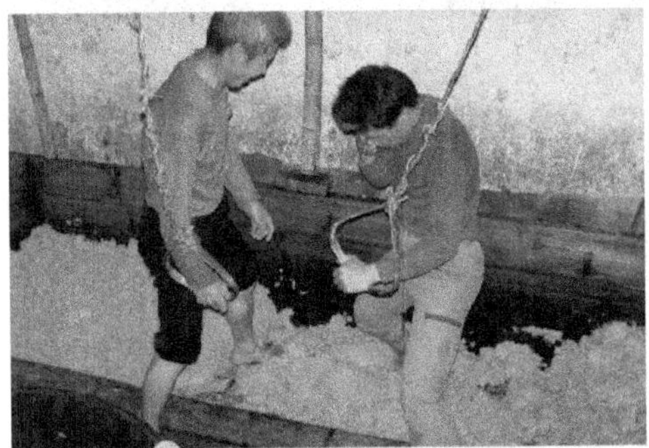
Pic 20&21
Pressing Bamboo Material and Trampling Bamboo into Pulp,
Photographs by Gui Shuzhong

(Pic 20&21 Pressing Bamboo Material and Trampling Bamboo into Pulp,
Photographs by Gui Shuzhong)

2. Sheet Formation:

The vat is filled with a blend of bamboo pulp and the prepared *lan* extract. Workers vigorously stir the mixture until perfectly even. Then comes the heart of the craft: sheet formation. Two workers—known as the front lifter (扛头) and the end lifter (扛尾)—lower a bamboo screen into the vat. With practiced movements, they agitate the pulp to create waves, letting the pulp waves roll across the bamboo screen. One edge of the screen is lifted quickly, allowing water to drain through the mesh, leaving a uniform, delicate sheet of wet paper. The screen is then flipped onto a flat wooden board; the sheet is gently transferred by peeling the screen away. Each team can produce around 1,400 sheets (seven *dao*) per day, or even more. This step is the soul of the papermaking process and requires a remarkably high degree of expertise. A well-made sheet must be thin but strong, evenly textured, and free from blemishes. For premium paper like Yukou paper, the pulp must be especially rich.

3. Pressing the Sheets:

The moist sheets are layered into a paper press. Its base and lid are made from thick wooden planks. Several trunks form crossbeams that lie over the lid, while heavier trunks as pressure beams atop them—all rough, solid logs. Wet sheets are stacked on the press base to a height of over ten centimeters, then pressed to remove moisture using lever principles. The goal is to squeeze out as much moisture as possible without overdrying the paper—a delicate balance that relies on the papermaker's experienced judgment.

4. Separating the Sheets:

After pressing, the stack of wet sheets—now compressed into a single mass—is moved to a smoothing table. Edges are trimmed, the stack is squared and smoothed, and clips are attached to separate the sheets. The water-squeezed wet paper sheets stick together and are hard to separate; thus, tweezers must be used by workers to peel the sheets apart one by one from the edge of the paper stack. Care is critical: the sheets are fragile and prone to tearing. If any sheets remain stuck together, a light mist of water helps loosen them. Once separated, the sheets are divided into stacks—with the number of sheets per stack determined by the length of the paper dryer—grouped by size before transferred to the drying room for the final stage.

2.2.4.　Paper Drying Stage

Drying the Paper:

Once the wet sheets are separated, they are carried by the drying master on his back to the paper-drying room. At the heart of this room stands a pair of back-to-back drying walls, typically 10 meters long and 1.6 meters wide. Viewed from the side, the narrowing from bottom to top structure forms a steep "A" shape. A clay stove is built at one end, where firewood is burned to heat the wall. The smoke travels through a channel within the wall and exits through a chimney at the opposite end. These walls, known as *bei bi* (焙壁, drying walls), were traditionally made using a bamboo frame, coated on both sides with a mixture of clay, sand, and straw, then finished with a layer of lime and tung oil. Modern workshops often use metal surfaces instead. As the fire heats the wall, two workers—one on each side—brush water onto the surface using long brushes made of pine needles. They then carefully press the moist sheets onto the wall, one by one. The heat gently evaporates the moisture, turning the wet sheets into dry paper. Timing is critical: the drying master must determine the exact moment to peel each sheet off the wall, ensuring ideal dryness without brittleness.

(Pic22 downy holly [Ilex pubescens], Photograph by Gui Shuzhong)

(Pic 23-25   Beating the Pulp, Sheet Formation, Wet Paper stack, Photographs by Gui Shuzhong)

(Pic 26-27   Pressing the Wet Paper, Pulling and Separating Sheets, Photographs by Gui Shuzhong)

2.2.5.   Packaging Phase

1. Trimming the Paper:

Once dry, the sheets are stacked neatly and trimmed to uniform dimensions according to specific length and width standards.

2. Packaging:

The sheets are bundled—200 sheets per *dao*. The bundles are then simply packaged and stacked in a formation known as the *si ma dui* (四马堆, four-horse pile) to further flatten the paper. Finally, the maker's *cao yin* (槽印, seal)—the equivalent of a trademark—is stamped onto the bundle, marking it ready for transport and sale.

(Pic 28-29   Drying Paper on Heated Wall, Photograph by Gui Shu-zhong)

Pic 30-31
Trimming the Paper, Packaging
Photographs by Gui Shuzhong

(Pic 30-31   Trimming the Paper, Packaging, Photographs by Gui Shu-
zhong)

2.3.   Workspaces and Tools

As the old saying goes, "To do a good job, one must first sharpen one's tools." In traditional papermaking, both the physical workspaces and the tools used are of critical importance. Before each production cycle begins, papermakers must thoroughly prepare, inspect, and clean the facilities and equipment to ensure smooth operations. Surveys from the Republican era already noted the typical layout of a papermaking workshop (especially for raw material papers). These facilities usually included a room for forming sheets, a drying room, and a space for cooking meals. Equipment require-ments were specific: six to ten soaking ponds, one raw material press, two stamping devices (for pulping), two wooden vats for storing pulp, one paper vat, four wooden barrels for holding the *langye* leaves extract, a paper press, two wooden rakes for beating pulp, two bamboo forks for dividing pulp, four paper tables, and one drying wall.[70] In reality, papermaking workshops were often built either beside the maker's own home or as standalone structures in remote mountain valleys. The full setup of buildings, tools, and materials was even more extensive and varied, reflecting not only production needs but also the daily life of paper workers. Since the core techniques for producing Yukou paper have changed little over the centuries, we can step into the centuries-old scene of hand papermaking in western Fujian's mountains by examining its key workspaces and tools.

2.3.1.   Workspaces

1. *Zhiliao* (纸寮, The Paper Shed)

Also known as the paper vat house, paper mill, or simply the workshop, *zhiliao* was both a workspace and a living area for papermakers. It typically included rooms for forming sheets, drying, cooking, and sleeping. Lin Zhaohe offers a description of such a facility of Maobian paper during the Republican era:

> The structures were generally simple, single-story, and rectangular—about 70 *chi* long and 25 *chi* wide—divided into two main areas: one for pulping, forming, pressing, separating, and meal preparation, and another for drying and sleeping. Building materials were usually inexpensive, such as loess and Chinese fir. The entire compound, including the open space, rarely exceeded 333 square meters and was typically situated at the base of a hill.

---

70 Zhang Yonghui, "A Survey of the Handmade Paper Industry in Shaxian County and Liancheng, Fujian (Industrial Investigation Report No. 1 by the Central Industrial Research Institute). *Industrial Center*, June 1937.

Typical internal equipment included six to ten soaking ponds, one raw material press, a trampling setup, one paper vat, four pulp barrels, a manual press, two wooden rakes for stirring, two bamboo forks for dividing pulp, four paper tables, one drying wall, four water buckets, and one paper knife.[71] Today in Zhiping, many abandoned paper sheds can still be seen. Some were single-story mud houses; others had two stories, with the upper floor used for lodging or storing paper—though conditions remained quite rudimentary.

2. The Soaking Ponds

These were large pits or ponds used to soak, rot, wash and cure bamboo fibers. A good pond had to retain water and was typically dug in areas with abundant, clean water sources and ample sunlight. Their size and depth could vary, but they could not be too shallow or too small, or they would not serve their purpose.

3. The Lime Shed

This was a small, temporary hut set up near the soaking ponds, used to store slaked lime.

2.3.2. Tools

1. Pulp Trampling Tools:

These are devices for trampling bamboo fiber. The main device, known in local dialect as the *cuogu* (蹉鼓), resembles a long trough and is about five meters long and one meter wide. Made with thick wooden planks on both ends and one side, its bottom is slightly sloped and fitted with a woven bamboo mat where the fibers are placed. The papermaker treads the bamboo fibers repeatedly with bare feet until they are fully broken down.

---

71 Lin Zhaohe, "An Overview of the Handmade Paper Industry in Fujian and Its Ongoing Improvements". *Construction Weekly*, Vol. 7, No. 6, 1938.

2. Pulp Rinsing Tools:

The rinsing tank is where the bamboo pulp are washed and stirred, while a special wooden rake is employed to agitate the pulp within this tank. The *Zhuma Huang* (竹麻榥, bamboo fiber vat) is a container for holding the trampled fibers. A *Na Zi* (纳子, skimmer) is used to repeatedly skim and remove long, coarse fibers or impurities from the pulp, ensuring a fine and clean texture.

3. Paper-Forming Tools:

The *Zhilian* (纸帘, paper screen)[72] is a crucial instrument, handwoven by specialized artisans using fine bamboo strips and silk thread, then coated with lacquer. These screens vary in size depending on the type of paper being produced and are highly perishable, so each workshop typically commissions several from professional screen makers before beginning a production cycle. Paper pulp is scooped using the screen inside a vat, traditionally made of wood (though sometimes stone or cement), with rectangular or square shapes. When making Yukou paper, since two workers operate on

---

72 The craft of making paper screens in Fujzhuling was included in the seventh batch of Fujian Province's Intangible Cultural Heritage in 2002. Chi Canghai and Chi Sihua are recognized as municipal-level inheritors of this tradition. The craft is practiced in Fuzhu village in Wan'an Town, Xinluo District, where all 136 households—comprising over 460 residents—bear the family name Chi. The origin of this tradition dates back over three centuries to the Yongzheng to Qianlong eras of the Qing dynasty, when Chi Yingchuan studied paper screen making under Master Weng Renyan in Xingguo County, Jiangxi Province. Since then, the entire village has built its livelihood on this skill, now passed down over 300 years through 15 generations. In the early 1990s, the 14th-generation inheritor Chi Yanqin led a group of villagers to Xiamen, where they launched a business and introduced technological innovations. As a result, Fuzhuling paper screens began to be exported widely—to provinces of Zhejiang, Anhui, Sichuan, and Taiwan, as well as Japan, South Korea, Thailand, and other countries. Fuzhuling paper screens are known for their smooth surface, even spacing, rounded bamboo slats, excellent resilience, resistance to corrosion and cold, and exquisite craftsmanship. Their long durability has made them the preferred choice for producing high-grade handmade papers.
This information is based on an oral history interview conducted by the author's research team with Mr. Chi Canghai on July 22, 2022, and on a written profile provided by Mr. Chi titled "An Introduction to the Craft of Fuzhuling Paper Screen Making."

the same side, rectangular vats are typically used—these vats are over two *chi* deep and can hold around two *dan* of pulp at a time.

(Pic 32-33   Residential Cluster at Xikeng, Xiaping Administrative Village, Zhiping She Ethnic Township and Hu Lanshan Paper Workshop, Photographs by Gui Shuzhong)

(Pic 34   Restored Paper Workshop at Zibei, Weixi, Yuankeng, Zhiping, Photograph by Gui Shuzhong)

(Pic 35   Testing Water Retention in the Soaking Pond, If the Pond Leaks, the Fibers Will Rot Quickly, Photographs by Gui Shuzhong)

*(Pic 36   Lime Shed,
Photographs by Gui
Shuzhong)*

(Pic 37-38   Cuogu and Material Preparation, Photographs by Gui Shuzhong)

***(Pic 39-42   Rinsing Tank, Tank Rake, zhuma huang [bamboo fiber vat],
and Na Zi [Skimmer], Photographs by Gui Shuzhong)***

4. Drying Tools:

The *zhibei* (纸焙, paper-drying wall) is used to dry wet sheets of paper. Traditionally made of mud or bricks, its surface is coated with lime, a mixture of lime, clay and sands, and tung oil. In modern times, metal drying walls are often used. A fire fueled with wood is built at the base, heating the wall from within. Wet sheets are brushed one by one onto the wall, where the heat dries them quickly. To maintain efficiency, the wall must be regularly protected, maintained, and repaired to keep its surface smooth and flat. A pine-needle brush is used to apply the wet paper, while a *Xibeiba* (ash-cleaning brush) is employed to sweep away accumulated ash and dust.

5. Paper-Trimming Tools:

A wooden table serves multiple purposes, including separating sheets and dining. Paper is flattened using a *tiezi* (贴子, pressing log). The cutting knife—a curved blade—is used to trim both freshly pressed wet stacks and fully dried sheets.

Local historians such as Gui Shuzhong and Lei Shaoqiu agree that the exceptional quality and purity of Yukou paper can be attributed to both its superior raw materials and the meticulous craftsmanship involved in its production. First, the paper workshops are strategically built in pristine mountain valleys, surrounded by abundant bamboo and clean water sources. The entire environment is kept free from smoke and dust, and production tools such as vats, presses, and pulp-troughs are diligently maintained to avoid contamination. Second, raw material processing—from harvesting and peeling bamboo to soaking and treading—follows time-honored protocols that rely not on precise scientific measurements but on the artisan's experience and feel for the craft. Every step is handled with extreme care and precision. Furthermore, every aspect of the papermaking process is done entirely by hand. Each stage is coordinated with the others in a rhythm dictated by natural conditions and the workers' internal discipline. The quality of the final product depends not only on skill but also on the attitude, patience, and collaborative spirit of the artisans involved.

From harvesting and trimming, to soaking, peeling, treading, pulping, forming, pressing, separating, and drying—though these procedures may seem simple when written down, they conceal the deeply intuitive, wordless knowledge passed down through generations. To this day, the traditional techniques of Yukou paper are transmitted through the age-old master-apprentice system. Learning the craft depends not only on instruction but on insight, observation, and long-term hands-on practice. Much of the skill cannot be captured by diagrams or measurements—it must be felt.

Thus, to truly master the art—from learning the basic techniques to honing their craftsmanship—workers must engage in patient, repeated practice under the guidance of mentors. Only through this can they refine their abilities and develop the resilience, dedication, and pursuit of perfection that define the craftsman's spirit. In essence, the survival and transmission of this exquisite handcraft are rooted not only in the rich natural conditions of mountainous Ninghua and Changting areas in western Fujian, but also in its people—their perseverance, attention to detail, and quiet pride in their work. The following section will focus on the heartland of Yukou paper—Zhiping She Ethnic Township in Ninghua County—and explore how this mountainous region nurtured and sustained both the unique tradition of raw material papermaking and the associated Yukou Paper industry from a social and cultural perspective.

(Pic 43-45   Vat, Screen Bed, and Bamboo Poles; Papermaking Screen; Screen Bed; Photographs by Gui Shuzhong)

(Pic 46 Paper Vat)

(Pic 47　Steel-Structured Paper-Drying Wall; Clay-Structured Paper-Drying Wall)

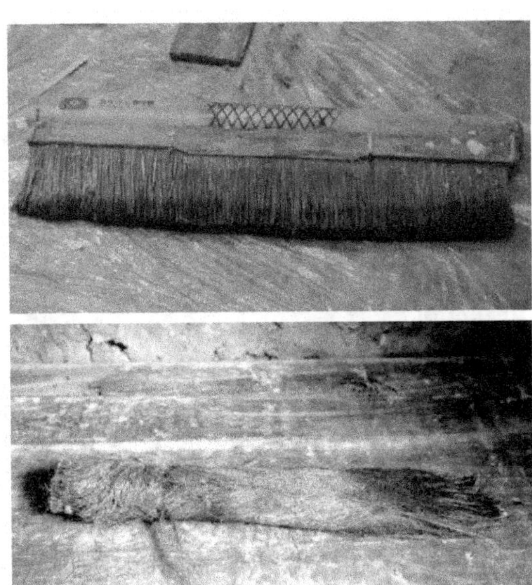

(Pic 48   Pine-Needle Brush; Xibeiba [Ash-Cleaning Brush])

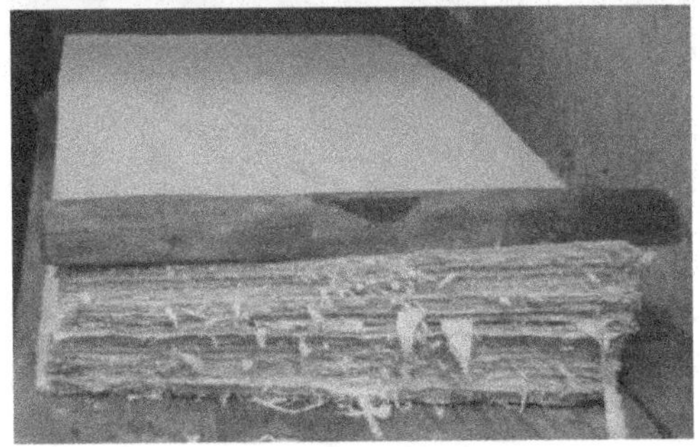

(Pic 49-50   Paper Table; Tiezi [pressing log]; The Image of Tiezi Was Provided by Gui Shuzhong)

112

(Pic 51   cutting knife; The Lower Image Was Provided by Gui Shuzhong)

3. The Beginning of Traditional Papermaking in Zhiping Township

The *Survey of Papermaking in Changting, Fujian*, published in 1946, notes with the observation that Fujian's mountainous terrain and abundant bamboo forests have made it one of China's naturally endowed papermaking regions. Fujian paper has not only held a prominent place among the province's export goods, but has also earned distinction nationwide for its superior quality and high output, playing a vital role in the country's traditional handmade paper industry. Of the more than 60 counties in the province at the time, as many as 46 once produced paper. According to the same survey, among 43 counties that still maintained active paper production at that time, only 2 specialized in *shuliao paper* (cooked material paper), while 31 focused on *shengliao paper* (raw material paper), and 10 counties produced both types. Cooked material paper from Gutian Town in Liancheng County was considered the finest of its kind, while raw paper from Changting enjoyed the highest reputation.[73] According to *A History of Papermaking in Changting*, the production of Yukou and Maobian paper in the Changting area was geographically divided into "upper mountain" and "lower mountain" zones. The upper mountain zone was further distinguished into "inner mountains" and "outer" mountain areas. Sibeiling in Ninghua County, for example, belonged to the inner mountain area. Papers produced in the upper mountain zone—especially from the inner mountains—were known for their superior quality: the soil was fertile, the bamboo stalk thick, the fibers thin, the water clear and low in impurities. Inner mountain Yukou paper, in particular, had long been renowned for its excellence.[74] By the 1990s, most Yukou paper from Ninghua's inner mountain area was sold through Changting's commercial networks and entered external markets under the name "Changting Yukou Paper." As a result, few

---

73 Southeast Changting Office of the Chinese Industrial Cooperatives Association (comp.), *Survey of Papermaking in Changting, Fujian*, 1946, p. 1.
74 Huang Majin (chief ed.). *A History of Papermaking in Changting*. China Light Industry Press, 1992, p. 17.

outside the region were aware of its true origins. In reality, what was widely known as "Changting Yukou" paper was largely produced in Ninghua. In terms of quality, it often surpassed paper made in Changting itself.[75]

The Sibeiling area of inner Ninghua—now part of Zhiping She Ethnic Township—was recognized in the 1950s as the principal production center of inner mountain Yukou paper, earning the nickname "Capital of Yukou Paper."[76] Earlier historical sources, such as the *Chorography of Ninghua County* of the Kangxi era, Qing dynasty, recorded a wide variety of local bamboo species—including Ci bamboo (慈竹), Mao bamboo (猫竹), Gui bamboo (筀竹), spotted bamboo, purple bamboo, square bamboo (方竹), human face bamboo (人面竹), arrow bamboo, bitter bamboo, large-leaved bamboo (箬竹), guanyin bamboo (观音竹), Jiangnan bamboo (江南竹), Chegan bamboo (车竿竹) and others—as well as limestone deposits. However, at that time, there was no clear evidence that the local population had adopted papermaking as an industry or trade.[77] By contrast, the *Chorography of Ninghua County* of the Republican era revealed a more developed paper industry. It noted that "Mao bamboo, suitable for papermaking, is found abundantly in the southeastern townships and is transported for sale throughout the provinces of Fujian, Guangdong, and the Yangtze re-

---

75 *Survey Report on Neishan Yukou Paper in Zhiping District, Ninghua County* (June 8, 1955), archived at the Ninghua County Archives, collected and provided by Lei Shaoqiu.
Mao Xing, "The Historical Origins of the Paper Industry in Ninghua and Tingzhou," in *Ninghua Historical and Cultural Materials (Special Volume on Industry and Commerce)*, compiled by the Committee for the Study of Historical Materials, CPPCC Ninghua County, 1990, p. 72.
76 *Survey Report on Neishan Yukou Paper in Zhiping District, Ninghua County* (June 8, 1955), archived at the Ninghua County Archives, collected and provided by Lei Shaoqiu;
Qingning County Bureau of Commerce, "The Indigenous Paper Purchasing Station Active in the 'Paper Capital' Zhiping" (September 23, 1959), archived at the Ninghua County Archives, collected and provided by Lei Shaoqiu.
77 *Chorography of Ninghua County*, Kangxi era edition, Chengwen Publishing House, 1967, pp. 94, 98–99.

gion."[78] In particular, "villages such as Sibeiling and Anle in the southern district, Quanshang and Wucun in the eastern district, and Kengzili in the west were home to villagers who cultivated bamboo not for food or shoots, but for papermaking."[79] How, then, did Zhiping—once a remote mountain township with lush bamboo forests and access to the headwaters of three rivers—transform into a major center for high-quality Yukou paper? This evolution began with the arrival of migrant settlers who developed the area step by step. To understand this transformation, we must begin with the natural landscape, the region's administrative changes, and the expansion of its villages. We must also examine when papermaking first took root among local residents and how the industry gradually developed. This book will take Zhiping as its focal point to trace the historical trajectory of the papermaking industry in western Fujian—its emergence, growth, and enduring legacy.

(Pic52   Scenery of Zhiping Township)

---

78 *Chorography of Ninghua County*, Republican era edition, vol. 6, "Treatise on Local Products," Shanghai Bookstore Publishing House, 2000, p. 570.
79 *Chorography of Ninghua County*, Republican era edition, vol. 10, "Treatise on Industry and Commerce," Shanghai Bookstore Publishing House, 2000, p. 615.

3.1.   A Brief History of Zhiping

Ninghua County lies on the eastern slopes of the Wuyi Mountains, in western Fujian Province. As one of the border counties between Fujian and Jiangxi, it spans from 25°58′ to 26°40′ north latitude and from 116°22′ to 117°02′ east longitude. It is bordered by Mingxi and Qingliu counties to the east, Changting County to the south, and the Jiangxi counties of Shicheng and Guangchang to the west, while to the north it adjoins Jianning County. Historically, Ninghua was known as Huanglian Dong. In the second year of the Qianfeng era, Tang dynasty (667 CE), it was established as Huanglian Town. By 725 (the thirteenth year of the Kaiyuan era, Tang dynasty), it had been elevated to the status of Huanglian County. A little over a decade later, in 738 (the twenty sixth year of the Kaiyuan era, Tang dynasty), it was incorporated into the jurisdiction of Tingzhou, with the nearby town of Changting serving as the regional political and economic center. In 742 , during the first year of the Tianbao era, Tang dynasty, the area was renamed Ninghua County. Throughout the Ming and Qing dynasties, Ninghua remained under the administration of Tingzhou Prefecture[80], with Changting as the prefectural seat. In the early years of the Republic of China, Ninghua fell under the jurisdiction of the Tingzhang Circuit of Fujian Province. From 1930 to 1934, it became part of the Soviet government in Fujian. On October 21, 1949, Ninghua was peacefully liberated, and on March 1, 1950, the Ninghua County People's Government was officially established under the Yong'an Regional Administrative Office of Fujian Province. At the time, the county was divided into five districts and sixteen townships. In February 1959, Ninghua was merged with neighboring Qingliu County to form Qingning County, with the county seat located in the town of Ninghua. This

---

80 Tingzhou Prefecture was established in the first year of the Hongwu era, Ming dynasty (1368), replacing the former Tingzhou Circuit. Its administrative seat was located in Changting County (present-day Changting County, Fujian Province). The prefecture was abolished in 1913. See: *Dictionary of Chinese Historical Place Names*, Institute of Historical Geography, Fudan University, Jiangxi Education Press, 1986, p. 224.

newly formed county was placed under the administration of the Longyan Prefecture. The merger was reversed in January 1962, with Ninghua and Qingliu reestablished as separate counties, both becoming part of the Sanming region. In November 1968, the Revolutionary Committee of Ninghua County was founded and remained in place until December 1980, when the Ninghua County People's Government was restored. Since then, the county has been governed by Sanming City. As of 2019, Ninghua County administered 11 towns and 5 rural townships, encompassing 19 residential communities and 210 administrative villages. By the end of that year, the county's population totaled approximately 288,000, consisting primarily of Han Chinese, along with a smaller She ethnic population. The She people live in close contact with Han residents, sharing a common language and many cultural practices.[81] Today, Zhiping She Ethnic Township remains under the jurisdiction of Ninghua County.

3.1.1. The Administrative Establishment of Zhiping She Ethnic Township

Zhiping She Ethnic Township, formerly known as Sibeiling, takes its name from Xingfu Temple, a Buddhist monastery built during the Song dynasty. Nestled in the southwestern part of Ninghua County, it sits at the border where Fujian's Ninghua and Changting counties meet Jiangxi's Shicheng County. It borders Caofang Township to the east, Guanqian and Anjie in Changting to the south, Shicheng County to the west, and Fangtian Township to the north. Deep in the mountainous interior, Zhiping remained largely isolated until the mid-20th century, with its only connection to the

---

81 Ninghua County Toponymy Leading Group Office (ed.), *Toponymic Directory of Ninghua County*, 1981, pp. 1–2;
Liu Shanqun (chief ed.), *Chorography of Ninghua County*, Fujian People's Publishing House, 1992, pp. 61–63;
"Overview of Ninghua," General Information Section, Official Website of the People's Government of Ninghua County (fjnh.gov.cn), accessed April 8, 2022.

outside world being County Road 781—a narrow highway completed in 1958 that runs through Caofang to central Ninghua.

Zhiping was first established as a rural market during the early Qing dynasty, under the jurisdiction of Huitong Li. The *Chorography of Ninghua County* compiled during the Kangxi era, Qing dynasty, lists 20 villages under Huitong Li, of which only Pengfang and Dengwu belong to present-day Zhiping She Ethnic Township.[82] In the early Republican era, Zhiping was incorporated into Datong Township. During the Chinese Soviet Republic period, it was renamed Changning District and placed under the administration of Tingdong County. Due to persistent local feuds, it was renamed Zhiping (literally meaning stability and peace) in 1942, and in 1943 a formal township government was established, overseeing 11 *bao* (保, administrative unit), including Sibei, Pingpu, Pengfang, Dengwu, Fukeng, Tianshe, Xiaping, Laiwu, Nikeng, Sixi, and Qishang. After the founding of the People's Republic of China in 1949, Zhiping came under the jurisdiction of the Third District (Caofang). In 1951, the Seventh District was established in Zhiping, overseeing 10 villages including Zhiping, Tianshe, Pengfang, Nikeng, Gaodi, Xiaping, Zhuwang, Nancheng, Fangtian, and Pingshang. The following year, Zhuwang, Nancheng, Fangtian, and Pingshang were reassigned to the Eighth District, while Sanhuang from the Third District was placed under Zhiping's jurisdiction. In 1954, Sanhuang returned to Caofang, while Sixi, Qiaoxia, Shetian, Liqi, and Pingpu were reassigned to Zhiping, bringing the total to 12 villages. The Zhiping People's Commune was founded in 1958, initially comprising 9 production brigades. By 1961, it had expanded to 25, then was consolidated to 12 production brigades in 1966. In 1984, the name was changed back to Zhiping Township, and in 2000 it was officially designated as Zhiping She Ethnic Township. Today,

---

82 Compiled by Li Jingzeng and Huang Zongxian, edited by the Fujian Provincial Local Chorography Compilation Committee, *Chorography of Ninghua County*, Vol. 1, "Table of Boundary Changes", Xiamen University Press, 2009, pp. 13–15.

Zhiping administers 12 villages and 100 villager groups, comprising approximately 3,619 households and 14,119 residents. Of these, 4,725 residents in 992 households belong to the She ethnic minority, accounting for 33.4% of the total population. Except for three Han-majority villages—Tianshe, Pengfang, and Dengwu—the remaining nine villages, including Zhiping, Gaofeng, Gaodi, Pingpu, Shefu, Hubeijiao, Xiaping, Nikeng, and Guangliang, are recognized as ethnic minority communities.[83]

Zhiping lies at the watershed of three major river systems—Min, Gan, and Ting. Its abundant, crystal-clear water is ideal for producing high-quality Yukou paper, known for its pure white texture. The Ting River originates from Laijia Mountain in Xiaping village, and within the township, three major streams—Gaoqikeng, Qiaoxia, and Zhiping—feed into the larger Min, Ting, and Gan rivers via Ninghua, Changting, and Shicheng, respectively. The terrain is rugged and elevated, with an average altitude of 678 meters; the highest peak, Jigongdong, rises to 1,389.9 meters above sea level. Zhiping is one of Fujian Province's key regions for *maozhu* (Phyllostachys edulis) cultivation, boasting 159,000 *mu* (亩, approximately 106,000,000 sq.m. in total) of bamboo forest—about 11 *mu* per capita. In contrast, per capita arable land is less than 0.6 *mu*. Of the 12 villages, only Pengfang and Dengwu rely primarily on farming. Until the 1980s and 1990s, the rest were heavily dependent on papermaking, earning Zhiping the title "Hometown of Bamboo Paper." In 1981, with the approval of the Sanming Regional Administrative Office, Zhiping was designated a special economic zone within the county for its focus on traditional papermaking.

---

83 Ninghua County Toponymy Leading Group Office (ed.), *Toponymic Directory of Ninghua County*, 1981, pp. 138–139;
Liu Shanqun (chief ed.), *Chorography of Ninghua County*, Fujian People's Publishing House, 1992, pp. 64–73, 81;
"Profile of Zhiping She Ethnic Township," General Information Section, Official Website of the People's Government of Ninghua County (fjnh.gov.cn), accessed April 8, 2022.

At that time, it was home to 166 handmade paper workshops and one small mechanized paper plant, with an annual output of around 30,000 *dan* valued at over 2 million yuan. Paper production formed the economic backbone of local life. In 1979, the average annual income per capita was 101.29 yuan. The township has never been self-sufficient in grain production and has always relied on external trade and government redistribution for its food supply.[84]

Table 1 Overview of Zhiping People's Commune in 1981

Name of Production Brigade	Jurisdiction	Number of Households	Population	Arable Lands (*Mu*)	Remarks
Zhiping	21 Villages	265	1425	1247	The commune was headquartered in this area, where members of the She ethnic group lived in scattered settlements. Papermaking served as the primary industry, though agriculture also played a considerable role in the local economy.
Gaodi	11 Villages	130	695	338	Papermaking served as the primary industry.
Nikeng	9 Villages, 6 Production Teams	114	591	680	Papermaking served as the primary industry.
Pingpu	13 Villages, 6 Production Teams	114	636	882	A total of 47 She ethnic minority households are scattered across 3 natural villages.
Pengfang	1 Village, 4 Production Teams	131	663	733	Agriculture served as the primary industry.

---

84 Ninghua County Toponymy Leading Group Office (ed.), *Toponymic Directory of Ninghua County*, 1981, pp. 138–139;
Zhiping She Ethnic Township Committee of the Communist Party of China and People's Government of Zhiping She Ethnic Township, *Research Report on the Development of the Yukou Paper Industry in Zhiping She Ethnic Township, Ninghua County*, December 2021.

Name of Production Brigade	Jurisdiction	Number of Households	Population	Arable Lands (*Mu*)	Remarks
Gaofeng	20 Villages, 7 Production Teams	175	1003	192	Papermaking served as the primary industry.
Xiaping	20 Villages, 8 Production Teams	210	1190	309	Adjacent to Changting (Fujian) and Shicheng (Jiangxi); 31 She ethnic minority households, 155 people. Papermaking served as the primary industry.
Hubeijiao	13 Villages, 5 Production Teams	114	565	410	Papermaking served as the primary industry.
Dengwu	3 Villages, 6 Production Teams	201	1046	1078	Agriculture served as the primary industry.
Shefu	10 Villages, 7 Production Teams	135	758	599	Papermaking served as the primary industry.
Guangliang	14 Villages, 5 Production Teams	91	538	218	She ethnic minority households are scattered here. Papermaking served as the primary industry.
Tianshe	23 Villages, 14 Production Teams	184	1124	312	Papermaking served as the primary industry.

Source: Ninghua County Toponymy Leading Group Office (ed.), *Toponymic Directory of Ninghua County*, 1981, pp. 140.

3.1.2.   Villages and Lineages in Zhiping

The villages of Zhiping She Ethnic Township are scattered across the landscape, each with its own distinct history of habitation and development. The 12 administrative villages—Pengfang, Dengwu, Zhiping, Hubejiao, Tianshe, Guangliang, Shefu, Gaofeng, Xiaping, Gaodi, Pingpu, and Nikeng—did not evolve simultaneously, and their respective trajectories require close historical scrutiny. Tracing the development of each village depends heavily on local genealogies, stone inscriptions, contracts, and other types of civil historical documentation. Drawing upon the work of Gui Shuzhong, and informed by extensive fieldwork conducted by five students from the 2020 undergraduate innovation project team of the Department of History, Xiamen University (titled "Historical Inheritance and Innovative Development of Traditional Handmade Papermaking in Western Fujian—A Case Study of Liancheng Lianshi Paper and Ninghua Yukou Paper")—Wang Siheng, Jiang Yunlin, Yu Yue, Dong Aijia, and Pan Yini—together with graduate student Lin Yun and Researcher Fu Huiling from the Quanzhou Overseas Chinese History Museum, in September 2021, October 2021, March 2022, July 2022, and September 2022, our investigation has involved multiple rounds of site visits and archival collection. Thanks to Gui Shuzhong's generous contribution of over 10 genealogical records, we have compiled the major surnames found in each of Zhiping's 12 villages. These are now matched with the family genealogies already collected for further historical analysis.

Table 2 Major Surnames and Genealogical Records in the Villages of Zhiping

Number	Village	Major Surnames	Genealogical Records
1	Pengfang	Peng, Fan, Lai	Pengfang, *Peng Clan Genealogy from Longxi Commandery* (1995); Pengfang, *The Sixth Revised Genealogy of the Fan Clan* (1993); Pengfang, *Lai Clan Genealogy of the Songyang Commandery* (1995).
2	Dengwu	Deng, Cao, Liu	Dengwu, *Deng Clan Genealogy of the Nanyang Commandery* (1995, Rear House); Dengwu, *Deng Clan Genealogy of the Nanyang Commandery* (1995, Front House); Shengheping, *Fan Clan Genealogy of the Gaoping Commandery* (1993); Yuankeng & Shaoguang, *Liao Clan Genealogy of the Xikeng, Wuwei Commandery* (2019).
3	Zhiping	Lai, Zeng, Liu, Zhang, Lian, Lei, Lan, Li, Luo, Jiang, Zou, Ma	Jiaoli, *Lan Clan Genealogy* (2016); Chengongkeng, *Liu Clan Genealogy of Pengcheng* (1992); Ge'ao, *Lai Clan Genealogy of the Songyang Commandery* (1993); Xiapingduan, *The Ninth Revised Genealogy of the Ma Clan of Fufeng Commandery* (1992).
4	Hubeijiao	Liao, Qiu, Li, Dai, Zhu, Zeng, Zhang, Huang, Lei	*Qiu Clan Genealogy of the Tianshui Commandery* (1993)
5	Shefu	Zeng	Tianshe, *The Third Revised Genealogy of Zeng Clan of Yunzhuang* (1880, Lower House—Line of Wulang and Balang);
6	Guangliang		
7	Tianshe		

Number	Village	Major Surnames	Genealogical Records
			Tianshe, *Zeng Clan Genealogy of Yunzhuang* (1879, Upper House—Line of Qilang); Fukeng, *Zeng Clan Genealogy of the State of Lu* (the Sixth Revision in 1945); Fukeng, *Zeng Clan Genealogy of Wucheng* (the Seventh Revision in 1996 in Fulukeng, joint revised with Tingzhou)
8	Pingpu	Lian, Zhang, Lei, Lan	Lianliping, Pingpu, *Lei Clan Genealogy of the Fengyi Commandery* (1926); Pingpu, *Lian Clan Genealogy of Shangdang Commandery* (1993); Zuokeng, *The Fourteenth Revised Genealogy of the Zhang Clan of Qinghe Commandery* (1991).
9	Gaodi	Chi, Ning, Wang, Diao, Ding, Lei, Zhang, Huang, Li	Gaodi, *Chi Clan Genealogy of Baixi* (the Sixth Revision in 1917, supplemented in the Seventh Revision in 1989)
10	Nikeng	Xie, Zhang, Lan, Zeng	Nikeng, The Eighth Revised Genealogy of the Zhang Clan of Qinghe Commandery (1993); Wubaikeng, Nikeng, *Xie Clan Genealogy of Dongjiafang* (the Sixth Revision in 1834); Wubaikeng, Nikeng, *Xie Clan Genealogy of Dongjiafang* (the Seventh Revision in 1866); Wubaikeng, *Nikeng, Xie Clan Genealogy of Chenliu Commandery (Fujian, Jiangxi, Hubei, Jianning)* (1991).
11	Xiaping	Li, Lai, Hu, Lei, Lan	Chushuling, Xiaping, *The Sixth Revised Genealogy of the Lan Clan of Runan Commandery* (1993); Xiaping, *The Third Revised Genealogy of the Li Clan of Longxi Commandery* (1879); Xikeng, *The Concise Genealogy of the Hu Clan* (1988), *The Fifth Revised Genealogy of the Lai Clan of Shangping* (1993); Rongzikeng, *Liu Clan Genealogy* (1993); Rongzikeng, *Liu Clan Genealogy* (2019).
12	Gaofeng	Lai, Chen, Lei, Hu, Wu	Fujikeng, *The Genealogy of the Chen Clan Descended from the Sanshisilang Gong* (1991), *The Genealogy of the Chen Clan of the Sanshisilang Gong in Shanhu, Shanghang* (1997); Gaofeng, *The Ninth Revision of the Lai Clan Genealogy, Hall of Respecting Ethics* (2014).

The history of settlement and development in the villages of Zhiping She Ethnic Township can be traced through three primary migratory patterns: She migrants into the mountainous areas, Han settlers in the plains, and Han migrants into the hills. Regarding the origins and migrations of the She people, *A Brief History of the She People* suggests that the She practiced slash-and-burn agriculture and moved from place to place in search of arable land. By the Sui and Tang dynasties (7th century), they had already established permanent settlements in the border regions of Fujian, Guangdong, and Jiangxi. It was not until the late Southern Song period that the term "She" came to officially designate these mountain-dwelling agriculturalists.[85] In Zhiping's mountainous terrain, many place names still bear the character "畲" (She), such as Sheli in Tianshe, Liangshe in Zhiping, and Shanheshe and Laishe in Gaofeng, as well as Liaoshuishe in Pengfang.[86] Today, most of the She people in Zhiping has moved down from the mountains and now live alongside Han communities. Intermarriage and assimilation over generations have led to significant cultural integration. Nevertheless, in more remote villages, residents with surnames such as Lei and Lan—common among She families—may still exhibit subtle differences in appearance, dialect, or mannerisms compared to their Han neighbors. A handful of She people even continue to practice traditional slash-and-burn farming and cultivate upland rice deep in the mountains.

When, exactly, the ancestors of the Lei and Lan clans first settled in Zhiping remains uncertain. The lack of written documentation makes it difficult to reconstruct a precise timeline.

---

85 Editorial Committee of *A Brief History of the She People*, *A Brief History of the She People*, Fujian People's Publishing House, 1980, pp. 7–9.
86 Ninghua County Toponymy Leading Group Office (ed.), *Toponymic Directory of Ninghua County*, 1981, pp. 141–146.

(Pic53   Practicing Traditional Slash-and-Burn Farming and Cultivating Upland Rice in Mountains of Zhiping, Photographs by Gui Shuzhong)

Today, Lan clan members of She ancestry are primarily found in natural villages such as Daling in Pingpu, Dayanli and Jiaoli in Zhiping village, and Shangping and Chushuling in Xiaping. Yang Yanjie, citing the *Lan Clan Genealogy*, notes that the founding ancestor of the Zhiping Lan line, Wan Yilang, migrated from Jianning to Shibi in Ninghua during the Song dynasty. However, local accounts from Chushuling claim that the Lan clan settled there even earlier than the Li clan of Xiaping, which dates to the Song dynasty as well. Curiously, though, the Lan people of Chushuling also venerate Lan Wenfu from the Qing dynasty as their founding ancestor, creating a chronological contradiction. A version of the *Lan Clan Genealogy* collected in Chushuling—titled *The Sixth Revised Genealogy of the Lan Clan of Runan Commandery* (compiled in 1993)—was produced by a branch of the clan in Shicheng, Jiangxi. It identifies a certain Youshan Gong as the ancestor who migrated to Ninghua. According to the record, in the second year of Later Zhou Taizu's Guangshun era (952 CE, Renzi year),, Youshan relocated from Lanwu Post in Shanghang to Lanjiazhuang in Huitongli, Ninghua, where he acquired more than 1,300 plots of farmland and mountain land, earning the title "Master of House-Building" (筑室翁).[87] One of the earliest surviving documents on clan affairs in this genealogy is an essay by the 19th-generation descendant Zhongjian, titled "A Narrative of Youshan Gong's Righteous Aid to the Community." This piece provides valuable clues for reconstructing the historical timeline of the Lan clan in Chushuling. The key excerpts from the essay are transcribed below.

Our forefather, Youshan Gong, migrated from Lanwu Post in Shanghang to Lanjiazhuang in Huitongli, Ninghua. There, he acquired expansive tracts of land and became known as "Master of House-Building." In the generations that followed, his descendants multiplied and spread far and wide, making it difficult to gather as one clan for ancestral rites or communal banquets. To address this, during the Kangxi era, Qing dynasty—specifically in the Renyin year—descendants of the 65th and 67th lineage branches who remained in Shicheng, including clan leaders Xingxiang, Xingzhi, and Zhongjian, initiated the collection of

---

87 Chushuling, *The Sixth Revised Genealogy of the Lan Clan of Runan Commandery*, vol. 2, "Biography of the First Ancestors," No. 4.

communal funds. The effort was renewed in the Bingchen year of the Qianlong era, Qing dynasty. Thereafter, annual contributions were levied based on each family branch's population size. Over time, through these pooled resources and careful accumulation of grain, they succeeded in purchasing several dozen *mu* of land to serve as rental income for the clan. However, a formal ancestral hall was never constructed. Instead, during the spring and autumn offerings, each family branch hosted its own commemorations, following a jointly agreed schedule. Notices were sent in advance to designate the date of the rites, and only those who had contributed to the fund were allowed to attend the ceremonial feasts. This initiative came to be known as the "Righteous Contribution Association."[88]

The author of the aforementioned text, Zhongjian, was born in 1695 (the 34th year of Kangxi era, Qing dynasty) and passed away in 1750 (the 15th year of Qianlong era, Qing dynasty). He was buried at Yangmeiling and his mother, Zeng, was the daughter of Gongxian from the same village.[89] Based on this information, the article must have been written between the first year of Qianlong era (1736, bingchen year) and Zhongjian's death in 1750. Yangmeiling, where Zhongjian was buried, lies within present-day Qingliu County and is relatively close to Zhiping. The text states that Youshan Gong migrated from Shanghang to Huitongli in Ninghua. However, "Huitongli" was an administrative division established in the early Qing period, and Zhiping itself fell within its jurisdiction. This suggests that the account of Youshan Gong's relocation to Huitongli may be a historical narrative that emerged or took shape in the early Qing dynasty.

---

88 Chushuling, *The Sixth Revised Genealogy of the Lan Clan of Runan Commandery*, vol. 6
89 Chushuling, *The Sixth Revised Genealogy of the Lan Clan of Runan Commandery*, vol. 3, "Biography of the Fifth Generation Ancestors,", p. 31.

The so-called "Righteous Contribution Association of Youshan Gong" appears to have been a clan-organizing initiative by the Lan lineage during the Kangxi–Qianlong eras. This early movement to consolidate family branches involved Lan clan members not only in Ninghua but also in neighboring regions such as Qingliu and Shicheng County in Jiangxi. In fact, the Lan clan's first successful compilation of a genealogical record also took place during the Qianlong era.[90]

As for Lan Wenfu, whom the Lan clansmen in Chushuling regard as their founding ancestor, his precise birth and death years are not recorded in the genealogy. However, given that his elder brother Wenhai was born in the fifth year of Qianlong era and his younger brother Wensong in the 12th year, Wenfu is believed to have been born in the early Qianlong era. He was laid to rest at Liren in Chushuling.[91] According to the genealogical biographies, Wenfu's father and grandfather were buried in "the ancestral mountains of our native *li*, at Liaobei, Shaluosheng." The closest village to this site, Liaobei, lies in Wuxing Village, Huaitu Town, in Ninghua County. Curiously, while all four of Wenfu's brothers eventually settled in Chong'an, he alone made his home in Chushuling. As the fourth son, Wenfu is the only one whose exact birth date is not recorded. Another notable difference is that, unlike his forebears—such as Youshan Gong and Zhongjian—Wenfu's descendants continued to practice intra-clan marriage with the Lei family well into the Republican era.

Beyond Chushuling, another branch of the Lan lineage—the Lan clan of Jiaoli (one of Zhiping's villages)—undertook a major revision and reprinting of their genealogy in 2016. For decades prior, their lineage records

---

90 Tingsheng, "Preface to *the Revised Genealogy of the Lan Clan of Runan Commandery*" (the 46th year of Qianlong era, Qing dynasty [1781]). In Chushuling's *The Sixth Revised Genealogy of the Lan Clan of Runan Commandery*, vol. 1.
91 Chushuling, *The Sixth Revised Genealogy of the Lan Clan of Runan Commandery*, vol. 6, "Biography of the Fourth Generation Ancestors,", p. 39.

had been destroyed during the Socialist Education Movement, leaving the clan uncertain of their origins, initial settlement, or lineage branches. In 2015, during the process of genealogical reconstruction, the Lan clan of Jiaoli traced their lineage back to Nian Qilang of Lufeng, Shanghang, recognizing him as their founding ancestor. Upon further cross-referencing with the Lan clan of Huanghu She Ethnic Village in Guanqian Town, Changting County, they confirmed that Qiansanlang Gong (the founding ancestor of the Lan clan of Huanghu) and Qianshilang Gong (the founding ancestor the Lan clan of Jiaoli) were the 24th-generation brothers, both direct descendants of Rishan Gong, their 22nd-generation forebear. Qianshilang Gong migrated to Jiaoli during the late Qianlong era, Qing dynasty, becoming the founding ancestor of that branch. He established an ancestral hall in the Jiaqing era, Qing dynasty, and passed away in 1810 (the Gengwu year of the Jiaqing era). He was married to Lei Nianshisiniang. For several generations, his descendants intermarried exclusively with members of the Lei family. It was not until the 30th generation that this practice of endogamy was finally broken.[92]

Due to the author's current access being limited to genealogies from only two branches of the Lan clan—those from Chushuling and Jiaoli—it remains difficult to reconstruct a clear and comprehensive picture of the migration history of the various Lan clans in Zhiping, Ninghua County, along the Fujian-Jiangxi border. However, based on the available materials, several broad patterns can be discerned. The Lan clan branches in Ninghua are notably complex in origin. Some of the earliest lines may have engaged in nomadic farming in the mountainous borderlands even before the Song dynasty. By the early Qing period, they began acquiring land and formalizing clan structures. During the Qianlong era, genealogical records were

---

92 Compilation Council of the *Lan Clan Genealogy*, Descendants of Nianqi of the Jiaoli Branch, Lineage of Ancestor Rishan. *Lan Clan Genealogy*. 2016, pp. 8–9, 72, 474–482.

compiled and ancestral halls were constructed. New branches continued to migrate into the area throughout the mid-Qing period, gradually being incorporated into the existing clan networks. These lineages did not share a single origin and varied in terms of marital customs. Nevertheless, most relied primarily on land-based agriculture as their means of subsistence and accumulation of property.

The Lei clan in Zhiping primarily resides in several villages: Lianliping of Pingpu Village, Shaluopai of Guangliang Village, Yangli of Zhiping Village, and Daji of Xiaping Village. According to local genealogical records from Xiasha in Zhongsha Township and from Zhiping itself—studied by researcher Yang Yanjie—the Lei clan traces its origins back to the fourth year of the Jianzhong era, Tang dynasty (783 CE), when their founding ancestor, Lei Fu, migrated from Fuzhou in Jiangxi Province to establish roots in Zhongsha and Xiasha. Beyond this, however, very little historical information has survived. On September 10, 2021, Lei Rongqing, Party Secretary of Pingpu Village, guided us to Lianliping, the ancestral settlement of the Lei She people in Zhiping. At his uncle's house, we viewed two volumes of Lei genealogies. Later, on November 20, Gui Shuzhong discovered the ancestral tomb of the Lei founding patriarch in Shaluopai, along with two inscribed tombstones. Then on March 31, 2022, Gui Shuzhong and Lei Shaoqiu identified another ancestral tomb in the "Lei Ancestor Ground" at Lianliping, this time bearing an uninscribed tombstone. These folk documents and physical relics have shed light on parts of the history of the Lei branches in Zhiping.

(Pic 54　Lan Tianfa, a Member of the Lan Clan from Shaluopai in
Zhiping She Ethnic Township)

Among the newly discovered gravestones, the uninscribed one marking the ancestral tomb of the Lei clan in Lianliping likely dates back to an
earlier period. The tombstone at Shaluopai, dated to the 43rd year of the
Qianlong era, Qing dynasty (1778), commemorates the renovated tombs of
"our honourable four ancestral figures: Lei Gong Xiaosanlang, Qianyilang,
Fayan, and Fayou." Another tombstone at the site was erected in the 15th
year of the Guangxu era, Qing dynasty (1889), to mark the grave of Lei
Maokui (see Pictures 55 and 56). Inscription on the Qianlong era tombstone
suggest that Xiaosanlang and Qianyilang were likely early settlers during
the Ming dynasty, while Fayan and Fayou were nearer ancestors at the time
of the tomb's restoration. By the 43rd year of Qianlong era, Qing dynasty
(1778), the Lei clan's tombstone had become remarkably similar to those of
the Han people, reflecting several key features. First, it evidences the Lei
family's adoption of Chinese characters. Second, it shows that the tomb's
feng shui orientation—"Xinshan Yixiang" (辛山乙向)—a term consistent

with the feng shui description of "Lei Maokui's tomb" in 1889 (the 15th year of Guangxu era, Qing dynasty) and with the Lei Clan Genealogy of the Fengyi Commandery, which mentions "Maokui Gong." This suggests that this branch of the Lei clan likely aligned itself with the Zhongsha-Xiasha Lei clan by adopting "Maokui Gong" as an ancestral figure, unifying their lineage. Third, by the Qianlong period, the Lei lineage had divided into three distinct sub-branches, with clearly recorded family lines. Fourth, records indicate a degree of endogamy during this time, and marital alliances were formed with the Lan clan. Fifth, many Lei names from this period still followed the customary naming patterns, including those using the "Lang" or "Fa" characters.

According to the *Lei Clan Genealogy of the Fengyi Commandery*, the founding ancestor of the Lei clan in Shaluopai, named Maokui, was the son of Wentai, who was born in 1695, the 34th year of the Kangxi era, Qing dynasty. The date of Wentai's death and his burial site are unknown. "He married a woman from the Wu family and had one son, Maokui, who later relocated to a village in the southern part of the county." The precise dates of Maokui's birth and death are also unrecorded. He was "buried in Shaluopai behind the family house, and was interred together with his wife, a woman from the Lan family, in a grave known as 'Tiger Shape,' facing the orientation of Xinshan Yixiang . Over the generations, Maokui's descendants frequently intermarried with members of the Lan clan.[93] This suggests that the Lei family may have migrated to Zhiping Township as early as the Ming dynasty. By the Qianlong era of the Qing dynasty, they had multiplied and established their own lineage branches. While it is possible that this particular branch of the Lei clan arrived in Zhiping later than those in Lianliping and Yangli, the precise timing remains unclear.

----

93 *Lei Clan Genealogy of the Fengyi Commandery*, Vol. 5, "Lineage and Biographies of the Descendants of Zichang", compiled in 1926.

Because the She people had no written language of their own and, for a long time, had no access to education in Han culture, they were unable to record their migration history in writing. The inscriptions on Lei family gravestones, along with genealogical records of the Lei and Lan clans, were likely compiled much later by descendants who had become literate in Chinese—some perhaps even having passed the imperial examinations. These texts were likely constructed from fragments of collective memory, written in the style of Han Chinese genealogy. According to local historian Lei Shaoqiu, the She people traditionally did not maintain genealogical records or ancestral halls. These customs only emerged through cultural assimilation with the Han. As the two groups integrated, the She began to invite Han genealogists to compile their family records and hire Han artisans to build ancestral shrines. For instance, one Lei branch in Zhongsha-Xiasha commissioned a Han genealogist to compile the *Lei Clan Genealogy* in 1610, the 38th year of the Wanli era, Ming dynasty. They subsequently hired Han craftsmen to build the Longmen Shrine, Taoyuan Shrine, and Xianggong Shrine in locations such as Tangkengli west of Ninghua county seat, Xia Dongmen, and Xiashagang in Zhongsha. Among them, Xianggong Shrine was completed in 1744 (the 9th year of the Qianlong era, Qing dynasty), with a commemoration: *Stele Inscription for the Construction of the Xiashagang Great Ancestral Hall*, written by the Qing-era Neo-Confucian scholar Lei Hong. With the establishment of genealogies and the construction of ancestral halls, the She people became further integrated into Han society.

At the same time, however, they retained some of their distinct cultural practices, including endogamous marriage, totem worship, and other traditional customs. The most important documents within She culture are the "ancestral painting" (see Pictures 59 and 60). In Lianliping, members of the Lei clan preserved such a painting—an exquisite handscroll approximately

10 meters long and 0.36 meters wide, painted in vibrant colors and meticulous detail. The painting is inscribed: "Commissioned by Lei Fagui for auspicious ancestral use, Autumn of the Jiaxu Year, the 19th year of the Jiaqing era, Qing dynasty" (1814). Rendered in a comic-strip style, the scroll depicts the ancestral legends of the She people.[94] Deng Xuanjiu, born in 1948 in the village of Dengwu, recalled that in his youth, he was ritually adopted by Lei Longwang of Zhongbian Jiaoli. Every Lunar New Year's Eve, he would accompany his father and uncles to Lei Longwang's home to celebrate. There, he witnessed the Lei family cleaning the main hall and setting off firecrackers after 3 p.m. They would then carefully unroll and display the ancestral portraits at the center of the hall floor. "Their ancestors," he remembered, "had the head of a dog and the body of a man, wore red court robes of an imperial son-in-law, had vivid eyes, a kindly face, and a tall, dignified figure." In the middle of the hall, they laid out traditional New Year's offerings—rice cakes, yellow cornbread, fish, meat, and other festive dishes. Each family member would ceremonially present dishes to the ancestors, praying for the health and longevity of all, and for an even greater harvest in the coming year.[95] This vivid account demonstrates that, even as late as the mid-20th century, the Lei clan in Zhiping continued to practice She traditions such as totem worship and ancestral rituals. At the same time, it also reflects the harmony and closeness that had developed between the She and Han communities over time.

---

94 Liu Shanqun (chief ed.), *Chorography of Ninghua County*, Fujian People's Publishing House, 1992, p. 786.
95 Deng Xuanjiu, *The Origins of the Lan and Lei Surnames*, Unpublished handwritten manuscript.

(Pic55   Tombstone of the Lei Clan Ancestors in Shaluopai Mountain, Guangliang Village, Zhiping She Ethnic Township, Renovated in the 43rd Year of the Qianlong Era, Qing Dynasty [1778])

(Pic56   Tombstone of the Lei Clan Ancestors in Shaluopai Mountain, Guangliang Village, Zhiping She Ethnic Township, Renovated in the 15th Year of the Guangxu Era, Qing Dynasty [1889])

(Pic57-58   Lei Clan Ancestral Residences in Lianliping, Pingpu Village, Zhiping She Ethnic Township; Depicted Are Lei Rongqing (left) and His Uncle Lei Guichun (right), along with a Copy of the Lei Clan Genealogy of the Fengyi Commandery)

Today, the Han residents who live alongside the She people in the small mountain plains of Zhiping are said to have migrated into the region after the Tang and Song dynasties. Among these villages, Pengfang and Dengwu stand out. These two villages occupy flat, fertile terrain well suited for farming and cultivation. Located closest to Caofang Township, they have long enjoyed convenient access to transportation and contact with the outside world. Historical records confirm their early development: both Pengfang and Dengwa are the first villages in the Zhiping area to appear in the *Chorography of Ninghua County* compiled during the Kangxi era, Qing dynasty.

According to local oral history in Pengfang, the founding ancestor of the Peng clan arrived during the late Tang dynasty, having migrated from Ningdu in Jiangxi province. The ancestral spirit tablet of the Peng family bears this inscription: "The founding ancestor of the Tang dynasty, Sanshilang Peng Fuxiang, of the Longxi lineage, and his wife Wu Siniang; their descendants—the second generation, Ershiyilang and his wife of the Deng clan; Ershierlang and his wife Liao; Ershisanlang and his wife Cao; Ershisilang and his wife Zeng." The *Peng Clan Genealogy of the Longxi Commandery*, revised in 1995, offers further insights and colorful accounts. The earliest text preserved in the genealogy is titled "Record of the Six Lands by the Mountain and Lake," dated to the 21st year of Kangxi era, Qing dynasty (1682), and authored by Wen Fu and others who oversaw the compilation. According to this record, the founding ancestor, Peng Fuxiang, "originally lived under the egret tree in Zhonggu Township, Ningdu County, Ganzhou Prefecture, Jiangxi Circuit of the Great Ming Empire. He later migrated to Longhu Village in Yidu, Huitong Li, Ninghua County, Tingzhou Prefecture, Fujian. In the second year of the the Later Tang's Tongguang era (924 CE), he moved again to reside at Qianchengqiu in Wugongduan. As the family grew and flourished, the settlement came to be known as Pengfang." The founding ancestor reportedly established "six ancestral estates on the surrounding hills of 'Pengjia Shanhu'," dividing them evenly among his four sons. Several historical traces attributed to him remain. First, the Ancestral Altar of Lord Xiao He was erected to commemorate a boundary dispute with the Zhang family of Nikeng. After a prolonged legal battle, the case was resolved favorably under Xiao He's spiritual protection. Second, an old village school was established. Third, an ancient well still remains. Fourth, the foundation site of Zhongshan Nunnery has been preserved. The text also records that four members of the Peng clan served as local chiefs. During the Jiajing era, Ming dynasty (1531), the magistrate of Ninghua, Mo from Guangxi, "initiated a campaign to demolish shrines and temples." One such chief, Peng Houchun, officially registered in the third division of Huitong Li, submitted a petition to Magistrate Mo to preserve the Datian Temple, claiming it was originally built in the Tang dynasty by ancestral monks.[96] While the timeline in "Record of the Six Lands by the Mountain and Lake" is inconsistent, its significance lies in this: in the genealogy preface written in the same year,[97] Wenfu and others made no mention of a late Tang migration. Although the document mentions the Tongguang era, Late Tang dynasty (924 CE), it simultaneously refers to "Great Ming" as the period of migration, suggesting historical confusion or purposeful anachronism. It is likely that, in an effort to protect ancestral temples from destruction during the Ming dynasty, the Peng clan emphasized the ancient origins of these sites, linking them to the Tang era. For this reason, from the Qianlong era, Qing dynasty, onward, successive editions of the family genealogy and the oral accounts of the Peng clan have uniformly maintained that their ancestors settled in Pengfang at the end of the Tang dynasty. According to the genealogy, the founding ancestor "assisted in the establishment of several religious and communal structures: Zhongshan Nunnery, a local altar, a shrine to Lord Xiao He, three ancient-tree-protecting Luodun earthen mounds, a sacred tree site, the old altar of Xianshang, and Shifo Nunnery. All these sites were built on land donated by the founding ances-

---

96 "Record of the Ancestral Land Plots, Residences, Altars, and Ancient Wells Left by the First Ancestor," in *Peng Clan Genealogy of the Longxi Commandery*, Vol. 1, Pengfang, 1995.
97 "Old Preface" (the 21st year of Kangxi era, Qing dynasty [1682]), in *Peng Clan Genealogy of the Longxi Commandery*, Vol. 1, Pengfang, 1995.

tor to house monks."[98] This legacy confirms the Peng as the earliest clan to establish a permanent settlement in Pengfang, possibly in the late Tang, and their name, fittingly, became attached to the place itself.

(Pic59 The Opening Section of the Ancestral Painting of the She People in Lianliping [commissioned by Lei Fagui in the Jiaxu Year of the Jia-qing era, Qing dynasty], Photographs by Gui Shuzhong)

---

98 "General Record of the Boundaries and Properties Left by Ancestor Fuxiang Gong," in *Peng Clan Genealogy of the Longxi Commandery*, Vol. 1, Pengfang, 1995.

(Pic60   A fragment of the Ancestral Painting of the She People in Lian-liping, Photographs by Gui Shuzhong)

The second-largest surname in Pengfang is Fan. According to *The Sixth Revised Genealogy of the Fan Clan*, the Fan family's founding ancestor, Fan Zhou, migrated from Guifu Li, Eighth District, Songxi County, Jianning Prefecture to Huitong Li's Pengfang in Ninghua County.[99] An alternate tradition claims he came from "Shuangjing Jingzhu"[100] in Songxi, Jianning. His arrival is dated to the third year of the Hongwu era (1370), early in the Ming dynasty. After settling in Pengfang, he "acquired land and established a household."[101] By 1993, the Fan clan had over 130 house-

---

99 "Original Preface to the Fan Clan Genealogy" (the fourth year of Shunzhi era, Qing dynasty [1647], by the eighth-generation descendant Guozhen, student at the Changting County School), in *The Sixth Revised Genealogy of the Fan Clan*, Vol. 1, Pengfang, 1993.
100 "Preface to the Revised Genealogy of the Fan Clan of Gaoping Commandery (the second year of Xianfeng era, Qing dynasty [1852], by the 14th-generation descendant Xiong), in *The Sixth Revised Genealogy of the Fan Clan*, Vol. 1, Pengfang, 1993.
101 "Preface of the Fan Clan Genealogy" (the 17th year of Jiaqing era, Qing dynasty

holds in Pengfang. The compilation of their genealogy began in the fourth year of Shunzhi era, Qing dynasty (1647), with further revisions undertaken in the sixth year of Qianlong era (1741), the17th of Jiaqing era (1812), the second of Xianfeng (1852), the seventh of Guangxu (1881), and again in 1917 and 1993.[102] The Fan genealogy notes that the Peng clan had resided in Pengfang since the third year of Tongguang, Late Tang dynasty (925 CE). The terrain of Pengfang is level, in contrast to the mountainous northwest and hilly southeast of the region. The village is ringed by hills, and has long been home to a mix of surnames and families.[103]

[1812], by the 13th-generation descendant Fang), in *The Sixth Revised Genealogy of the Fan Clan*, Vol. 1, Pengfang, 1993.
102 "Preface to the Sixth Revision of the Genealogy of the Fan Clan of Gaoping Commandery" (1993, by the 18th-generation descendant Tianpei), in *The Sixth Revised Genealogy of the Fan Clan*, Vol. 1, Pengfang, 1993.
103 "Local Geography and Land Records" (the second year of Xianfeng era, Qing dynasty[1852], by Meng Ying), in *The Sixth Revised Genealogy of the Fan Clan*, Vol. 4, Pengfang, 1993.

(Pic61   Ancestral Hall of
Peng Clan in Pengfang)

The Lai clan, the third largest surname in Pengfang, claims that their 16th-generation ancestor, Bingying Gong, moved from Guanqian to settle in Pengfang. Bingying, "a virtuous descendant of Langui Gong, was described as gentle in manner, sincere in nature, and fond of landscapes. Versed in feng shui, he traveled through this area, marveled at its clear waters, lush mountains, and majestic dragon veins (a feng shui term refers to channels of energy flowing through mountain ranges), and deemed it an ideal place to settle, thus becoming the founding ancestor. He had three sons: Guofo, Guotang, and Guodou." Thereafter, the clan purchased farmland, built ancestral halls, established sacrificial properties, and took root to thrive in

Pengfang.[104] In the Lai clan's genealogy, the birth and death dates of ancestors before the 20th-generation Enchun are unknown. Enchun, styled Yingyuan, was recorded as born in the fifth year of the Yongzheng era, Qing dynasty (1727, Dingwei year), and married Guo Jinnniang, who was born in the second year of the Kangxi era (1663, Guimao year). They had three sons, including Jinghui. Jinghui, styled Wencai, was born in the 20th year of the Kangxi era, Qing dynasty (1681, Xinyou year) and died in the 14th year of the Qianlong era, Qing dynasty (1749, Yisi year); his tomb was relocated to Longyaoli, Guanqian, in the 24th year of Qianlong era, Qing dynasty (1759).[105] If these dates hold true, Enchun's own birth year (1727) would be chronologically implausible. It is more likely he was born in the Dingwei year of Kangxi era, Qing dynasty (1667). Based on an average generational span of 25 to 30 years, we can infer that Bingying was born sometime between 1547 and 1567, suggesting that the Lai clan's migration to Pengfang occurred during the mid to late Ming dynasty.

As recorded in "Record of the Six Lands by the Mountain and Lake" from *The Sixth Revised Genealogy of the Fan Clan*, the Peng clan of Pengfang placed strong emphasis on the possession of arable land and water resources. By the end of the Ming dynasty, they had become the principal family from which local chiefs were selected, indicating that early settlers focused their livelihood on land development and agricultural production.[106] The Peng founding ancestor is said to have "cleared the wilderness, toiled through rain and clouds, enduring decades of hardship to leave behind fer-

---

104 "Preface to the Revised Genealogy of the Lai Clan of the Songyang Commandery" (the 34th year of Qianlong era, Qing dynasty [1769], by the 22nd-generation descendant Qigeng), "Genealogical Account of Bingying Gong's Migration to Pengfang," in *Lai Clan Genealogy of the Songyang Commandery*, Vol. 1, Pengfang, 1995.
105 "Complete Generational Record of the Lai Clan of the Songyang Commandery," in *Lai Clan Genealogy of the Songyang Commandery*, Vol. 2, Pengfang, 1995.
106 "Record of the Ancestral Sites, Altars, and Wells Left by the First Ancestor in the Six Lands by the Mountain and Lake," in *Peng Clan Genealogy of the Longxi Commandery*, Vol. 1, Pengfang, 1995.

tile fields and hillside land as the 'back dragon' foundation for his descendants." In August of the 41st year of the Qianlong era, Qing dynasty (1776), the Peng clan undertook a major reconstruction of their ancestral hall.[107] The Fan clan of Pengfang similarly valued irrigation and water infrastructure.[108] In the second year of Daoguang era, Qing dynasty, they spent over 2,800 pieces of She silver to build the ancestral hall of Shiyuan Gong. They continued acquiring neighboring properties to expand the ancestral complex, and later they had become the most populous and powerful lineage in Pengfang.[109] The Lai clan began acquiring land near Pengfang from the Fan family during the Yongzheng era, Qing dynasty as well. This land acquisition process frequently sparked disputes between the Lai clan and Fan clan over fields, house lots, and burial grounds.[110] It was not until 2011 that the Lai clan finally expanded the ancestral hall of Jingxin Gong into a full clan temple.[111] This historical trajectory reveals a common pattern: the Peng, Fan, and Lai clans, though arriving at different times, all relied on agriculture for their livelihood. As more families settled in Pengfang during the early Qing period, land became increasingly scarce. Newcomers could only secure a foothold through land purchases, and inter-lineage conflicts over property rights grew increasingly common.

---

107 "General Record of the Boundaries and Properties Left by the First Ancestor Fuxiang Gong," in *Peng Clan Genealogy of the Longxi Commandery*, Vol. 1, Pengfang, 1995.
108 "Local Geography and Land Records" (the second year of Xianfeng era, Qing dynasty[1852]), in *The Sixth Revised Genealogy of the Fan Clan*, Vol. 4, Pengfang, 1993.
109 "Record of the Ancestral Hall of Shiyuan Gong," in *The Sixth Revised Genealogy of the Fan Clan*, Vol. 4, Pengfang, 1993.
110 "Epitaph and Burial Record for the Seventh-Generation Ancestor by Yingyuan Gong" (Yongzheng era, Qing dynasty), "Homestead Deed and Development Record of Wencai Gong" (the wuzi year of the Qianlong era, Qing dynasty [1768]), "Relocation Burial Record of Jinghui Gong (Style Wencai) to Guanqian" (the 24th year of Qianlong era, Qing dynasty [1759]), "Geographic Survey of Tomb Boundaries and Land Allocation for Enchun Gong" (the 21st year of the Qianlong era, Qing dynasty [1756]), and "Yezhupai Land Transaction Contract" (the eighth year of Qianlong era, Qing dynasty [1743]), in *Lai Clan Genealogy of the Songyang Commandery*, Vol. 1, Pengfang, 1995.
111 "Preface to the Ancestral Shrine of the Lai Clan," 2015.

(Pic62 Fan Clan Ancestral Hall and Lai Clan Ancestral Hall in Pengfang Village)

Adjacent to Pengfang lies the village of Dengwu, whose residents predominantly bear the surname Deng. According to local accounts, their founding ancestor, known as Ershiliulang Gong, migrated from Ganzhou in Jiangxi province during the final years of the Southern Song dynasty to establish his lineage in this area. It is said that during Wen Tianxiang's campaign to lead volunteer troops against the Mongol invasion, Deng ancestors joined the resistance and eventually settled in Ninghua. Their chosen dwelling came to be known as "Dengwu" ("Deng's Hamlet"). From the third generation onward, the descendants of Ershiliulang Gong divided into two primary branches: the elder branch, descended from the Shiqilang

Gong, settled in what became known as the "Front House" (*Waiwu*), while the younger branch, descended from the Shiyilang Gong, resided in the "Rear House" (*Liwu*). These two lineages developed independently and formed the core structural divisions within the Deng clan. By the 1990s, the Deng lineage had reached its 32nd generation. The Front House branch comprised around 140 members, while the more populous Rear House had grown to about 800 individuals. Each branch maintained its own ancestral hall. Locals recall that prior to the Qianlong era of the Qing dynasty, the genealogies of the two houses were compiled jointly. However, apart from joint ancestral tomb rituals, the two groups generally operated independently.[112] According to the preface of the genealogy preserved by the Front House, the Deng ancestors reportedly fled wartime turmoil in the third year of the Tongguang era (925 CE) of the Later Tang dynasty, leaving their home "under the white poplar tree in Shangsandu, Ningdu County, Ganzhou Prefecture, Jiangxi." Disguised as hunters, they settled at Hantian'ao in Huitong Li of Ninghua County, under Tingzhou Prefecture in Fujian before moving to the southern foothills, and named the locality Dengwu after their family name.[113] The genealogical record of the Front House was first compiled in the 18th year of the Kangxi era, Qing dynasty (1679), with subsequent editions completed in 1760 (the 25th year of Qianlong era, Qing dynasty), 1813 (Guiyou year, the 18th year of Jiaqing era, Qing dynasty), 1870 (the ninth year of Tongzhi era, Qing dynasty), and 1946.[114]

The genealogy kept by the Rear House presents a slightly different origin story. It records that the Ershiliulang was once appointed a prefect

---

112 Yang Yanjie, "The Rotating Worship Circle: Huaguang Dadi Worship in Zhiping, Ninghua," in *Into the Hakka Historical Field: Local Society and Cultural Traditions*, Guangdong People's Publishing House, 2018, p. 6.
113 "Preface to the Old Genealogy" (the 18th year of Kangxi era, Qing dynasty [1679]), in *Deng Clan Genealogy of the Nanyang Commandery* (Front House), Dengwu, 1946.
114 "New Preface to the Revised Genealogy of the Deng Clan of Nanyang Commandery" (1946), in *Deng Clan Genealogy of the Nanyang Commandery* (Front House), Dengwu, 1946.

during the Song dynasty. "After resigning his post, he settled temporarily in Hantian'ao, drawn by the area's scenic beauty, before moving to the southern foothills to establish a permanent home."[115] By the 18th year of Kangxi era, Qing dynasty, the genealogy preface further specifies that Ershiliulang had served as prefect of Zhangzhou during the Song dynasty, later relocating to Yaolijing Hantian'ao, in Huitongli of Tingzhou-Ninghua, and founding the hamlet of Dengwu beneath the southern hills. The village was initially named "Dengfang" (Deng's Hamlet) after the clan. The family branched in the third generation into the Shiqilang and Shiyilang, giving rise to the Front and Rear Houses, respectively.[116] The Rear House's genealogy was first compiled in the Bingzi year, i.e. the ninth year of the Chongzhen era, Ming dynasty (1636) and revised multiple times thereafter: in 1679 (Jiwei Year, the 18th year of Kangxi era, Qing dynasty), 1780 (the 45th year of Qianlong era, Qing dynasty), 1813 (the 18th year of Jiaqing era, Qing dynasty), 1839 (the 19th year of Daoguang era, Qing dynasty), 1866 (the fifth year of Tongzhi era, Qing dynasty), 1897 (the 23th year of Guangxu era), 1930 (the 19th of the Republic era), and finally in 1995. As for ancestral halls, the Shiyilang Gong's ancestral hall in the Rear House was constructed in 1792 (Renzi year, the 57th year of Qianlong era, Qing dynasty) and renovated in 1829 (the ninth year of Daoguang era, Qing dynasty), with subsequent expansions over time.[117] In addition, a branch ancestral hall built by descendants of Ziwen Gong in the Rear House begun in 1808 (the 13th year of Jiaqing era, Qing dynasty) and was completed in

---

115 "Preface to the Genealogy of the Deng Clan of Nanshan" (the ninth year of Chongzhen era, Ming dynasty [1636]), in *Deng Clan Genealogy of the Nanyang Commandery* (Rear House), Dengwu, 1995.

116 "Preface to the Deng Clan Genealogy" (the 18th year of Kangxi era, Qing dynasty [1679]), in *Deng Clan Genealogy of the Nanyang Commandery* (Rear House), Dengwu, 1995.

117 "Record of the Ancestral Hall of the Ershiliulang Gong (the 23rd year of Guangxu era, Qign dynasty [1897]), in *Deng Clan Genealogy of the Nanyang Commandery* (Rear House), Dengwu, 1995.

1821 (the first year of Daoguang era, Qing dynasty).[118] The joint ancestral hall of the entire clan, dedicated to the Ershiliulang Gong, was built later, in 1881 (the seventh year of Guangxu era, Qing dynasty).[119] Like many lineages in the region, the Deng clan of Dengwu was primarily engaged in agriculture. One entry in the clan genealogy notes that, "in the 25th year of the Wanli era, Ming dynasty (1597), the entire clan collaborated to dig irrigation channels and cultivate farmland at the ancestral site in Hantian'ao. By 1601 (the 29th year of Wanli era, Ming dynasty), the land was surveyed and registered for tax purposes, and the clan assumed corvée duties. In the first year of the Chongzhen era, Ming dynasty (1628), a local acquaintance named Zhang Wu was invited to till the land and, as tenant, paid an annual rent of six *dou* of rice and one livestock animal. The rice was split equally between the Front and Rear Houses—three *dou* each—and the livestock was divided between them. The two houses alternated in performing the annual ancestral rites for this land.[120] During the late Ming dynasty, a member of the Rear House branch of the Deng lineage, known as Maocong (between the 18th year of the Jiajing era, Ming dynasty, and the sixth year of the Chongzhen era, Ming dynasty, i.e., 1539–1633), "was entrusted with overseeing grain taxes and corvée duties for three local *Jia*. Records praise him as upright and conscientious in his duties," and "he was issued official credentials by the Grain Office to manage taxation matters."[121] By the Kangxi era of the Qing dynasty, we read that "a clan member, Deng Wanqin, had originally paid grain taxes through the household of a prominent figure named Zhang Shixian in Longtou. For years, however, exorbitant extra lev-

---

118 "Record of the Ancestral Shrine of the Ziwen Gong" (the first year of Daoguang era, Qing dynasty[1821]), in *Deng Clan Genealogy of the Nanyang Commandery* (Rear House), Dengwu, 1995.
119 "Record of the Ancestral Shrine of the Shiyilang" (1995), in *Deng Clan Genealogy of the Nanyang Commandery* (Rear House), Dengwu, 1995.
120 "On the Sacrificial Lands" (the 18th year of Kangxi era, Qing dynasty [1679]), in *Deng Clan Genealogy of the Nanyang Commandery* (Front House), Dengwu, 1946.
121 "Biography of Maocong" (the ninth year of Chongzhen era, Ming dynasty [1636]), in *Deng Clan Genealogy of the Nanyang Commandery* (Rear House), Dengwu, 1995.

ies were imposed. In response, the clan elders collectively decided to resolve the matter by offering twelve *liang* of silver, along with pork and wine, to the Zhang household, stipulating that henceforth, Deng's household could pay taxes directly to the official granary. Thereafter, they would only deliver a modest annual tribute of eight *qian* in the form of a 'shoe and boot tribute,' ensuring no further excessive demands. This pragmatic solution, inspired by the wishes of their ancestor Ji Gong, was seen as a fresh start for the clan's fiscal autonomy. In the 22nd year of the Qianlong era, Qing dynasty (1757), a census was carried out. During this time, a man named Zhang Bing, exploiting his position as a village chief, behaved with arrogance and disregard for the rights of registered households. Outraged by such abuses, members of the Deng clan—both uncles and nephews—rallied together. They unanimously agreed to withdraw from their current administrative jurisdiction and purchased the position of *li yi* (local service duty) for 30 *liang* of silver under the name of Deng Wanqin. Specifically, the slot of 'Wuchanghou Li, Fourth Jia, Third Tu, Xingshan Li,' at a cost of thirty *liang* of silver. From this point onward, they adopted the name of Renmei Gong as the official designation for this *li yi* duty."[122] In the years that followed, both the Front House and Rear House branches of the Deng clan steadily accumulated extensive farmlands and ritual estates dedicated to ancestral worship.

Within the jurisdiction of present-day Dengwu village lies the natural village of Shaoguang, which is predominantly inhabited by the Liao surname. Local tradition holds that these Liaos originally came from Huaitu Township in Ninghua County. According to the *Liao Clan Genealogy* from Huaitu, their founding ancestor, Jing Gong, migrated from Malan Temple in Ningdu, Jiangxi, to Hekeng in Huaitu during the second year of the

---

122 "Preface to the Office of the *Li yi* of Renmei Gong" (dated the 18th year of Kangxi era, Qing dynasty [1679], authored by a distant descendant Mingning, styled Zi'an), in *Deng Clan Genealogy of the Nanyang Commandery* (Front House), Dengwu, 1946.

Hongwu era, Ming dynasty (1369). Subsequent migration from Huaitu to Zhiping likely occurred in the early Ming period or later. Another genealogy, the *Liao Clan Genealogy of the Xikeng, Wuwei Commandery (Yuankeng, Shaoguang)*, discovered in Xiaping village's Xikeng area, asserts that their forefather, Siyilang Gong, moved from Qi'xia in Huaitu to Xikeng, Zhiping, during the Southern Song dynasty's Qiandao era (1165–1173). He is revered as the founding ancestor of Xikeng. His descendants included Fu Bao, who fathered Xingchang and Xingzhi. Xingzhi later migrated from Xikeng to Yuankeng, whose descendant Zesheng had two sons. One of their lines, stemming from Chenghuang, eventually settled in Shaoguang. Regrettably, the original *Liao Clan Genealogy* was destroyed. Much of the ancestral lore and clan records were not preserved in the newer versions.[123]

Traveling further into the mountains from the villages of Dengwu and Pengfang, one arrives at the administrative center of today's Zhiping She Ethnic Township. Although the terrain remains relatively flat here, it marks the threshold of the mountainous zone and serves as a crucial gateway to the uplands. The area is now divided into two administrative villages—Zhiping and Hubeijiao. From Zouwuba in Hubeijiao, the road forks: one route to the left leads through Shefu and Guangliang to Tianshe, while the path to the right winds toward Xiaping, Gaofeng, and ultimately reaches Jigongdong, the highest peak in Ninghua County. Another road from Zhiping Street, branching right halfway between Pengfang and Zhiping, leads to Pingpu, Gaodi, and Nikeng. As the mountain population continues to dwindle and road construction costs remain high, more than half the mountain roads within Zhiping Township remain unpaved. Motorcycles are the primary means of transportation for mountain dwellers, though some still travel on foot. Most residents descend the mountain to stock up on supplies

---

123 "Lineage and Origins," in *Liao Clan Genealogy of the Xikeng, Wuwei Commandery (Yuankeng, Shaoguang)*, compiled by descendants of the Siyilang Gong of Zhiping, Ninghua County, Fujian Province, 2019, pp. 31–32.

only on market days, which occur on dates ending in four or nine, a testament to the difficulty of accessing the mountains. Zhiping and Hubeijiao serve not only as the administrative hubs of the township but also as its commercial and cultural centers. The population here is multi-surnamed, with many residents having relocated from other, especially mountainous, villages within the township.

The Qiu clan of Hubeijiao settled here relatively late, likely in the early Qing period. According to the *Qiu Clan Genealogy*, "the seventh-generation ancestor Lilang Gong moved to Shuixi in Ninghua, and the 14th-generation ancestor Ershilang Gong later branched off to settle in Gaoling. By the 20th generation, the family's forefather Yunlang moved from Gaoling to Shangshe village in Zhiping in the second year of the Hongwu era, Ming dynasty (1369), founding the clan base at Guantang, where they lived and thrived."[124] It was not until the next generation of Fuheng, the eldest son of Rongchun Gong, that the Qiu clan first connected with Zhiping, with his descendants eventually settling there. Fuheng was born in the 60th year of Kangxi era, Qing dynasty (1721, Xinchou year) and passed away in the 41st year of Qianlong era, Qing dynasty (1776, Bingshen year). He was buried in Hengkengli of Lishangli. His wife, Xiangniang of the Wen clan, was born in the fourth year of Yongzheng era, Qing dynasty (1726, Bingwu year) and died in the gengshen year of Jiaqing era, Qing dynasty (1800), buried at Zhangpai, Sibeiling in Huitongli. They had five sons, of whom Shouxiang and Shoupeng continued the lineage. Shouxiang, born in the Wuchen year of Qianlong era, Qing dynasty (1748) and deceased in Wuxu year of Guangxu era, Qing dynasty (1838), lived to the age of 91. He was buried in Mukenli and "was remembered for his sincerity and integrity. From a young age, he was cautious with words and

---

124 "Preface to the Eighth Revision in the Guiyou Year" (1993), in *Qiu Clan Genealogy of the Tianshui Commandery*, Vol. 1, 1993.

deeds, devoted to virtue and duty, avoiding idle affairs. He tilled the land diligently, lived frugally, and through hard work amassed considerable wealth. With increasing prosperity, he acquired fertile land and built an ancestral hall at Sibeiling." His brother Shoupeng was born in Wuzi year of Qianlong era (1768) and died in Bingxu year of Daoguang era (1826), also buried at Zhangpai.[125] The Qiu clan have since taken root in Zhiping, though their population remained relatively small. To this day, they are not among the surnames recognized with formal representation in community rituals such as the Ten-Village Rotating Worship of Lingguan Dadi (灵官大帝, a powerful protective deity), discussed in the next section.

The earliest Han Chinese settlers in the mountain areas date back to the Song dynasty. Among them, the Zeng clan is the most populous in Zhiping. The major surnames in Shefu, Guangliang, and Tianshe administrative villages are Zeng, which branch into the "Lower House" lines of Wulang and Balang (founders of the Lower Gate) and the "Upper House" line of Qilang (founder of the Upper Gate). From the relatively flat lands of Shefu, the road into the mountains leads deeper into remote territory, culminating in Tianzhe village—a landscape of "towering peaks, lush forests, and thick bamboo forests." According to Zeng clan oral history, their founding ancestor, Zeng Qinglu, migrated from Nanfeng in Jiangxi province to Huitongli in Ninghua during the Song dynasty. He first settled at Peizhukeng before the family branched out into other areas. The Zeng ancestral hall originally built in Peizhukeng was unfortunately destroyed by fire before 1949 and has never been rebuilt. According to the genealogy of the Upper House line, Tianzengshe (modern-day Tianshe) lies 120 *li* south of the Ninghua county seat, under Huitongli jurisdiction, and is 70 *li* from the prefectural capital of Changting. The region is described as "its valleys

---

125 "Descendants of Shirui Gong within the Line of Wenxian Gong," in *Qiu Clan Genealogy of the Tianshui Commandery*, Vol. 14, 1993.

are majestic, home to dense family settlements, with a simple and unpretentious custom—few studied, many tilled the land. Its proximity to Changting has led to a blend of ritual practices and dialect."[126] The founding ancestor of the Upper House in Tianzengshe was the 60th-generation Zeng clan member, Qilang Gong, who moved to the village and began that line's settlement.[127] The genealogy for the Wulang and Balang lines from the Lower House was first compiled in the 59th year of Qianlong era, Qing dynasty (1794), revised again in the 28th year of Daoguang era, Qing dynasty (1848), and underwent a third revision in the sixth year of Guangxu era, Qing dynasty (1880).[128] The Upper House Qilang line's genealogy followed a similar pattern, with compilations in 1794, 1847, and 1879 respectively.[129]

The largest surname group in Xiaping village is the Li clan, which is also believed to be the earliest to settle in the area. According to the *Li Clan Genealogy*, the clan's founding ancestor was Chongfu Gong, who, along with his son Liulang Gong, is credited with initiating the family's migration. The genealogy records that Chongfu held the post of tax supervisor in Tingzhou, Fujian, under the title "Southern Sword Commandery" and was exceptionally versed in astronomy, geography, and feng shui. "In the first year of the Taiping Xingguo era of Emperor Taizong of the Song dynasty (976 CE), the Jiazi year, he journeyed through Huitongli and discovered an auspicious site at Jiuxu Gorge in Xiaping, a place believed to bring forth

---

126 "Record of the Alternate Name 'Yunzhuang' of Tianzengshe," in *Zeng Clan Genealogy of Yunzhuang* (Upper House—Line of Qilang), Vol. 1, 1879.
127 "Preface to the Genealogy of Lu State Commandery Compiled in the Qing Dynasty" (the 59th year of Qianlong era, Qing dynasty [1794]), in *Zeng Clan Genealogy of Yunzhuang* (Upper House—Line of Qilang), Vol. 1, 1879.
128 "Preface to the Third Revision of the Zeng Clan Genealogy" (the sixth year of Guangxu era, Qing dynasty [1880]), in *Zeng Clan Genealogy of Yunzhuang* (Lower House—Line of Wulang and Balang), 1880.
129 "Preface to the Re-revision of the Genealogy in Jimao Year" (the fifth year of Guangxu era, Qing dynasty [1879]), in *Zeng Clan Genealogy of Yunzhuang* (Upper House—Line of Qilang), Vol. 1, 1879.

countless descendants and enduring fortune." He then moved to Shihui'ao in Huitongli. His son Liulang later migrated from Shihui'ao to Wuchangqiu in Xiaping in the first year of Emperor Zhenzong's Xianping era (998 CE), where he "cleared the land and built a homestead—thus becoming the founding forefather of the Xiaping branch of the Li clan." The Li clan compiled its first genealogy in 1797 (the second year of Jiaqing era, Qing dynasty, Ding-si year), followed by revisions in 1836 (the 16th year of Daoguang era, Qing dynasty), 1879 (the fifth year of Guangxu era, Qing dynasty), and again in the 1990s.[130]

(Pic63 Tianshe Administrative Village, Zhiping She Ethnic Township)

Within Xiaping Administrative Village, the Hu clan traces its ancestry back to their founding forefather Wulang Gong, who first settled in Huling. In the 12th generation, Xianyi Gong migrated from there to Shifu in Changting, establishing a new branch of the family. From Xianyi to Hu Lanshan (born in 1951), a recognized intangible cultural heritage inheritor of the Yukou papermaking technique, the lineage spans 27 generations.[131] The

---

130 "Preface of the Li Clan Genealogy of Longxi Commandery" (the second year of Jiaqing era, Qing dynasty [1797]), "Preface of the Li Clan Genealogy of Longxi Commandery", (the 16th year of Daoguang era, Qing dynasty [1836]), "Preface of the Li Clan Genealogy of Longxi Commandery", (the fifth year of Guangxu era, Qing dynasty [1879]), in *The Third Revised Genealogy of the Li Clan of Longxi Commandery*, Vol. 1; "Lineage Biography of the Founding Ancestor", in *The Third Revised Genealogy of the Li Clan of Longxi Commandery*, Vol. 3, 1879.
131 *Concise Genealogy of the Hu Clan*, transcribed by Hu Youtao (manuscript), 1988.

Lai clan of Shangping, another settlement within Xiaping, took root on Lai-jia Mountain, a key point along a mountain path leading to Jiangxi. Their founding ancestor, Hongkai Gong, and his two sons, settled in Shangping during the Ming dynasty, where they "cleared thorns and opened up the wilderness," laying the foundation for future generations.[132] The clan restored Hongkai's tomb in 1700 (the 39th year of Kangxi era, Qing dynasty), located beneath the rocks of Anhu Lake and described as "Xinshan Yixiang, shared by husband and wife." In 1893 (the 19th year of Guangxu era, Qing dynasty), they established the clan's ancestral hall, Zhenxiang Tang. The Lai family's genealogy was first compiled in 1797 (the second year of Jiaqing era, Qing dynasty), then revised in 1837 (Ding-you year of Daoguang era), 1869 (Ji-si year of Tongzhi era), and 1903 (the 29th year of Guangxu era, Qing dynasty).[133]

In Gaofeng Administrative Village, the major surnames are Chen and Lai. Among them, the Chens are concentrated in Fujikeng village, where they regard Zhenxian of the 18th generation, descended from the Yanjiu Gong lineage, as the founding forefather. The birth and death dates of Zhenxian and his father Gongjun remain unknown, but Zhenxian's uncle Gongyong was born in 1690 (the 29th year of Kangxi era, the Gengwu year). It is known that Zhenxian later moved to Jimawo in Ninghua's Fujikeng, where he died and was buried,[134] suggesting that the Chen family migrated to the area in the mid-Qing dynasty.

The Lian clan of Pingpu She ethnic village also claims to have settled in the area as early as the Song dynasty. According to the *Lian Clan Genealogy of Shangdang Commandery*, a man named Chaolang, styled Shiping,

---

132 "Old Preface" (Gengchen year of the Kangxi era, Qing dynasty [1700]); "Preface to the Lai Clan Genealogy" (the second year of Jiaqing era, Qing dynasty [1797]), in *The Fifth Revised Genealogy of the Lai Clan of Shangping*, 1993.
133 "New Preface to the Fifth Revised Genealogy," in *The Fifth Revised Genealogy of the Lai Clan of Shangping*, 1993.
134 *Genealogy of the Sanshisilang Gong Branch of the Chen Clan in Shanhu, Shanghang*, 1997, p. 303.

fled to Anhu in the First District in Huitongli, Ninghua, during local authorities' conscripted militia in the fifth year of the Qiandao era, Song dynasty (1169). He was born in the 20th year of Shaoxing era, South Song dynasty (1150) and died in the 4th year of Jiading era, South Song dynasty (1211), buried in the "goose-shaped" terrain within the narrow part of Anhu's water gap. The Lian clan's ancestral hall, located at Shishengduan in northern Anhu of Pingpu, was first built in 1807 (the 12th year of Jiaqing era, Qing dynasty) and rebuilt in 1833 (the 13th year of Daoguang era, Qing dynasty). It honors Lianchao as the founding ancestor of the clan in Anhu.[135]

---

135 "Lineage of the Descendants of Yilang Gong," in *Lian Clan Genealogy of Shangdang Commandery*, Pingpu, 1993.

(Pic64   Laijia Mountain, Xiaping Administrative Village, Zhiping She Ethnic Township)

(Pic65   Lian Clan Ancestral Hall, Pingpu Village, Zhiping She Ethnic Township, Photograph by Gui Shuzhong)

Gaodi Administrative Village lies nestled in the mountains at an altitude of 800 meters, straddling the border between Ninghua County in Fujian Province and Shicheng County in Jiangxi Province. The village is surrounded by mountain ranges on all sides. Among its oldest inhabitants, the Chi clan holds a prominent place. The clan's founding ancestor, Yulang Gong, migrated from E'yatang in Ningdu, Jiangxi, to Chijiabei in Ninghua during the first year of the Kaixi era of the Southern Song dynasty (1205). Later, in 1242 (the second year of Chunyou era, Southern Song dynasty), his descendant Tianbao Gong moved once again, settling in Chijiadong in Huitongli.[136] According to the *Chi Clan Genealogy*, "In earlier times, this area was still a desolate frontier, home to only a few families of mountain tenants dwelling in thatched huts." "The transformation began when the Fan clan sold the surrounding hills and fields to Jishi Gong, an early ancestor of the Chi clan. He cleared thorns and tilled the barren land, gradually turning it into fertile soil." In the early Qing dynasty, "to honor his pioneering efforts, village elders rebuilt and expanded the family shrine he had established, acknowledging the labor and legacy of this forefather."[137] By the 1980s, the Chi clan numbered over 520 people. They cultivated 100 *mu* of farmland and 70 *mu* of agricultural land, and managed 11,603 *mu* of forest-

---

136 "Origins and Branches of the Baixi Genealogy" (the 39th year of Qianlong era, Qing dynasty [1774]), in *Chi Clan Genealogy of Baixi*, Gaodi, Vol. 3, sixth revision in 1917, supplemented in the seventh revision in 1989; "'The seventh revised genealogy contains both printed and handwritten texts; all printed characters are original from the old genealogy'" ("Preface to the Seventh Revised Genealogy" [1988]), in *Chi Clan Genealogy of Baixi*, Gaodi, Vol. 1, sixth revision (1917), supplemented in the seventh revision (1989).
137 "Origins and Branches of the Baixi Genealogy" (the 39th year of Qianlong era, Qing dynasty [1774]), in *Chi Clan Genealogy of Baixi*, Gaodi, Vol. 3, sixth revision in 1917, supplemented in the seventh revision in 1989; "'The seventh revised genealogy contains both printed and handwritten texts; all printed characters are original from the old genealogy'" ("Preface to the Seventh Revised Genealogy" [1988]), in *Chi Clan Genealogy of Baixi*, Gaodi, Vol. 1, sixth revision (1917), supplemented in the seventh revision (1989).
137 "Record of Baixi" (Renyin year of Daoguang era, Qing dynasty [1842]), in *Chi Clan Genealogy of Baixi*, Gaodi, Vol. 2, sixth revision (1917), supplemented in the seventh revision (1989).

ed hills, including 8,358 *mu* of bamboo forests."[138] The Chi genealogy has a long history of compilation: the first edition was completed in 1694 (the 33rd year of Kangxi era, Qing dynasty, Jiaxu year), followed by updates in 1774 (the 39th year of Qianlong era, Jiawu year), 1807 (the 12th year of Jiaqing era, Dingmao year), 1842 (the 22nd year of Daoguang era, Renyin year), 1874 (the 13th year of Tongzhi era, Jiaxu year), and 1917 (the sixth year of Republican era). A seventh edition was published in 1989.[139] Local Chi clansmen recount that, one fascinating cultural tradition preserved by the Chi clan is the Lantern Array Dance, introduced from Qixing Town in Ganzhou, Jiangxi, during the Qianlong era of Qing dynasty. It is locally known as the Chi Family Civil and Martial Lanterns or Chi Clan Civil and Martial Guandao (Broadsword) Lanterns, combining ritual and artistry. It is a form of ancestral worship, staged annually in the ancestral hall from the second to the fifteenth day of the first lunar month.

Nikeng Administrative Village lies at the boundary between Zhiping and Fangtian townships. Its main surnames include Xie, Zhang, Lan, and Zeng. Among them, the Xie family is particularly prominent in Wubaikeng, a hamlet originally under the jurisdiction of Sixi Village in Fangtian. The clan traces its migration to Fujian back to the Zhishun era, Yuan dynasty (1330-1333), when a man named Renfu moved from Shaowu to Dongjiafang in Jianning. His grandsons, Yanglang and Pulang, later relocated to Ninghua, becoming the founding ancestors of the Xie clan in the region.[140] A genealogical record collected by Gui Shuzhong—the Sixth Compilation of the *Xie Clan Genealogy of Dongjiafang*, dating from the

---

138 "My Hometown" (1988), in *Chi Clan Genealogy of Baixi*, Gaodi, Vol. 1, sixth revision (1917), supplemented in the seventh revision (1989).
139 "Preface to the Sixth Revised Genealogy" (1917), in *Chi Clan Genealogy of Baixi*, Gaodi, Vol. 1, sixth revision (1917), supplemented in the seventh revision (1989).
140 Yuanlang, "Genealogical Origins through the Ages" (1368), preface to the *Xie Clan Genealogy of Dongjiafang*, Nikeng, sixth revision, 1834;
Fuxiu, "Preface to the Third Genealogical Revision" (1725), preface to the *Xie Clan Genealogy of Dongjiafang*, Nikeng, sixth revision, 1834.

Daoguang era, Qing dynasty—is known as the Lion edition. It was held by "descendants of Dengxiang Gong from Wubai Keng, Sixi Dam, Ninghua, Tingzhou Prefecture, of the Wensheng Branch." Dengxiang Gong, the 13th-generation ancestor in the line, was the fifth son of Bisheng Gong (12th generation). Bisheng Gong was born in 1663 (Guimao year of Kangxi era, Qing dynasty) and died in 1674 (Jiayin year of Kangxi era, Qing dynasty)—a date the author notes may be uncertain. Bisheng was buried at Pengkeng in Huaitu. His son, Dengxiang, was born in 1709 (Jichou year of Kangxi era) and deceased in 1771 (Xinmao year of Qianlong era), was buried in the unmarked cemetery at Henglutou in Nikeng.[141] He is considered the founding ancestor of the Xie clan in Nikeng. The Xie genealogy has a rich history of revisions, first compiled in 1368 (the first year of Hongwu era, Ming dynasty) and subsequently updated in 1725, 1773, 1790, 1814, 1834, and 1866—amounting to seven major editions by the late Qing.[142] A more recent version published in 1991 marks the 11th known edition. Interestingly, the fourth revision came less than thirty years after the third and fifth editions—an unusual pattern possibly linked to the unification of multiple clan branches into a consolidated genealogy.[143] It is worth noting that the Xie clan of Nikeng migrated relatively late, and as a result, the available genealogies—being linked-lineage compilations—include relatively scant information on this particular branch.

---

141 "Lineage of Wensheng, Zhongming, and Shixian of the Bo'an Branch," in *Xie Clan Genealogy of Dongjiafang*, Nikeng, Vol. 3, sixth revision, 1834;
Xie Clan Genealogy of Chenliu Commandery (Fujian, Jiangxi, Hubei, Jianning), revised in 1991.
142 Dao Xin et al., "Preface to the Sixth Revised Genealogy of the Xie Clan" (1834), preface to the *Xie Clan Genealogy of Dongjiafang*, Nikeng, sixth revision, 1834; Buying, "Preface to the Seventh Revised Genealogy" (1866), preface to the *Xie Clan Genealogy of Dongjiafang*, Nikeng, seventh revision, 1866.
143 Riguang, "Preface to the Fifth Revised Genealogy" (1814), preface to the *Xie Clan Genealogy of Dongjiafang*, Nikeng, sixth revision, 1834.

166

(Pic66   Chi Clan Ancestral Hall, Gaodi Village, Zhiping She Ethnic Township)

In summary, Han Chinese migration into the region of Zhiping likely began as early as the late Tang to Song dynasties. The earliest settlers mostly came from Jiangxi, a pattern closely tied to Zhiping's geographic proximity to that province. These early migrants either cultivated small plains nestled within the mountains or ventured deeper into the highlands to clear and farm new land, with agriculture as their primary livelihood. By the Ming and Qing periods, a larger wave of new migrants had arrived and taken root within the area now known as Zhiping Township. Village populations expanded, surnames diversified, and clan-based organizations gradually took shape. As a result, local power structures within the villages grew increasingly intricate. Alongside this influx of Han settlers, She people had already begun inhabiting and developing the mountainous areas of Zhiping. Inevitably, there were moments of friction and conflict, but the broader trajectory was one of gradual integration. The complex dynamics between the Han and She peoples can be explored in depth through the operation and performance of Zhiping's most significant inter-clan village alliance ritual: the Ten-Village Rotating Worship of Lingguan Dadi.

3.2. Procession of Deities Among Ten Villages

The Ten-Village Rotating Worship of the deity Lingguan Dadi refers to a shared religious practice among ten Han-majority villages within Zhiping Township, in which each village takes turns hosting the worship and festivities for Lingguan Dadi, a powerful protective deity in local folk belief. According to oral accounts from residents, the original ten villages included Dengwu, Pengfang, Huangtianguan (now part of Caofang Township), Shaoguang, Liangshe, Xiajie, Shangjie, Xiaping, Tianshe, and Pingpu. Of these, Liangshe, Xiajie, and Shangjie are currently administrative villages under Zhiping, while Shaoguang and Dengwu fall within the Dengwu administrative unit. Thus, the concept of "ten villages" in this rotating worship is a geographically defined community shaped by folk culture, not entirely aligned with modern administrative divisions.

3.2.1.   Field Observation of Lingguan Dadi Worship

On September 10, 2021, guided by Gui Shuzhong, I visited Pengfang Village with a few colleagues. The village head, Fan Renning, warmly received us and led us to visit both the Peng Clan Ancestral Hall and the Fan Clan Ancestral Hall. To our delight, we discovered that the Peng Clan Ancestral Hall was, at that very moment, serving as the host site for the rotational worship of Lingguan Dadi, also known as Wuxian Wutong Lingguan Dadi (the Great Lord with Five Manifestations and Five Spiritual Powers). Inside the hall, Lingguan Dadi's altar was flanked by a pantheon of revered figures: Dongyue Dadi (the Great Deity of Mount Tai), Mazu Niangniang (the Sea Goddess), Wugu Zhenxian (the Immortal of the Five Grains), Qianliyan and Shunfeng'er (Thousand-Mile Eye and All-Hearing Ear), as well as Faguan (Divine Judge) and Panguan (Underworld Recorder). On the table in front of all deities was a dragon plaque inscribed with "Long Live the Emperor." Among locals, belief in Lingguan Dadi runs deep. His arrival for worship is regarded as a momentous event in the village, drawing the entire community into ritual celebration. Just a year prior, on the 28th day of the ninth lunar month of 2020, it was Pengfang's turn to host the deity. The entire village mobilized for the welcome procession. After completing a year-long stay in the combined villages of Shaoguang and Huangtianguan (collectively referred to as Shaohuang), the deity was ceremonially sent to Niushou Temple on the 27th for a *jiao* ritual (打醮, a Taoist ceremonial ritual to pray for blessings and exorcism), and then welcomed by Pengfang on the 28th. That day, the procession was a grand spectacle. Firework bearers led the way, followed by a lead figure carrying incense lanterns and a horse lantern. A lively drum and gong band played without pause. The crowd wielded two to three hundred banners of varying sizes, along with ritual implements and ceremonial regalia. Lingguan Dadi's palanquin was borne aloft by villagers, followed by those of Dongyue Dadi, Mazu, Wugu Zhenxian, Qianliyan, Shunfeng'er, and other deities. Each palanquin and incense burner was carried by a team of four, with different teams rotating throughout the procession. As the divine entourage entered the village, every household had prepared incense tables outside their doors to welcome the gods. The air filled with the thunder of firecrackers, gongs, and ritual firearms—a deafening symphony of devotion. The procession circled the village before finally delivering the statues to a prearranged ancestral hall. Once Lingguan Dadi's statue was safely installed, the local management committee initiated the carefully prepared *jiao* ritual. Members of the host lineage then took on the responsibility of tending to the deity—offering daily incense, lighting ritual lamps, and ensuring his presence was honored with the utmost reverence throughout his stay.

(Pic67   Lingguan Dadi and Other Deities Enshrined at the Peng Clan Ancestral Hall in Pengfang during the 2021 September Rotating Worship)

It is said that each clan' ancestral hall conducts the *jiao* ritual at different times and with varying frequency. Generally speaking, the ritual must be held both when the statue of Lingguan Dadi is welcomed into a village and when it is sent away. Take Pengfang village as an example. In 2020, when Lingguan arrived, the *jiao* ritual was held in the ancestral hall of the Fan clan starting on the 28th day of the ninth lunar month. Five months later, the statue was moved to the ancestral hall of the Lai clan, and two months after that, it was transferred again to the ancestral hall of the Peng clan. Each time the deity changed residence, a *jiao* ceremony was held to mark the occasion. Beyond this, in the year when Lingguan's statue was enshrined in Pengfang as part of the rotation, residents from the other nine villages could also prearrange to invite the deity to their own villages for a *jiao* ritual.

During a visit on September 10, 2021, we learned that the following day would witness such a moment: Tianshe village was preparing to travel to Pengfang to formally invite Lingguan back for a *jiao* ritual. On the morning of September 11, we arrived at Tianshe village and, under the guidance of Deputy Village Head Mr. Zeng Youchun, participated in the full process of welcoming the deity. After sharing a communal breakfast in front of the ancestral hall of the Zeng clan, the villagers traveled together by trucks to Pengfang to greet the deities. Several students, including Wang Siheng, observed the scene closely: out of reverence for the deities, most villagers remained standing during the ride. The sounds of suona horns and long trumpets echoed through the early morning mountains as the procession made its way. The order of the vehicles carrying the statues was also strictly regulated: the statue of the Lingguan Dadi led the way, followed by the Dongyue Dadi and Mazu, with lesser deities trailing behind. The three principal deities were carried on palanquins, while the rest were simply transported by hand. Notably, due to population decline in rural areas, women have increasingly taken on key roles in carrying and escorting the deities.

Through firsthand observation and interviews, we came to understand just how significant the arrival of Lingguan Dadi and the *jiao* rituals are to the residents of the ten villages of Zhiping. Each village is responsible for organizing its own delegation to welcome the deity, carefully preparing offerings and ceremonial arrangements in advance, while also take turns hosting *ya hui* (communal sacrificial feasts). These rituals not only embody the rights of participating clans—each with a stake in the proceedings—but also reflect unity and cooperation among different surnames, laying bare the core framework of Zhiping's social structure. According to members of the Lingguan Dadi Council, this governing body comprises representatives elected from all ten villages. Acting in the common interest, the council addresses communal affairs through annual or ad hoc meetings, thus creating an organic system of coordination across village boundaries. This layered organizational framework, combined with the enduring popular devotion to Lingguan Dadi, explains the lasting vitality of the ten-village rotating ritual system. At the same time, it serves as an effective mechanism for maintaining local social order. In this light, the rotating worship of Lingguan Dadi is far more than a religious tradition—it is perhaps the most important grassroots social institution in Zhiping. It expresses the region's norms, rules, and communal practices from the ground up and deserves our close attention as a mirror of village-level governance and social organization.

(Pic68-69   The Zeng Clan of Tianshe Administrative Village Performing a Deity-Welcoming Jiao Ritual at the Zeng Clan Ancestral Hall, September 11, 2021; Welcoming and Worshipping Lingguan Dadi at the Liao Clan Ancestral Hall in Yuankeng Village, Hubeijiao Administrative Village, February 28, 2022)

3.2.2.   Faith in Lingguan Dadi and Village Society

Building on Yang Yanjie's 1990 survey report[144]—and supplementing it with our own recent fieldwork and collected texts—we turn to an in-depth discussion of the largest ritual practice in Zhiping: the "Ten-Village Rotat-

---

144 Yang Yanjie, "The Rotation Circle: Worship of Emperor Huaguang in Zhiping, Ninghua" in *Entering the Historical Fields of the Hakka: Local Society and Cultural Traditions*, Guangdong People's Publishing House, 2018, p.6.

ing Worship of Lingguan Dadi." This ceremonial institution provides key insights into the region's social structure before the rise of the papermaking industry.

A central question arises: When did the ten villages first come together to jointly venerate Lingguan Dadi in this rotating worship? A historical clue lies in the "Preface to the Recasting of Lingguan Dadi's Statue," found in the 1981 *Record Book of the Reestablished Lingguan Dadi*. It states: "Our Wuxian Wutong Lingguan Dadi has, since the Song Dynasty, shown remarkable merit and divine power. All prayers are answered; no request goes unheeded. Under his radiant blessing, the faithful of the ten villages in Yidu, Huitongli, Ninghua, have enjoyed timely winds and rains, national prosperity, and peace for over a thousand years."[145] This suggests that local people believe the rotating worship began in the Song dynasty, and has endured for over a millennium. However, Yang Yanjie offers a more critical view. Drawing on the historical record that Caofang village only established its Wutong Temple during the Tianshun era of the Ming dynasty—along with genealogical evidence about the migration of clan ancestors into Zhiping—Yang argues that the ritual practice likely began not in the Song, but in the Ming dynasty.

The Ten-Village Rotating Worship of Lingguan Dadi in Zhiping involves more than a dozen lineages, including those of Peng, Zeng, Deng, Fan, Liao, Lai, Li, Lian, Chen, Liu, Luo, Zou, Zhang, and Wu. These surnames did not all arrive in Zhiping at the same time. As noted earlier, the Peng clan is said to be the earliest, having settled in Pengfang during the late Tang dynasty. The Zeng clan arrived in the Song dynasty and founded their ancestral base in Tianshe, while the Deng clan established Dengwu

---

145 *Record Book of the Reconstruction of Lingguan Dadi*, 1981, preserved in Shangjie of Zhiping, provided by Deng Xuanjiu of Dengwu. A total of 11 volumes were compiled, with one copy held by each village and an additional general copy kept with the deity's statue for recording events as they occurred.

during the end of the Southern Song. Other lineages came much later. For instance, the Fan clan of Pengfang migrated and established their base during the third year of the Hongwu era (1370) in the Ming dynasty, while the Liao clan of Shaoguang also arrived after the beginning of the Ming. Yet both Fan and Liao have long been recognized participants in the rotating worship of Lingguan Dadi. Based on such evidence, Yang Yanjie argues that the formation of the Ten-Village Rotating Worship alliance could not have taken place before the early Ming period. Further support for this view comes from the case of the Cao clan in Dengwu. Their ancestor Wanyun Gong, the 19th-generation forebear who moved from Caofang to establish the Dengwu branch, lived around the Kangxi to Qianlong eras of the Qing dynasty. Prior to this, the Cao clan was not included in the worship circle. This suggests that the Ten-Village alliance had already solidified before the Kangxi–Qianlong period—yet it likely did not emerge earlier than the Ming dynasty. Since lineage formation requires time for growth and consolidation, the rotating system probably came into being in the mid-Ming period at the earliest, or by the late Ming to early Qing at the latest.

Local accounts maintain that the Ten-Village alliance refers specifically to ten participating village communities. These were originally divided into the "Inner Five Villages" and the "Outer Five Villages." The Inner Five Villages were located closer to the mountainous interior of Zhiping and included Shangjie (Upper Street), Xiajie (Lower Street), Xiaping, Tianshe, and Pingpu. Among them, Shangjie served as the core. Zhiping was formerly known as Sibeiling, named after the Huaguang Temple at the foot of Mount Mabeiling—where the ceremonial handover of the Lingguan Dadi traditionally took place. In contrast, the Outer Five Villages lay closer to the outer edge of the region, bordering Caofang. These included Liangshe, Pengfang, Dengwu, Shaoguang, and Huangtianguan. For the Outer Five,

Niushou Temple in Dengwu served as the ceremonial center, where the transfer of Lingguan Dadi also occurred.

It is unclear when the Huaguang Temple and Niushou Temple were originally built. By the time Yang Yanjie visited in 1990, both temples had fallen into ruin. In 2016, the Lingguan Dadi Council built a new "Wutong Temple" at Baishiji in Hubeijiao Village, replacing the original Huaguang Temple, which had been repurposed for other uses. At the same time, the council undertook the restoration of the Niushou Temple, which was re-named "Fengtian Temple."[146] According to the council, Niushou Temple was originally known as Zhonglin Temple. It was first established during the Jiajing era of the Ming dynasty by Mao Cong, the 15th-generation ancestor of the Deng clan in Dengwu. Later, the 18th-generation ancestor Kui En funded the construction of the Guanyin Hall, enshrining the Sakyamuni Buddha, the Bhaisajyaguru Buddha and the Amitabha Buddha. The temple was jointly maintained by five villages: Dengwu, Pengfang, Liangshe, Shaoguang, and Huangtianguan.[147] The temple's origins thus coincide with the era when the ten-village rotating worship system appears to have been established.

Local accounts recall that prior to the Cultural Revolution, the traditional rotation order for the ten-village worship cycle was: Huangtianguan → Pengfang → Shaoguang → Dengwu → Liangshe → Xiajie → Shangjie → Xiaping → Tianshe → Pingpu, and then back to Huangtianguan. When the worship of Lingguan Dadi was revived in 1982, the rotation resumed with Dengwu as the first host. However, both the sequence and the composition of participating villages were modified. Huangtianguan and

---

146 Wutong Wuxian Lingguan Dadi Council of Zhiping She Ethnic Township, "Application for Religious Activity Venue Certification for 'Wutong Temple' and 'Fengtian Temple'", May 4, 2017, provided by Deng Xuanjiu of Dengwu.
147 Wutong Wuxian Lingguan Dadi Council of Zhiping She Ethnic Township, "Application for Religious Activity Venue Certification for 'Wutong Temple' and 'Fengtian Temple'", May 4, 2017, provided by Deng Xuanjiu of Dengwu.

Shaoguang merged into a single unit—referred to as "Shaohuang"—while a new member, Gaofeng Village, was added, keeping the total number at ten. Gaofeng's inclusion was partly due to their own request and partly because the newly merged Shaohuang had too few residents to shoulder a full year of ritual responsibility on their own. With the consent of all participating villages, Gaofeng was officially accepted into the rotation. As a result, the original division between "five inner villages" and "five outer villages" shifted to a "six inner villages, four outer villages" arrangement. The revised order of the ten village rotation is as follows: Dengwu, Liangshe, Xiajie of Zhiping, Shangjie of Zhiping, Xiaping, Gaofeng, Tianshe, Pingpu, Shaohuang, and Pengfang—then returning to Dengwu to begin the cycle anew.[148]

Yang Yanjie observed that the Ten-Village Rotating Worship of Lingguan Dadi was a collective form of religious devotion. Since each village was home to one or more clans, the entire ritual cycle carried a strong undertone of clan alliance. One of the most distinctive features of this worship system was the establishment of a representative council, which reflected a high level of organizational structure. Important decisions were carefully documented, resulting in a rich archive that preserved detailed records of nearly all major issues encountered during the rotation process. When the ritual cycle was restored in 1981, a total of 31 representatives attended the preparatory meeting. These included 3 from Dengwu, 3 from Liangshe, 3 from Xiajie, 5 from Shangjie, 4 from Xiaping, 2 from Gaofeng, 2 from Tianshe, 3 from Pingpu, 3 from Shaohuang, and 3 from Pengfang. Analyzed by surname, the representatives included 6 surnamed Zeng, 4 Lai, 5 Li, 3 Deng, 3 Fan, and 3 Lian, while the Peng, Liao, Jiang, Zou, Zhang, and Wu families each had one delegate. Notably, there was also one repre-

---

148 *Record Book of the Reconstruction of Lingguan Dadi*, 1981, preserved in Shangjie of Zhiping.

sentative surnamed Lei from Xiajie, which stands out as an exception in a predominantly clan-based structure.[149]

During the 1981 re-sculpting of the statue of Lingguan Dadi, villagers from all ten communities donated money and goods to support the rotation activities, collectively Purchasing necessary assets. The total donations from all villages amounted to 5,924.9 yuan. Contributions by village were as follows: Tianshe – 706 yuan, Shangjie of Zhiping – 939 yuan, Pingpu – 507 yuan, Xiajie – 548 yuan, Liangshe – 602 yuan, Pengfang – 522.1 yuan, Shaohuang – 412.8 yuan, Gaofeng – 766 yuan, Xiaping – 422 yuan, and Dengwu – 500 yuan. Among these figures, the donation from Gaofeng is particularly striking. With a contribution of 766 yuan, Gaofeng ranked second, just behind Shangjie. Given that Gaofeng was located in the mountainous interior of Zhiping Township and, according to 1981 data, had a smaller population than larger villages like Shangjie, Xiaping, Dengwu, or Tianshe, Yang concluded that the villagers of Gaofeng were especially committed to participating in the Lingguan Dadi worship.[150]

Thereafter, the ritual cycle of Lingguan Dadi among the ten villages gradually became institutionalized. In 1990, the ten villages held a new round of elections for ritual representatives and appointed two general representatives to oversee the entire process. A total of 42 individuals were elected, including 4 from Dengwu (with the addition of one member from the Cao lineage), 4 from Liangshe, 3 from Xiajie, 4 from Shangjie, 4 from Xiaping, 4 from Gaofeng, 5 from Tianshe, 3 from Pingpu, 5 from Shaohuang, and 5 from Pengfang. When classified by surname, the representatives included 9 with the surname Zeng, 5 Lai, 5 Li, 4 Deng, 4 Fan, 3 Lian, 2 Peng, 2 Liao, and 2 Chen. Other surnames such as Liu, Luo, Zou, Zhang,

---

149 *Record Book of the Reconstruction of Lingguan Dadi*, 1981, preserved in Shangjie of Zhiping.
150 *Record Book of the Reconstruction of Lingguan Dadi*, 1981, preserved in Shangjie of Zhiping.

Wu, and Cao each had one representative.[151] According to Yang Yanjie, the distribution of representatives closely reflected the demographic composition of the village populations at the time. The Zeng clan, for example, numbered around 3,500 to 4,000 individuals, making it the largest clan in the area. The second largest, the Lai clan, counted about 2,000, while the Li, Deng, and Fan families each had over 1,000 members. It is worth noting that while the Lei surname was absent from the 1990 list of representatives, it reappeared in 1995 when a Lei representative was once again appointed for Xiajie. This same individual continued to serve as the representative for Xiacun (Xiajie) in subsequent cycles, including in 1999 and even as recently as 2020.[152]

The Ten-Village Rotating Worship of Lingguan Dadi not only established a representative conference system but also had various established rules and arrangements during the rotation process of each village. These not only reflected the interests of each clan but also fostered cooperation among clans, making the entire worship activity proceed in an orderly and vibrant manner. The handover of the Lingguan Dadi statue took place annually on the 28th day of the ninth lunar month. On the day before the handover, the hosting village was required to carry the statue to a designated temple—either the Wutong Temple or the Niushou Temple—where *jiao* ritual would be held for one to three days. Once the handover was completed on the 28th, the receiving village would welcome the statue back with drums and gongs, marking the beginning of its yearlong stay. Because each village was typically composed of one or more clans, once the statue arrived, an internal allocation would take place. The clans—and even branches within a single clan—would negotiate how long each would host the deity.

---

151 *Record Book of the Reconstruction of Lingguan Dadi*, 1981, preserved in Shangjie of Zhiping.
152 *Record Book of the Reconstruction of Lingguan Dadi*, 1981, preserved in Shangjie of Zhiping; Ten-Village Council, *Meeting Minutes*, 28 September 2020, provided by Deng Xuanjiu of Dengwu.

Dengwu is currently inhabited by two surnames—Deng and Cao. In the early days of the rotating worship of Lingguan Dadi, only the Deng lineage was granted the privilege. As a result, when the deity visited the village, the statue was enshrined alternately in the Front House and the Rear House of the Deng clan: first in the Rear House for six months, then in the Front House. The Cao clan, although they had built their own ancestral hall after migrating to the area in the early Qing dynasty, held no right to participate in the worship rotation. Instead, they were only allowed to attend Deng clan's rituals as guests or supporters. By 1992, however, this custom changed. With the Cao lineage numbering over a hundred people and the Deng branch of the Front House relatively diminished in population, the Cao clan formally petitioned for inclusion. It was agreed that two months would be carved out from the Front House's six-month period and allotted to the Cao clan. From that point on, the Cao family gained the right to worship Lingguan Dadi in their own ancestral hall—a significant shift in ritual privilege.

The village of Pengfang presents an even more intricate picture, as it is home to three different lineages: Peng, Fan, and Lai. Among them, the Peng family were the original settlers, with the Fan and Lai clans arriving later. By the 1990s, Pengfang had over 800 residents. The Fan surname had become the most numerous, accounting for over 500 individuals; the Peng family had around 200; and the Lai family, about 100. According to local elders, when Lingguan Dadi is hosted in Pengfang, the Lai clan is allotted two months, typically in the middle of the year. The remaining ten months are split evenly between the Peng and Fan families, with each receiving five months. These two lineages continue to draw lots to determine the order of hosting—a tradition that persists to this day. The current system of rotation among the ten villages reflects the cumulative outcome of historical negotiations and evolving clan dynamics. In 2020, when it was Pengfang's turn to host the deity, representatives from the Peng, Fan, and Lai clans not only arranged the reception affairs for that year but also jointly drafted a formal agreement outlining the rotating order for the next thirty years. The full text reads as follows:

Agreement

Regarding the scheduling of enshrining the statue of Wutong Wuxian Lingguan Dadi among the Peng, Lai, and Fan clans of Pengfang Village, after consultations held by the council members of the three clans at the Pengfang Village Office on January 31, 2020, the rotation and time allocation for each clan's enshrinement are as follows:

1. In 2020, the statue of Wutong Wuxian Lingguan Dadi shall first be enshrined at the Fan Clan's Ancestral Hall.

2. In 2030, the statue shall be enshrined at the Peng Clan's Ancestral Hall.

3. In 2040, the statue shall be enshrined at the Lai Clan's Ancestral Hall.

Schedule for Enshrinement and Transfer:

For 2020: The Fan Clan's Ancestral Hall shall host the statue for 6 months, the Lai Clan's Ancestral Hall for 2 months, and the Peng Clan's Ancestral Hall for 4 months, with the Peng Clan's Ancestral Hall handling the final transfer.

For 2030: The Peng Clan's Ancestral Hall shall host for 4 months, the Fan Clan's Ancestral Hall for 6 months, and the Lai Clan's Ancestral Hall for 2 months, with the Lai Clan's Ancestral Hall handling the final transfer.

For 2040: The Lai Clan's Ancestral Hall shall host for 4 months, the Peng Clan's Ancestral Hall for 4 months, and the Fan Clan's Ancestral Hall for 4 months, with the Fan Clan's Ancestral Hall handling the final transfer.

This agreement shall be perpetually followed by all descendants without alteration. Four copies of the agreement have been prepared: one copy for each of the three clans, and one copy to be archived at the Pengfang Village Committee.

Signed by:

Representatives of the Peng Clan's Ancestral Hall (4 signatures omitted)

Representatives of the Lai Clan's Ancestral Hall (3 signatures omitted)

Representatives of the Fan Clan's Ancestral Hall (5 signatures omitted)

Date: January 31, 2020[153]

In villages such as Shaohuang, Xiaping, Tianshe, and Pingpu, where a single surname or a few dominant lineages prevail, the internal order of rotating worship for the Lingguan Dadi follows a structure similar to that of Dengwu and Pengfang. However, in Liangshe, Xiajie, and Shangjie—now all part of Zhiping Village—the situation is far more intricate. Historically, Shangjie was a market hub and remains a natural village with a mix of surnames, including Zeng, Luo, Li, and Zou, all of whom share a role in the rotation of Lingguan worship. The natural villages involved in this collective veneration include Shangjie, Anziqian, Hubeijiao, Jiantouji, Yuankengwei, Zhongyuankeng, Goudaoling, Yuanling, Shetian, and Fukeng. To

---

153 Provided by Deng Xuanjiu of Dengwu

accommodate this complexity, the annual cycle of worship is divided into four segments: four months are assigned to Shangjie, two to Yuankeng, three to Shetian, and three to Fukeng. Wherever the deity resides during a given rotation, it is typically enshrined within the ancestral hall of the corresponding surname. Based on this pattern, Yang Yanjie observes that the defining feature of the ten-village rotation system is its grounding in kinship lineage. Whether a particular clan has a "share" in the worship depends on its ability to bring the Lingguan statue into its ancestral hall for veneration. This "share" is a historically contingent concept—mutable across time—yet, in local consciousness, which ancestral halls are entitled to host the deity is a relatively fixed and well-understood arrangement.

Another fascinating aspect of this worship system is the monthly ritual gathering known as the *ya hui*—also referred to as the *peng* (棚) or *penghui* (棚会). This is a community-wide sacrificial ceremony held according to a fixed calendar during the period when the ten villages jointly host the Lingguan Dadi deity. The organization of each *peng* is based on local population size and aligned with the scheduling of sacrificial dates. According to local custom, the deity is worshiped two or three times per month while residing in a given village. In the case of two ceremonies, they take place on the 6th and 16th of the lunar month; if three, they occur on the 6th, 16th, and 26th. Villages with smaller populations typically hold two ceremonies, requiring 24 households (one per ceremony, 12 months a year). For villages observing three offerings per month, the number rises to 36 households. Once the members of each *peng* are determined, they assign internal duties and arrange the rotation order. On each sacrificial day, one designated household takes responsibility for the rituals. The ritual involves offering a whole pig to Lingguan Dadi. After the ceremony, the host family returns home to prepare a grand feast. The banquet, often featuring more than 20 dishes per table, is attended by relatives, friends, and members of the same *peng* (each represented by one delegate). These gatherings are lively and well-attended. Importantly, a separate table with matching dishes is also prepared exclusively for Lingguan Dadi. This sacred offering remains on display until the end of the banquet, after which it is taken back and dedicated to the host family's altar.[154]

Yang Yanjie notes that the historical population of the ten Zhiping villages was relatively sparse. To accomplish large-scale collective tasks like deity worship, local families adopted the *peng* system, organizing themselves based on residence or lot drawing. For instance, the Fan clan of Pengfang had reached its 13th generation by the sixth year of the Qianlong era, Qing dynasty (1741), yet counted only about 50 households. According to a 1941 census, the entire Zhiping area contained 1,047 households and 4,937 individuals.[155] From this, we can infer that the number of families participating in the rotating Lingguan system was likely only a few hundred—meaning each village had just a few dozen households. With such limited numbers, sustaining an entire year of sacrificial obligations was an enormous burden. The *peng* system thus emerged as a practical and ingen-

---

154 Organizing ritual activities in the form of *peng* is a common practice in western Fujian. This structure appears not only within individual clans but also in broader communal worship of shared deities. Its exact meaning and function may vary depending on the context. In an article by Yang Yanjie, he cites a contract from 1712 (the 51st year of the Kangxi era, Qing dynasty), signed by descendants of the Cao clan of Louxia, Liancheng County, regarding the collection of taxes and levies on behalf of their ancestor Zongheng Gong and his "Taiqi Peng" lineage group. In the author's view, this document reflects a folk mechanism for the mobilization of taxes and corvée labor. In the contract, the eighth and ninth *peng* are collectively termed "the group," while the tenth *peng* is represented by an individual named Hengyu who had not yet joined the *peng* system. This contract is, in fact, a procedural document, showing that some members of the "groups" and individuals like Hengyu were joining this cooperative group to fulfill corvée obligations.
See: Yang Yanjie, "The Rotation Circle: Worship of Emperor Huaguang in Zhiping, Ninghua" in *Entering the Historical Fields of the Hakka: Local Society and Cultural Traditions*, Guangdong People's Publishing House, 2018, p. 23.
155 Liu Shanqun (ed.), *Chorography of Ninghua County*, Fujian People's Publishing House, 1992, p. 134.

ious response, distributing responsibilities in a manageable and equitable way.

The annual ritual of rotating the worship of the Lingguan Dadi among the ten villages of Zhiping reveals a strong regional alliance rooted in clan-based organization. Locals claim this regional ritual alliance was established by the ten villages of Yidu in Huitongli, and it likely emerged in the mid-to-late Ming Dynasty. This connection evokes the *lijia* household registration and corvée system of that era, where ten villages formed ten *Jia*. In this context, the *peng* system—used to organize ritual responsibilities—may have functioned not only as a religious calendar but also as a mechanism to manage mandated labor services imposed by the government. Moreover, though the rotating worship of the Lingguan Dadi resumed in 1981, and representatives from the Lei surname have occasionally been seen among village delegates, local accounts suggest that in earlier times, the She ethnic minority was not included among the ten-village representatives. This implies that the ritual alliance may have also acted as a form of social boundary—separating state-registered Han households from She communities in the mountainous periphery, who had historically not been fully integrated into the government's corvée and taxation systems. As a result, She people tended to reside in the surrounding hills, while Han Chinese clans dominated the ritual core of Zhiping in the central basin. Today, however, many She families have settled among Han neighbors and participate in festivals and *ya hui* gatherings. Although they still lack representation and are not entrusted with hosting the Lingguan Dadi's stature during its rotation, the relationship between the two groups has become notably harmonious. This shift is closely tied to the rise of the local papermaking industry.

3.3.   The Rise of Papermaking

The origins of papermaking in Zhiping, and how this craft made its way into the mountainous interior, remain largely undocumented in official records. Fragmentary insights can only be gleaned from sifting through clan genealogies. Fortunately, the ancestral records of several prominent Han families in the mountains—including the Zeng clan of Tianshe, the Chi clan of Gaodi, the Lai clan of Shangping, and the Li clan of Xiaping—contain scattered references to papermaking and paper trade in the Qing dynasty. These scattered notes provide a valuable window into the early development of the industry. More importantly, recent efforts led by the Zhiping She Ethnic Township government have taken steps toward a more systematic recovery of this cultural legacy. With the help of Gui Shuzhong, a digital platform—The Ninghua Zhiping Papermaking Heritage Sites Network—has been launched, offering a comprehensive geographic and historical account of the rise and decline of papermaking in the region.

3.3.1.   The Early Emergence of Papermaking in Genealogies

According to the historical materials currently available, the earliest family in Zhiping's mountainous villages to enter the papermaking and paper trade business appears to be the Lai clan of Laijia Mountain, Shangping, Xiaping Village. The Lai clan began engaging in the paper trade during the mid-Qing period. Their genealogy records Lai Rongding as the family's pioneer in this craft. Lai Rongding, styled Guo'an, was born in the Genshen year of the Qianlong era, Qing dynasty (1740) and died in the 19th year of Jiaqing era, Qing dynasty (1814). "Orphaned at a young age and raised in extreme poverty, he endured many years of hardship. Later, he traveled to the county seat and began selling paper alongside merchants from Yuzhang (present-day Nanchang, Jiangxi). Over a decade of industrious labor and frugal living eventually brought modest prosperity. Finally, he married, built a house, and gradually earned a reputation as a leading figure in the township. He was generous to his neighbors in need—feeding the hungry, aiding struggling relatives, and contributing what he could to the construction of bridges and temples."[156] Rongding's fifth son, Lai Huajing—also known as Tingguang, styled Hanzhang—was born in the seventh year of Jiaqing era, Qing dynasty (1802) and passed away in the 10th year of Xianfeng era, Qing dynasty (1860). "He faithfully carried on his father's enterprise, managing the papermaking operation and expanding trade to Guangdong and Jiangxi. Under his stewardship, the family's name grew ever more prominent. Known for his harmonious relations with neighbors and his teachings of thrift and diligence to younger generations, he was also active in relieving hardship, mediating disputes, and contributing to public works such as road and temple repairs."[157] Records show that Huajing's property included at least 22 water reservoirs and 3 paper mills, scattered across various sites: one pond at Jianfeng; twelve in Shanliao; one in Taiyangbeikeng; four stretching from Niuhu to Shazihang; one across from Zhuzhangpingtang; two at the entrance to the village temple; one at the slope near Duanshangliao; two paper workshops in Shanliao; and one in Shazihang."[158] These genealogical entries reveal that Han people in the mountainous regions of Zhiping began engaging in papermaking and paper trading as early as the latter half of the 18th century. Their involvement was likely influenced by the flourishing paper industry in neighboring Jiangxi. In the decades that followed, the economy of these remote villages would come to depend heavily on papermaking and the trade it enabled.

---

156 "Biography of Guoan Gong" (the 17th yeaf of Daoguang era, Qing dynasty [1837]), in *The Fifth Revised Genealogy of the Lai Clan of Shangping*, Vol. 1, 1993; see also Vol. 3.
157 "Biography of Uncle Sheng, Han Zhang" (the 17th yeaf of Daoguang era, Qing dynasty [1837]), in *The Fifth Revised Genealogy of the Lai Clan of Shangping*, Vol. 1, 1993.
158 *The Fifth Revised Genealogy of the Lai Clan of Shangping*, Vol. 2, 1993.

After the rise of the Lai family, members of the Zeng clan in Tianshe also joined the paper-making economy. In the sixth year of the Guangxu era, Qing dynasty (1880), when the Zeng clan of Lower House, Tianshe, compiled their genealogy, they commissioned a *linsheng* (廪生 , county-sponsored scholar) Ma Qian to write biographies for notable ancestors. Among them, the life stories of Zeng Yingqing and Zeng Ying'en recount the family's prosperity through papermaking. Zeng Yingqing, born in the Jiashen year of Daoguang era, Qing dynasty (1824), "styled Liangfu and Murong. His family had long resided in Tianzengshe. His father, Wanrong Gong, apart from farming, had opened up mountain land to cultivate bamboo and engage in papermaking, which brought considerable prosperity. Yingqing inherited this legacy, expanding the enterprise through hard work and frugality. Known for his integrity and generosity, he would donate to good causes within his means and mediate disputes in his community." Yingqing's father, Wanrong Gong, was born in the Jiyou year of the Qianlong era, Qing dynasty (1789) and died in the 24th year of Daoguang era, Qing dynasty (1844).[159] This indicates that the Zeng clan in Tianshe had begun planting bamboo and making paper to profit from it by the early 19th century at the latest. Zeng Ying'en, born in the 12th year of Daoguang era, Qing dynasty (1832), passed an imperial grace examination in the Dingmao year of Tongzhi era (1867), earning himself an honorary scholarly title as a distinguished tribute student and a candidate for the director of a local Confucian school. "Styled Liangrong and with the courtesy name Tinghui, he was the eldest son of Wanhe. He too lived in Tianzengshe for generations. As a scholar (*Mingjing* 明经, a scholar well-versed in Confucian classics), he inherited his ancestors' undertakings. Beyond farming, he managed

---

159 "Biography of Elder Brother Zeng Mu Ru", (the sixth year of Guangxu era [1880]), in *Zeng Clan Genealogy of Yunzhuang*, Tianshe (Lower House—Line of Wulang and Balang), Vol. 1, 1880;
see also: "Lineage of the Lower House Branch", in *Zeng Clan Genealogy of Yunzhuang*, Tianshe (Lower House—Line of Wulang and Balang), Vol. 3, 1880.

bamboo forests and produced fine-grade *yu ban* (jade plate) *paper*, from which he reaped generous profits. Building on his father's foundation, he expanded the family business and wealth. He even built a grand residence at a place called Xiongkeng, nestled behind their ancestral mountain. Shortly thereafter, he honorably became a tribute student in accordance with established regulations." Hence he was called "Mingjing." His father Wanhe was born in the Dingsi year of Jiaqing era, Qing dynasty (1797) and passed away in the Yimao year, the fifth year of Xianfeng era, Qing dynasty (1855).[160] The fact that Ying'en's rise through papermaking occurred slightly later suggests that by the mid-19th century, paper production had already become a widespread practice in Tianshe.

The Chi family of Gaodi claims their ancestor Tianbao Gong settled in the Chijiadong Ridge during the second year of the Chunyou era, Southern Song dynasty (1242), acquiring expansive mountain land.[161] The earliest record of paper-related commerce among the Chi appears with Chi Kaitang's household. Kaitang, personal name Kunyang and styled Zhaoting, was born in the 45th year of Qianlong era, Qing dynasty (1780). In the 19th year of Jiaqing era, Qing dynasty (1918), he, as a commoner of good standing, followed the regulations to donate through the Guangdong provincial treasury, thereby being selected as a student of the Imperial College. He died in the first year of Tongzhi era, Qing dynasty (1862). Family accounts recall that he "profited immensely from his enterprise under the brand name Xutang Paper." Kaitang's sons—Chi Taibin (styled Danshan, 1807–1883) and Chi Taixiang (courtesy Jingnan, 1822–1880)—both joined the paper

---

160 "Sketch of the Life of Elder Brother Zeng Liangrong", (the sixth year of Guangxu era, Qing dynasty [1880]), in *Zeng Clan Genealogy of Yunzhuang*, Tianshe (Lower House—Line of Wulang and Balang), Vol. 1, 1880;
see also: "Lineage of the Lower House Branch", in *Zeng Clan Genealogy of Yunzhuang*, Tianshe (Lower House—Line of Wulang and Balang), Vol. 3, 1880.
161 "Genealogical Origins of the Baxi Lineage", (the 39th year of Qianlong era, Qing dynasty [1774]), in *Chi Clan Genealogy of Baixi*, Gaodi, Vol. 1, sixth revision (1917), supplemented in the seventh revision (1989).

trade. Taixiang's son, Chi Yuncai (personal name Zhongzao, courtesy Panlin), was born in the 26th year of Daoguang era, Qing dynasty (1846), was promoted to a "zengsheng" (增生, augmented student) through supplementation in the seventh year of Tongzhi era, Qing dynasty (1868), and died in the 13th year of Guangxu era (1887). At one point, Yuncai "laid down his brush and took up the market battle, stockpiling Cai Lun paper and following in the footsteps of the legendary merchant Fan Li. Within a short time, he achieved tremendous wealth, shaking the market with his success."[162] In the 13th year of Tongzhi era (1874), Chi Taibin left behind a detailed autobiographical account while overseeing the revision of the clan genealogy. In it, he describes his father, brother-in-law, himself, and his younger brother's experience in running the paper business in Jiangxi. He writes: "During the period when my father was greatly enhancing the family's reputation, he was busy increasing property and building houses, leaving no idle days. In the 10th year of Daoguang era (1830), my father and brother-in-law Zhang Xianyao began trading paper in Jiangxi, entrusting household affairs to me. At that time, my younger brother Taixiang was only eight, and our youngest brother Qi was still nursing. I managed operations for more than ten years, supported by my wife, and expanded both production and income, continuing my father's path." Eventually, the paper trade in Jiangxi was handed over to his brother Taixiang.[163]

The Chi clan of Gaodi village, beyond the well-known lineage of Chi Kaitang, also included many clan members actively engaged in papermak-

---

162 "Biography of Panlin Gong and His Wife Huang" (the sixth year of Republican era [1917]), in *Chi Clan Genealogy of Baixi*, Gaodi, Vol. 3, sixth revision (1917), supplemented in the seventh revision (1989);
see also: "Portrait Inscription and Preface for Uncle Jingnan" (the 13th year of Tongzhi era, Qing dynasty [1874]), Vol. 3, sixth revision (1917), supplemented in the seventh revision (1989); Vol. 6; Vol. 8.
163 "Self-Account of Danshan" (the 13th year of Tongzhi era, Qing dynasty [1874]), in *Chi Clan Genealogy of Baixi*, Gaodi, Vol. 3, sixth revision (1917), supplemented in the seventh revision (1989).

ing and the paper trade. Chi Kailing (styled Yongqing), born in   the third year of Jiaqing era, Qing dynasty (1798), began life with modest means. "After separating households with his brothers, he inherited little. Yet through diligence in both farming and commerce, he gradually accumulated wealth, acquiring bamboo mountains and rice fields. Over time, his family attained a level of modest prosperity."[164] Chi Taipei, courtesy name Qinghe and styled Jinyun, was born in the 16th year of Daoguang era, Qing dynasty (1836). In the first year of Guangxu era (1875), as a commoner of good standing, he followed regulations to donate through the Hubei provincial treasury, gaining admission to the Imperial Academy as a student. For over a decade, he oversaw operations and eventually acquired over 300 *dan* of land devoted to paper-making, passing away in the 31st year of Guangxu era, Qing dynasty (1905).[165] Chi Yunyan (given name Ronghui), was born in the 11th year of Tongzhi era, Qing dynasty (1872). "Since he followed regulations to enter the Imperial Academy in the Guimao year of the Guangxu era (1903), he has engaged in making Cai Lun's paper and farming like Yi Yin (a legendary sage-turned-statesman). Within a few years, his family fortune thrived even more."[166] By the early 20th century, the Chi clan in Chijiadong remained primarily dependent on the paper trade, producing up to 1,500 *dan* of paper annually, which was sold to Hengjiang Town in Shicheng County, Jiangxi.[167] These records from the Chi genealogy about papermaking and paper trade clearly reveal that papermaking in the mountainous Gaodi area had begun by at least the early 19th century.

---

164 "Biography of Great-Uncle Yongqing" (the 13th year of Tongzhi era, Qing dynasty [1874]), in *Chi Clan Genealogy of Baixi*, Gaodi, Vol. 3, sixth revision (1917), supplemented in the seventh revision (1989); Vol. 5.
165 "Biography of Chi Jinyun, My Maternal Uncle-in-Law" (the 5th year of the Republic era [1916]), in *Chi Clan Genealogy of Baixi*, Gaodi, Vol. 3, sixth revision (1917), supplemented in the seventh revision (1989); Vol. 5.
166 "Biography of My Clan Uncle Yunyan" (the 6th year of the Republic era [1917]), in *Chi Clan Genealogy of Baixi*, Gaodi, Vol. 3, sixth revision (1917), supplemented in the seventh revision (1989); Vol. 8.
167 "My Hometown," in *Chi Clan Genealogy of Baixi*, Gaodi, Vol. 1, sixth revision (1917), supplemented in the seventh revision (1989).

They also point to trade with Jiangxi as early as the tenth year of Daoguang era (1830), and the establishment of the Xu Tang paper firm as a vehicle for expanding commercial activity. Profits from papermaking enabled Chi merchants to acquire official titles through donations, thereby enhancing both their social status and community prestige. This, in turn, further facilitated the growth and stability of their paper enterprises.

In addition, the Li clan of Xiaping similarly played a major role in the local paper industry during the late Qing and Republican periods. For instance, Li Ronglin, born in the 15th year of Guangxu era (1889), began papermaking in his early years. "Through careful accumulation, he gradually acquired land and eventually brought his family to a comfortable standard of living." Another figure, Li Rongbang (1883–1932), dedicated himself to managing the paper trade and running his household with meticulous order.[168]

Beyond this, in the records of ancestral sacrificial estates within the genealogies, it is easy to discern that assets related to papermaking—such as bamboo forests, paper workshops, and ponds (vital for raw materials and production sites)—were designated as *chang chan* (尝产, public estates belonging to a clan with income mainly used for sacrificial ceremonies) and thus not divided during family separations. For instance, the ancestral sacrificial estates registered under the name of the seventh patriarch of the Zeng clan in Tianshe included cedar and bamboo forests as well as a pond.[169] Similarly, in Gaodi the Chi clan's patriarch Jing'a was recorded to have owned a paper workshop in Chijiadong Creek and a pond in Kanshang Shaba.[170] In the Li clan's genealogy from Xiaping village, extensive rec-

---

168 "Genealogical Records of the Jianlang Branch," in *The Third Revised Genealogy of the Li Clan of Longxi Commandery*, Vol. 3, 1879.
169 "List of Sacrificial Estates of Qilang Gong," in *Zeng Clan Genealogy of Yunzhuang*, Tianshe (Upper House—Line of Qilang), Vol. 6, 1879.
170 "Sacrificial Estates of Jing'a Gong," in *Chi Clan Genealogy of Baixi*, Gaodi, Vol. 2,

ords point to holdings of bamboo forests, paper workshops, and ponds: Shixing (1767–1847) held a single cedar-bamboo mountain as part of his *Chang chan*; Shichai (1780–1842) owned multiple bamboo plots and two ponds as part of his *Chang chan*; Changbing (1788–1848) had a cedar-bamboo mountain as part of his *Chang chan*; Changli (1795–1864) and Changhe (1799–1860) each held several bamboo forests as part of their *Chang chan*, with Changhe also owning a paper workshop. Changyu (1803–1826) was noted for one cedar-bamboo mountain as part of his *Chang chan*, while Changlong (1805–1861) held multiple bamboo plots as part of his *Chang chan*. Later generations, such as Changmen (1833–1879), owned both paper workshops and multiple bamboo mountains and ponds as part of his *Chang chan*. Longdang (1856–1904) had four ponds and two paper workshops as part of his *Chang chan*, while Longgui (1863–1930) owned a paper workshop, a worker's lodge, two lime kilns, eleven ponds, and numerous bamboo plots as part of his *Chang chan*.[171] Even this incomplete dataset suggests a growing accumulation of such properties over time, reflecting the rapid expansion of the local paper industry.

The origins of this papermaking boom can be traced primarily to Han Chinese communities in the mountainous areas. Prominent families like the Zengs of Tianshe, the Lis and Lais of Xiaping, and the Chis of Gaodi were deeply involved in its development. But what changes did this industry bring to local mountain societies? Genealogies of the Zeng clan—long settled in the villages of Tianshe, Shefu, and Guangliang—document their interactions with nearby She ethnic communities, particularly the Lei and Lan clans. During the Ming and Qing periods, Han Chinese households were formally registered by the government and subjected to tax and labor obligations. Their land ownership was often backed by written deeds and rec-

---

sixth revision (1917), supplemented in the seventh revision (1989).
171 "Genealogical Records of the Jianlang Branch," in *The Third Revised Genealogy of the Li Clan of Longxi Commandery*, Vol. 3, 1879.

ognized by the state. As Han settlers gradually acquired more land, She families found themselves with less uncultivated land to claim and increasingly became tenant farmers under Han landlords. The Zeng genealogy carries stigmatizing descriptions of the She, noting that in the mountains of Tianzengshe, "there lived several families surnamed Lan and Lei—neither Yao nor Zhuang ethnics. Men and women tilled the fields together, and their customs were deemed crude and uncouth; the locals all shunned them, regarding and calling them 'wild people.'" In farming arrangements, She tenants were required to "pay rent in kind to the Zeng family, typically on the 16th day of the tenth lunar month."[172] Furthermore, genealogical records from the Zhiping show numerous examples of Lei and Lan tenants farming land owned by Han families. These tenant relationships, though initially based on economic necessity, grew into more frequent social exchanges over time. By the Qing dynasty, such interactions deepened. In one case, Zeng Jingxiu provided financial aid to a destitute Lei tenant involved in a wife-selling crisis. Additionally, intermarriage between the Zeng clan and She families also had became increasingly common by the early Qing period.[173]

---

172 "Account of Tianzengshe, Also Known as Yunzhuang," in *Zeng Clan Genealogy of Yunzhuang*, Tianshe (Upper House—Line of Qilang), Vol.1, 1879.
173 "Biography of Mr. Zeng Jingxiu" (the 59th year of the Qianlong era, Qing dynasty [1794]), in *Zeng Clan Genealogy of Yunzhuang*, Tianshe (Upper House—Line of Qilang), Vol.1, 1879;
"Biography of Tianqiu Gong, the Village Elder" (the 27th year of the Daoguang era, Qing dynasty [1847]), in *Zeng Clan Genealogy of Yunzhuang*, Tianshe (Upper House—Line of Qilang), Vol.1, 1879.

***(Pic70   A Paper Workshop Established During the Daoguang Era, Pre-
served in Guangliang Administrative Village)***

With the rise of the papermaking industry, the demand for labor increased significantly. As a result, She people also joined the paper production workforce, living and working alongside Han villagers. This daily cooperation gradually deepened the integration between She and Han communities. Mr. Deng Xuanjiu, a member of the Deng clan's Rear House
branch in Dengwu, recounted the close relationship between the She families—especially those bearing the surnames Lan and Lei—and their Han
neighbors in Zhiping: "For a living, the Lan and Lei clans in Zhiping mainly relied on bamboo cultivation, forestry, and a small amount of farmland.
Most were chronically short of grain and had to purchase food from outside.
When bamboo shoots matured around *Guyu* (Grain Rain, the 6th solar term
in the traditional Chinese lunisolar calendar), they harvested and processed
zhuma (bamboo fiber for papermaking) to produce *Yukou* paper. Each production site housed a paper workshop employing about 14 workers: two for
forming the paper and lifting the finished sheets, two for drying, two for
pounding the bamboo fibers, two for stripping, one or two for carrying materials, two for collecting firewood, one for gathering *lan* leaves, and one
managing the vats. Workers from the Lan and Lan She ethnic clans labored

alongside Han workers day in and day out, forming close and seamless bonds. Over time, this led to intermarriage, friendships, and alliances. I saw this firsthand—my father and uncle became close friends with Lei Long-wang and others from Jiaoli Village in Zhongbian. Our family had rented a few *mu* of land to them at a very low grain rent and entrusted parts of our bamboo forests to their care. These ties made our relations especially warm and close."[174] This account offers a vivid and valuable insight: the emergence of new industries like papermaking opened up collaborative spaces where communities once divided by lifestyle and legal status—such as the She and Han—began to break down barriers and forge new, cooperative relationships that transcended old boundaries.

3.3.2.   A Detailed Map of Paper Workshops in the Region

Papermaking emerged as a burgeoning industry in the mountainous region of Zhiping since the late 18th century, gradually expanding to become a pillar of the local economy well into the 1980s and 1990s. According to the *Toponymic Directory of Ninghua County*, published in 1981 by the county's Toponymy Leading Group Office, paper workshops had been established across multiple communes including Zhiping, Quanshang, Hucun, Jijun, Hekou, Fangtian, Anle, and Caofang. The map of Zhiping Commune stands out in particular, as it carefully marks the names and locations of 25 paper workshops. Yet in the *Toponymic Directory of Ninghua County*'s section on "Important or Locationally Significant Administrative and Enterprises Units (Specialized Farms, Stations)," Zhiping is recorded as having 65 paper workshops in total—suggesting that at least 40 were not geographically pinpointed at the time the map was compiled.

In recent years, the Zhiping She Ethnic Township Government launched a renewed effort to map and document these historical sites. Local

---

174 Deng Xuanjiu, *The Origins of the Lan and Lei Surnames*, Unpublished handwritten manuscript, pp. 14–16.

village heads and committee members, most of whom are native to the area, conducted a new round of surveys to locate the remains of former paper workshops—aiming to preserve this facet of intangible cultural heritage through detailed historical geography. While they were generally familiar with the locations of more recent paper mills, tracing older, long-abandoned sites required extensive fieldwork. They interviewed elderly villagers, cross-referenced old maps, and created tables to record findings. The collective memory and participation of villagers proved vital in reconstructing the once-vibrant landscape of Zhiping's papermaking industry. Building on the survey materials submitted by each village, Guishu Zhong conducted further field investigations, incorporating information on newly discovered paper workshops. He also established an online website titled the "Ninghua Zhiping Papermaking Cultural Heritage Site Group" (https://yukoupaper.com/).

Thanks to this meticulous work, the website is now publicly accessible and searchable, with ongoing updates and improvements. According to its data, Zhiping once boasted over 500 paper vats at the height of papermaking prosperity. So far, the precise locations of 272 paper workshops have been identified. By village, the distribution is as follows: 61 in Xiaping, 54 in Gaofeng, 32 in Tianshe, 23 in Gaodi, 16 in Guangliang, 14 in Nikeng, 25 in Hubeijiao, 20 in Zhiping, 11 in Pingpu, 10 in Shefu, 4 in Pengfang, and 2 in Dengwu. These figures show a clear pattern: the more mountainous the village, the more paper vats were found. The flatter the terrain, the fewer mills there were—Xiaping and Gaofeng alone accounted for nearly half of Zhiping's total. The surname data offers further insight into local social structures. Among the paper workshop households, the Lai surname leads with 56 vats, followed by Zeng (28), Chen (14), Li (13), Hu (11), Zhang (11), Lei (7), Liu (5), Lian (4), Wu (4), Fan (4), Liao (4), Zhan (2), Lan (2), Xie (2), and Wang (1). Some workshops were collectively owned by village groups or cooperatives. In Gaodi, for instance, all registered paper workshop owners were listed under place names rather than personal ones, omitting the number of workshop owners in Chijiadong, though it is reasonable to infer that most of these vats were operated by families of the Chi surname.[175]

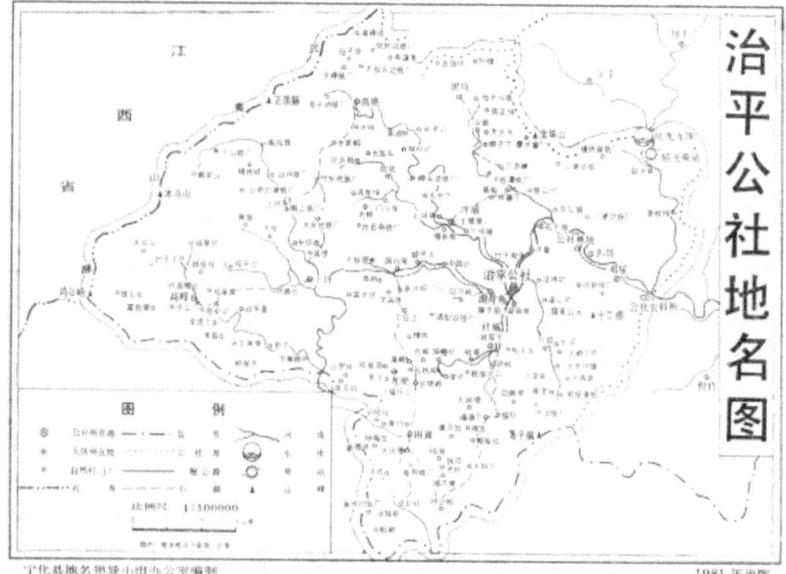

(Pic71 The Map of Zhiping Commune, Ninghua County Toponymy Leading Group Office (ed.), Toponymic Directory of Ninghua County, 1981, p. 140)

---

175 Ninghua Zhiping Papermaking Cultural Heritage Site Group (https://yukoupaper.com/), accessed June 8, 2022.

(Pic72-73   Survey map used by Zeng Shaoqun, First Secretary of Tianshe Village, Zhiping She Ethnic Township; Survey form used by Zeng Shaoqun, First Secretary of Tianshe Village, Zhiping She Ethnic Township)

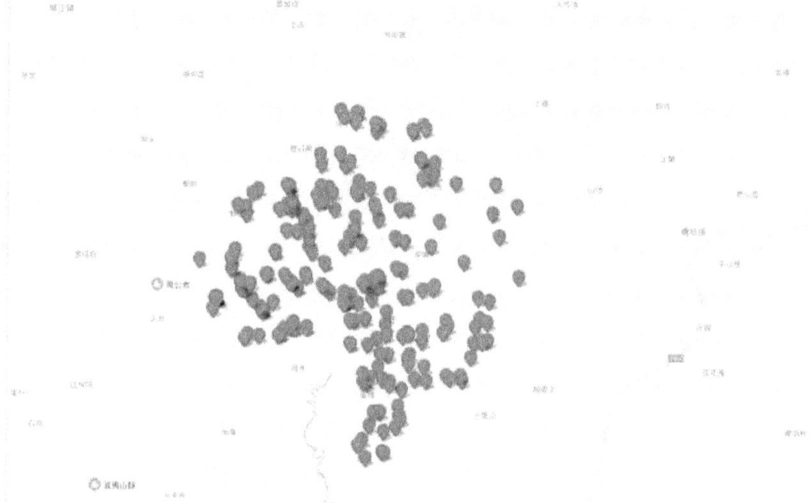

(Pic74   Schematic diagram of the distribution of paper workshops in Zhiping, Ninghua)

Based on the available data, a total of 271 papermaking workshops in Zhiping can be confirmed in terms of their establishment dates, while 264 have known closure dates. Though the precision of these records may warrant further verification, the dataset already reveals clear patterns in the rise and fall of papermaking activity in the region. To begin with, papermaking in Zhiping began with the earliest paper workshops built in the mid-to-late 18th century, aligning roughly with accounts found in local genealogies. According to field investigations, the Cooperative Workshop in Gaoling Group of Guangliang Village was established in 1770, operating continuously until 1957—its structures remain well preserved to this day. Secondly, the Republican period (1912–1949) witnessed an extraordinary boom in papermaking. At least 110 workshops were established during these decades, marking it as the most prosperous and rapidly expanding phase in Zhiping's papermaking history. Thirdly, after the founding of the People's Republic of China in 1949, although the overall number of new workshops decreased, the industry continued to grow vigorously between 1950 and 1967, during which 44 new workshops were launched. Following a brief downturn, a revival period began in 1972, bringing forth another 68 newly built facilities. Fourthly, while the 1980s saw some continued expansion, the end of the decade marked a dramatic decline. Most paper workshops were forced to cease operations, ushering in the end of a historical chapter.

Taken as a whole, this dataset offers a compelling outline of the rise and decline of Zhiping's papermaking industry. Yet, if we wish to fully grasp the scale of its prosperity during the 20th century, and the unique historical significance it brought to the region, we must turn to more specific and detailed historical materials. The following sections will explore the commodity chain of *Yukou* paper, the ups and downs of the industry during the Republican era, and the boom-and-bust cycles during the People's Republic period.

Zhiping's development in papermaking was no accident. The region, like much of western Fujian, is richly endowed with bamboo species wide spread and suitable for papermaking, including *Mao Zhu* (Phyllostachys pubescens), *Ma Zhu* (Dendrocalamus latiflorus), *Ku Zhu* (Pleioblastus amarus), *Mian Zhu* (Bambusa emeiensis), *Fen Zhu* (Yushania falcatiaurita),

Chijian Zhu, Huang Zhu (Indocalamus tessellatus), and several others. With a cool, humid climate year-round, the area provides ideal growing conditions for bamboo. Today, Zhiping She Ethnic Township still boasts 159,000 *mu* (approximately 106,000,000 sq.m. in total) of *Mao Zhu*, along with abundant clear spring water from the headwaters of three rivers, and high-quality limestone from the surrounding mountains—making it perfectly suited for traditional handmade paper production. From the Tang and Song dynasties through to the Ming and Qing, both She and Han communities gradually migrated into what is now Zhiping. Their livelihoods were primarily based on agriculture, involving forest clearing and farming small mountain plains. For centuries, the two ethnic groups lived side by side, yet largely maintained separate social spaces, cultural customs, and institutional identities. However, beginning in the mid-18th century, the mountainous Han settlers, influenced by the papermaking techniques of neighboring Jiangxi, began to adopt papermaking as a livelihood. As the industry expanded, it drew She villagers into the production chain as laborers. Through shared residence and shared labor, the two groups gradually broke down traditional boundaries, collaborating in the economic life of the paper industry, and forging the ethnic integration that characterizes Zhiping's social landscape today.

Table 3 Timeline of Paper Workshop Establishment and Cessation in Zhiping, Ninghua (1770–2023)

Time Period	Number of Newly Established Paper Workshops	Number of Paper Workshops That Ceased Production
1770-1799	1	0
1800-1829	3	0
1830-1859	9	0
1860-1889	7	0
1890-1919	29	0
1920-1949	107	2
1950-1979	63	7
1980-2009	51	251
2009-2023	1	4
Sum	271	264

4. The Paper Industry of Western Fujian in Turbulent Times

As the data in the previous chapter reveals, at least 136 new papermaking workshops were established in the Zhiping region between the late 19th century and the mid-20th century, with an astonishing 107 built during the 1920s to 1940s alone. This surge marked a golden era for papermaking in Zhiping—yet it was not an isolated phenomenon. As illustrated in Chapter 2, four surveys conducted during the Republican era (1912–1949) on papermaking techniques and industry conditions across Fujian reveal the widespread attention paid by government bodies, professional associations, and the general public to the thriving paper industry in western Fujian. A rich array of Republican-era documents—surveys, newspaper articles, government archives, and more—have preserved a record of how the paper industry in western Fujian's mountainous regions matured and expanded during this period, spanning every link in the chain: production, transportation, distribution, and consumption. During the Central Soviet Area period and the War of Resistance against Japanese Aggression, the paper industry in this region gained even greater significance. At one point it became a vital pillar supporting the Soviet base areas' economy and finances. Under the influence of revolutionary education in political philosophy of the Red political power, countless papermaking workers joined the Communist cause. Later, in the wartime, they sustained the national resistance by producing paper through industrial cooperatives, contributing much-needed resources to the nation's effort to resist against Japanese aggression. This chapter first explores how Yukou paper—handmade by papermakers in remote mountainous villages like Zhiping—was transported by shoulder and boat across great distances, eventually reaching the port cities along the southeastern coast, and even being exported in large quantities overseas. There, admirers of its quality found inventive ways to incorporate it into daily life. The chapter then turns to the disruptions and reconstructions that this intricate paper production and distribution network underwent during the Soviet period and the war years. It also considers how individuals working in the paper trade navigated the difficult choices of their time and shaped their destinies amid sweeping historical change.

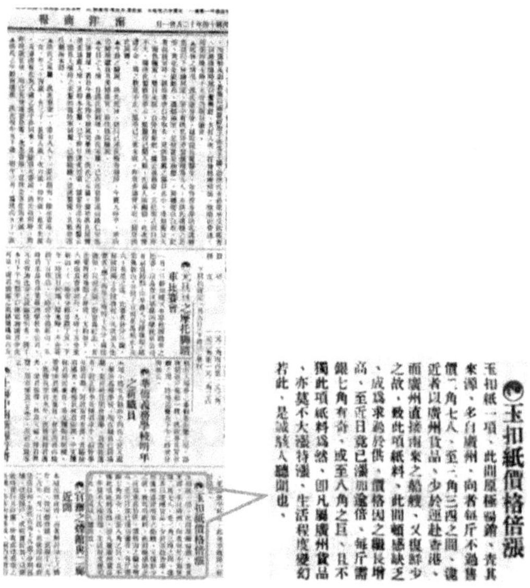

(Pic75 Report Titled "More than Double Yukou Paper Prices ", Nanyang Commercial Daily, December 31, 1925, p. 4)

4.1. Production, Transportation, Distribution, and Consumption

According to anecdotes from the paper industry cited in *A History of Papermaking in Changting*, the production of Yukou paper in the Changting region during the Qing dynasty reportedly reached as high as 4,166.67 tons annually[176]—making it the leading producer in Fujian and a front-runner of handmade paper landscape across China. Yukou paper originated in the mountainous regions where the Ting and Gan Rivers rise—most notably in Laijiashan of Zhiping Township, Ninghua County, and its surrounding hills. From there, Yukou paper was transported downriver via the Ting River,

---

176 One ton of Yukou paper equals 24 *dan* (担), each *dan* contains 7 *dao* (刀), and each *dao* consists of 200 sheets. Maobian paper is measured at 10 *dao* per *dan*, each *dao* also with 200 sheets. This is its conversion standard.
See Lin Jingliang, "An Investigation of the Papermaking Industry in Changting, Fujian," *China Construction (Shanghai)*, Vol. 14, No. 5, 1936; Huang Majin (chief ed.). *A History of Papermaking in Changting*. China Light Industry Press, 1992, p. 41.

passing through Changting and joining the Han River (韩江) at Sanheba in Dapu, Guangdong, before flowing into the sea near Chaozhou. Alternatively, some routes followed the Heng River into the Gan River, distributing the paper to cities such as Ganzhou and Jiujiang, and from there across the country. By the mid-Qing period, Yukou paper had already gained wide popularity, being sold in provinces such as three provinces in Northeast, Shandong, Henan, Jiangsu, Zhejiang, Anhui, Guangdong, Jiangxi, as well as in Taiwan and Hong Kong. After the opening of five treaty ports for foreign trade, the paper entered international markets, with exports reaching Singapore, Malaya, Indonesia, Siam, the Philippines, Japan, and beyond. Changting merchants not only established themselves in the paper markets of Chaozhou and Guangzhou but also founded paper trading houses overseas. Yukou paper served many purposes. It was widely used for accounting books, writing paper, cigarette paper, and napkins—and even found its way into culinary applications.[177] Building on this general overview, the following sections delve further into Yukou paper's modern trajectory, examining its production, transportation, distribution, and usage.

4.1.1. Production

In traditional Yukou papermaking, production was organized around small-scale, manually operated paper workshops known as *zhicao* (literally "paper vats" or "paper troughs") or paper workshops. The name derived from the most crucial tool of the trade—the papermaking vat. Each paper vat functioned through a clearly defined division of labor. The owner or operator, known as *caozhu* or *caohu* (paper workshop owners), either held direct ownership of the workshop or rented it to oversee production. Their responsibilities encompassed all aspects of management, including financing, hiring and assigning workers for material preparation (such as main-

---

177 Huang Majin (chief ed.), *A History of Papermaking in Changting*, China Light Industry Press, 1992, pp. 10, 35–36.

taining the mountain and soaking ponds, felling *zhuma*, and transporting lime), and supervising both raw material handling and the paper production process. They also ensured the quality of the final product, managed logistics and distribution, and handled all other related matters. In their dealings with paper wholesalers and financiers, *caozhu* represented the paper workshops, managing loans and paper transactions with paper merchants. By the Republican era, they were also held legally accountable to the government for the workshop's activities.[178]

Beyond *caozhu* and the preparatory workers, a typical production team required at least nine additional laborers once papermaking began. The first step involved peeling the outer layer of *zhuma*, a job for two workers. On average, they could peel over 400 *jin* (200 kg in total) of material per day—enough to produce one *dan* of paper. The second stage, known as *ta liao* (踏料, treading pulp), also required two workers, who also handled pulp beating. The third phase was *chao zhi* (抄纸, sheet forming), carried out by two workers—a senior master papermaker, respected for his technical expertise and years of experience, and an apprentice assistant known as *kang wei* (扛尾, the end lifter), typically a novice who could be promoted after four to five years of diligent learning. The fourth step was *bei zhi* (焙纸, drying the paper), which involved two more workers. Lastly, a general helper took on miscellaneous tasks such as gathering firewood, cooking, stoking the fire, and occasionally gathering *lan* leaves and preparing its extract used in the process.[179] Once production commenced, it had to proceed

---

178 Lin Zhaohe, "An Overview of the Handmade Paper Industry in Fujian and Its Ongoing Improvements". *Construction Weekly*, Vol. 7, No. 6, 1938;
Lin Jingliang, "An Investigation of the Papermaking Industry in Changting, Fujian," *China Construction (Shanghai)*, Vol. 14, No. 5, 1936.
179 Lin Zhaohe, "An Overview of the Handmade Paper Industry in Fujian and Its Ongoing Improvements". *Construction Weekly*, Vol. 7, No. 6, 1938;
Lin Jingliang, "An Investigation of the Papermaking Industry in Changting, Fujian," *China Construction (Shanghai)*, Vol. 14, No. 5, 1936.

continuously until all the materials—namely the peeled and soaked *zhuma*—had been processed into paper. A typical workday for these laborers spanned up to 12 hours, beginning in the dim light of dawn around four or five a.m. and ending only as darkness fell in the evening.

According to Xie Shenchu, a Xiamen University professor who relocated to Changting during the War of Resistance Against Japanese Aggression, the relationship between *caozhu* and workers was marked by mutual respect. He observed that *caozhu* did not exploit their workers, writing in his analysis:

> These papermakers were simple, honest farmers by nature—far removed from modern industrialists, who, driven by intense market competition, would often resort to unscrupulous tactics to satiate their insatiable greed for profit. In contrast, paper workers in these rural workshops were relatively few in number and highly sought after by different papermaking households. This competition elevated their status significantly. Moreover, the quality of the paper depended entirely on the skill and diligence of these workers, compelling the proprietors to treat them with considerable respect and generosity.[180]

But how much capital was required to operate a single paper vat, and what kind of income could a workshop expect to generate? What wages did workers earn? Given the variability of both working hours and output in traditional papermaking, few records of financial accounts from either workshop owners or paper merchants have survived. As a result, it is difficult to calculate exact figures for costs and revenues. Nevertheless, a rough estimate can be made from scattered historical sources. Lin Zhaohe's ob-

---

180 Xie Shenchu, "A Study on the Papermaking Industry in Changting," *Journal of Economic and Commercial Studies* (Xiamen), No. 1, 1941.

servations on the capital and wages in Fujian's papermaking industry during the Republican period offer some clues:

The required capital could be divided into two categories: fixed capital and working capital. The average fixed capital for each paper vat was approximately 450 yuan, covering the cost of building and equipment. Working capital varied depending on the production volume. For a vat operating year-round—roughly 300 days annually—he estimated the following:

1. Raw materials: around 300 loads of pulp per year, at 5 yuan per load, totaling 1,500 yuan.

2. Wages and miscellaneous expenses: about 6.5 yuan per day, based on a 60-day cycle, totaling around 390 yuan.

Together, this amounted to an annual working capital of approximately 1,890 yuan. Thus, the total capital needed to run a standard paper workshop would not exceed 2,340 yuan.

As for wages, the highest-paid workers earned about 60 cents a day, while the lowest earned around 30 cents. Daily operating expenses for a single vat—including wages, meals, fuel, and miscellaneous costs—averaged about 6.5 yuan, which accounted for roughly 61.9% of the total production cost (taking the cost of a load of maobian paper as 11.5 yuan as an example).[181]

Based on Lin Zhaohe's data, the annual wage expenditure for a standard paper workshop operating 300 days a year would amount to 1,950 yuan. Therefore, the total annual working capital invested would amount to about

---

181 Lin Zhaohe, "An Overview of the Handmade Paper Industry in Fujian and Its Ongoing Improvements". *Construction Weekly*, Vol. 7, No. 6, 1938.

3,450 yuan. The figure of 11.5 yuan as the cost per load of maobian paper is derived from dividing this 3,450 yuan by 300 loads.

Lin further observed that a single paper workshop could typically produce one *dan*—equivalent to seven *dao*—of Yukou paper per day. Each *dao* contained 200 sheets, weighing roughly 10.5 *jin*, and was valued at around 2 yuan in national currency at the time. Alternatively, a vat might produce ten *dao* of Changxing paper (a lighter variant of maobian paper), also weighing one *dan* or one load in total. Each *dao* weighed just over 7 *jin* and was similarly priced at 2 yuan.[182] This meant that one *dan* of Yukou paper sold for approximately 14 yuan, while Changxing paper, "due to its lighter weight and higher production cost, often fetched the same price—or even more—than heavier paper", at around 20 yuan per *dan*. Based on Lin's cost estimate of 11.5 yuan per *tiao*, the gross profit per load was 2.5 yuan for Yukou paper and a considerable 8.5 yuan for Changxing paper.[183] If a workshop operated year-round, the annual profit could reach 750 yuan for Yukou and up to 2,550 yuan for Changxing paper. These figures included not only the depreciation of fixed capital but also the owner's own wages—typically around 180 yuan. However, whether Lin's pricing estimates for Yukou and Changxing paper accurately reflected the market remains open to question.

---

182 Lin Zhaohe, "An Overview of the Handmade Paper Industry in Fujian and Its Ongoing Improvements". *Construction Weekly*, Vol. 7, No. 6, 1938.
183 According to the 1926 (the 15th year of Republican era) edition of *Chorography of Ninghua County*, the paper produced in Sibeiling sold for just over 12 yuan per *dan* (with 10 or 7 *dao* per *dan*); paper from Anle and Kengzili was priced slightly above 8 yuan per *dan*; from Quanshang and Wucun, it was just over 6 yuan (Daguang) and 4 yuan (Xizhuang), respectively. Lin Zhaohe's 1938 report noted fluctuating prices of Fujian paper in recent years: Changxing paper ranged from 0.8 to 2.5 yuan per *dao*; Yukou paper from 1.5 to 2.5 yuan per *dao*; Gaolian paper cost 20–30 yuan per *dan* (10 *dao*, 85 sheets per *dao*); Jia zhi was worth 2.5–3.8 yuan per *dan* (2 blocks, 6 *dao* per block, 120 sheets per *dao*); Hai zhi was priced at 1.5–2 yuan per block (10 *dao* per block, 330 sheets per dao). See: *Chorography of Ninghua County* (Republican era), Vol. 10, "Industry", Shanghai Bookstore Press, 2000, p. 615; Lin Zhaohe, "An Overview of the Handmade Paper Industry in Fujian and Its Ongoing Improvements". *Construction Weekly*, Vol. 7, No. 6, 1938.

Meanwhile, Lin Jingliang's survey of the paper trade in Changting revealed a different layer of complexity: many vat owners relied heavily on credit arrangements and advance purchase agreements with paper merchants, further entangling the economics of production and profit:

> Each winter, paper produced by workshop owners was used to repay the capital and interest borrowed between the previous September and the current year. The interest rate varied depending on the loan amount, typically ranging from 1% to 1.5% per month. However, interest was calculated only up until the date when the first load of paper was delivered to the merchant. Any subsequent deliveries incurred no additional interest. For instance, if a workshop owner delivered a load of paper on August 1st, interest would no longer accrue after that date. The quantity of paper produced by each vat was relatively stable, with daily deliveries falling within a predictable range. If a vat's output decreased or fell short of expectation, the creditor would send someone to investigate. In cases where the borrower secretly sold paper without repaying the debt, the guarantor was held responsible for recovery. If a vat ceased production for over a month, the creditor could hire workers to resume operations directly. After deducting wages and the outstanding debt (including interest), the paper would be sold by the creditor to recover the loan. Borrowers were not strictly required to sell paper to the creditor, but they were obliged to notify them first so that the owed amount could be deducted accordingly.[184]

These conditions meant that when workshop owners borrowed money to produce paper, the cost of interest charged by paper dealers had to be

---

184 Lin Jingliang, "An Investigation of the Papermaking Industry in Changting, Fujian," *China Construction (Shanghai)*, Vol. 14, No. 5, 1936.

added to their total production expenses. In Ninghua County, it was customary for paper-makers without capital to borrow money by signing a note, "using *zhuma* as collateral, upon delivering paper, each load would be discounted by 30–40 or 40–50 cents, and the remaining debt would be repaid with 2% monthly interest." If the borrower's business failed and could not repay the principal and interest, their property would be used to settle the debt. A telling example is Fan Chunhe, a full-time paper manufacturer in Ninghua. Between 1917 and 1925, he suffered losses in at least four different years (1917, 1919, 1924, and 1925). By 1925, he was 2,800 *xiao yang* (small silver coins, equals to 280 yuan) in the red, overwhelmed by debt. After settlement, it emerged that he had borrowed a principal of 6,293 *xiao yang* from Fan Chaowei, with accrued interest of 2,169 *xiao yang*. To clear the debt, Fan Chunhe was forced to pawn four mountain plots, half a house, and an ox. In Changting County, it was common for vat owners to borrow from paper merchants. In return, they had to sell an agreed quantity of paper to the creditor. Failure to do so would not only make it impossible to secure loans the following year, but would also oblige the vat owner to pay brokerage fee.[185] These customary lending and purchasing arrangements between paper workshop owners, paper dealers, and merchants persisted well into the mid-20th century.[186]

According to Lin Jingliang's investigation, paper workers "were paid daily. Master papermakers earned 10 *xiao yang* per day, paper dryers 9, pulp treaders 5, and materials sorters and wood carriers each received 5 as well. In addition to wages, vat owners were responsible for providing room and board. On average, each load of paper of each workshop required a supplement of 5 to 6 yuan's worth of oil, salt, firewood, and rice for the

---

185 Yu Ruxian, *A Study of Rural Informal Lending in Western Fujian from the Qing to the Republican Era*, Tianjin Ancient Books Publishing House, 2010, pp. 165, 167.
186 See Appendix I of this book, "Hu Lanshan's Personal Account."

workers."[187] General Peng Shengbiao, who began working in the 1920s and 30s, reportedly became a skilled papermaker during this time. He was said to have been capable of producing over a thousand sheets a day, earning between 3 and 4 *xiao yang* per day.[188] Other reports suggest that raw material maobian paper sold for around 80 cents to 1 yuan per *dao*, with a production cost of roughly 85 cents—40 of which went to labor.[189]

By the 1940s, the price of Yukou paper had skyrocketed from 18 yuan per load before the war to 60 yuan per load. Yet, during this time, the general price level and wages had also risen sharply. The table below (Table 4) illustrates the average cost per load of Yukou paper in those years.

Table 4 Detailed Production Cost Breakdown for Yukou Paper in Changting (Survey Conducted in 1941)

Item		Amount (Yuan)	Notes
Raw Materials	Purchase of Hillside Woodlots	7.00	Rent paid by some *caohu* for hillside plots
	Lime	4.50	Includes boat transport, porterage, and brokerage fee
	Subtotal	11.5	
Labor Costs	Miscellaneous labor	2.40	Before harvesting and trimming *zhuma*, used for trail clearing, pond maintenance, lime collection; approximately 2 laborers at 1.2 yuan/day

187 Lin Jingliang, "An Investigation of the Papermaking Industry in Changting, Fujian," *China Construction (Shanghai)*, Vol. 14, No. 5, 1936.
188 Peng Shengbiao was born in March 1909 in Liangkeng Village, Gucheng Township, Changting County, Fujian Province. Many bamboo farmers in Liangkeng relied on papermaking for their livelihood. For three generations, Peng's family made their living by producing paper for paper workshop owners. His grandfather Peng Xiangrui and father Peng Dongqian were both highly skilled papermakers. Peng began working as a papermaking apprentice at age 13, and once skilled, could produce over 1,000 sheets per day. His daily wage was 0.3–0.4 yuan—barely enough to support the family. He often had to borrow wages in advance from the workshop owner, with interest deducted from future pay. See: Wang Qisen and Zhang Hongxiang, "Peng Shengbiao: From Papermaker to General," *Changting Historical and Cultural Materials*, Vol. 39, 2006, pp. 67–68.
189 Zhang Yonghui, "A Survey of Handmade Paper Industry in Shaxian and Liancheng, Fujian (One of the Industrial Survey Reports by the Central Industrial Experiment Institute)," *Industrial Center*, June 1937.

Item		Amount (Yuan)	Notes
	Harvesting and trimming	8.00	Average 4 laborers (local & non-local), at 2 yuan/day
	Washing and bleaching	2,00	Includes lake soaking, washing and bleaching, lake raking, and cutting grass
	Sheets forming	5.00	2 workers, each paid 2.5 yuan
	Paper drying	4.00	2 workers, each paid 2 yuan
	Pulp trampling	4.00	2 workers, each paid 2 yuan
	Peeling	3.00	2 workers, each paid 1.5 yuan
	Firewood cutting	2.00	1 worker
	Vat management	2.00	1 worker
	Transport labor	3.50	Average distance of 40 *li* to town
	Subtotal	35.90	
Consumables & Provisions	Meals for harvesting and trimming laborer	3.00	4 people consume 6 *sheng* of rice, each person 1.5 *sheng* per day; calculated at 2 *sheng* per yuan
	Food & wine for hillside work	2.00	Extra meals and wine traditionally provided when going up/down the mountain
	Meals for papermaking workers	8.20	10 workers each vat; each person consumes 1.5 *sheng* of rice, total 1.5 *dou*; includes rice and pickles
	Miscellaneous supplies (e.g. oils)	2.00	Includes gelatinous leaves, oil roasting, tung oil, blade oil, brush oil, etc.
	Festival expenses	2.00	During holidays, extra meat and wine were customarily provided to workers
	Subtotal	17.20	
Miscellaneous Expenses	Interests	1.20	Interest on borrowed capital; average interest per *dan* of product
	Harvesting and trimming tools wear	2.00	Includes axes, machetes, raincoats, bamboo hats, etc., provided by workshop owner
	Papermaking tools wear	1.00	Includes paper screens, screen beds, cutting knives, bark cords, bamboo & iron tools, etc.
	Subtotal	4.20	
Total		68.80	

Source: Xie Shenchu, A Study of the Paper Industry in Changting, *Journal of Economics and Commerce* (Xiamen), No. 1, 1941.

According to the table above, the production cost for each *dan* (担) of Yukou paper amounted to 68.8 yuan. Compared to the market price of 60 yuan at the time, this meant that papermakers incurred a loss of 8.8 yuan per *dan*, highlighting the severe hardships faced by paper producers during the war.

In terms of output, after the 25th year of the Guangxu era, Qing dynasty (1899), the total annual value of handmade paper produced in Fujian province averaged around five million yuan. During World War I, the export of foreign machine-made paper declined sharply, creating a window of opportunity for local handmade paper. Fujian's exports peaked at about 10 million yuan annually, reaching 13 million in 1926. According to data from the Fujian Provincial Statistics Bureau, the province's paper production and output value between 1934 and 1939 reached their highest point in 1939, with a total output of 36,925.42 tons and a production value of 12,388,820 yuan (in the old Chinese National Currency). Among all production areas, the Tingjiang River basin led the province, with counties such as Changting, Liancheng, Shanghang, and Wuping standing out—each generating an annual value of approximately 400,000 to 500,000 yuan.[190]

In fact, the Tingzhou region consistently led the province in paper production. During the 1920s, "Changting alone produced around 50,000 *dan* annually, Liancheng 30,000 *dan*, and Shanghang about 10,000 *dan*."[191] The region produced a variety of paper types—including dagong, xiaogong, yangzhuang, zhengpi, and shouben—with a combined yearly value of over 3 million yuan. Of this, over 2 million yuan worth was shipped to Guangdong, and more than 1 million to cities like Tianjin and Shanghai.[192]

---

190 Lin Cunhe (ed.), *Papers of Fujian* (Fujian Survey and Statistics Series No. 4), issued by the Statistical Office of the Fujian Provincial Government, 1941, pp. 5, 7, 42.
191 Peng Wangshu, "A Nationwide Survey of the Paper Industry," *Agricultural and Commercial Bulletin*, Vol. 11, No. 1, 1924.
192 "Overview of the Paper Industry in Fujian Province," *Monthly Bulletin of the Brit-*

Changting was the foremost producer among all counties in western Fujian. In its peak year of 1927, its paper exports alone were valued at 2 million yuan.[193] Statistics from the Ministry of Industry and Commerce of the Wang Jingwei regime at the time noted that prior to 1929, Changting's "annual production of the paper industry exceeded 100,000 *dan*, valued at over 1 million yuan—making paper one of its primary rural industries and an economic backbone for the region."[194]

By the 1940s, Guangzhou alone consumed 1.19 tons of Yukou paper per day just for cigarette rolling.[195] The neighboring county of Dapu in Guangdong also consumed Yukou paper from Changting worth 20,000 to 30,000 yuan annually.[196] According to a survey by the Changting Papermaking Industrial Cooperative, there were 625 paper vats operating across 11 rural townships in the region, with a combined annual output of 3,913.75 tons. Key production areas included: Tie'an in the Inner Mountain area (161 vats, 1,127.08 tons); Guanqian in the Outer Mountain area (25 vats, 208.33 tons); Qingyan (55 vats, 293.75 tons); Luofang (60 vats, 395.83 tons); Zhongzheng (17 vats, 166.67 tons); Sibao (14 vats, 67.08 tons); Datong (19 vats, 145.83 tons); Jiushui in Gucheng (14 vats, 79.17 tons); Gucheng in the West Road Region (79 vats, 479.42 tons); Zhongshan in the South Road Region (8 vats, 64.58 tons); Hecai (14 vats, 50 tons); Nanye and surrounding areas in Gucheng (21 vats, 133.33 tons); Cewu (12

---

ish-American Tobacco Company, Vol. 5, No. 3, 1925.
193 "Key Points in the Reform of the Changting Paper Industry," *Women and National Goods*, Vol. 2, No. 4, 1936.
194 Statistical Office of the Ministry of Industry and Commerce, *Monthly Bulletin of the Ministry of Industry and Commerce*, Vol. 1, No. 9, 1936.
195 Huang Majin (chief ed.), *A History of Papermaking in Changting*, China Light Industry Press, 1992, pp. 35–36.
196 *Revised Chorography of Dapu County* (Republican Era), Vol. 10, Shanghai Bookstore Publishing House, 2003.

vats, 65.625 tons); Nanxuan (36 vats, 213.96 tons); Tufang in Sanping (12 vats, 77.08 tons); and Sidu (78 vats, 346.25 tons).[197]

4.1.2. Transportation

In the mountainous regions where Yukou paper was produced, transportation to urban paper markets relied primarily on manual labor—porters carrying the goods on their shoulders. After production was completed in Neishan of Zhiping and its surrounding areas, *caozhu* would hire several trusted local porters, sometimes up to a dozen, to carry the freshly made paper on foot along mountain paths to markets in Changting or to Hengjiang Town in Shicheng County, Jiangxi. Each load typically contained seven *dao* of paper, simply wrapped in waste paper or low-grade paper, tied together for ease of transport. This so-called "Neishan Yukou Paper" from Ninghua traveled with minimal packaging during its journey to Changting or Hengjiang. Most of it was sold via paper shops in Changting and re-branded as "Changting Yukou Paper," though in reality, much of it originated in Ninghua. [198] The Ninghua Yukou paper exported through Hengjiang's paper shops, meanwhile, became known as "Hengjiang heavy paper."[199]

---

197 Southeast Changting Office of the Chinese Industrial Cooperatives Association (comp.), *Survey of Papermaking in Changting, Fujian*, held at the Changting County Archives, 1946, p. 19.

198 A survey conducted in the 1950s noted: "It is understood that the Yukou paper produced in Ninghua is of higher quality than that made in Changting. Since Ninghua was under the jurisdiction of Tingzhou Prefecture during the Qing dynasty, and was administered by the Changting Special Region during the early Republican era, at that time people tended to consider Ninghua as part of Changting. Moreover, Zhiping is geographically close to Changting, and most of the Yukou paper from Neishan was exported via Changting. Today, it is exclusively distributed by the Changting Local Products Company and packaged in Changting for outward transportation. As a result, the outside world only knows of 'Changting Yukou paper,' while remaining unaware of 'Ninghua Yukou paper.'"
See *Survey Report on Neishan Yukou Paper in Zhiping District, Ninghua County* (June 8, 1955), archived at the Ninghua County Archives, collected and provided by Lei Shaoqiu.

199 Liu Shanyong, *Walking through Tingzhou*, Jiangxi Science and Technology Press,

Zeng Youchun, a native of Tianshe Village in the She ethnic township of Zhiping, was intimately familiar with the region's terrain. According to his account, the ancient footpath over Yunxiao Mountain (also known as Xiuyun Mountain), which connects Changting County to Shicheng in Jiangxi, once served as a vital route for transporting goods. Tianshe Village lies directly on this narrow, secluded mountain trail. The route wound its way from Changting's Xinqiao, through Sankengkou Pass, Dongkengjiao, and Beikengba, over Zijin Ridge to Tianshe, then descended into Zhiping or continued across the border into Jiangxi. Until a modern road was built into Zhiping, all materials—both for daily life and paper production—were carried in and out via this trail by porters. From Tianshe, porters would descend with loads of Yukou paper to Sankengkou Pass, where the goods could be transferred to riverboats.[200] The Ting River and its tributaries formed the main waterways for transporting handmade paper from western Fujian counties like Ninghua, Changting, and Liancheng to Dabu and Chaoshan in Guangdong, where it was transshipped for export.

There were two main footpaths from Zhiping to Hengjiang, Jiangxi. The first passed through Kaizi Mountain, climbed Muma Mountain, continued to Xiangluwo and Min-Gan Pavilion (a landmark marking the Fujian-Jiangxi border), then descended Lannikeng into Hengjiang. The second trail began at Xiaping, went through Nanfengduan, crossed Jiangjuncha, entered Jiangxi, descended to Zhuji Village—a fellow producer of Yukou paper (particularly the heavier variety)—and then continued downhill to Hengjiang Town. From there, the paper was shipped downriver via the Qin

---

2019, pp. 67–69, 97–101;
Wen Xiaoxing, "The Transformation and Preservation of Traditional Hakka Papermaking Techniques: A Case Study of 'Hengjiang Heavy Paper' in Shicheng," *Journal of Gannan Normal University*, No. 4, 2016.
200 See the author's oral interview with Zeng Youchun in Hubeijiao and Tianshe villages, Zhiping Township, on February 27, 2022.

River into the Gan River.[201] During the Republican era, Hengjiang Town served as the commercial hub for both Maobian and heavy paper (Yukou paper) in this region. Part of the Fourth District of Shicheng County, Hengjiang had over 200 households and lay 50 *li* (roughly 25 km) southeast of the Shicheng county seat. The steep mountains 30 to 40 *li* southeast of Hengjiang were rich in bamboo—its dense bamboo forests stretching deep into the hills. Straddling the border of four counties in two provinces—Changting, Ninghua, and Ruijin in Fujian, and Shicheng in Jiangxi—local mountain-dwelling farmers made their living from papermaking. Hengjiang District had 49,630 *mu* of bamboo forests, with papermaking in 15 villages involving 360 households and 167 paper vats. The local heavy paper was used for writing letters, official documents, archives, contracts, registers, accounting ledgers, and books. Its distribution extended throughout Jiangxi Province and further into Jiangsu, Zhejiang, and Hubei via Nanchang.[202]

During the Republican era, handmade paper products such as Yukou paper were transported out of the mountainous regions primarily via two major water routes. One route led from Changting down the Yin River to Fengshi, where it was transferred to the Han River, eventually reaching Chaozhou and Shantou in Guangdong.[203] Another route began from Hengjiang in Jiangxi Province, where the paper was shipped along the Gan River. Some of it crossed the Dayuling Ridge to Guangzhou, while other shipments traveled down the Yangtze River to inland provinces such as Hubei. A portion was also transported eastward to Fuzhou, the provincial

---

201 See Appendix I, "Hu Lanshan's Personal Account," as well as the author's oral interview with Hu Lanshan in Xikeng, Xiaping Village, Zhiping Township, on July 23, 2022.
202 Wu Zhenya, "Recent Survey on the Production and Marketing of Hengjiang Maobian Paper in Shicheng County, Jiangxi Province," *China Farmers' Bank Monthly: Investigations*, 1936.
203 Ming Qiang, "Changting's Papermaking Industry in Urgent Need of Rescue," *Weili*, Vol. 2, No. 10, 1939.

capital. Paper that reached Chaozhou, Shantou, and Guangzhou served both local consumption and, more importantly, export markets in Southeast Asia and beyond.[204]

During the War of Resistance against Japanese Aggression, the Industrial Cooperatives of Changting Paper Industry investigated paper transportation along the Ting River. Their findings indicated that, aside from limited volumes sent from Dapu in Guangdong to Meixian, the majority of paper produced along the Ting River was shipped from Changting to Gan County in Jiangxi. From there, it continued on to Hunan and other parts of southwest China. Changting thus emerged as a critical hub for the distribution of Fujian-made paper to markets beyond the province. Domestically, Fujian-made paper was shipped in large quantities each year to provinces such as the three northeastern provinces, Hebei, Shandong, Jiangsu, Zhejiang, Jiangxi, Anhui, and Guangdong, with only relatively small amounts reaching northwest and southwest provinces. Overseas markets leaned heavily toward destinations such as Japan, the Philippines, Hong Kong, Annam (present-day Vietnam), Taiwan, the Kwantung Leased Territory, and Southeast Asia. Among these, Annam, Taiwan, and the countries of Southeast Asia were the most significant markets.[205]

In sum, Changting and Hengjiang served as the primary trade centers for Yukou and Changxing paper from western Fujian. Paper was typically carried on foot by porters, who shouldered their loads over rugged mountain paths to river ports. From there, the goods were transferred onto boats

---

204 Peng Wangshu,"A Nationwide Survey of the Paper Industry," *Agricultural and Commercial Bulletin*, Vol. 11, No. 1, 1924;
Lin Zhaohe, "An Overview of the Handmade Paper Industry in Fujian and Its Ongoing Improvements". *Construction Weekly*, Vol. 7, No. 6, 1938;
Wu Zhenya, "Recent Survey on the Production and Marketing of Hengjiang Maobian Paper in Shicheng County, Jiangxi Province," *China Farmers' Bank Monthly: Investigations*, 1936.
205 Southeast Changting Office of the Chinese Industrial Cooperatives Association (comp.), *Survey of Papermaking in Changting, Fujian*, 1946, p. 35.

and continued downstream. The transportation network consisted of three main routes: the first went through Changting via the Ting River, connecting to the Han River to reach the Chaoshan region; the second passed through Hengjiang Town in Jiangxi, following the Gan River and crossing the Dayu Ridge to link with the Bei River for water transport to Guangzhou; the third followed the Gan River to Jiujiang, from where paper was distributed to Hankou and Shanghai. New modes of transportation such as steamships, railways, and motor roads only gradually transformed the commercial transport routes of this region after the founding of the People's Republic of China.

(Pic 76 Topographical Sketch Map of the Area Surrounding Tianshe Village, Ting River, and Sankengkou Village)

(Pic77 The Min-Gan Pavilion at Xiangluwo on an Ancient Mountain Trail Used to Carry Yukou Paper from Zhiping to Jiangxi, Photograph by Gui Shuzhong)

4.1.3.   Distribution

As the seat of Tingzhou Prefecture, Changting was nestled deep within the mountainous interior of Fujian, long isolated by difficult terrain and limited transportation. Local merchants rarely ventured beyond the region to conduct trade. However, with the rise of the papermaking industry, this began to change. Paper merchants began establishing offices and agencies in the city, shipping their goods to markets in Chaoshan, Guangzhou, Hong Kong, Changsha, and Jiangxi.[206] Merchants from Guangdong, Jiangxi, Hunan, and across Fujian set up shops in Changting to manage large-scale transactions on-site in local paper, rice, timber, and other bulk commodities. Among these, Ting paper gained considerable renown, both domestically and abroad.

During the late Qing and Republican eras, most of Changting's paper businesses were concentrated on Shuidong Street. Among the two or three

---

206 *Chorography of Changting County* (Republican era), Vol. 18 "Industry Records," Shanghai Bookstore Publishing House, 2000, p. 495.

dozen establishments were Zheng Taicheng, Tai'an Hang, Chang Fengrong, Sichang Hang, Jiucheng Hang, and Dexin Hang. The largest of these was Zheng Taicheng, which operated branches in both Guangzhou and Hong Kong. Later, Li Shuming rose to prominence as the leading figure in Changting's paper industry. He not only founded Duofu Paper Firm in Changting, but also established Chang'an Paper Firm in Guangzhou.[207] Some of these paper firms functioned solely as intermediaries. As described by Lin Jingliang, their role was "to act between paper merchants and papermaking workshops, helping to introduce merchants to invest in workshops and guaranteeing the safety of investment. Once a deal was secured, the paper firm would charge a brokerage fee—five cents per *dan* from the investor and ten cents from the workshop owner. After production, the finished paper would be transported by the workshop owner to the paper firm, which then handled the sale."[208] According to the study by Xie Shenchu, many paper merchants not only lent capital to the workshop owners (a practice known as *jiaocao*, or "funding the vats") but also demanded high interest—typically no less than 1.5% per month. In return, they secured priority purchasing rights. They could dispatch agents to the countryside at any time to inspect production. Once the paper was made, they would buy it at prices three to five yuan per *dan* below the market rate. This monopolistic setup was difficult to challenge. Since the merchants maintained close networks among themselves, one firm would never buy paper funded by another. As a result, workshop owners had little leverage and were forced to accept the

---

207 Mao Xing, "Fragments of Commerce and Trade in Changting before the Founding of the PRC," *Changting Historical and Cultural Materials*, Vol. 12, 1987, p. 35.

208 Lin Jingliang later noted that "[paper workshop owners] are not bound to sell to the original creditor, but are free to choose a paper merchant offering a higher price. After the merchant purchases the paper, the goods can be stored at a paper firm; even if Paper Firm A purchased the paper, it could be stored at Firm B without additional warehouse rent, because when the merchant initially invested, a five-cent commission had already been collected by the firm, and the workshop owner paid ten cents as well." These statements do not quite reflect the competitive dynamics among paper firms at the time. See: Lin Jingliang, "An Investigation of the Papermaking Industry in Changting, Fujian," *China Construction (Shanghai)*, Vol. 14, No. 5, 1936.

depressed prices. Paper merchants profited not only by squeezing the producers but also by hoarding stock and selling it at inflated prices—often reaping a hundredfold profit.[209] This exploitative relationship between capital and production became increasingly apparent as the papermaking industry matured during the Qing,[210] and by the Republican period, workshop owners still had limited bargaining power.

Most prominent paper merchants lived in Changting itself. A typical example was Li Hongdong, who resided on Dongmen Street. His family had been in the paper business for generations and operated paper firms in Changting, Chaozhou, and Guangzhou. Through savvy business practices, he became one of the wealthiest paper merchants in the region.[211] Led by figures like Li, Changting merchants established more than 30 paper firms in major trading ports such as Chaozhou, Guangzhou, and Hong Kong, as well as inland cities like Shaoguan, Huizhou, Laolong, and Meixian in Guangdong, and Ganzhou, Ji'an, and Nanchang in Jiangxi.[212] On one hand,

---

209 Xie Shenchu, "A Study on the Papermaking Industry in Changting," *Journal of Economic and Commercial Studies* (Xiamen), No. 1, 1941.
210 Xu Jianqing, "Papermaking Industry in the Qing Dynasty." *Journal of Chinese Historical Studies*, No. 3, 1997.
211 Liang Xinbin, "Mr. Li Hongdong: A Devoted Supporter of Local Education," *Changting Historical and Cultural Materials*, Vol. 18, 1990, p. 91.
212 Notable paper firms included: Chang'an Paper Firm (founded by Xu Weiyun), Rongfeng Paper Firm (founded by Tong Ziyi), and Changfeng Paper Firm (founded by Li Hongkai), among more than a dozen in Chaozhou; Jin'an Paper Firm, Lianxingchang Paper Firm, and Gongxing Paper Firm in Shantou; Changxing Paper Firm (founded by Li Tisheng), Gong'an Paper Firm (founded by Luo Zuoheng), Dehe Paper Firm (founded by Chen Xuhe), Yongfeng Paper Firm (founded by Chen Bochun), Anle Paper Store (founded by Lan Qiwei), and Jianchanglong Paper Firm (founded by Tong Xiaoqing) among others in Guangzhou; Changlian, Changxing, and Jianxing Paper Firms among others in Foshan; Tingzhou Paper Firm (founded by Zheng Yunsong) and Nanlianchang Paper Firm (founded by Zhou Yangyun) among others in Hong Kong; and Rongchang Paper Firm (founded by Mao Huanzhang) in Shanghai.
See: Lin Renfang (chi ed.), *Guarding and Exploring: Selected Works of Directors of the Fourth Hakka Association in Western Fujian*, China Yanshi Publishing House, 2017, pp. 280–281;
Zou Zibin, "'Skilled Papermakers in Tingzhou Prefecture'—Interviews with Veteran Papermakers and Industry Elders on the Overview of Tingzhou's Handmade Paper Industry," *Changting Historical and Cultural Materials*, Vol. 5, 1983, p. 108;

these merchants secured control over local paper production by issuing loans in exchange for pre-purchase rights, binding the workshop owners in long-term debt relationships to manipulate local paper production, purchase, and sales. On the other, they expanded outward, setting up distribution networks in both coastal port cities and inland towns to sell Tingzhou paper.

As for external markets, the opening of five treaty ports for foreign trade at the end of the Qing dynasty significantly expanded the commercial reach of Fujian's paper products. With Fuzhou and Xiamen among the new treaty ports, trade flourished. Merchants from other provinces came to Fujian to set up purchasing agencies, and the export of *Hai zhi*—"overseas paper"—to Northeast China and Southeast Asia soared.[213] By the early Republican era, most of Changting's native paper was sold either to other provinces or to foreign markets. Changxing paper was mostly shipped to the Yangtze River basin and the northern provinces. *Jia zhi* was exported in large quantities to Northeast and North China, while Jiangsu, Zhejiang, and parts of Fujian also formed smaller markets. Almost all *Hai zhi* went to the northeast and northern provinces. Gaolian paper was commonly exported to Annam (modern-day Vietnam), and Yukou paper was sold not only in Guangzhou, but also in Annam and Siam (modern-day Thailand).[214]

The rapid development of the paper trade in the counties along the Ting River basin was largely fueled by the expansion of external markets. "In earlier times under the Qing dynasty, handmade bamboo papers like Yukou paper were sold only within China. However, with the advent of the Republic era, their market reach gradually extended to Southeast Asia and beyond. By the 16th and 19th years of the Republic era (1927 and 1930),

---

Mao Xing, "Fragments of Commerce and Trade in Changting before the Founding of the PRC," *Changting Historical and Cultural Materials*, Vol. 12, 1987, p. 35.
213 Fujian Provincial Local Chorography Compilation Committee (ed.), *Fujian Provincial Chorography: Light Industry Records*, Fangzhi Publishing House, 2000, p. 127.
214 Lin Zhaohe, "An Overview of the Handmade Paper Industry in Fujian and Its Ongoing Improvements". *Construction Weekly*, Vol. 7, No. 6, 1938.

the paper industry had entered a period of remarkable prosperity, flourishing to its peak. Demand surged, prices climbed, and profits soared than ever before—yielding an average profit of 400 to 500 yuan per *zhi* (只)."[215] A 1925 report in the *Nanyang Commercial News* further attested to this boom: "Yukou paper, once in great demand here and primarily imported from Guangzhou, used to sell at just 0.27 to 0.34 yuan per *jin*. But recently, as less goods came via Hong Kong and direct shipments from Guangzhou became scarce, local supplies fell short. Demand quickly outpaced supply, pushing prices ever higher. In fact, the price has more than doubled—now reaching 0.70 yuan per *jin*, and even as high as 0.80 yuan."[216] Another report, titled "Investigation of Fujian's Rich Resources," published in the *Nanyang Commercial News* on December 28, 1934, noted that in 1933, over 200,000 *dan* of handmade bamboo paper were exported through customs—including around 48,000 *dan* of premium-grade paper and more than 80,000 *dan* of mid-grade varieties. From the ports of Fuzhou, Xiamen, and Shantou alone, the total annual export value of paper exceeded 5 million silver *liang*. A significant share of this trade consisted of Yukou paper.[217]

By 1943, the Changting Paper Industry Trade Guild counted 141 registered members. Due to the government's policy of commercial regulation, most paper merchants had joined the trade guild. According to *The Membership List of Paper Industry Trade Guild, Changting County, Fujian Province*, the firm with the largest declared capital was Yulong Paper Firm, located at No. 47 Tai'an Road, with 140,000 yuan in capital. Its manager,

---

215 Lin Jingliang, "An Investigation of the Papermaking Industry in Changting, Fujian," *China Construction (Shanghai)*, Vol. 14, No. 5, 1936. One *zhi* equaled 20 *dan* (担), and one *dan* was 7 *dao* (刀).
See: "Changting's Papermaking Industry in Urgent Need of Rescue," *Weili*, Vol. 2, No. 10, 1939.
216 "Prices of Yukou Paper Soar," *Nanyang Commercial Daily*, December 31, 1925, p. 4.
217 "Investigation of Fujian's Rich Resources," *Nanyang Commercial Daily*, December 28, 1934, p. 11.

Zheng Diqun—a 37-year-old native of Changting, university-educated and a member of the Kuomintang—was among the most prominent figures in the trade. Six other firms reported capital of 100,000 yuan each, including Duofu, Guangrongtai, Linji, Zhenxinglong, Guang'an, and Yuechang. Three companies were capitalized at 80,000 yuan, two at 60,000 yuan, and seven more at 50,000 yuan. Another six fell within the 40,000–45,000 yuan range, while 18 reported 30,000–35,000 yuan. Ten firms listed capital of 20,000 yuan, and 42 more declared between 10,000 and 15,600 yuan. The lower tiers included 21 firms with 5,000–5,600 yuan and 11 with capital ranging from 1,000 to 4,000 yuan. Fourteen firms operated on a modest base of just 400–500 yuan.[218] Together, these 141 paper merchants in Changting amassed a total registered capital of approximately 3.0158 million yuan. Over 82% of them operated with less than 35,000 yuan in capital, and nearly one-third with less than 10,000 yuan. Businesses with around 10,000 yuan were especially common.

By the late 1940s, however, surveys conducted by the Industrial Co-operatives of Changting Paper Industry painted a much gloomier picture of the industry's development after the War of Resistance Against Japanese Aggression, stating:

> Since the outbreak of the War of Resistance against Japanese Aggression, Fujian paper began to lose its markets. At first, sales routes to Shanghai were obstructed; soon after, those to northern China were entirely severed. Then, as the government imposed export restrictions to prevent domestic resources from falling into the enemy's hands, paper exports were further curtailed. As a result, nearly all of Fujian paper's pre-war markets

---

218 *The Membership List of Paper Industry Trade Guild, Changting County, Fujian Province* (Reported on October 20, 1943 [Year 32 of the Republic]), Changting County Archives, Paper Industry Guild Files, Archive No. 81–6–704, pp. 76–88.

were cut off. During the war, as cities like Xiamen, Fuzhou, and Shantou successively fell, Fujian paper had to find new routes. Some products were transported overland to Zhejiang and Jiangxi provinces. Lishui in Zhejiang and Gan County in Jiangxi became key distribution centers beyond Fujian, from which the paper was re-routed to southern Zhejiang, southern Jiangxi, and even further inland—to Hengyang, Guilin, Guiyang, Kunming, and Chongqing. By the days following the victory of the War of Resistance, though Fujian's traditional foreign markets for paper had gradually recovered, the overall situation remains difficult. Domestic instability and limited transportation networks continue to hinder trade, and international routes remain largely inaccessible. Moreover, the postwar influx of foreign paper, aggressively dumped across both domestic and overseas markets, has made it increasingly difficult for Fujian paper—burdened by higher production costs and outdated technology—to compete. A return to the thriving sales of the pre-war years now seems out of reach.[219]

4.1.4. Consumption

A History of Papermaking in Changting offers a detailed account of the various uses of Yukou paper and explains why it has long been favored by consumers in both domestic and overseas markets. Chinese communities in Hong Kong, Macau, and the Southeast Asian archipelago often used Yukou paper for printing account books. When processed into writing paper such as *jiugong pei* (九宫胚, grid paper for calligraphy practice), *xizi pei* (习字胚, calligraphy practice sheets), and *miaohong bu* (描红簿, copybooks for learning calligraphy), Yukou paper became especially popular among users in Japan and Southeast Asia. In the Pearl River Delta, where

---

219 Southeast Changting Office of the Chinese Industrial Cooperatives Association (comp.), *Survey of Papermaking in Changting, Fujian*, 1946, pp. 1–2.

rolling one's own cigarettes is a common habit, the finest Yukou paper was widely used as cigarette paper. It was favored not only for its strength—resistant to breaking when held between the lips—but also for its hygienic, non-toxic quality, which did not cause throat irritation or inflammation. In regions like Guangzhou, Xingning, and Meixian, Yukou paper was also used to wrap the famed "salt-baked chicken," turning the dish into a culinary specialty known for both flavor and presentation. In some areas, maobian paper even served as napkins.[220]

In truth, the paper products from Changting were both abundant and diverse. They were crafted into various colored papers, account books, red and white couplets for celebratory or funeral occasions, spirit money, and woodblock-printed books. Civilian paper goods included large and small eight-column letter paper, envelopes of various sizes, and "heaven-reaching" grid paper. Official papers encompassed forms such as *chengwen zhi* (呈文纸, memorial paper), ten-column formats, official document paper, and petition and lawsuit paper. For bookkeeping, there were daybooks, general ledgers, square-format account books, strip-format account books, and multiple types of accordion-fold accounts.[221] As for Yukou paper specifically, different classes and types served different purposes. The Grade 2 and Grade 3 Prime Yukou paper were primarily shipped to commercial ports in Guangzhou, Hong Kong, Macau, and the Southeast Asian archipelago. There, they were used mainly for printing account books, continuing a tradition among overseas Chinese of using Tingzhou's Yukou paper for their bookkeeping needs. The Grade 3 and Grade 4 Prime Yukou papers were also popular in the Guangzhou, Hong Kong and Macau markets, especially for cutting into cigarette paper. The Grade 5 Yukou was widely sold in the

---

220 Huang Majin (chief ed.), *A History of Papermaking in Changting*, China Light Industry Press, 1992, pp. 35–36.
221 Mao Xing, "Fragments of Commerce and Trade in Changting before the Founding of the PRC," *Changting Historical and Cultural Materials*, Vol. 12, 1987, p. 36.

Han River and Mei River trade hubs in Guangdong, especially in the Cha-oshan region. In addition to cigarette paper, it was also used for making bright-colored printing sheets such as "Da Bei Yan" and "Vermilion Red." The Grade 7 Yukou was more commonly used for colored paper, as well as packaging in traditional Chinese medicine shops, cloth stores, and general merchandise retailers.[222]

A 1932 report in the *Nanyang Commercial Daily* noted that "Chinese-made paper materials exported annually to Siam were of considerable quantity, with account books and practical varieties of Yukou paper comprising the majority. As the year's end approached, shops customarily had to replace their account books. However, due to the high cost of Yukou paper, many buyers were deterred. Seeing such high prices for Chinese paper, bookbinders increasingly turned to cheaper foreign *lianshi* papers or even newspaper stock for binding, taking advantage of their lower costs."[223] This highlights that in Siam and other parts of Southeast Asia, Yukou paper was widely used for account book production. Its popularity stemmed from the tradition among overseas Chinese merchants of replacing account books every year—a custom that ensured steady demand. Yet, the rising price of Yukou paper led many manufacturers to seek affordable alternatives. During the War of Resistance Against Japanese Aggression, imported papers became scarce. In response, Changting artisans developed an improved version of maobian paper, treating it with glue to allow for smooth writing with a fountain pen. These refined paper products became popular and found a wide market both within and beyond the province.[224]

---

222 Zou Zibin, "'Skilled Papermakers in Tingzhou Prefecture'—Interviews with Veteran Papermakers and Industry Elders on the Overview of Tingzhou's Handmade Paper Industry," *Changting Historical and Cultural Materials*, Vol. 5, 1983, p. 106.
223 "Recent Developments in Chinese Paper Industry in Siam." *Nanyang Commercial Daily*, Jan. 4, 1932, p. 9.
224 Mao Xing, "Fragments of Commerce and Trade in Changting before the Founding of the PRC," *Changting Historical and Cultural Materials*, Vol. 12, 1987, p. 36.

Another notable export was tinfoil spirit money, made from Yukou paper. Crafted from tender bamboo shoots, the paper had fine fibers, which burned cleanly with little ash and left a white residue. This quality made it especially favored among Chinese communities in Southeast Asia and turned it into one of Changting's major export paper products. By the 1930s, over 30 paper firms in Changting specialized in producing such spirit money, categorized into varieties such as the "old six-cut" or "seven-cut" formats. Each bundle was half-dyed yellow using sophora flower water to represent gold, while the rest remained silver-colored—collectively known in the market as *jinyin zhi* (gold and silver paper).[225]

By this time, it had become a clear trend for some functions of local paper to be replaced by foreign paper. Observations of the Guangzhou market revealed the following general situation:

In recent years, the domestic handmade paper market has been more than half overtaken by imported paper. For cultural and public uses—such as newspapers, books, flyers, and other printed materials—foreign paper has become virtually indispensable. Even coarse paper once used for simple wrapping is now being increasingly replaced by machine-made imports. As a result, the traditional handmade paper industry in China has seen its market shrink dramatically, inversely mirroring the rapid rise of foreign paper in both volume and influence. Yet, not all is lost. Some uses still rely on traditional handmade paper due to long-standing cultural habits—needs that imported paper has yet to displace. Among these are specialty papers used for traditional accounting ledgers, receipts, and ritual offerings such as joss paper or spirit money. These retain strong demand. According to

---

225 Mao Xing, "Fragments of Commerce and Trade in Changting before the Founding of the PRC," *Changting Historical and Cultural Materials*, Vol. 12, 1987, p. 36.

investigations, Guangzhou alone consumes a significant quantity of such paper annually, with total sales valued at around five million yuan. Foshan ranks second, with yearly sales exceeding two million yuan. These figures do not even account for sales in other prefectures or shipped to other cities. Thus, although the hand-made paper trade is clearly in decline, such numbers indicate it still holds a notable place among domestic products.[226]

During the War of Resistance Against Japanese Aggression, to meet growing demand from various provinces for printing paper—especially for newspapers, books, and publicity materials—the paper industry in Changting undertook a series of experimental innovations. Drawing on years of experience, local craftspeople developed an "improved paper" by applying a glue-sizing method typically used for single-sided colored sheets. This new paper was suitable for fountain pen writing: it didn't smudge or leak, dried quickly, and maintained its color. Later, inspired by imported products, they produced student exercise books with green grid lines printed using wooden blocks, or subtle ruled lines pressed into the paper—offering a budget-friendly alternative to costly foreign brands like Dowling paper. These products quickly gained popularity in the market. A further breakthrough came through collaboration among the Chemistry Department of Xiamen University, the Fujian Provincial Trade Company, and the Southeast branch of the Chinese Industrial Cooperative Association. Together, they developed a low-cost rosin soap solution for paper sizing. They also adapted the sheet size to match that of machine-made paper, facilitating newspaper and book printing. Their efforts resulted in a successful, affordable "improved paper." At a time of extreme scarcity of machine-made paper, this innovation met pressing wartime needs. Suitable for printing newspa-

---

226 "Special Report from Guangzhou." *Nanyang Commercial Daily*, Apr. 17, 1931, p. 15.

pers, magazines, books, official documents, letters, forms, ledgers, and notebooks, Changting's improved paper found wide circulation throughout the rear areas in southeast and southwest China. It not only contributed significantly to the local economy of the mountainous Tingzhou area, but also played an important role in supporting the national war effort.[227]

4.2. The Papermaking Industry in the Soviet Areas

By the late 1920s, the people of the mountainous regions of Western Fujian still relied on traditional means of livelihood—primarily farming and papermaking. In March 1931, the Central Committee of the Chinese Communist Party established Tingdong County[228] at the border between Changting and Ninghua. A county committee and a Soviet government were formed at the same time, governing key areas such as Tongfang, Guanqian, Xinqiao, Changning[229], Sibeiling, Caofang, Pengfang, and Zhangdi—all of which lay at the heart of the region's papermaking economy. In the autumn of 1931, the 36th Regiment of the 13th Division of the Red Fourth Army dispatched troops to Sibei Township in Changning District to set up a Soviet administration and establish a local government and a peasant associa-

---

227 Zou Zibin, "'Skilled Papermakers in Tingzhou Prefecture'—Interviews with Veteran Papermakers and Industry Elders on the Overview of Tingzhou's Handmade Paper Industry," *Changting Historical and Cultural Materials*, Vol. 5, 1983, p. 107; Mao Xing, "A Brief Discussion of Changting's Improved Paper," *Changting Historical and Cultural Materials*, Vol. 18, 1990, pp. 93–95.

228 When Tingdong County was established, its administrative offices were located in Guanqian. In October 1934, the county was merged into Changting County, Ninghua, and placed under the jurisdiction of the Min–Gan Provincial Government. See The Party History Materials Collection and Research Committee of the CPC Longyan Prefectural Committee, *History of the Revolutionary Base Areas in Western Fujian*, Huaxia Publishing House, 1987, p. 266.

229 Changning District, under Tingdong County, comprised seven townships—Sibeiling (now Zhiping), Chengongkeng, Pengfang, Tianshe, Xiaping, Qiaoxia (now Gaofeng), and Dawubei (now part of Changting). It was one of the principal papermaking areas in western Fujian, employing some 3,000 paper workers. See All-China Federation of Trade Unions, "Survey of the Paper Workers' Union in Changning District," *Ninghua Historical and Cultural Materials*, Vol. 5, 1985, p. 38.

tion.[230] After the Red Army entered Fujian and took control of transportation hubs like Changting, merchants involved in the paper trade fled, and the papermaking industry suffered a sharp decline. Many paper workshops halted production due to a lack of capital, and external sales plummeted. Transportation and sales to external markets became difficult, with exports collapsing.[231] The Kuomintang's economic blockade further strangled the region, cutting off distribution channels and preventing locally produced handmade paper from reaching markets in the non-Soviet areas or overseas. Moreover, the land reform policies implemented in the Soviet areas also dealt a blow to the traditional social and economic structure of the mountainous regions, creating additional pressure on the struggling papermaking trade. Faced with this crisis, how did papermakers in the Soviet areas rebuild and sustain the complex chain of production, transportation, and commerce?

4.2.1. Initial Recovery of Papermaking in the Soviet Areas

In terms of paper production, the first impact fell on the ownership of bamboo forests—the raw material essential for papermaking. After the establishment of Soviet governments in the villages, land survey campaigns and land reforms were launched to redistribute land and forest rights on the basis of village units. Building on the old system of land ownership, the policy of "taking from those with surplus to supplement those with deficiency, and taking from fertile lands to supplement barren ones" was implemented, distributing land equally among peasants according to population.[232] According to a survey by the Paper Industry Union, in Changning

---

230 All-China Federation of Trade Unions, "Survey of the Paper Workers' Union in Changning District," *Ninghua Historical and Cultural Materials*, Vol. 5, 1985, pp. 38-39.
231 Statistical Office of the Ministry of Industry and Commerce, *Monthly Bulletin of the Ministry of Industry and Commerce*, Vol. 1, No. 9, 1936.
232 For details, see The Party History Materials Collection and Research Committee of the CPC Longyan Prefectural Committee, *History of the Revolutionary Base Areas in*

District, ownership of bamboo forests was converted into paddy field equivalents: one *dan*[233] of paper-producing mountain land was valued at two *dan*[234] of rice paddy. Following the principle that "poor and landless workers and peasants receive better mountains and fields, while landlords and rich peasants receive poorer ones," these resources were allocated to individual households. In practice, the specific outcomes varied by township. Some areas received more forest than farmland, others the opposite; some villages were allocated only forestland, others only paddy fields. The actual amount distributed to each person also differed—from seven to nine and a half *dan* per capita. The land reform policy aimed to abolish the old rent-extraction system, under which one *dan* of bamboo forest could be taxed two *dao* of paper. By eliminating this exploitative rent, the reform sought to boost the enthusiasm of papermakers and restore production momentum.[235]

In the early days of the Chinese Soviet Republic (the "Soviet areas"), paper production in Changting faced severe challenges. Under the economic blockade imposed by the Kuomintang and the flight of paper merchants from the region, the greatest difficulty faced by paper workshop owners was the acute shortage of financial resources. Confronted with the economic struggles, the local Communist Party organizations and the Soviet government in western Fujian initiated a cooperative movement aimed at ensuring people's livelihoods. On February 28, 1930, they issued *A Teaching Outline*

Western Fujian, Huaxia Publishing House, 1987, pp. 208–215;
Jiang Boying, "An Investigation into the Land Revolution in the Soviet Areas of Western Fujian," *Fujian Party History Newsletter*, No. 11, 1985.
233 Here, the term *dan* (石) refers to a unit of paper weight carried by workers—one *dan* equals seven *dao*, each *dao* weighing approximately 11 *jin*. See Lin Jingliang, "An Investigation of the Papermaking Industry in Changting, Fujian," *China Construction (Shanghai)*, Vol. 14, No. 5, 1936.
234 In this instance, *dan* (担) refers to a measurement unit of grain yield.
235 All-China Federation of Trade Unions, "Survey of the Paper Workers' Union in Changning District," *Ninghua Historical and Cultural Materials*, Vol. 5, 1985, pp. 38-39.

on Cooperatives, which offered comprehensive explanations on cooperatives' roles, principles, types, organizational systems, membership rules, capital shares, dividend distribution, the relationship between cooperatives and the government, and procedures for establishing cooperatives. In the following month, the First Congress of Workers, Peasants, and Soldiers in western Fujian officially adopted the *Cooperative Regulations*, leading to the creation of large-scale paper production cooperatives. At the beginning of the movement, merchants and wealthy peasants were permitted to join, which soon led to these cooperatives being dominated by these groups, who used them to manipulate local economies. In response, the Second Congress held in September 1930 passed *Revised Cooperative Regulations*, explicitly banning merchants and rich peasants from cooperative membership.[236] From then on, paper workshop owners and paper workers voluntarily pooled their resources to form their own cooperatives. The rules stipulated that "each share would cost 50 cents, with a maximum of ten shares per person, and only laboring people were eligible for membership."[237] Freed from exploitation by paper merchants and loan sharks, workshop owners and workers flocked to join these cooperatives, which in turn promoted the recovery and development of the paper industry in the Soviet Area.

Notably, in the early stages, however, due to the extreme scarcity of public and private funds, most cooperatives relied heavily on government-run funds. After 1931, as institutions matured and confidence grew, cooperatives increasingly turned to raising capital from among the people. Government-run cooperatives gradually gave way to privately operated ones.

---

236 Guo Tiemin and Lin Shanlang, *A History of the Development of China's Cooperative Economy*, Contemporary Economy Publishing House, 1998, p. 512.
237 Huang Majin (chief ed.), *A History of Papermaking in Changting*, China Light Industry Press, 1992, p. 38.

The recovery of the paper economy also owed much to the work of local trade unions, particularly the All-China Federation of Trade Unions and the Paper Workers' Union. In February 1932, under the leadership of the Ninghua All-China Federation of Trade Unions, the Minguang Paper Workers' Union was established in Changning District, headquartered in the home of a former local landlord in Zuokeng village, Zhiping township. The union elected Qiu Daonan from Anziqian village as its director. When Qiu stepped down due to illness and age, Zeng Xueqin—then the head of the Peasants' Association in Fukeng, Shefu village, Zhiping Township[238]—took over the post.[239] The Minguang Paper Workers' Union oversaw six branches across Zhiping, Pengfang, Tianshe, Xiaping, Gaodi, and Kaizishan, and counted 390 members. Many branch chairmen also served as chairs of local Soviet governments.[240] After its formation, the union followed strategic directives from the Min-Gan Regional Paper Workers' Union[241] to "break through paper trade blockades." They soon revived over 300 shuttered paper workshops, mobilized local paper production, and boosted the paper economy. To support this, the trade union leaders Zeng Xueqin and Liang Hongbiao personally sought loans from the Tingdong County gov-

---

238 The primary task of the Peasants' Association was to assist in establishing the Changning District Committee and the District Soviet Government, and to lead local residents in confiscating land from landlords and redistributing it. See materials on Zeng Xueqin, Director of the Changning District Paper Workers' Union, compiled by Lei Shaoqiu, as well as the author's interview notes with Zeng Linggui, son of Zeng Xueqin, conducted in Fukeng Village, Shefu on February 27, 2022.

239 In the spring of 1931, the Red Army first entered Fukeng Village, Shefu. In September, Company Commander Shen led his unit to liberate the entire township. In October 1931, with Shen's assistance, a Peasants' Association was organized, with Zeng Xueqin serving as its chairman. See the author's interview notes with Zeng Linggui in Fukeng Village, Shefu, on February 27, 2022.

240 See All-China Federation of Trade Unions, "Survey of the Paper Workers' Union in Changning District," *Ninghua Historical and Cultural Materials*, Vol. 5, 1985, pp. 38-39.

241 The Min–Gan Paper Workers' Union was established in Tianshe, Changning District, Tingdong County, slightly earlier than the Minguang Paper Workers' Union, which was founded in Zuokeng, Zhiping Township, Changning District. Owing to the similarity of their names, the two are often confused. — Oral account by Zeng Youchun, Tianshe Village, Zhiping She Ethnic Township, February 27, 2022.

ernment. With assistance from the local paper company, loans were issued based on projected output—two or three silver dollars per *dan* of paper. Once produced, the paper was transported to Hengjiang in Shicheng County, Jiangxi Province, where it was purchased by the Soviet government. The proceeds were then used to repay the loans. Amid the rallying cry of "Workers Above All," large numbers of paper laborers joined the union. Members paid a monthly fee of 10 cents, with some villages contributing 0.7% of total paper sales as union dues. All dues collected in the district were redistributed by the union to support the families of fallen soldiers. The paper workers of Changning became a formidable force within the county trade union. Operating more than 300 paper workshops and producing over 30,000 *dan* of paper annually, they played a critical role in both resisting the Kuomintang's economic blockade and caring for the dependents of revolutionary martyrs.[242] According to *A History of Papermaking in Changting*, the Changning District alone sustained over 300 active workshops during this period with an annual output of 1,250 tons.

---

242 All-China Federation of Trade Unions, "Survey of the Paper Workers' Union in Changning District," *Ninghua Historical and Cultural Materials*, Vol. 5, 1985, pp. 38-41.

(Pic 78 Former site of the Minguang Paper Workers' Union in Changning District)

4.2.2. Opening Up Distribution Routes for the Paper Industry in the Soviet Areas

Because of the Kuomintang's economic blockade, industrial goods rarely made their way into the Soviet areas, while agricultural products from within the Soviet areas found few opportunities to be sold outside. Local paper, too, was mostly consumed and used within the districts themselves. Revolutionary proclamations and leaflets—such as the *Proclamation of the Fourth Red Army, Documents of the 6th National Congress of the Communist Party of China*, and the Ten-Point Program—as well as Marxist works like *A Brief Introduction to Communism* and the Central Bureau of the Communist Youth League's newspaper *The Youth's True Voice* were all printed on local paper. The Ministry of Finance of the Central Soviet Government even used Yukou paper to print public bonds for economic development, postage stamps, and cooperative shares. In the Red Army hospitals, Yukou paper also substituted for cotton wool, alleviating shortages caused by the blockade. The domestic sale of local paper not only helped meet daily expenses but also became a medium for spreading revolutionary ideas throughout the Soviet area.[243]

While developing cooperative and state-run economies, the Soviet authorities did not completely exclude private commerce or small merchant groups. In April 1930, the Western Fujian Soviet Government issued a special proclamation to protect merchants, requiring "all levels of government to safeguard the transport of paper, timber, tobacco, and all other goods, without detention or confiscation." The following month, the First Congress of Workers, Peasants, and Soldiers of Western Fujian adopted the *Regulations on Merchants*, which stipulated that "merchants shall trade freely, and the government shall not restrict their prices."[244]

Under the guidance of a series of new economic policies introduced by the Soviet government, the problem of distribution routes was partially eased. Some Yukou paper began to cross the blockade lines and reach the border areas or the so-called "white zones," thus expanding trade between Red and White areas. On June 30, 1932, the Fujian–Jiangxi Paper Workers' Union issued a notice entitled *On the Issue of Exporting Paper*, which reads:

> The most pressing matter now is the export of paper. If paper can be regularly shipped out, the economy will circulate, prices will improve, unemployed workers will be partially alleviated, and production in the Soviet area will be stimulated.

> The following decisions are made regarding paper export:

---

243 Li Zhibui & Yu Shulan, "The Dissemination of the Soviet Area Revolution and the Rise and Fall of the Paper Industry in Jiangxi and Fujian," *Journal of Jiangxi Normal University (Philosophy and Social Sciences Edition)*, No. 3, 2015.
244 Central Archives and Fujian Provincial Archives (comp.), *Collected Revolutionary Historical Documents of Fujian: Soviet Documents (1930)*, 1985, pp. 102–103.

1. For paper already stored along rivers en route, paper dealers must be urged to find ways to keep it moving out of the Soviet area, thereby circulating the economy. The provincial economic department, together with the paper-workers' and boatmen's unions, shall organize supervisory committees to ensure that the proceeds from paper sales are brought back to the Soviet area for business. Hoarding, speculation, shutdowns, or fleeing will not be tolerated.

2. Make every effort to find more small paths and establish transportation routes. For paper from Xinquan, Wuping, and Shanghang, with Shanghang as the hub, two routes shall be established: one connecting Shanghang city to the border regions, and another bypassing Shanghang to Lanjiadu. Use all available connections—or send personnel—to engage merchants in Fengshi for border trade. Those willing to operate in the Soviet area may be issued travel permits, on condition they refrain from political activity and abide by Soviet law. (The Paper Workers' Unions of Wuping, Xinquan, Shanghang, etc., shall discuss this jointly with the government's Economic Department.)

3. All localities shall collaborate with cooperatives and boat porters to sell and transport paper for export. Production of paper in Shanghang, Wuping, and Xinquan shall be prepared for improvement. When sending personnel to communicate with merchants in White Areas or Lanjiadu to purchase paper, ask them what types of paper sell best and bring back samples for research and improvement. Production upgrades will be addressed in a separate notice.

4. Use economic strength and mutual aid to resist capital, raise paper prices, and organize marketing cooperatives. Increase

cooperative capital to sell paper at the border or in White areas. The purpose of these cooperatives is not mere profit but to secure better prices and keep exports flowing, while assisting each other in sales. Individual small producers with voting rights may also export; wealthy producers without such rights are forbidden to do so.

5. Establish four major routes for paper from Changting, Tingdong, Ninghua, Ruijin, and Shicheng as well as Changxing paper:

(1) toward Shanghang;

(2) from Changning and Ninghua to Yangkou and Fuzhou;

(3) from Ruijin and Henggang down to Ganzhou;

(4) from Ruijin down to Huichang, Junmen, Jiaoba, and Dapu in Guangdong.

Use merchants to help open each route, but also rely on our own hard work to establish them. Based on these routes, attract merchants from White Areas to do business, negotiate with them, or purchase goods at the border, and sign business agreements mutually.

6. In exporting paper, whether through cooperatives or individuals, avoid sending large batches straight to the border without reconnaissance. First, scout whether it is safe. In cities, pose as small traders and never disclose Soviet information. Ideally, draw buyers to the border to purchase. Exchanging paper for cash or goods is the safest option. Exercise extreme caution when transporting paper out; never act recklessly, to avoid confiscation.

7. Since paper export work is of great importance, each county shall assign two cadres to handle and carry out this task.

8. Upon receiving this notice, all levels of the union must discuss its decisions and make concrete arrangements.

Printed on June 30[245]

The directive laid out a detailed plan to address the pressing challenges of paper exports. It called for strict measures to prevent paper firm owners from engaging in speculation, shirking work, shutting down operations, or fleeing. It urged the expansion of sales channels for local paper, pushing exports toward border areas and attracting merchants from the "White Areas" to engage in trade or purchase directly at the frontier under mutually agreed business contracts.

In order to secure supplies for the revolutionary war and improve the livelihood of the Soviet-area populace, Mao Zedong called for an immediate economic mobilization—launching all feasible and necessary construction projects on the economic front. On August 26, 1932, *Order No. 20 of the Council of People's Commissars of the Provisional Central Government of the Chinese Soviet Republic*, issued in the name of Chairman Mao Zedong and Vice-Chairmen Xiang Ying and Zhang Guotao, stipulated that all agricultural products from the Soviet Area—including local paper—sold in White Areas would be subject to a 50% tax reduction. In February 1933, the Central Committee of the Communist Party of China established a Bureau of Foreign Trade under the People's Committee for National Economy, directing counties to develop public-sector commerce, which included

---

245 "Notice from the Min–Gan Paper Workers' Union—On the Issue of Paper Transportation and Export," in CPC Ninghua County Committee Party History Office (ed.), *Collected Historical Materials on the Revolutionary Struggle in Ninghua County*, Vol. 2, 1962, pp. 67–68.

promoting paper production and creating export routes.[246] In Changting County, the China Paper Company was formed[247], forming a distribution model centered on the paper company, supplemented by cooperatives and paper merchants. Through armed communication networks in western Fujian,[248] the company liaised with merchants in the White Areas to coordinate shipments. In the Changting region, the process generally followed this pattern: the China Paper Company advanced production funds to paper workshop owners to secure orders; part of the collected paper was allocated to printing houses for revolutionary books and publicity materials, while the rest broke through the Kuomintang blockade to be sold in areas like Chaoshan and Guangzhou.[249]

By June 1933, paper production across much of western Fujian had made a remarkable recovery. According to *Red China* (June 11, 1933), Tingzhou had restored over 40 paper cooperatives and private paper workshops, producing on average 1.33 tons of maobian paper per day. With a market price of 2.5 yuan per *dao*, the daily output value reached 715 yuan.

---

246 Fu Rutong, "Overview of Commerce in Tingzhou in the Soviet Areas," in *Changting Historical and Cultural Materials*, Vol. 10, 1986, p. 23.

247 China Paper Company, formed in 1933 during the Soviet period in Changting as the first industrial–commercial paper–trading institution, organizing production and sales for all paper cooperatives and handmade paper workshops in the county, see Huang Majin, (chief ed.), *A History of Papermaking in Changting*, China Light Industry Press, 1992, p. 58. After the Red Army's Long March in 1934, the China Paper Company was taken over by the Kuomintang government and, following the resolution passed at the third provisional meeting of the Rehabilitation Committee, a state-owned paper manufacturing company was established, see "Overview of Papermaking in Changting," *Shen Bao*, February 8, 1935, p. 16.

248 The Armed News Agency, founded in 1930, was responsible for underground communication and also tasked with protecting the transportation of materials. It leveraged various connections to make contact with shop owners in the White Areas, using them to procure supplies through covert means and smuggle them into the Soviet Area. This played a significant role in the struggle to break the Kuomintang's economic blockade. See Kong Yongsong & Qiu Songqing, *Economic Construction in the Western Fujian Revolutionary Base Area*, Fujian People's Publishing House, 1981, p. 58.

249 Lai Luan, "Summary of Industry and Commerce Administration in Changting during the Central Soviet Period," in *Changting Historical and Cultural Materials*, Vol. 18, 1990, p. 29.

The paper, famed for its quality, was shipped to Guangzhou, Shanghai, Shantou, and beyond. The Fujian Provincial Committee of the Communist Party reported that "paper production in Changting has recovered by two-thirds."[250] In August 1933, the same committee noted that the largest industry in western Fujian—papermaking—had been brought nearly to a standstill under the enemy's tight economic blockade. Yet, since August of that year, through the steadfast struggle of paper workers and the leadership of the Party, government, and workers' unions, more than 90 workshops had resumed operations, and paper prices had doubled.[251] By late 1934, however, with the Red Army's main forces withdrawing from the Central Soviet Area, Changting fell back under Kuomintang control. The assets of the China Paper Company in Changting were confiscated. Although detailed company accounts were lost, surviving invoices from subordinate paper workshops indicate the firm had once held over 100,000 yuan in capital and produced more than 20,000 *dan* of paper[252]—evidence of the considerable scale of the Soviet area's paper industry.

Under the Soviet government's new economic policies, and with the active involvement of the All-China Federation of Trade Unions, the Changning District Trade Union, and the Minguang Paper Workers' Union, papermakers in the mountains of western Fujian made full use of their abundant bamboo resources. They produced bamboo paper, sold it beyond the Soviet borders, raised local incomes, and strengthened the Soviet area's economic base. Surveys from the time reveal the dramatic improvements: before the revolution, paper workers earned at most 10 yuan a month; dur-

---

250 *Red China*, Issue No. 84, June 11, 1933, p. 7; Huang Majin, (chief ed.), *A History of Papermaking in Changting*, China Light Industry Press, 1992, pp. 37, 41.
251 "Competition Agreements at the Economic Construction Conference of Seventeen Counties in the Southern Central Soviet Area (August 15, 1933)," in *Selected Historical Materials on the Economy of Revolutionary Base Areas*, Vol. 1, Jiangxi People's Publishing House, 1986, pp. 145–150.
252 "Overview of Papermaking in Changting," *Shen Bao*, February 8, 1935, p. 16.

ing the Soviet period, the highest wage reached 35 yuan. The lowest wage, once only 3 yuan, rose to 31 yuan.[253]

4.2.3.   The Expansion of the Red Army in Western Fujian and the Participation of Papermakers in the Revolution

On October 18, 1933, the Central Government of the Soviet Area issued an *Urgent Mobilization Order to Smash the Fifth Encirclement and Suppression Campaign*, calling on the masses in the Soviet Area to join the Red Army. In late October, the Third Congress of the Fujian Provincial Party Committee and the Congress of the Provincial Soviet were both convened in Changting. These meetings implemented the central mobilization order, requiring all levels of government to meet the goal of expanding the Red Army by 10,000 soldiers before the convening of The Second National Soviet Congress of the Chinese Soviet Republic in Fujian. Citizens aged 18 to 40 were to be mobilized into the Red Guards, while ordinary workers and peasants were encouraged to join the Young Pioneers and other mass organizations. In December 1933, the Central Military Commission launched a new campaign across the Soviet Area to recruit an additional 25,000 fighters.[254] *Red China* reported repeatedly on the fervor: "Local armed units from Ninghua, Shanghang, and Xinquan joined the Red Army en masse"; "The entire branch of the Farm Laborers' Union in Wukeng Township enlisted"; "A new Western Fujian regiment was created."[255] These dispatches captured the momentum of the time, as peasants and workers poured into the revolutionary ranks. In Changting County alone, from January to April 1934, 3,214 people joined—far exceeding the Military Commission's target of 864—making it "the leading county in Fujian

---

253 Huang Majin, (chief ed.), *A History of Papermaking in Changting*, China Light Industry Press, 1992, p. 40.
254 Tang Jiaqing, "The Revolutionary Struggle in Western Fujian Before and After the Long March of the Red Army and Its Historical Contribution," *Party History Data and Research*, June 1986.
255 *Red China*, Issue No. 84, June 11, 1933, p. 7.

for Red Army recruitment."[256] The Party in western Fujian pursued the expansion drive with deliberate organization. Through meetings and publicity tours, cadres fanned out into the districts, strengthened political and military training for model Young Pioneer battalions, and implemented policies to care for Red Army families. The results were particularly striking in areas like Ninghua, where recruitment exceeded all expectations.

The main targets for reorganization in this expansion were local armed forces. In Changning District, for example, one of the greatest threats to the papermaking industry was the scourge of bandit roadblocks. The Party had repeatedly organized anti-bandit campaigns and helped form workers' guerrilla units to escort shipments of handmade paper. Around 1930, under the leadership of local Party representative Zeng Yigang[257] and with Red Army support, each paper workshop in the village of Tianshe contributed one or two strong men to form a factory defense unit, totaling nearly 50 members. Yet, because Tianshe's natural villages were scattered among the hills and lacked unity, the unit still struggled to repel raids.[258] In the spring of 1931, the 36th Regiment of the Red Fourth Army was dispatched to Changning to assist. Their first move was to organize a 78-member Fujian–Jiangxi Papermakers' Guerrilla Unit in Tianshe. According to exhibits at the former site of the Minguang Paper Workers' Union in Changning, in late October

---

256 Tang Jiaqing, "The Revolutionary Struggle in Western Fujian Before and After the Long March of the Red Army and Its Historical Contribution," *Party History Data and Research*, June 1986.

257 Based on the oral account of Zeng Youchun and the stub of the Martyr Certificate: Zeng Yigang, born in 1908 in Tianshe, was mobilized to join the Red Army and the revolution in 1931, serving as Party representative of Tianshe. In 1932, he became secretary of the Tingdong County Paper Workers' Union. In December 1933, he served as chief of the Changting Military Section and concurrently as retreat commissioner. He was killed in action while dismantling the Taiping Bridge in Changting to prevent the Kuomintang from entering the city. In the same battle, Zeng Congtai survived and was later commended by the government in 1985. Zeng Laorong, captain of the Tianshe guerrilla detachment, was his comrade-in-arms. Oral history given by Zeng Youchun of Tianshe Village, Zhiping She Ethnic Township, on February 27, 2022.

258 Oral history given by Zeng Youchun of Tianshe Village, Zhiping She Ethnic Township, on February 27, 2022.

and early November 1933, papermakers and peasants from the district gathered in Zhiping to form the Minguang Papermakers' Guerrilla Unit. Its ranks soon swelled to 486 members, who were later absorbed into the Red Army and placed under the Ning–Qing–Gui (Ninghua, Qingliu, Guihua) Military Subdistrict Command. The local people contributed not just manpower but also resources—"a thousand *dan* of paper and ten thousand *dan* of grain"—to the revolutionary cause, earning western Fujian the nickname "the Ukraine of the Red Soviet Area."

The Communist Party of China's anti-bandit campaigns played a vital role in keeping the paper industry running smoothly and also shaped paper workers' perceptions of the Party. According to the oral account of Zeng Xueqin[259], then head of the Minguang Paper Workers' Union in Changning District, a workers' guerrilla unit was first formed in the Zhiping area in the third lunar month of 1931. It numbered 80 to 90 members, led by Zeng Huomu with Zeng Xueqin as political instructor. The unit operated in such places as Guanqian, Zhushouli, Nancaikeng, and Litian. It was organized into three platoons, commanded respectively by Lian Jiayi of Pingpu, Lai Qingxiu of Chengongkeng, and Zeng Lisheng of Fukeng. By July that year, however, the unit was disbanded, and its members returned to papermaking. Zhiping organized another Minguang Papermakers' Guerrilla Unit in 1933, this time under the command of Lei Ximei from Zuokeng, with Chi Baolin of Gaodi as political instructor. Later, a larger guerrilla battalion was established in Xiaping, led by Lai (full name unknown) with Zhong Shenmin as political instructor. According to the recollections of Zeng Youchun, the Minguang Papermakers' Guerrilla Unit eventually had four detachments. The first, led by Zeng Zhongfu, operated in Sheli of Tianshe and Huangzhujie area. The second, commanded by Zeng Zhaohong, was active in

---

259 Party History Working Committee of the Ninghua County CPC Committee, *Ninghua Party History Materials*, Vol. 9, 1988, p. 118.

Huangnitian, Qiji, Rongkeng, and Laiwukeng. The third, under Zeng Wei-cun—grandfather of Zeng Youchun—worked in Jizhuawo, Beikeng, Yegongling, and Chuandong. The fourth, led by Zeng Zhihua, operated around Guangliang. When the Western Fujian Soviet mobilized for Red Army expansion, 48 of the 78 members of the Minguang Papermakers' Guerrilla Unit set out for Caoxieling in Datong, Changting County, to join the Red Army and undergo reorganization. Along the way, Zeng Congshi joined them temporarily and enlisted alongside them.

(Pic79 Revolutionary Martyr Certificate of Liao Chugu from Yuankeng, Hubeijiao Village

Liao Chugu, born in 1889, was a soldier of the 8th Red Army Corps. He joined the revolution in 1933 and sacrificed his life in 1934 while fighting against the enemy in Taihe County, Jiangxi.)

(Pic80 Revolutionary Martyr Certificate of Zeng Yigang from Tianshe Village

Zeng Yigang, born in 1908, joined the revolution in 1931. He served as Secretary of the Tingdong County Paper Workers' Union and was killed by the enemy in December 1933 while dismantle   Changting's Taiping Bridge to block the enemy's entry into the city.)

(Pic81 Revolutionary Martyr Certificate of Deng Xuanzhong from Dengwu Village

Deng Xuanzhong, born in 1890, joined the revolution in 1933. He served as Chairman of the Changning District Soviet and was arrested by the enemy in 1934, then killed in Qingliu County.)

After the Central Red Army embarked on the Long March in October 1934, the Kuomintang regained control of western Fujian and unleashed harsh reprisals. Zhiping Township had originally comprised 29 natural villages; before 1949, only 22 remained. Seven villages were wiped out entirely, and in only three of them retain a few households.[260] Nearly all houses in the destroyed villages were burned to the ground. Even by 1938, a quarter of the population still lived in thatched huts or shacks.[261] Many Soviet cadres were arrested and executed, including Chi Jiusheng, deputy county magistrate of Tingdong; Zeng Yigang, secretary of the Tingdong Papermakers' Union; Deng Xuanzhong, chairman of the Changning Soviet; Liao Zilong, land minister; Deng Minghua, judicial minister; and Zeng

---

260 See *Investigation Report on the Old Revolutionary Base Area of Zhiping Township*, provided by Lei Nianfu.
261 *Summary Report on Old Base Area Work in the Seventh District of Ninghua County* (April 2, 1953), Ninghua County Archives, Archive No. 0057–003–0031–0001.

Zhongfu, chairman of the Tianshe Soviet.[262] According to the family of Deng Xuanzhong, he had become chairman of the Changning Soviet in 1933, was captured by the Kuomintang in 1934, and executed in Qingliu.[263] Zeng Qinyuan, son of Zeng Yigang, recalled that his father had joined the Red Army in 1931 as Party representative for Tianshe, later becoming secretary of the Tingdong Paper Workers' Union in 1932. In December 1933, he served as head of the Military Section in Changting and as evacuation commissioner. He died heroically while demolishing the Daping Bridge in Changting to block the Kuomintang army from entering the city.[264]

During the Soviet period, more than 600 people from Changning District enlisted and fought; Zhiping alone recorded 170 martyrs,[265] most of them unnamed.[266] Over 200 papermakers from the district joined the Third, Fifth, Eighth, and Ninth Red Corps, the Fourth and Twelfth Armies, the Thirteenth Division, the Nanfeng–Guangchang–Jianning Independent Regiment, and the Young Communist International Division. In the history of China's paper industry, the sacrifices of these western Fujian papermakers during the Soviet era stand as a chapter written in blood and courage.[267]

4.3. The Failure of Control

In 1934, the Kuomintang returned to Fujian. With the Red Army embarking on the Long March, western Fujian once again fell under the au-

---

262 *Survey of Old Revolutionary Cadres in Zhiping District, Ninghua County During the Land Revolution* (December 22, 1956), Ninghua County Archives, Archive No. 6–9–19–148.
263 Oral history given by the grandson and great-grandson of Deng Xuanzhong of Dengwu Village, Zhiping She Ethnic Township, on February 27, 2022.
264 Oral history given by Zeng Qinyuan in Tianshe Village, Zhiping She Ethnic Township, on February 27, 2022.
265 All-China Federation of Trade Unions, "Investigation of the Changning District Paper Workers' Union", *Ninghua Literature and History Materials*, Vol. 5, 1985, p. 41.
266 Oral history given by Zeng Youchun in Tianshe Village, Zhiping She Ethnic Township, on February 27, 2022.
267 All-China Federation of Trade Unions, "Investigation of the Changning District Paper Workers' Union", *Ninghua Literature and History Materials*, Vol. 5, 1985, p. 41.

thority of the Nationalist government. The new rulers sought to use administrative power to promote a cooperative system, aiming to bring the rural economy of Western Fujian—centered on Changting—firmly under state control, with particular attention to its pillar industry: papermaking. Merchants who had fled during the Soviet period now returned to Changting, eager to restore the old commercial order in the paper trade. Yet they soon found themselves constrained by the wartime economic regime imposed by the Nationalist government—a system of economic regulation mediated through trade guilds in every sector. In the 1930s and 1940s, the handmade paper industry of western Fujian faced a dual crisis: the disruptions of wartime conditions and fierce market competition from imported machine-made paper. How to break free from such dire straits became a question of real urgency.

4.3.1.   From Papermaking Cooperatives to the Collapse of Control

After taking over the papermaking regions of western Fujian, the Paper Workers' Union conducted a survey of Changting's 1935 paper output. The figures were stark: sales totaled only around 400,000 yuan—a drop of four-fifths compared to earlier years. The blow was felt across local commerce and industry, and the livelihoods of papermakers grew increasingly precarious.[268] To quickly revive paper production, the Nationalist government continued to use the *Cooperative Law* issued in 1927, promoting paper production cooperative organizations and planning to assist paper workshop owners in restarting operations through loans.

In October 1935, the Fujian Provincial Rural Cooperative Committee established a Cooperative Instructor's Office in Changting County, tasked specifically with organizing cooperatives and handling papermaking loans.

---

268 "Key Points of the Changting Paper Industry Reform," *Women and Domestic Products* (Fuzhou), 1936, Vol. 2, No. 4.

By spring 1936, Qin Zhenfu, commissioner of the Seventh Administrative Inspection District of Fujian and concurrently county magistrate of Changting, traveled to the provincial capital to petition Governor Chen Yi and the Rural Cooperative Committee. He proposed securing a loan of 100,000 yuan from the Farmers' Bank of China, to be managed for the county government by a Paper Industry Cooperative Committee in collaboration with the Changting office of the Rural Cooperative Committee. This fund would be distributed to papermaking credit cooperatives in the major production areas. Loans would go directly to individual workshops as working capital to resume production,[269] with interest set at 0.8% per month. A Paper Industry Maintenance Committee—composed of respected local figures and representatives from relevant agencies—would oversee the loan distribution. Subsequently, Changting's cooperative instructors traveled to rural areas to organize paper industry credit cooperatives. By March 10, 1936, the Cooperative Instructor's Office had organized 33 papermaking credit cooperatives with 501 members, collectively pledging 15,587 *dan* of paper as collateral for the full 100,000 yuan in loans. The northeast of Changting dominated in numbers, accounting for 20 cooperatives, 6,771 *dan* of planned paper output, and 44,566 yuan in loans. This region dominated due to its high paper production and superior quality, unmatched by other areas. As part of the arrangement, each pledged *dan* of paper immediately earned an advance of 2 yuan to cover lime purchases. The remainder of the loan was disbursed in stages—once in April for bamboo cutting, and again in July when papermaking began in earnest to ensure that workshops could sustain production through the season.[270]

---

269 "Turning Point of the Changting Paper Industry in Fujian," *Monthly Bulletin of the Ministry of Industry and Commerce* (Nanjing), 1936, Vol. 1, No. 9; "Supporting the Changting Paper Industry," *Fujian County Administration*, 1937, Vol. 2, No. 3.
Also refer to Yu Ruxian, *A Study of Rural Informal Lending in Western Fujian from the Qing to the Republican Era*, Tianjin Ancient Books Publishing House, 2010, p. 168.
270 "Key Points of the Changting Paper Industry Reform," *Women and Domestic*

After some time, the provincial government instructed the committee to send inspectors to western Fujian to review the progress of the papermaking credit cooperatives. In the northeastern part of Changting, the cooperative movement in the villages was already complete, with a considerable number of cooperatives in operation. The inspectors were impressed not only by the solid, honest character of the rural population but also by the diligence of the women engaged in labor. Most members, however, voiced two grievances. First, while the bank's loan carried a monthly interest rate of only 0.8%, the Paper Industry Maintenance Committee had added a surcharge of 0.7%, bringing the total to 1.5% per month. Many members felt this was excessive and asked that 0.2% be reserved as a cooperative fund. Second, they complained that paper prices had fallen too low, while workers' wages in papermaking remained based on old rates—or were sometimes entirely without standard—causing significant losses for the workshop owners. The inspectors accepted both points as reasonable and promised to seek remedies. On the interest issue, they gave a preliminary explanation: since the loans were guaranteed by the county government, the county had established the Paper Industry Maintenance Committee to ensure that the funds were issued safely. The committee's role was to verify the creditworthiness of members and to monitor the use of the loan funds. Maintaining this oversight required over 300 yuan per month—around 4,000 yuan per year—hence the additional interest.[271]

The Paper Industry Maintenance Committee itself had been created by the Changting county government as part of an effort to rescue the local paper industry, working in coordination with the county chamber of commerce. In reality, however, it was dominated by paper merchants who had returned to Changting after the Red Army's Long March. In 1936, follow-

---

Products (Fuzhou), 1936, Vol. 2, No. 4.
271 "Key Points of the Changting Paper Industry Reform," *Women and Domestic Products* (Fuzhou), 1936, Vol. 2, No. 4.

ing the disbursement of the 100,000 yuan loan, the Rural Cooperative Committee reclaimed the funds, leaving the county's paper industry once again in difficulty. At the end of that year, Lu Zelin, chairman of the county chamber of commerce, negotiated with the committee for a renewal of the loan. After investigation, the committee agreed that an extension was necessary and arranged for the Farmers' Bank of China and the Provincial Bank to issue a joint loan. In 1937, the two banks agreed to provide 150,000 yuan—100,000 from the Farmers' Bank and 50,000 from the Provincial Bank—to be released in four installments. The loans would again be guaranteed by the Paper Industry Maintenance Committee and the county chamber of commerce. Interest remained at the original 0.8% per month, and the lending procedures followed the same pattern: loan contracts were signed between the Rural Cooperative Committee's county offices and the borrowers, submitted to the committee for approval, and then forwarded to the banks for fund allocation.[272]

An article in *Weili* magazine, titled "An Overview of Changting's Papermaking Industry," drew on information provided by the Paper Industry Maintenance Committee, County Chamber of Commerce Chairman Lu Zelin, and Paper Workers' Union leader Zhang Yangjing. The article concluded that the Maintenance Committee had been a powerful force in supporting the industry's revival. Thanks to its establishment, papermaking households no longer had to borrow from private paper merchants—who would often require exclusive rights to all their paper output. Instead, they could access government-backed loans and sell freely to customers of their choosing, thereby securing better prices. Under such conditions, the article asserted, the revival of Changting's papermaking was all but assured. It noted that the industry's peak had been in the 17th year of Republican era

---

272 "Relief for the Changting Paper Industry," *Fujian County Administration*, 1937, Vol. 2, No. 4.

(1928), when annual production exceeded 100,000 *dan*, with a total value of two to three million yuan. While far from that height, statistics from the Changting Paper Workers' Union showed a rising trend between 1936 and 1938: 36,600 dan in 1936, 40,180 dan in 1937, and 12,503 dan in the first four and a half months of 1938.[273] From this, the article argued, it was clear that the Maintenance Committee's early work in organizing credit cooperatives had been necessary, and that government loans had played a positive role in jumpstarting the industry.

In 1938, investigator Lin Zhaohe also reported optimistic findings. He observed that after order was restored in Changting, annual paper output reached about 25,000 *tiao*—roughly 75% of production in the prosperous early Republican era. Once the Cooperative Instructor's Office of the Paper Industry in Changting was set up and 150,000 yuan was loaned to local papermakers, output quickly doubled to over 50,000 *tiao*. By 1937, loan amounts had risen further, from 150,000 to 180,000 yuan. Given these figures, Lin expressed strong confidence in the industry's future: paper output would surely continue to grow, and most of the papermakers' economic hardships had been eased. "The outlook for the industry," he wrote, "is indeed most promising."[274]

Yet by 1941—just five years after the county government had launched its loan guarantee and cooperative program—the optimism of 1938 had given way to sharp decline. Xie Shenchu, a professor from Xiamen University who had relocated to Changting during the war, conducted a meticulous study of papermaking cooperatives and loan records over the five-year period. He compiled his findings into the following table:

---

273 Shen Zuxin, "An Overview of Changting's Papermaking Industry," *Weili*, 1938, No. 10.
274 Lin Zhaohe, "An Overview of the Handmade Paper Industry in Fujian and Its Ongoing Improvements". *Construction Weekly*, Vol. 7, No. 6, 1938.

Table 5 1935–1940 Paper Industry Cooperatives and Loan Conditions in Changting

Year	Number of Cooperatives	Number of Members	Number of Shares	Total Share Capital (Yuan)	Paper Delivered (*dan*)	Loan per *dan* (Yuan)	Total Loans (Yuan)
1935	27	430	1,250	2,500	—	—	—
1936	51	727	2,626	5,250	over 9,000	8	over 73,000
1937	46	779	2,947	5,294	over 8,000	8	over 68,000
1938	46	779	2,647	5,294	over 21,000	8	over 170,000
1939	48	802	2,698	5,396	15,000	12	over 190,000
1940	67	1,005	4,104	9,500	over 7,000	17	over 130,000

(Original table note: In 1940, 19 new paper production and marketing cooperatives were established, but all were reorganized from existing paper credit cooperatives. Therefore, the membership and share capital figures are duplicated, and in reality there was no substantial increase. For convenience, these were not deducted here.)

Source: Xie Shenchu, "A Study on the Papermaking Industry in Changting," *Journal of Economic and Commercial Studies* (Xiamen), No. 1, 1941 pp. 73–74.

According to the table notes and annotations, the paper industry cooperatives were newly established in 1935, and no loans had been issued at that time. In 1937, a re-registration process took place, during which 12 cooperatives were dissolved and 7 new ones formed, reducing the total number from 51 to 46. However, the actual membership remained largely unchanged. By 1940, although it appeared that 19 new paper cooperatives had been founded, these were in fact reorganizations of the existing paper credit cooperatives. Therefore, from 1936 onwards, both the number of cooperatives and their membership remained relatively stable. Examining the share capital reveals a steady increase in both the number of shares and total capital. Generally, each share was valued at 2 yuan per year. However, in 1937, the unit share price dipped below 2 yuan, only to rise sharply by 15% in 1940. Looking at the amount of paper delivered (measured in *dan*), production by the cooperatives peaked in 1938, then plunged by 53% in 1939, and dropped even more drastically in 1940. Despite the steep decline in output, the loan amount per *dan* of paper increased rapidly in 1939 and 1940, causing the total loans for those years to soar and placing heavy financial pressure on the borrowers.

In 1941, Xie Shenchu observed that the cooperative movement was facing a bleak future. Through oral interviews with paper workers, he learned that from the very beginning, the cooperatives had been undermined by the Paper Industry Maintenance Committee, which was controlled by paper merchants. This committee monopolized loan disbursements and engaged in corrupt practices, rendering the cooperatives' administration and regulations powerless. By 1938, the Maintenance Committee was dissolved, and loan management was transferred to the borrower-organized Changting County Cooperative Joint Office, gradually eliminating the deep-rooted problems. That year, a surge in production reflected a renewed enthusiasm. Nevertheless, Xie Shenchu remained deeply concerned about the cooperatives' prospects. He summarized seven major reasons for their troubled future, based on his field research:

1. Influenced by the Maintenance Committee, many borrowers were suspicious and fearful of the cooperatives, some even mistaking them for mere loan associations, preventing the development of genuine trust.

2. A number of paper merchants and local tyrants were either infiltrated the cooperatives or sabotaged them from the outside, hypocritically complying while pursuing selfish interests.

3. Loan administration was inconsistent. For example, in that year, the Provincial Trade Company independently issued loans amounting to 200,000 yuan without charging interest and with minimal procedures—only requiring purchasing rights as collateral. Many borrowers were thus lured by this convenience. However, once the company gained the purchasing rights, it arbitrarily suppressed paper prices, causing borrowers losses even heavier than interest payments, thereby shaking their faith in cooperatives and government loans.

4. Borrowers lived deep in the mountains with scattered households, making geographical gatherings difficult and hampering cooperative business activities.

5. Cooperatives required a multitude of forms and records, and loan procedures were cumbersome. Many borrowers were illiterate, which bred feelings of fear and aversion.

6. The government deducted share capital repeatedly, and paper workshop owners fell into many misunderstandings, confusing "borrowing money" with "depositing money."

7. The loan disbursement process was excessively slow and often lost its timeliness, forcing borrowers to turn to paper merchants for high-interest loans, thus eroding their confidence in the cooperatives.[275]

In 1941, the Changting County Cooperative Joint Office was reorganized into the Changting Industrial Cooperative Federation, legally formed by the various paper-making cooperatives under the Rural Cooperative. Wang Wenming served as its first chairman, overseeing the prima-

---

275 Xie Shenchu, "A Study on the Papermaking Industry in Changting," *Journal of Economic and Commercial Studies* (Xiamen), No. 1, 1941.

ry-level cooperatives engaged in the production and marketing of handmade paper. That year, the number of paper-production cooperatives—composed entirely of paper workshop owners—declined to 49, with 601 members (representing 601 workshops) and a total share capital of 4,778 yuan in legal currency.[276] Although these paper cooperatives, led by the Rural Cooperative, were composed solely of workshop owners, they functioned in practice as loose alliances. Once loans were disbursed, each member simply used the funds for his own purposes, hired laborers, and ran production independently. There was no pooling of welfare benefits or collective accumulation of capital. After the victory of the War of Resistance against Japanese Aggression, inflation eroded the value of currency, the loans lost much of their usefulness, and the cooperatives gradually disintegrated. By 1948, the Federation existed in name only.[277]

In retrospect, the implementation of the cooperative policy—together with the establishment of the Paper Industry Maintenance Association—did provide tangible support to the recovery of Changting's paper industry between 1936 and 1938. Yet the old problems were never fully resolved. In December 1941, after consultations with the Fujian Provincial Bank, the Changting County Government established a Preparatory Office for a County Cooperative Treasury, with supplementary investment from the Provincial Bank, in an effort to sustain the industry's revival.[278] However, inflation soon intensified. Commercial profits dwindled by the day. Investment from the Provincial Trading Company, the rural and industrial cooperatives, and paper merchants steadily dried up. The downturn in the local

---

276 *Chorography of Changting County* (Republican era), Vol. 18 "Industry Records," Shanghai Bookstore Publishing House, 2000, p. 539.
277 Huang Majin, (chief ed.), *A History of Papermaking in Changting*, China Light Industry Press, 1992, pp. 44-45.
278 Xie Shenchu, "A Study on the Papermaking Industry in Changting," *Journal of Economic and Commercial Studies* (Xiamen), No. 1, 1941.

economy was by then irreversible, and no single institution or policy—least of all a cooperative treasury—could halt the decline.[279]

In an attempt to reverse this trend, the Fujian provincial government issued a set of paper trade control regulations in June 1940. The main provisions were as follows:

1. Establish purchasing offices and export offices in paper-producing areas and provincial transport hubs to regulate all transactions in handmade paper.

2. Purchasing offices would operate on a joint public–private basis, including the Provincial Trading Company and local paper merchants' cooperatives, whereas export offices would be fully state-run, barring direct participation by merchant cooperatives.

3. Purchasing offices would buy paper from workshop owners at 50 percent above the highest price in the 28th year of Republican era (1939), take an 8 percent fixed profit margin, and then deliver the goods to export depots for onward shipment.

4. Half of the stations' surplus would go to reserve funds and staff bonuses, with the remaining half distributed to members according to their share capital.[280]

---

279 Huang Majin, (chief ed.), *A History of Papermaking in Changting*, China Light Industry Press, 1992, pp. 52-53. Many paper workshop owners went bankrupt due to inflation. For example, Yang Xizhen of Ninghua County, whose livelihood was papermaking, had long relied on government loans to resume production each year. In 1939, deceived and manipulated by paper merchants from Jiangxi and others, he signed a loan contract agreeing to sell paper at low prices (just over 10 to 20 yuan per *dan*). Unexpectedly, beginning that winter, prices soared and wages rose sharply: producing a *dan* (ten *dao*) of paper, which had previously required five to six yuan in wages and food, now cost more than 20 yuan. Unable to fulfill the contract, Yang requested that the merchants subsidize wages and food, but they ignored him. Consequently, in 1940 Yang and others petitioned the government to mediate. See Yu Ruxian, *A Study of Rural Informal Lending in Western Fujian from the Qing to the Republican Era*, Tianjin Ancient Books Publishing House, 2010, pp. 171–172.

These measures provoked fierce resistance from the merchants. They repeatedly sent representatives to petition the provincial government for the policy's repeal, and in protest, they suspended loans to workshop owners and halted paper purchases—pressuring the workshop owners themselves to oppose the regulations. Within three months, the government was forced to rescind the policy, restoring free trade and transport in the paper industry. Yet the repeal came with a price. The government seized the opportunity to impose heavier levies on producers and traders within the province. An export license for each *zhi* of paper (about 200 *dao*) now cost 80 yuan, with 48 yuan in workshop owners' contributions deducted by the merchants, a special business tax of 14.4 yuan, a 20-yuan contribution to the Paper Workers' Union, and additional local security fees and taxes. The burden on both workshop owners and merchants was substantial, and much of the merchants' cost was inevitably passed down to the workshop owners and paper workers.[281] The Nationalist government's ever-changing systems and policies—ranging from cooperatives and loan programs to trade control schemes and layered taxes—did, on occasion, provide a short-lived boost to production enthusiasm. But in the long run, the impact was more damaging than beneficial. By the time the Nationalist government collapsed, the long-hoped-for recovery of the paper industry had never materialized.

4.3.2. Internal Divisions among Paper Merchants and the Failure of Controls

In Changting County, the paper merchants possessed considerable wealth and influence within both the local business community and society at large. They not only took part in organizing the Paper Industry Maintenance Committee and assisting the county government in implementing its

---

280 Xie Shenchu, "A Study on the Papermaking Industry in Changting," *Journal of Economic and Commercial Studies* (Xiamen), No. 1, 1941.
281 Xie Shenchu, "A Study on the Papermaking Industry in Changting," *Journal of Economic and Commercial Studies* (Xiamen), No. 1, 1941.

paper-production cooperative program, but also employed various tactics that ultimately frustrated the Nationalist government's paper industry control policies ineffectual. The commercial elite of Changting had long traditions of organized activity. As early as 1907, during the 33rd year of the Guangxu era, local merchants from various trades jointly founded the Tingzhou Chamber of Commerce. 16 directors were elected, with Zheng Keming[282] chosen as director-general, and the headquarters located in the Ruyi Palace. Among its members, the paper merchants held a dominant position.[283] In 1915, the Tingzhou Chamber was renamed the Changting County Chamber of Commerce, the title of director-general changed to president, and its headquarters moved to the former site of the prefectural school. The chamber ceased operation in 1929 after the Communist Party of China entered Changting.[284]

The Changting County Paper Industry Trade Guild was established on February 27, 1935, with its first headquarters in the Xianyin Temple. Zhang Yangjing, a key figure in the county's commercial circles, served as its inaugural chairman, followed by figures such as Lu Zelin and Zeng Yulin.[285]

---

282 Zheng Keming, a native of Changting, obtained the title of *Jinshi* (the highest and final degree in the imperial examination in Imperial China) in the 15th year of the Guangxu era, Qing dynasty (1889) and rose to the position of *Neige Zhongshu* (secretary in the Grand Secretariat). "A man of profound learning, admired by the scholarly community," he was, during the Republic era, superintendent of Tingzhou Middle School and head of the Tingzhou branch of the Bureau of Commerce. See *Chorography of Changting County* (Republican era), Vol. 14, "Elections," p. 481.
283 *Chorography of Changting County* (Republican era), Vol. 18 "Industry Records," Shanghai Bookstore Publishing House, 2000, p. 539.
284 *Chorography of Changting County* (Republican era), Vol. 18 "Industry Records," Shanghai Bookstore Publishing House, 2000, p. 539.
285 In October 1939, the Changting County Paper Industry Trade Guild was ordered to reorganize under the new law. 15 executive committee members and seven supervisory committee members were elected, with Lu Zelin chosen as chairman. The guild had 97 members and relocated its headquarters to Yunxiang Pavilion. On October 1, 1941, Zhang Yangjing was re-elected as standing chairman, with 87 member units. On October 2, 1943, Zeng Yulin was elected as director-general, leading 141 member units. On December 28, 1945, Zhang Yangjing was again elected as director-general, with 128 member units. In 1948, Zheng Diqun served as director-general, but on September 10, 1948, Zeng Yulin was re-elected to the post. By 1949, the guild had 126 members and 12 staff.

The following month, on April 2, 1935, the county Chamber of Commerce was reestablished under Zhang's initiative, with its headquarters moving between the Ruyi Palace and the Yunxiang Pavilion. Membership reached 138, and Lu Zelin was elected as the chamber's leader.

In practice, the Paper Industry Trade Guild wielded the greatest influence among the various guilds and urban associations in Changting. Its first chairman, Zhang Yangjing, was a merchant who had returned to Changting after the Red Army's northward march. He founded the Xinting Printing Bureau, invested in the paper trade, and was appointed president of the Changting County Chamber of Commerce by Lin Sixian, the county's Nationalist administrative inspector.[286] The second chairman, Lu Zelin, was a local warlord who co-founded the Tingzhou Electric Company with fellow military leader Guo Fengming. He also served as director of the county relief institute, head of the Chamber of Commerce, and president of the Paper Industry Trade Guild.[287] Lu's successor, Zeng Yulin, was a powerful local gentry figure. He held the presidency of the Chamber of Commerce, chaired the paper guild, and served as county assembly president, exerting considerable influence in both political and commercial affairs.[288] From the backgrounds of these three men, it is clear that the chairmanship of the Paper Industry Trade Guild also served as presidents of the Changting County Chamber of Commerce. Its leaders were not merely trade representatives but towering figures in Changting's political, military, and commercial spheres.

See *Chorography of Changting County* (Republican era), Vol. 18 "Industry Records," Shanghai Bookstore Publishing House, 2000, p. 539.

286 Lin Sixian, "My Recollections as Administrative Inspector of Changting," in *Selected Historical and Cultural Materials*, Vol. 4, "Politics and Military" Series, Vol. 5, compiled by the Committee on Historical and Cultural Materials of the CPPCC Fujian Provincial Committee, 2006, pp. 264–272.

287 Zhong Min, "A Brief History of the Electric Power Industry in Changting," *Changting Historical and Cultural Materials*, Vol. 12, 1987, pp. 32–33.

288 Mao Xing, "The 'Changting Chaos-Suppression Committee' on the Eve of Liberation," *Changting Historical and Cultural Materials*, Vol. 15, 1989, pp. 58–60.

(Pic82 Present Condition of the Ruyi Palace in Changting County, Photograph by Hu Shiya)

Nor were these three men exceptional cases. In fact, the leading positions in the Changting County Chamber of Commerce and in the 20 trade guilds—including the Paper Industry Trade Guild—were largely held by local warlords and powerful gentry. Before the Red Army's entry into Fujian, these warlords and landed gentry had entrenched themselves across western Fujian as regional separatist forces. When the Red Army arrived, some were eliminated in battle, while others fled the province. Yet by the end of 1934, after the Red Army's northward march, they quickly returned to Tingzhou Prefecture. With Kuomintang support, they reorganized themselves into a network of trade guilds. Correspondence between the Paper Industry Trade Guild and both the Changting County and Fujian provincial governments reveals that these gentry-led associations placed particular emphasis on maintaining close coordination with official bodies.[289] In 1936,

---

289 "Report on the Date of Re-election and Request for an Official to Attend and Su-

recognizing that "the paper industry in recent years has been in steady decline, with inland paper workshops closing down one after another," the Fujian Provincial Department of Finance reduced or exempted certain special business taxes and county surcharges on the paper trade.[290]

The Articles of Association of the Changting County Paper Industry Trade Guild, Fujian Province (hereafter Articles) was a printed, standardized document. The cover required only the insertion of "paper" or the name of another trade; by signing it, the Paper Industry Trade Guild committed itself to operating under its prescribed rules and regulations. The Articles made clear that the guild had the authority to intervene in its members' business activities. Four principal functions were defined:

1. The joint purchase, storage, and transportation of members' goods, along with other necessary facilities.

2. The regulation of members' commercial operations.

3. The guidance, research, investigation, and statistical monitoring of members' businesses.

4. Other activities consistent with the objectives outlined in Article 3. Any project under the first function required a formal plan, approval by at least two-thirds of the guild's committee, and authorization from the com-

---

pervise the Election" (September 22, 1941), Archives of the Paper Trade Guild of Changting County, Archive No. 81–6–704, held in the Changting County Archives, p. 4; "Report on the Results of the Re-election and the Date of Oath-taking of Executive and Supervisory Committee Members for Verification and Record" (October 7, 1941), ibid., p. 5;
"Report on Changes to the Serial Number of the Originally Issued License, the Name of the Party-appointed Supervisor, Whether the Constitution Has Changed After Re-election, Together with Four Copies Each of the Constitution and the List of Officers and Members" (October 19, 1941), ibid., p. 10.
290 "Reduction of Special Business Tax on the Paper Industry," *Statistical Record of Political Achievements Under the Guidance of the Kuomintang*, No. 4, 1936, p. 224.

petent government office before implementation.[291] Furthermore, all paper merchants within Changting County were required to join the guild.

Article 6 stipulated: "Any company, firm, or factory engaged in the paper trade within this district, regardless of whether the business is public or private—except for state enterprises related to national defense or other legally designated state monopolies—must be a member of this guild. The aforesaid members shall appoint representatives to attend the meetings of the guild, to be known as a member representative." Article 12 further declared: "A member may not withdraw from the guild unless relocating to another district, ceasing operations, or receiving a permanent closure order."

The system became even more centralized over time. For example, the Colored Paper Trade Guild of Changting County—originally part of the county chamber—was ordered in November 1939 to "cease independent operations," and in January 1941 its 18 member units were absorbed into the Paper Industry Trade Guild.[292] By October 1942, the guild's president, Zhang Yangjing, went so far as to petition the county government, citing government control policies to demand punishment for non-member merchants. He wrote: "During the emergency period, the measures for compulsory membership in professional organizations and restrictions on withdrawal have long been formulated by the central government, and orders have been issued to counties for implementation, with official records on file. Reports indicate that a few merchants in various districts are still oper-

---

291 *The Articles of Association of the Changting County Paper Industry Trade Guild, Fujian Province* (October 19, 1941), Archives of the Paper Trade Guild of Changting County, Archive No. 81–6–704, held in the Changting County Archives, p. 11.
292 The Coloured Paper Trade Guild of Changting County was founded on February 15, 1935, electing Qiu Yinhe as chairman, with 19 members. On February 6, 1939, Yang Weipan was elected standing committee member, with 15 member units. See Qiu Renyuan, "Overview of Commercial Organizations (Guilds) in Changting County during the Republican Era," *Changting Historical and Cultural Materials*, Vol. 14, 1988, pp. 46–50.

ating shops without completing the required membership procedures, which is wholly improper. In order to strengthen management, henceforth all commercial firms in the province must, as required, join their respective trade guilds. Those failing to comply within the stipulated time may, at the request of the association concerned, be subject to fines or suspension of business by the competent authority."[293]

This makes it clear that the Changting Paper Industry Trade Guild bore a distinctly authoritarian economic character. All paper merchants in the county were compelled to join this single guild and to submit to its interference in their business operations. Such a mandate was bound to provoke resistance. In the county seat, long-established firms with deep roots in the trade—Da Cheng Zhuang, Qun Yi Hao, Sheng Li Hao, Li Tai Sheng, Yong Tai Hao, De He Hao, Jian Cheng Hao, and Yu Sheng Hao—refused to cooperate. The guild's chairman, Zhang Yangjing, sought to bring these merchants into line through pressure from the county government, declaring: "This guild has repeatedly and formally ordered you to enroll as members, yet you have dared to willfully disobey. Such defiance is nothing less than contempt for government decrees. If we do not report this and request an investigation and punishment, future efforts at industry control and price assessment will be seriously obstructed."[294] It was plain that the policy of control did little to foster healthy competition or the free growth of the paper trade. The scheme met with staunch opposition from certain merchants,

---

293 "Petition to Enforce the Order on Paper Merchants Who Have Been Notified Repeatedly but Still Refuse to Join the Guild as Members, Requesting Approval for Investigation and Punishment to Uphold Government Decrees, and Asking for Implementation Instructions," Archives of the Paper Trade Guild of Changting County, Archive No. 81–6–704, held in the Changting County Archives, pp. 38–39.
294 "Petition to Enforce the Order on Paper Merchants Who Have Been Notified Repeatedly but Still Refuse to Join the Guild as Members, Requesting Approval for Investigation and Punishment to Uphold Government Decrees, and Asking for Implementation Instructions," Archives of the Paper Trade Guild of Changting County, Archive No. 81–6–704, held in the Changting County Archives, pp. 41–42.

and by 1942 had still not been fully implemented. In 1943, the guild count-ed 141 members—while the eight original holdouts still refused to join.[295]

4.3.3.   Paper-making Cooperatives in the Industrial Cooperative Movement

When the War of Resistance against Japanese Aggression erupted in full scale in 1937, efforts were made to break the economic blockade im-posed by Japanese forces and implement a plan to establish industrial coop-eratives in China's rear areas. On August 5, 1938, the Chinese Industrial Cooperatives was founded, with Kong Xiangxi as chairman and Soong Mei-ling as honorary chairwoman. The movement's prominent international friend, Rewi Alley, was appointed technical adviser, alongside patriotic democrats and Communist Party members took on roles as council mem-bers. The Industrial Cooperative Movement emerged as a key economic front in the United Front against Japan between the Kuomintang and the Communist Party. Zhou Enlai and Bo Gu personally guided the early or-ganization, making it clear that its aim was to "spur Chiang Kai-shek to fight the war" while "winning as much American and foreign support for the Industrial Cooperatives as possible." They advised that the movement should coordinate with the Nationalist government, yet maintain the ap-pearance of an independent social organization. On May 4, 1939, the Changting Office of the Southeastern District of the Chinese Industrial Co-operatives was formally established.[296] Over the following decade, up until 1949, the Industrial Cooperatives in Changting played an active and con-structive role in the county's industrial production and development.

---

295 *The Membership List of Paper Industry Trade Guild, Changting County, Fujian Province* (Reported on October 20, 1943 [Year 32 of the Republic]), Changting County Archives, Paper Industry Guild Files, Archive No. 81–6–704, pp. 76–88.
296 See Rewi Alley, "An Account of the Gonghe Movement," in *Selected Historical and Cultural Materials*, Vol. 71, 1980, p. 103.

In 1939, soon after the Changting Office was established, it first organized urban cooperatives for knitting, umbrella-making, printing, and machinery, along with nine rural paper industry cooperatives.[297] In the spring of 1942, Dr. Chen Hansheng—renowned economist and Executive Secretary of the International Committee for the Promotion of Chinese Industrial Cooperatives ("Gonghe")—toured the principal papermaking regions of southeastern China. Writing afterwards, he observed: "From Pucheng and Nanping in northern Fujian; to Shanghang and Changting in western Fujian; across to Ningdu and Suichuan in Jiangxi; through Nanxiong, Heping, Shixing, and Renhua in northern Guangdong; and as far as Shaoyang, Xinhua, and Hengshan in Hunan—this forms one of China's great papermaking zones. Among them, maobian paper from Changting is the most renowned."[298] Dr. Chen also noted that, of Changting's 35,000 households, fully 70 percent were connected directly or indirectly with the paper industry. The most successful Fujian branch of the Industrial Cooperatives was located in Changting, which lies closest to the Jiangxi border. Even during wartime, a machinery cooperative and a cluster of papermaking cooperatives thrived here,[299] all founded and sustained with the support of the Southeastern Changting Office of the Chinese Industrial Cooperative Association.

In October 1943, the Cooperatives—seeking both to improve handicraft production and to lay the groundwork for rural industry—chose

---

297 Mao Xing, "Ten Years of the Gonghe in Changting: 1939–1949," in *Changting Historical and Cultural Materials*, Vol. 10, 1986, p. 37.

298 Chen Hansheng, *Gonghe: A Brief History of Chinese Cooperatives* (1947), in Wang Xi and Yang Xiaofu (eds.), *Collected Works of Chen Hansheng*, Fudan University Press, 1985, p. 188.

299 Li Yangmin, "Industry and Handicrafts in Changting during the War of Resistance against Japanese Aggression," in *Changting Historical and Cultural Materials*, Vol. 26, 1995, p. 61;

Geng Sheng, "Work and Writings of the Gonghe in Changting during the War of Resistance against Japanese Aggression," in *Changting Historical and Cultural Materials*, Vol. 26, 1995, pp. 18–19.

Changting as its papermaking hub. In the county's northeastern district, famed for its Neishan paper, it gave strong backing to the creation of 11 new papermaking cooperatives. At the same time, three existing cooperatives—Dakeng, Shangcun, and Xiakeng—were reorganized into the Nanxuan Township Papermaking Cooperative, operating a total of 14 papermaking vats. The Chinese Farmers' Bank provided modest start-up loans for this experiment; yet the sum was too small, and papermaking production struggled to gain momentum.[300]

Table 6 Statistics on Paper-making Cooperatives Established under the Guidance of the Changting Office, Southeast District, Chinese Industrial Cooperatives, 1944–1946

Year	Number of Cooperatives	Number of Members	Total Share Capital (yuan)	Total Output Value (yuan)	Total Loans (yuan)
1944	12	162	70,000	865,428	910,000
1945	12	162	86,800	6,126,000	1,251,900
1946	12	160	87,000	79,331,490	7,440,000

Source: *Survey of Papermaking in Changting, Fujian*, Chinese Industrial Cooperatives, Southeast District, Changting Office, 1946.

After 1940, hyperinflation in China entered a phase of rapid escalation, and the worsening economy dealt a severe blow to paper production in western Fujian. Against this backdrop, the Changting County Industrial Cooperative Federation was reorganized in April 1945 into a specialized paper industry federation. Its primary functions were to market the products

---

300 From 1944 to 1946, the number of papermaking cooperatives remained at 12, though membership in 1944 fell from 162 to 160. The 12 cooperatives were: Nanxuan Township Papermaking Cooperative, Haozhukeng Papermaking Cooperative, Yezhupai Papermaking Cooperative, Nanfengkeng Papermaking Cooperative, Chi'aobei Papermaking Cooperative, Qiaozitou Papermaking Cooperative, Hulikeng Papermaking Cooperative, Shenkeng Papermaking Cooperative, Dongxiashan Papermaking Cooperative, Wendi Papermaking Cooperative, Hanqian Papermaking Cooperative, and Chenwukeng Papermaking Cooperative. See Southeast Changting Office of the Chinese Industrial Cooperatives Association (comp.), *Survey of Papermaking in Changting, Fujian*, 1946, pp. 33–35.

of its member cooperatives, supply them with raw materials, coordinate the transfer of funds between cooperatives, and oversee their educational and welfare initiatives. As shown in Table 6, the Chinese Industrial Cooperatives established 12 paper-making cooperatives in Changting, 10 of which were located in the renowned Neishan (Inner Mountain) paper-making district. In 1946, these Neishan cooperatives produced 1,000 *dan* of paper. In addition, the Nanlu Cooperative operated three paper workshops, with an annual output of 200 *dan*, while the Xilu Cooperative produced 100 *dan*. It was said that the specialized paper industry federation made full use of cooperative principles, especially in August and September of 1945 when paper prices plummeted below production cost. Through its coordination of funds between member cooperatives, the federation alleviated the financial strain considerably.[301] According to the 1946 accounts, the cost of producing one *dan* of paper was 63,740 yuan, while the selling price ranged from 70,000 to 80,000 yuan—a razor-thin profit margin. For paper workshop owners who also relied on high-interest loans, there was virtually nothing left after repayment.[302]

What was life like in Changting's mountainous paper-producing villages at the time? The village of Chi'ao Bei in Anjie Township offers a vivid example. Director Yan Huizi of the Changting Industrial Cooperatives Office led an economic survey there. The cooperative planned to transform Chi'ao Bei into a fully cooperative village. Nestled in the northern corner of Tie'an Township, 70 *li* from Changting and only 5 *li* from the Ninghua border, Chi'ao Bei was encircled by mountains, forming an isolated area of just 5 *li* in circumference. The village had 50 households and 208 residents, but only 115 able-bodied laborers. Of its 1,000 *dan* of farmland, much con-

---

301 Southeast Changting Office of the Chinese Industrial Cooperatives Association (comp.), *Survey of Papermaking in Changting, Fujian*, 1946, p. 35.
302 Huang Majin, (chief ed.), *A History of Papermaking in Changting*, China Light Industry Press, 1992, p. 54.

sisted of "field skins" (tenant farming rights) rather than full ownership, meaning villagers had to pay more than 200 *dan* of rent grain annually to landlords in Ninghua. With limited arable land, bamboo forests became the farmers' main livelihood. In a good year, the area could yield over 1,000 *dan* of bamboo. Except for one household without bamboo groves, two households held 70 *dan* each, six held 50 *dan*, thirty held 10–20 *dan*, five held 5 *dan*, and six held 3 *dan*. Whether farming or papermaking, the villagers could not escape the grip of high-interest moneylenders. After the cooperative began its work, 30 of the 50 households joined the paper-making society, contributing about three-fifths of the area's bamboo resources. Yet, due to limited funds, some papermakers remained trapped in debt. The local office therefore drew up a loan plan, requesting additional funds from the central association to establish two more paper cooperatives in Chi'ao Bei, with the aim of making it a fully cooperative village.[303]

Among the 10 Neishan paper-making cooperatives, some had to venture to the borderlands between Changting and Ninghua to harvest bamboo and make paper. The hills there were covered with bamboo, but the local population and resources were insufficient, so bamboo forests were often rented out. The Neishan district's paper was considered superior, and bamboo forests rents were correspondingly higher. These forests were primarily located in the mountainous areas of Zhiping Township. During the war, Zhiping was outside the official scope of the Changting cooperatives' assistance, yet it still maintained an impressive 155 paper workshops. As Table 7 shows, these workshops were largely run by prominent clans in each village.

Table 7 Number of Paper Workshops and List of Managers in the Villages of Zhiping Township, Tingdong County, during the Second World War

---

303 Mao Xing, "Several Works and Writings of the Gonghe in Changting," in *Changting Historical and Cultural Materials*, Vol. 13, 1987, p. 41.

Village Name	Number of Paper Workshops	List of Managers
Zhiping	6	Chen Bingxing, Lei Xuefu, Lei Xuefa, Zhang Fengfen, Zhang Fengdao, Zhang Fengqin
Nikeng	3	Wang Qinshui, Wang Fadong, Wang Fayuan
Gaodi	9	Chi Renkuan, Chi Xianfen, Chi Renhuo, Chi Renfu, Chi Zhulin, Chi Ren'ai, Chi Xianrong, Chi Renze, Chi Binghui
Shangping	9	Lai Yuanxing, Lai Rifeng, Lai Rixiang, Lai Rigui, Lai Ribang, Lai Xiangfeng, Lai Tianyong, Lai Yueqiu, Lai Guangrong
Xiaping	11	Li Liangbiao, Li Liangkui, Li Liangyou, Liu Shichang, Liu Shilong, Liu Shitang, Liu Zhiqing, Pan Youneng, Lai Yuehe, Lai Yuehuo, Lai Yonghuo
Kuzhuwo	8	Wu Liangji, Wu Liangkui, Hu Wentong, Lai Huafen, Lai Bangtao, Lai Yongyong, Lai Guofen, Lai Dade
Fuqikeng	6	Chen Xianglin, Chen Shangui, Chen Shankun, Chen Hongzeng, Chen Guofa, Chen Fuxing
Fukengbao	9	Zeng Chengdong, Zeng Chenggui, Zeng Xiangwen, Zeng Xiangzhen, Zeng Helin, Zeng Youxin, Zeng Chongzhou, Zeng Zhonghe, Zeng Chonghan
Tianxinshe	53	Zeng Jusong, Zeng Xuelin, Zeng Xiangxing, Zeng Guihua, Zeng Juting, Zeng Litian, Zeng Congyu, Zeng Qinyuan, Zeng Ju'an, Zeng Jutang, Zeng Lizheng, Zeng Zeyu, Zeng Litang, Zeng Lixiang, Zeng Weishui, Zeng Zeyi, Zeng Xuewen, Zeng Jumo, Zeng Juhui, Zeng Yinying, Zeng Juneng, Zeng Qinzhong, Zeng Congzheng, Zeng Jusi, Zeng Zeyan, Zeng Zhengjing, Zeng Zhiwen, Zeng Lishun, Zeng Xiangcai, Zeng Qinlin, Zeng Shaoxun, Zeng Chuidong, Zeng Youfu, Zeng Chang, Zeng Youcai, Zeng Julu, Zeng Qinsheng, Zeng Youkuan, Zeng Zhijin, Zeng Zhishi, Zeng Zhilian, Zeng Zhikui, Zeng Zhifu, Zeng Yousheng, Zeng Youjin, Zeng Youmei, Zeng Qinde, Zeng Zexin, Zeng Qinrong, Zeng Qinchang, Zeng Zegen, Zeng Youtang, Zeng Congsuo, Zeng Yanggao
Gu'ao	5	Liu Qinji, Lai Yuezhong, Lai Xiangji, Lai Hua'an, Lai Dasen
Laiwu & Qiaoxia	17	Lai Bangmo, Lai Sizong, Lai Bangyi, Lai Bingwen, Lai Zinan, Lai Banglin, Lai Binghuo, Lai Yongsheng, Lai Qirong, Lai Xianghui, Lai Guohuang, Lai Guojun, Lai Guomo, Lai Bangjin, Lai Zhanchun, Lai Qingquan, Lai Xinwen
Anle	10	Ma Zegao, Luo Jinquan, Liao Changqing, Lei Chunshui, Zeng Chengxin, Xia Changming, Luo Jingwen, Zhou Yicai, Shen Jiacai, Zeng Yiqing
Fuzaiwo & Daping	4	Wu Liangkui, Wu Renchang, Lai Tianyong, Lai Yueqiu
Diqian'ao,	5	Lai Guogan, Fan Xingjin, Zeng Qinquan, Zeng

Village Name	Number of Paper Workshops	List of Managers
Pengfang, Yangwuding, Dadongkeng & Rongzikeng		Fanpeng, Liu Shisheng

Source: Mao Xing, "The Historical Origins of the Paper Industry in *Ninghua and Tingzhou,*" in *Ninghua Historical and Cultural Materials (Special Volume on Industry and Commerce)*, compiled by the Committee for the Study of Historical Materials, CPPCC Ninghua County, 1990, pp. 73–75.

The Industrial Cooperatives Movement lasted barely seven or eight years and faced formidable obstacles, yet there is no denying that it achieved certain results. In Changting, while the movement "could not yet generate the full force of economic reconstruction," it nevertheless managed to invest 16 million yuan of cooperative funds and increase output by 91 million yuan—"a contribution of real significance to the rural economy."[304] In the papermaking sector, where the growth of *Mao Zhu* alternated between "good years" and "lean years," independent paper workshop owners tended to produce more in good years and less in poor ones. The cooperatives introduced a notable improvement: "harvest in good years, refrain from cutting in poor years, and reserve bamboo for propagation," thereby expanding bamboo resources and stabilizing production. This marked a significant improvement in paper production during the movement's period.[305]

Looking across the first half of the 20th century, western Fujian's handmade papermaking industry weathered repeated upheavals yet achieved remarkable growth. Production areas expanded, output surged, and sales routes extended to markets across China and even overseas. Gov-

---

304 Southeast Changting Office of the Chinese Industrial Cooperatives Association (comp.), *Survey of Papermaking in Changting, Fujian*, 1946, p. 35.
305 Mao Xing, "Several Works and Writings of the Gonghe in Changting," in *Changting Historical and Cultural Materials*, Vol. 13, 1987, p. 39.

ernments at all levels, the business community, and scientific researchers alike showed keen interest in papermaking technology. This period even saw the rise of a renowned regional paper—the Yukou paper—celebrated throughout Southeast Asia. Papermaking once stood as a vital economic pillar of the Central Soviet Area, and papermakers themselves took an active role in supporting the Chinese Red Army, leaving a distinct "red" chapter in the cultural history of the region.

From the perspective of the entire production–transport–sales chain, however, the lending and advance-purchase practices of paper merchants had a markedly negative impact. On one hand, they stifled capital accumulation among paper workshop owners and bamboo farmers, trapping them in long-term poverty and forcing the industry to rely on merchant loans rather than grow independently. On the other hand, by monopolizing the export trade, they exerted lasting influence over price fluctuations in domestic and overseas markets. The sheer power of Changting's paper merchants can be glimpsed in how the Nationalist government's attempts to regulate paper production and merchant activities faltered time and again. With the birth of the People's Republic of China, a fresh chapter unfolded for western Fujian's paper industry.

5. The Rise and Fall of
Yukou Paper Industry

After the founding of the People's Republic of China, Yukou paper became the largest specialty product of Ninghua County, enjoying strong demand both domestically and internationally. Zhiping People's Commune (today's Zhiping She Ethnic Township) was its principal production base, accounting for 95% of Ninghua's total Yukou paper output and, remarkably, ranking first among all communes nationwide in papermaking volume. Over the past seven decades, Zhiping's Yukou paper industry has experienced dramatic highs and lows. In the 1957–1958 production cycle—locally referred to as one *dangban* (当班, a combined "big year" and "small year")—output reached a historic peak of 34,410 *dan*. Yet, following the large-scale felling of bamboo forests, production plummeted to 15,600 *dan* in 1959–1960. Recovery was slow, and although output nearly returned to peak levels by 1966–1967, the industry subsequently suffered chronic setbacks, with recovery still incomplete as late as 1981.[306] Around 1974, Yukou paper temporarily regained national prominence when it was designated by the Central government and State Publishing Bureaus,[307] with shipments sent to Beijing for printing Mao Zedong's works. The Reform and Opening period brought further changes: Zhiping's paper workshops expanded by 45 vats and underwent rapid mechanization.. However, from

---

306 Ninghua County Committee of the Communist Party of China, *Investigation Report on Establishing the Zhiping Paper-Making Area*, April 3, 1981, Ninghua County Archives, archive number 57-31-7.
307 The State Council Publishing Office was abolished in July 1973, after which the National Publishing Administration (commonly referred to as the National Publishing Bureau) was established, directly under the leadership of the State Council. Until September 1976, prior to the death of Mao Zedong, the National Publishing Bureau was responsible for the central government-assigned task of printing large-character thread-bound editions of Mao's works.
See: Song Muwen, "Reforms in the State News, Publishing, and Copyright Administration (Part I)," *China Publishing*, No. 10, 2005;
Gen Huo, "The Secret Printing of the Large-Character Editions in Shanghai," *Memories and Archives*, No. 4, 2015;
Fang Houshu and Wei Yushan, *A General History of Publishing in China: Volume on the People's Republic of China*, China Books Publishing House, 2008, p. 130.

the 1990s onward, the number of paper workshops declined sharply; more than 200 ceased production altogether.

In the modern era, the Yukou paper industry in Ninghua had to adapt to the realities of a new political order and the implementation of new institutions. How was an entirely new mode of production and livelihood established and then maintained in Zhiping, the heartland of Yukou paper? How did local paper farmers adapt to the post-war reconstruction, the implementation of state monopoly for purchasing and marketing, the trend toward mechanization, and the new market environment after reform and opening-up? These questions warrant deep exploration. Fortunately, valuable records and testimonies remain. The Ninghua County Archives and the Zhiping She Ethnic Township Government Archives preserve an extensive body of documents on the contemporary Yukou paper trade. Equally important are the voices of local participants—especially those in their seventies and eighties—who almost all, in one way or another, took part in producing, transporting, or selling Yukou paper. Their memories bear witness to both the industry's golden age and its gradual disappearance.

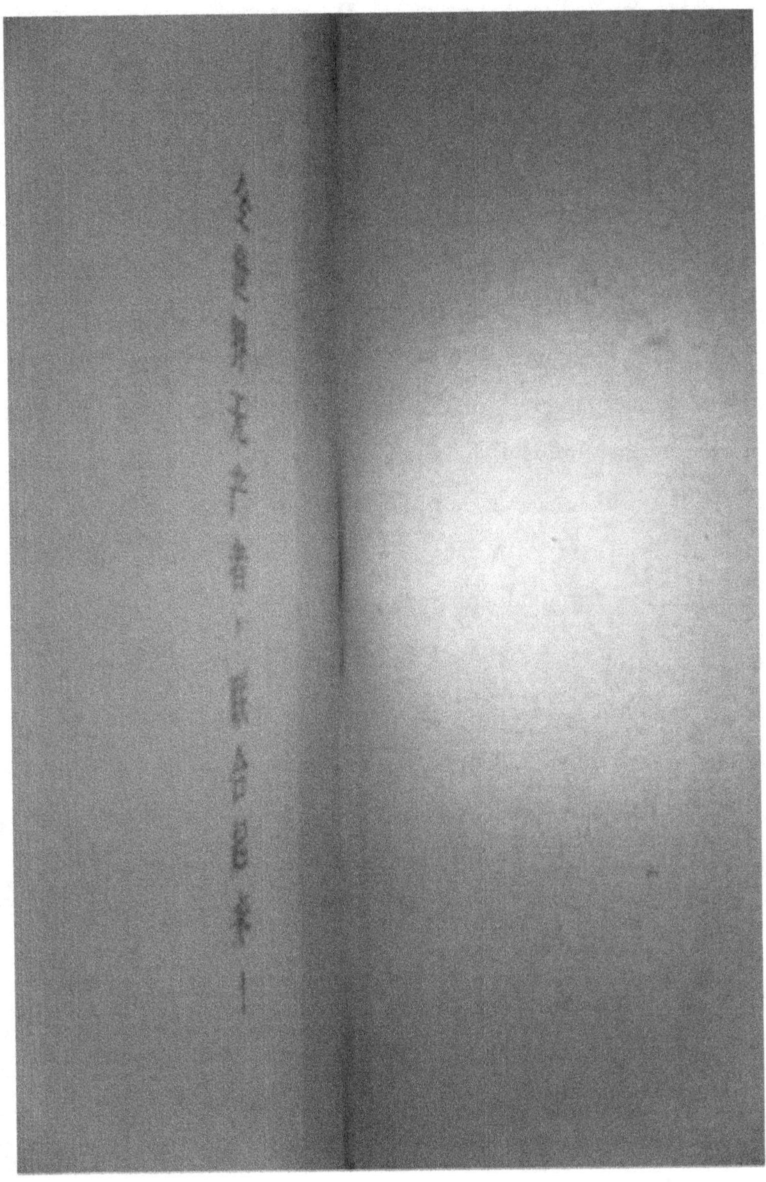

(Pic83 Flyleaf of Chairman Mao's Request Poem [Large-Character Edition])

5.1. State Monopoly for Purchasing and Marketing

Following the founding of the People's Republic of China, the State Council implemented a policy of planned procurement for major categories of agricultural and specialty products that are of overall significance. The aim was to stimulate production while ensuring both national development needs and people's livelihoods. Any goods designated for planned procurement were to be purchased exclusively by state-run enterprises or by supply and marketing cooperatives entrusted by the state, with prices uniformly set by the provincial authorities. From 1961 onward, China also introduced an award-for-purchase policy for items under quota procurement and planned purchase, a measure that remained in effect until the early 1980s, when it was gradually phased out.[308]

The production of Yukou paper rose and fell in tandem with the degree of state attention it received. In 1950, Ninghua County produced 531 tons of handmade paper; by 1952, output had surged to 1,951 tons. From 1953 to 1957, annual production averaged 1,448.8 tons. However, during the Great Leap Forward, excessive logging of commercial bamboo severely depleted raw materials, causing the 1960–1963 annual average to plummet to just 461.25 tons. After 1963, the Ninghua County People's Committee and relevant management departments gave special support to the Yukou paper-producing areas, enabling the industry to recover. Between 1964 and 1972, annual output averaged 1,106 tons, and from 1973 to 1979, production remained consistently above 1,000 tons for seven consecutive years,

---

308 Editorial Office of the Compilation Committee for the Chronicle of Supply and Marketing Cooperatives in Ninghua County, *Chronicle of Supply and Marketing Cooperatives in Ninghua County, Fujian Province (1931–1985)*, 1988, p. 84.

reaching an annual average of 1,160.43 tons—firmly establishing Ninghua as one of the country's major handmade paper bases.[309]

5.1.1.　The Purchase and Sale System for Category II Goods

On March 1, 1950, the People's Government of Ninghua County was established under the jurisdiction of the Yong'an Special Administrative Office of Fujian Province. Initially, the county was divided into five districts and 16 townships. Zhiping initially belonged to the Third District (Caofang). In 1951, the Seventh District was established in Zhiping, encompassing 10 townships: Zhiping, Tianshe, Pengfang, Nikeng, Gaodi, Xiaping, Zhuwang, Nancheng, Fangtian, and Pingshang. Over the following years, administrative boundaries were repeatedly adjusted: in 1952, Zhuwang, Nancheng, Fangtian, and Pingshang were reassigned to the Eighth District, while Sanhuang of the Third District was added to Zhiping; in 1954, Sanhuang was returned to Caofang, while Sixi, Qiaoxia, Shetian, Liqi, and Pingpu were added to Zhiping, bringing its jurisdiction to 12 townships. In 1958, the Zhiping People's Commune was formed, comprising nine production brigades; by 1961, there were 25 brigades; and in 1966, they were reorganized into 12 brigades.

From 1949 to 1951, the production and marketing of Yukou paper largely continued the pre-1949 model, with paper workshop owners, paper firms, and merchants dominating production, distribution, and sales. However, in 1953, Ninghua County began the socialist restructuring of private paper trading firms and shops, laying the groundwork for state monopoly for purchasing and marketing. Institutions such as the Ninghua Purchasing

---

309 Liu Shanqun (ed.), "Statistical Tables of the Main Agricultural and Special Local Products Purchased by the Commercial Departments of Ninghua County in Various Years," *Chorography of Ninghua County*, Fujian People's Publishing House, 1992, p. 385;
Editorial Office of the Compilation Committee for the Chronicle of Supply and Marketing Cooperatives in Ninghua County, *Chronicle of Supply and Marketing Cooperatives in Ninghua County, Fujian Province (1931–1985)*, 1988, p. 25.

Office of the China Native Products Company (Yong'an Branch) and the Ninghua County Supply and Marketing Cooperative were established. The Zhiping Supply and Marketing Cooperative began preparations in August 1952 and officially opened for business on September 20 of the same year. At its founding, it had 1,348 members and was engaged only in supply, not in the purchase of local specialties.[310]

In 1953, as the state introduced the state monopoly for purchasing and marketing for grain and oil, and implemented planned distribution for cotton cloth, it further classfied major agricultural and sideline products into three categories: Category I (unified procurement), Category II (quota procurement), and Category III (negotiated purchase). While maintaining stable prices, supply and marketing cooperatives gradually adjusted unreasonable purchase prices for agricultural and sideline products in a planned and phased manner. For Category I and II goods, the state-mandated prices were strictly enforced. For Category III goods, prices were negotiated based on market supply and demand, following the principle of benefiting both producers and traders. Ultimately, purchase prices for agricultural and specialty products were determined and issued by the county-level cooperative.[311]

In 1953, Yukou paper from Zhiping was officially classified as a Category II goods under the national procurement system. From that point on, its purchase was centralized through the Zhiping Supply and Marketing Cooperative, the local handmade paper purchasing station, and the Ninghua County Supply and Marketing Cooperative, in coordination with relevant departments of the County Commercial Bureau. These agencies not only handled procurement but also integrated it with the acquisition and

---

310 *Supply and Marketing Cooperative of Zhiping Township, Seventh District, Ninghua County* (1952). preserved in Ninghua County Archives, collected and provided by Lei Shaoqiu.
311 Editorial Office of the Compilation Committee for the Chronicle of Supply and Marketing Cooperatives in Ninghua County, *Chronicle of Supply and Marketing Cooperatives in Ninghua County, Fujian Province (1931–1985)*, 1988, pp. 193-194.

transport of military-support goods. Export quotas were arranged at the regional level, with trading companies at each port sending representatives to Ninghua to assist. Yukou paper quickly became one of the county's main export commodities, earning valuable foreign exchange for the nation.[312] To facilitate centralized buying and selling, the Ninghua County Supply and Marketing Cooperative set up a dedicated handmade paper purchasing station in Zhiping. Its primary tasks were to guide production, organize purchases, and manage outbound shipments of Yukou paper. At the same time, the Zhiping Supply and Marketing Cooperative ensured a stable supply of both production inputs and daily necessities—delivering, according to plan each year, essential materials such as lime, papermaking screens, tung oil, raw lacquer, jute, and tea oil. Over time, the cooperative established close ties with local production teams, providing loans, grain subsidies, and production guidance.[313]

Yet 1953 was not without challenges. That year, the market for Fujian's handmade paper was shaken by the influx of cheap machine-made paper, leaving the Yong'an Special District Cooperative with large unsold inventories. The result, as one report put it, was "buying at high prices in production areas, selling at a loss in sales areas," which depleted state funds

---

312 Malaysia has long been a key market for Yukou paper exports. Datuk Lee Yong Kwang (born 1952), Chairman of the Shunde Association in Penang, Malaysia, traces his family's connection to the trade: his grandfather, Li Hengbao, was born in 1886 in Shunde, Guangdong, China. As a young man, Li moved to Penang and opened Hengji, a grocery store on Yi Fu Street selling grain and oil. Since the 1940s, Hengji has imported Yukou paper, sourcing it from mainland China via Hong Kong. The paper arrived in Penang in its original basket packaging, primarily used locally as toilet paper, wrapping paper, and for account books. When Mr. Li Yongguang took over Hengji in the 1970s, the market for Yukou paper gradually declined. (Based on the author's oral interviews with Mr. Li Yongguang conducted on September 13–14, 2023, at Penang Chinese Seafood Restaurant and the Penang Shunde Association.)

313 Zhiping Handmade Paper Procurement Station, Agricultural Products Division, Ninghua County Supply and Marketing Cooperative, *How the Zhiping Handmade Paper Purchasing Station Participates in Production, Improves Quality, and Enhances Business Management* (May 6, 1964). Ninghua County Archives, collected and provided by Lei Shaoqiu.

and dampened private merchants' enthusiasm. To address this, the Ninghua County Cooperative submitted two proposals to the Fujian Branch of the China Native Products Company and to the Yong'an Special District Cooperative: first, to reach a unified agreement on the official prices of Yukou and Maobian paper across all relevant authorities, and then to implement those prices uniformly; second, to focus marketing efforts on traditional markets such as Guangzhou and Hong Kong, in hopes of reopening sales channels.[314] Beyond these measures, 1954 saw the county conduct a comprehensive survey of the Yukou paper industry in key producing areas such as Xiaping and Gaodi Townships of the Seventh District. Investigators traced back every link in the production, transport, and sales chain. Thanks to these coordinated and concerted efforts, by 1955 Zhiping's Yukou paper had won back both market recognition and government support.[315]

That year marked a decisive breakthrough. On February 15, 1955, the Yong'an Branch of the Fujian Native Products Company and the Yong'an Special District Supply and Marketing Cooperative jointly relayed a provincial directive to the counties of Ninghua, Qingliu, and Mingxi. The notice announced that Maobian and Yukou paper from the Yong'an region had

---

314 Yong'an Special District Cooperative General Association: "Adjusting the Purchase Prices for Handmade Paper" (March 24, 1953), Ninghua County Archives, archival number 35–2–8;
Ninghua County Cooperative General Association: "Request for Prompt Readjustment of the Purchase Prices for Maobian Paper and for Setting Prices for Yukou Paper Produced in Zhiping" (April 2, 1953), Ninghua County Archives, collected and provided by Lei Shaoqiu.
315 In the document *Survey Report on Neishan Yukou Paper in Zhiping District, Ninghua County* (June 8, 1955), the original printed text stated: "We believe it has no prospect for development and will eventually be eliminated; thus, we have not provided leadership, and it has essentially been left to its own course. We are still unclear about the development direction of this industry. We request instructions." This passage was crossed out, with a handwritten amendment alongside: "Because we have not fully recognized the importance of developing a diversified economy and integrating agriculture and forestry in the mountain areas, we, on the contrary, believed its development prospects were limited. As a result, we failed to provide proper leadership, leading to a state of drift." This revision indicates that Ninghua County authorities had by then become aware of its inadequacies in leading the Yukou paper industry.

secured export orders. To meet the specifications of overseas markets, Maobian paper from six counties—Jiangle, Shunchang, Shaxian, Mingxi, Ninghua, and Qingliu—was to be purchased exclusively by the cooperatives and shipped according to seasonal export schedules. Paper meeting export standards would be sent to the provincial trading office to fulfill foreign trade quotas, while paper for domestic sale would be distributed under a quota system: 31.17% to state enterprises, 27.83% to cooperatives, and 1% to private merchants, as set by the Provincial Planning Commission. For 1955, the Yong'an Special District was assigned an annual export quota of 57,500 *dao*, with the first quarter's target set at 12,000 *dao*. Ninghua's share was 6,600 *dao*, followed by Qingliu with 3,600 and Mingxi with 1,800. The Ninghua County Supply and Marketing Cooperative leadership was instructed to personally oversee procurement and to "fully grasp the sources of supply," with an explicit reminder that "the export task is of strategic importance to the nation's industrialization."[316] On August 10, 1955, the First Wholesale Department of Shanghai Branch of the China Native Products Company signed a contract with the Ninghua County Supply and Marketing Cooperative for Maobian and Yukou paper, including orders for 285 *dao* of Grade 4 Yukou paper (at 6.435 yuan per *dao*), 480 *dao* of Grade 5 (6.20 yuan), and 195 *dao* of Grade 6 (5.965 yuan)—a total of 960 *dao*.[317] Then, on September 1, Ninghua once again mobilized Zhiping and Caofang to ship 10,000 *dao* of Yukou paper. By this point, "earning foreign exchange, fulfilling the nation's export quotas, and supporting the nation's industrialization effort" had become not just an economic goal, but a politi-

---

316 China Native Products Company, Yong'an Branch, and Fujian Province Yong'an Special District Supply and Marketing Cooperative, *On Arranging the Task of Maobian Paper Export and Hoping for Firm Implementation* (February 15, 1955), N inghua County Archives, collected and provided by Lei Shaoqiu.
317 *Yukou Paper Supply and Marketing Contract* (August 10, 1955), Ninghua County Archives, collected and provided by Lei Shaoqiu.

cal mission for the Yukou paper-producing areas.[318] In 1956, the provincial government took a further step, placing handmade paper under the planned-procurement system and entrusting the Supply and Marketing Cooperative with exclusive purchasing rights, with both quotas and prices set by the province.[319]

Based on surveys conducted in 1954 and 1955, Zhiping, then part of Ninghua County's Seventh District, administered 12 townships—each home to its own paper workshop. Out of the district's 1,657 households, 1,327 (about 90%) possessed bamboo forests suitable for papermaking. The local workforce numbered around 530, supplemented by roughly 1,000 migrant workers from Changting and Liancheng. In total, the district had 218 paper workshops, with 213 in active operation. In 1954, the district harvested 74,605 *dan* of *zhuma* (bamboo fiber)—enough to make 196,000 *dao* of paper. Actual production reached 130,000 *dao*, with the remaining 66,000 partially processed and carried over into 1955. The year's output value exceeded half a million yuan. Remarkably, the district's agricultural output value was less than one-third of that generated by papermaking. A closer look at Xiaping Township reveals the same picture. Out of its 206 households, only three had no bamboo forests. The township had 41 paper workshops and 95 skilled papermakers. In a good year, its bamboo forests could yield 74,605 *dan* of *zhuma*—enough for more than 42,000 *dao* of paper.[320]

---

318 Ninghua County Government, *Mobilize Laborers to Rush the Transport of Native Paper for Export within September* (September 6, 1955), Ninghua County Archives, collected and provided by Lei Shaoqiu.
319 Editorial Office of the Compilation Committee for the Chronicle of Supply and Marketing Cooperatives in Ninghua County, *Chronicle of Supply and Marketing Cooperatives in Ninghua County, Fujian Province (1931–1985)*, 1988, p. 87.
320 *Survey Report on Neishan Yukou Paper in Zhiping District, Ninghua County* (June 8, 1955), archived at the Ninghua County Archives, collected and provided by Lei Shaoqiu.

Before the simple road linking Zhiping and Caofang was completed in 1958, paper from Zhiping and Xiaping had to be carried by shoulder pole to Xialai in Caofang, then transported by cart to Shantou or Guangzhou. Some shipments also traveled via Changting and Hengjiang in Jiangxi before reaching Guangzhou. [321] By 1956, Zhiping produced approximately 138,000 *dao* of Yukou paper, solidifying its position as the largest producer of Ninghua's premier local specialty. From 1959 onward, Zhiping gained a string of honorary titles—"Capital of Yukou Paper," "Paper Capital of Zhiping," "Paper Capital of Ninghua," "Paper Capital of Qingning," and even "Paper Capital of Western Fujian." In good years, production reached 31,500 *dan*; in lean years, it never fell below 3,000. Average annual output was around 18,000 *dan* (126,000 *dao*), making papermaking the backbone of the local economy. In 1958 alone, the commune's 6,328 residents earned 180,147.55 yuan from agriculture but a staggering 1,020,000 yuan from papermaking—85% of total income. In the Xiaping administrative area (Xiaping and Qiaoxia brigades at that time), papermaking in 1958 brought in 252,000 yuan from 8,400 *dan* of paper, while agriculture contributed only 14,265 yuan—just 5% of total income. Therefore, as locals put it, they "relied on the mountains, lived off the mountains, and clothed themselves with materials from the mountains." Based on this, to coordinate production, the Zhiping Commune set up a Papermaking Production Command Headquarters, with a nine-member leadership department. Each brigade formed its own Papermaking Production Committee of five members, with deputy party secretaries heading committees in Pengfang, Zhiping, Fukeng, and Pingpu. Brigades with significant papermaking activity—such as Xiaping,

---

321 Ninghua County Government, *Mobilize Laborers to Rush the Transport of Native Paper for Export within September* (September 6, 1955), Ninghua County Archives, collected and provided by Lei Shaoqiu;
Request for Review of Constructive Opinions on Issues Concerning the Circulation of Ninghua Zhiping Yukou Paper (November 1, 1955), Ninghua County Archives, collected and provided by Lei Shaoqiu.

Laiwu, Gaodi, Nikeng, and Tianshe—were typically headed by the Party secretary, supported by one or two deputy directors and three to four committee members. At the production team level, small papermaking leadership groups were established, usually headed by the team leader, with three to five forestry workers (who oversaw workshop operations) directing daily production.[322]

At the grassroots level, unified procurement of handmade paper was handled by the Zhiping Supply and Marketing Cooperative and the local Paper Purchasing Station. The station signed purchase contracts with each brigade's paper workshops, distributed advance loans and grain subsidies and allowances, provided production guidance, and arranged for government procurement and transport. In 1959, the Ninghua County Party Committee issued a explicit directive: Zhiping must prioritize papermaking over agriculture. The Paper Station allocated labor accordingly—85% to papermaking, 15% to farming—and organized training courses, production demonstrations, and mentorship systems where skilled veterans taught newcomers, producing 176 trained papermakers, 79 of them women, "a historic first." Beyond labor and training, the Paper Station addressed grain subsidies, shortages of lime, and the distribution of papermaking income. It also promoted the recycling of waste materials (old bark, scrap bamboo, and paper scraps) to increase output while improving quality. As a result, the quality of Yukou paper rose from the lower Grade 5 to 6 to a steady Grade 3 to 4.[323]

In 1955, the Ninghua Seventh District Federation of Industry and Commerce carried out an unprecedentedly detailed cost analysis of Yukou

---

322 Communist Party Committee of Zhiping Commune, *Summary Report on the Current Situation of Handmade Paper Production* (May 24, 1959), Ninghua County Archives, collected and provided by Lei Shaoqiu.
323 Qingning County Bureau of Commerce, *The Handmade Paper Purchasing Station Active in Zhiping, the "Paper Capital"* (September 23, 1959), Ninghua County Archives, collected and provided by Lei Shaoqiu.

paper. The conclusion was striking: <u>regardless of the grade</u>, the production cost for each *dan* was 21.66 yuan—a finding that revealed many deeper issues. The original report read as follows:

Cost of Material Preparation for Zhiping's Handmade Paper Industry (1954), Calculated as 1 *dan* = 7 *dao* of Yukou Paper:

1. For 1 dan of paper, 1.5 days are spent on bamboo forest maintenance. With daily wages (including meals) at 0.70 yuan, this totals 1.05 yuan.

2. Each *dan* of paper requires 75 *jin* of lime. Lime is sold at 0.75 yuan per *dan* (where 1 *dan* of lime = 70 *jin*), amounting to 0.80 yuan.

3. Transportation costs for lime vary by distance, ranging from 1 to 1.60 yuan per 100 *jin*; an average of 1.30 yuan per 100 *jin* is calculated here. For 75 *jin* of lime, this comes to 0.99 yuan (including food expenses for laborers).

(Pic84 Site of the Zhiping Handmade Paper Station in Mabeiling)

4. Pond maintenance: Each pond processes 30 *dan* of bamboo baskets on average, yielding 23 *dan* of paper. Maintenance work includes 1 day for locating water sources and installing bamboo pipes, 1 day for cleaning the pond, 3 days for renovation, and roughly 2 days for drying and upkeep (done 8–10 times)—totaling 7 days. With daily wages (including meals) at 0.70 yuan, this totals 4.90 yuan. Averaged over 23 *dan* of paper, this adds 0.21 yuan per *dan*.

5. Depreciation of tools and equipment: For a household producing 30 *dan* of paper:

Two axes: Each weighs 42 *liang*, at 0.08 yuan per *liang*, costing 3.36 yuan each (total 6.72 yuan).

Two paring knives: Each weighs 21 *liang*, at 0.08 yuan per *liang*, costing 1.68 yuan each (total 3.36 yuan).

Together, axes and knives cost 10.08 yuan, with a 5–6 year lifespan—annual depreciation 2.01 yuan. Averaged over 30 *dan*, this is 0.07 yuan per *dan*.

Other items: 4 straw raincoats (3.80 yuan each), 3 straw rain capes (1.55 yuan each), 2 mountain pruning knives (1.12 yuan each), 3 firewood knives (1.76 yuan each), 4 bamboo hats (0.72 yuan total), 2 straw mats (1.36 yuan total), and 2 manure baskets (1.35 yuan total). These total 30.80 yuan, with a 3-year lifespan—annual depreciation: 10.26 yuan. Averaged over 30 *dan*, this is 0.34 yuan per *dan*.

6. Labor for *zhuma* processing:

Harvesting bamboo: 30 *dan* processed daily yields 2.5 *dan* of paper. With daily wages (including meals) at 1.15 yuan, this is 0.46 yuan per *dan*.

Slide *Zhuma*: 35 *dan* processed daily yields 2.8 *dan* of paper. With daily wages (including meals) at 1.05 yuan, this is 0.37 yuan per *dan*.

Peeling and Splitting *zhuma* (two workers): 20 *dan* processed daily yields 1.6 *dan* of paper. With total wages (including meals) at 2.30 yuan, this is 1.44 yuan per *dan*.

Carrying *zhuma*: On average, daily carried *zhuma* yields 1 *dan* of paper, with wages (including meals) at 1.05 yuan per *dan*.

Soaking with lime: 100 *dan* of material (including lime) processed daily yields 8 *dan* of paper. With daily wages (including meals) at 1.15 yuan, this is 0.14 yuan per *dan*.

7. Washing *zhuma*: 100 *dan* washed daily yields 8 *dan* of paper. With wages (including meals) at 2.00 yuan, this is 0.25

yuan per *dan*. (Another arrangement involves providing meals with a base wage, where workers receive a larger quantity of food—this is equivalently balanced in overall terms.)

8. Bleaching: For each pond, the process includes 2 days of preparing with bamboo husks, 1 day of stirring and repairing banks, 1 day of collecting pine needles, 3 days of bleaching (over 10 rounds), and 3 days of trimming and covering—totaling 10 days. With daily wages (including meals) at 0.70 yuan, this totals 7.00 yuan. Averaged over 23 *dan* of paper, this adds 0.30 yuan per *dan*.

Total raw material cost: 7.47 yuan per *dan* of paper.

Expenses for Finished Products:

1. Production of one paper-drying wall: 130 *jin* of hide (13 yuan), 300 *jin* of lime (7.11 yuan), 40 stone bricks (1.50 yuan); 12 workdays for processing hide (6 yuan), 6 yuan for felling and transporting logs, 5 days for felling bamboo, 4 days for carrying paper-drying wall clay, 32 days for mixing clay, 10 days for plastering the clay, setting up the wall, and transporting firewood—totaling 57 workdays (wages including meals: 39.90 yuan); builder's wage (including meals) for one wall: 13 yuan; 2 days for sawing wall corners (2.20 yuan). Total: 82.71 yuan. This wall is capable of producing 200 *dan* of paper, with a depreciation of 0.38 yuan per *dan*.

2. Production of one paper vat, one paper press, one *zhuma* press, six barrels (large and small), one set of water buckets, four wooden buckets, one treading trough, two water basins, one rice steamer, and two pot lids: requiring 22 fir logs; 6 workdays for felling trees, 16 workdays for peeling and transporting logs (22

workdays total, with daily wages including meals: 13 yuan); 4 workdays for sawing (4.40 yuan); 6 workdays for making the paper press (6.60 yuan); 2 workdays for making the *zhuma* press (2.20 yuan); 10 workdays for making six barrels (11 yuan); 1.10 yuan for one set of water buckets; 11 workdays for four wooden buckets (2.20 yuan); 2 workdays for the treading trough (2.20 yuan); 2.20 yuan for miscellaneous basins, rice steamer, and lids; 4 workdays for one paper table (4.40 yuan). Total for materials: 67.40 yuan. With a lifespan of 5 years, producing 120 *dan* of paper annually, annual depreciation is 13.50 yuan, averaging 0.11 yuan per *dan*.

3. Depreciation of bamboo utensils: 3 baskets for carrying *zhuma* (3 yuan), 10 bamboo sieves for *zhuma* (2.5 yuan), 1.50 yuan for large and small troughs, 2 yuan for one bamboo-splitting tool, 0.40 yuan for one small leaf sieve; 3 workdays for felling bamboo (2.12 yuan). Total for bamboo utensils: 13.7 yuan. Capable of producing 120 *dan* of paper, with a depreciation of 0.11 yuan per *dan*.

4. Two cart wheels (9 yuan), two woks (10.40 yuan), one screen bed (4.20 yuan). Total: 23.60 yuan. With a lifespan of 2 years, producing 240 *dan* of paper, depreciation is 0.10 yuan per *dan*.

5. Two paper-cutting knives (18 yuan), one wok spatula (0.90 yuan), one kitchen knife (1.12 yuan), three drying wall hooks (2.40 yuan). Total: 22.42 yuan. With a lifespan of 8 years, annual depreciation is 2.80 yuan, averaging 0.02 yuan per *dan*.

6. Miscellaneous labor for repairs and cleaning (including felling bamboo, opening sluices, and fixing leaks, vat adjust-

ments, and miscellaneous work): 12 workdays, totaling 8.40 yuan in wages. Depreciation: 0.07 yuan per *dan*.

Total depreciation for utensils above: 0.81 yuan per *dan*.

7. For one *dan* of paper, workers are paid 1.2 *dao* of Yukou paper (with the Grade 4 paper sold at 3.96 yuan per *dao*, totaling 6.72 yuan) plus 2 yuan for meals. Total wages for making one *dan* of paper: 8.73 yuan.

8. Rice consumed by workers in the factory over 10 days (during which 8 *dan* of paper is produced): 24.12 *jin* daily, averaging 30.15 *jin* per *dan*, costing 2.32 yuan.

9. For one *dan* of paper: 0.30 yuan for *zhuma*, 0.25 yuan for 10 *liang* of jute, 0.21 yuan for 3 *jin* of *lan* leaves, 0.12 yuan for 10 *liang* of salt, 0.16 yuan for 4 *liang* of kerosene, 0.08 yuan for 2 *liang* of tea oil, 0.06 yuan for tung oil and beans. Total: 1.18 yuan per *dan*.

10. Miscellaneous labor wages: 0.80 yuan; expenses for transporting to the purchasing station (including meals): 0.30 yuan; stationery costs (paper, brushes, ink, account books, and stamps): 0.05 yuan per *dan*.

Total: 1.15 yuan per *dan*.

Total expenses for finished products: 14.19 yuan per *dan* of paper.

Overall, regardless of class, the cost of each *dan* of Yukou paper is 21.66 yuan. (Excluding mountain rent—land remuneration—and agricultural taxes)

The statement that "regardless of class, the production cost for each *dan* was 21.66 yuan" carried an important implication: in any era, so long as Yukou paper was made by hand from raw materials, the cost remained relatively stable. What changed the outcome was not the cost, but the care of the workmanship. Attentive, meticulous labor yielded fine sheets; careless, hasty work produced inferior ones. Before the mid-20th century, it was precisely the market's pricing mechanism that directly spurred papermakers to aim for high-quality Yukou paper. The price-by-grade system did not disappear in later years. However, it came to be overlaid by state control of the overall purchase price and by new methods of profit distribution—factors that, in fact, had an even greater impact on the attitudes of the papermakers and on the quality of the sheets they produced.

In 1955, for example, the purchase price for the Sub-Grade 2 Yukou paper—produced in very small quantities—was 4.76 yuan per *dao*. The price generally dropped by 0.20 yuan per *dao* for each grade, down to Grade 8: Grade 3 sold for 4.56 yuan, Grade 4 for 4.36 yuan, Grade 5 for 4.16 yuan. Between Grades 8 and 9, the gap widened to 0.60 yuan; from Grade 9 to Grade 14 the drop was again 0.20 yuan per *dao* per grade. The lowest, Grade 14 paper, brought only 1.50 yuan per *dao*. Under these rates, producing one *dan* of Sub-Grade 2 paper yielded a profit of 11.66 yuan. A *dan* of Grade 4 brought 8.86 yuan. But a *dan* of Grade 14 paper meant a loss of 11.16 yuan—and this calculation still excluded agricultural taxes and other levies. That same year, sales to Shanghai told another story: Yukou paper sold there for 6.435 yuan per *dao* for sub-Grade 4, 6.20 yuan for Grade 5, and 5.965 yuan for Grade 6—prices far above the purchase rates in Zhiping. The 1955 investigation drew blunt conclusions: with backward production techniques, costs could not be reduced; when costs were identical but a workshop turned out more low-grade than high-grade paper, the wide price gap between grades meant the business could quickly sink into loss. In addition, papermakers complained that the purchase prices were too low and profits too thin, sapping their incentive. Purchasing agencies, however, countered that while the paper still sold readily at current prices, any price rise would choke off demand.[324]

In response, the authorities set two standards for papermakers' wages, based on the volume of local paper output and the satisfaction of the community. Agriculture-first, papermaking-second regions—or areas with a roughly equal mix of farming and papermaking—such as Pengfang, Zhiping, Fukeng, and Pingpu brigades: workers' pay would be uniformly determined through a proportional profit-sharing system. As to those papermaking-first regions, with farming as a sideline—such as Xiaping, Gaodi, Laiwu, Tianshe, and Nikeng brigades: workers' pay could be calculated mainly according to the grade of paper produced, with work points assigned accordingly. Earnings would be pooled at the brigade level and distributed through unified profit-sharing. The specific standards were as follows:

(Pic85 Group Photo of the Advanced Native Paper Producers' Representatives Conference, Qingning County, 1959)

---

324 *Survey Report on Neishan Yukou Paper in Zhiping District, Ninghua County* (June 8, 1955), archived at the Ninghua County Archives, collected and provided by Lei Shaoqiu.

(1) For each *dan* of Grade 1 Yukou paper produced, workers were assigned 17.5 work points for papermaking, 16 points for lifting bamboo screens, 15 points for drying and treading, and 14 points for stripping bark. For Grade 2 Yukou paper, the respective figures were 16.5, 15, 14, and 13 points; for Grade 3 paper, 15.5, 14, 13, and 12 points; for Grade 4, 14.5, 13, 12, and 11 points; and for Grade 5, 13.5, 12, 11, and 10 points. All grades above Grade 6 were paid at the Grade 5 rate.

(2) For colored paper, Grade 1 paper was assigned work points according to the work-point rate for Grade 4 Yukou paper, and Grades 2–3 according to the Grade 5 rate.

(3) When production was interrupted due to paper workshop accidents, an additional 4 points were granted to workers whose worksite was over *10* li away, and 3 points to those within 10 *li*.

(4) Group leaders in charge of vat management were assigned work points according to the papermakers' rate if their worksite was far, or according to the drying and treading workers' standard if it was near. No additional points were given for distances within 5 *li*; beyond that, points were calculated based on the distance equivalent to carrying a *dan* of rice.

(5) For paper delivered to the workshop, no extra points were granted within 20 *li*. Beyond that distance, every additional 10 *li* would entitle the workers to an additional 6 work points.

(6) Wages for gathering *lan* leaves were paid entirely in cash at 0.05 yuan per *jin*, with no work points awarded.[325]

---

325 Communist Party Committee of Zhiping Commune, *Summary Report on the*

With the transformation to the commune system, the earlier policy of "equalitarian distribution, uncompensated reallocation, and mandatory loan recovery" was gradually adjusted. In its place came a system of "payment according to labor, four-tier management, four-tier assessment, and accounting for profit and loss at each level." This shift did bring a modest boost to workers' enthusiasm for production.[326] Yet in the broader picture, the incentives remained undercut. In 1953, the purchase price for a *dao* of Grade 5 Yukou paper in Ninghua County was 4.38 yuan. After several years of fluctuations, it was only in 1961 that the price was restored—and slightly increased—to 5.05 yuan.[327] This prolonged suppression of purchase prices was the root cause of the decline in papermaking motivation.

5.1.2.　Collective Economy and the Income of Papermaker

Between 1960 and 1962, native paper production in Zhiping People's Commune went through several lean years. The setbacks came partly from two major flash floods and other natural disasters, and partly from poor production management. Output dropped, and papermakers struggled to make ends meet. By 1963 and 1964, recovery was gradually underway. According to reports from the Zhiping native paper purchasing station, the commune was characterized by its high, forested mountains and a sparse population in some areas. Of its total 8,094 *mu* of arable land, more than 300,000 *mu* were bamboo-covered hills. In a good year, the commune could produce over 30,000 *dan* of Yukou paper, while in a poor year, output might fall to around 5,000 *dan*. Out of the commune's 24 brigades

---

Current Situation of Handemade Paper Production (May 24, 1959), Ninghua County Archives, collected and provided by Lei Shaoqiu.
326 *Paper Industry Production Plan of Zhiping People's Commune* (June 10, 1959), Ninghua County Archives, collected and provided by Lei Shaoqiu.
327 Editorial Office of the Compilation Committee for the Chronicle of Supply and Marketing Cooperatives in Ninghua County, *Chronicle of Supply and Marketing Cooperatives in Ninghua County, Fujian Province (1931–1985)*, 1988, p. 207.

(spanning 182 villages), 10 lived entirely on papermaking, 9 combined farming with papermaking, and 5 farmed as their mainstay while producing paper on the side. All the grain and lime needed for papermaking had to be brought in from neighboring districts. Year after year, papermaking accounted for more than 80 percent of the commune's gross income and about 70 percent of total county output. In 1963, the Zhiping native paper station purchased 406 tons of handmade paper. The number of paper workshops, which had fallen from 215 before the downturn to just 36 in 1961, rebounded to 60 by 1963. In 1964, raw material reserves in the commune surpassed 1,250 tons, enough to keep 96 workshops running. To greet the great production drive of that year, the goal was to open 140 workshops, with a planned output of 550 tons, and an ambitious target of 600.[328]

In November 1964, the Ninghua County Planning Commission notified the county supply and marketing cooperative that the original annual export quota for native paper—150 tons—was raised to 200 tons. The directive called for seizing the moment and fulfilling the export task.[329] In response, Zhiping launched a mass campaign in which men and women, the elderly and children alike, contributed their labor to the collective:

In Chuandong production brigade, 78-year-old member Zeng Zhikui and his 65-year-old sister Zeng Zhinyu each climbed the hills daily, stripping and splitting 29 *dan* of *zhuma*. 13-year-old Xu Jinmei, too young to shoulder a carrying pole, hauled the *zhuma* on her back. In the Gaofeng brigade,

---

328 Zhiping Handmade Paper Procurement Station, Agricultural Products Division, Ninghua County Supply and Marketing Cooperative, *How the Zhiping Handmade Paper Purchasing Station Participates in Production, Improves Quality, and Enhances Business Management* (May 6, 1964). Ninghua County Archives, collected and provided by Lei Shaoqiu.
329 Ninghua County Planning Committee, *Notice on Implementing the 1964 Handmade Paper Export Plan* (November 9, 1964), archived at Ninghua County Archives, collected and provided by Lei Shaoqiu.

eight-year-old Chen Dimei gathered bamboo strips by the ponds and assisted in loading lime. In the ethnic-minority Daji brigade, 36 members of the 19 households went to the mountains, leaving only three elderly women at home to take care of the children and guard the village. They trained six women as skilled splitters, while children of eight or nine carried meals to the hills. Of the brigade's three schoolchildren, each used the early mornings and evenings to haul *zhuma* and tend cattle. Lan Lisao, another member, herded cattle in the hills while carrying *zhuma* on her back.[330]

In this fervent, high-intensity labor, every hand was turned to the collective task. But in the end, one question was still left unanswered—what did all this effort mean for the papermakers' own income?

Table 8 Preliminary Calculation of Production Costs for Handmade Paper Material Preparation in Zhiping Commune, 1964

Item	Amount (yuan)	Description
Lime	1.98	Each *dan* of paper uses 90 *jin* of lime; price per 100 *jin*: 2.20 yuan
Lime transportation fee	4.05	Calculated from Shangping as the central point to Shirenkeng in Changting, round trip 130 *li*; freight per 100 *jin*: 4.50 yuan
Mountain maintenance	1.50	Maintenance once every two batches; about one workday per *dan* of paper
Pond maintenance	0.60	Each pond holds an average of 20 *dan* of paper; requires 8 workdays, costed at 1.50 yuan/day, apportioned
Tool depreciation	1.00	Includes palm-fiber rain capes and skirts, bamboo hats, straw mats, knives for trimming mountain vegetation, axes, baskets, bowls, cooking utensils, etc.
Zhuma cutting/splitting wages	6.65	On average, cutting to soaking takes 3.5 days per *dan* of paper; daily wage: 1.90 yuan

---

330 Communist Party Committee of Zhiping Commune, *Work Summary Report on the Handmade Paper Raw Material Preparation Phase in 1964* (June 4, 1964), archived at Ninghua County Archives, collected and provided by Lei Shaoqiu.

Item	Amount (yuan)	Description
Zhuma washing wages	0.40	Washing 100 *dan* of *zhuma* costs 3 yuan, apportioned based on the fact that this quantity yields about7.5 *dan* of paper
Miscellaneous labor	0.75	One cook delivering meals and buying supplies, 2.5 trips per person down the mountain, totaling 50 days; wage: 1.50 yuan/day; apportioned over 100 *dan* of paper
Raw material administrator wages	0.55	For tasks such as unblocking bamboo water pipes, opening and cleaning pond sluices, cutting weeds around ponds, and monitoring water levels; about 37 days at 1.50 yuan/day; apportioned
Miscellaneous raw material expenses	0.13	Inspecting 100 *dan* of lime costs 3 yuan (total 4.50 yuan), plus oil and kerosene for soaking *zhuma*, 8.30 yuan; apportioned
Interest	0.58	Each *dan* of paper financed at 10 yuan; annualized monthly interest rate 4.8% applied
Subtotal	18.19	
Papermaking wages	18.38	For Grade 5 Yukou paper per *dan* (1 *dan* = 7 *dao*) at purchase price 52.50 yuan; 35% allocated as wages
Vat management wages	1.60	One person per workshop; average daily production one *dan* of paper; wage: 1.60 yuan/day; responsible for managing production, daily life, rice transport, delivery, and settlement
Production expenses	2.40	0.5 *jin* jute: 0.24 yuan; 3 *jin lan* leaves: 0.30 yuan; 2 *jin* each tung oil and beans: 0.20 yuan; kerosene/oiling brushes 0.15 *jin*: 0.60 yuan; transport out of mountains: 0.70 yuan; large/small thread: 0.10 yuan; others: 0.11 yuan
Workshop drying tool depreciation	2.50	Includes paper workshop, paper-drying walls, vats, barrels, buckets, paper press, racks, grain sieves, cooking pots, cooking utensils, etc.
Mountain rent	1.50	
San Jin (Three Contributions)	2.41	Paid at 5% rate
Taxes	1.21	Levied at 2.5% rate
Subtotal	30	
Total	48.19	

Source: *Preliminary Cost Estimate for Raw Material Preparation in Handmade Paper Production, Zhiping Commune, 1964* (May 9, 1964), Ninghua County Archives, collected and provided by Lei Shaoqiu.

According to Table 8, the cost of raw material preparation for Zhiping's handmade paper in 1964 had more than doubled compared to 1955. This rise was closely linked to the increased prices of production inputs such as lime and other materials and utensils, as well as higher labor wages. Correspondingly, the purchase price also rose: for Grade 5 Yukou paper, it reached 7.5 yuan per *dao*, an 80% increase over the 4.16 yuan per *dao* in 1955.

Regarding income, the commune adhered to the principle of "more work, more reward; those who do not work receive nothing." Zhiping Commune meticulously arranged cash wages for migrant workers and labor-point evaluations for local members. This led to a vigorous Five Inspections and Five Comparisons campaign—examining quantity and quality, attendance and efficiency, progress and diligence, planning and measures, as well as ideological commitment and collective spirit. Production brigades in Zuokeng, Huoyue, Xiaping, Gaodi, Qiaoxia, Laiwukeng, and Fukeng set records, with daily paper outputs exceeding 30 *dan*, which not only boosted productivity but also nurtured a new generation of skilled technicians. In 1963, for example, Gaofeng team members earned 1.05 yuan per 10 labor points; in the five Shangping teams, the daily minimum wage was 1.6 yuan, while the highest reached over 2 yuan. By 1965, Shangping team members received 2.6 yuan per 10 labor points as a dividend. That year, Zhiping's Yukou paper procurement totaled 370 tons, a 111% increase over 1962, and the quality improved substantially: Grades 1–3 accounted for 35.21% of production, Grades 4–5 for 42.15%, representing quality improvements of 40.02% and 24.93%, respectively, compared with 1962. The 1963 re-evaluation indicated a 95% compliance with the established grade standards. Samples of Grade 1 Yukou paper, selected from Zhiping Handmade Paper Station at the provincial handmade paper quality review meetings in Longyan and Sanming, gained recognition and were satisfactory to foreign trade export units.[331] After rapid recovery and development, handmade paper production across counties in Fujian approached or even surpassed historical highs by 1964.

In 1966, the Zhiping Commune sought to the consolidate collective economic gains, maintain high output, enhance product quality, and further develop the paper industry. The commune proposed "Thorough rectify the past practices of diverse and fragmented individual operations in the paper industry where production was contracted to groups or workshops in various forms and resolutely uphold the principle of taking production teams as the foundation, conducting collective production and operation, and implementing unified administration." Practices such as contracting for production, contracting for quality, over-fulfillment, or returning output to the workshops were considered forms of "private work" and had to be stopped. Instead, management was organized according to clearly defined quotas and labor-point evaluation for each stage of production.[332] Moreover, under the influence of the "Learn from Dazhai in Agriculture" campaign and socialist education movements, more local labor was directed to agricultural production and water conservancy projects, while the movement of migrant workers was strictly controlled. To cope with labor shortages in paper production, Zhiping Commune and its production teams mobilized local residents, including women, the elderly, and children.[333] As shown in Table 9, production recovered to historically high levels in 1965–1966. Despite a low period between 1970 and 1972, hand-

---

331 Zhiping Handmade Paper Procurement Station, Agricultural Products Division, Ninghua County Supply and Marketing Cooperative, *How the Zhiping Handmade Paper Purchasing Station Participates in Production, Improves Quality, and Enhances Business Management* (May 6, 1964). Ninghua County Archives, collected and provided by Lei Shaoqiu.
332 *Zhiping Commune's Opinions on the Management of Handmade Paper Production and Operations in 1966* (February 8, 1966), Ninghua County Archives, collected and provided by Lei Shaoqiu.
333 *Notice on Several Issues in Current Handmade Paper Production* (November 13, 1966), Ninghua County Archives, collected and provided by Lei Shaoqiu.

made paper production rebounded between 1975 and 1978, reaching annual outputs of over a thousand tons. Overall, during the Cultural Revolution, handmade paper production in Ninghua County and Zhiping Commune remained relatively stable, with the purchase price of Grade 5 Yukou paper remaining at 6.7 yuan per *dao*.[334] However, this stability was largely superficial and reflected only the general trends.

Table 9 Statistics on Purchases and Exports of Handmade Paper in Ninghua County

Year	Handmade Paper Purchases (tons)	Handmade Paper Exports (tons)
1965	1199.8	113.92
1968	1110.4	154.2
1970	896.5	
1972	980.1	365.78
1975	1146.9	205.27
1976	1028.8	187.52
1978	1065.7	275.20

Source: "Statistical Tables of the Main Agricultural and Special Local Products Purchased by the Commercial Departments of Ninghua County in Various Years" and "Statistical Tables on the External Sales of Several Major Export Products in Various Years in Ninghua County" (Liu Shanqun (ed.), *Chorography of Ninghua County*, Fujian People's Publishing House, 1992, pp. 385, 395)

In 1974, the Ninghua County Planning Commission, the Bureau of Commerce, the Native Products Company, and the Zhiping Supply and Marketing Cooperative formed a joint investigation team. With the close cooperation of the Zhiping Commune Party Committee and the broad participation of cadres and the masses, the team conducteded a comprehensive survey of the production costs of Yukou paper in Zhiping. The resulting report, rich in detail, offered a candid and factual depiction of the

---

334 Editorial Office of the Compilation Committee for the Chronicle of Supply and Marketing Cooperatives in Ninghua County, *Chronicle of Supply and Marketing Cooperatives in Ninghua County, Fujian Province (1931–1985)*, 1988, p. 207.

commune's handmade paper production between 1966 and 1974. It noted that Zhiping was among the main Yukou paper–producing areas in Fujian Province, and indeed a paper-making commune at its core. In 1973 alone, the paper industry contributed 75% of the commune's total income. The commune's population exceeded 9,300, with more than 3,300 laborers; it cultivated 8,020 *mu* of farmland and maintained 71,000 *mu* of bamboo forests. Of its 12 production brigades, five specialized in paper production, five combined farming with paper production, and two were primarily agricultural. Among the 77 production teams, 73 were engaged in the paper trade, operating a total of 173 paper workshops. Between 1966 and 1974, Zhiping delivered 131,000 *dan* of Yukou paper.[335]

For this investigation, the team conducted multiple interviews with commune cadres, vat managers, and paper-making farmers. They chose four representative production teams for a comprehensive and in-depth survey of the Yukou paper-making process: the Lower Pingpu team of the Pingpu Brigade, Gaodi Team No. 2, Lower Ping Team No. 7, and Tianshe Team No. 1. The basic profile of these four teams is presented in Table 10.

Table 10 Table of Basic Conditions of the Four Production Teams

Item	Unit	Pingpu Brigade, Lower Pingpu Team	Gaodi Team No. 2	Lower Ping Team No. 7	Tianshe Team No. 1
Number of households	households	20	31	33	28
Population	persons	114	158	181	120
Labor force	persons	48	45	51	46
Cultivated land	*mu*	163	54.5	48	40.4
Bamboo forests	*dan*	600	1,000	1,300	780
Total grain output in 1973	*jin*	65,300	26,855	40,122	27,170
Number of paper workshops	units	1.5	6	6	2

---

335 *Materials from the Zhiping Commune's Yukou Paper Production Cost Investigation* (July 30, 1974), Ninghua County Archives, Archive No. 57–24–15.

Item	Unit	Pingpu Brigade, Lower Pingpu Team	Gaodi Team No. 2	Lower Ping Team No. 7	Tianshe Team No. 1
Yukou paper output, 1972–1973	*dan*	387	971	1,307	588
Total income (1972–1973)	yuan	32,957.47	53,631.42	68,327.03	32,989.65
of which: Agriculture	yuan	11,470.48	5,124.44	8,094.07	5,297.12
Paper-making	yuan	17,662.00	46,287.61	57,302.95	27,153.75
Sideline activities	yuan	2,837.22	2,219.37	2,832.20	462.01
Others	yuan	987.77	124.87	77.81	76.77
Share of paper-making in total income	%	53.6	86.3	84.25	82.31
Share of agriculture in total income	%	34.8	9.37	11.84	16.06
Workpoint value in 1972	yuan per 10 points	0.77	0.91	1.11	1
Average self-produced grain per capita in 1972	*jin*/person	356	137	232	220
Workpoint value in 1973	yuan per 10 points	0.55	0.92	1.11	0.623
Average self-produced grain per capita in 1973	*jin*/person	356	134	185	201

From Table 10, it is evident that in 1972 the work-point value of these four production teams was far lower than that of Shangping Brigade in 1964. In fact, two of the teams experienced a sharp further decline in 1973. The investigation also verified the complete income and expenditure records for the paper industry during 1972–1973. Based on this, the team calculated the actual production cost per *dan* of Yukou paper in 1973 and made a preliminary discovery of several major issues in its production.

The first and foremost problem was that production costs were, in general, higher than the average purchase price. The breakdown of production costs for the four teams is shown in the following table.

Table 11 Detailed Cost Breakdown for the Four Production Teams

Unit	Type	1973 Production Cost per *dan* of Yukou Paper (Yuan)	1973 Average Purchase Price per *dan* of Yukou Paper (Yuan)	Difference between Cost and Purchase Price (Yuan)
Pingpu Brigade, Lower Pingpu Team	Mixed paper and farming	50.29	46.01	4.28
Gaodi Team No. 2	Paper-dominated	50.74	47.68	3.06
Lower Ping Team No. 7	Paper-dominated	49.28	43.8	5.48
Tianshe Team No. 1	Paper-dominated	50.3	46.03	4.27

The survey materials indicated that the main factors behind rising production costs were the general increase in prices and transportation fees for auxiliary raw materials such as lime and *lan* leaves, the higher wages paid to hired (migrant) laborers, and the inflated cost yet inferior quality of production tools—such as papermaking screens, paper presses, and iron drying plates—which further pushed up expenses.

A second problem identified was a noticeable decline in the overall quality of Yukou paper. In 1968, the average selling price per *dan* in Zhiping commune stood at 47 yuan; by 1972 it had fallen to 46 yuan, and in 1973 it dropped again to 45.07 yuan. The downward trend continued in the first half of 1974, dropping to 43.63 yuan. Historically, Gaodi Team No. 2 had produced mostly Grade 2 to 4 paper, yet by 1974 the majority had slipped to Grades 4 and 5. The other three production teams also experienced varying degrees of quality decline. With production costs unchanged, each drop in quality by one grade meant over 2 yuan less in revenue per *dan*. In 1973 alone, Zhiping commune purchased 20,000 *dan* of Yukou paper, earning roughly 40,000 yuan less than in previous years.

According to the survey report's analysis, this decline was mainly due to the lack of clear quality standards during factory production, a lack of attention from papermakers to improving quality during the process, and insufficient diligence from purchasing departments in enforcing quality checks to drive improvements. Additionally, the poorer quality of lime directly affected the final product.

Drawing on interview findings, the report offered several recommendations for improving Yukou paper production. These included increasing the grain reward for each metric ton of Yukou paper to 650 *jin*, making a moderate upward adjustment to the official purchase price of handmade paper (based on the 1966 pricing revision), and advising the tax authorities to exempt handmade paper from income tax.[336]

Table 12 Comparison of Production Costs and Benefits of Yukou Paper

Item	Unit	Year						Increase/Decrease in 1980 compared to 1959		Increase/Decrease in 1980 compared to 1975		Increase/Decrease in 1980 compared to 1979	
		1959	1961	1975	1977	1979	1980	Amount	%	Amount	%	Amount	%
Gross Output Value	Yuan	733.13	861.72	1044.94	1169.72	1497.99	1563.96	830.83	113.3	519.02	49.7	65.97	4.4

---

336 *Materials from the Zhiping Commune's Yukou Paper Production Cost Investigation* (July 30, 1974), Ninghua County Archives, Archive No. 57–24–15. According to the supply and marketing system, handmade paper had long been a key sideline industry in Ninghua County and the single largest product handled by the supply and marketing cooperative, accounting for about one-third of total procurement value. Each year it contributed over 200,000 yuan in taxes and profits to the state, hence the high level of government attention.
See: Editorial Office of the Compilation Committee for the Chronicle of Supply and Marketing Cooperatives in Ninghua County, *Chronicle of Supply and Marketing Cooperatives in Ninghua County, Fujian Province (1931–1985)*, 1988, p. 87.

Item		Material Costs	Labor (Work Days)	Unified Wage Rate	Amount	Amount	Cost as % of Gross Output Value
			Labor Payment Amount			Total Cost	
				Per Ton			
Unit		Yuan	Days	Yuan	Yuan	Yuan	%
Year	1959	191.22	387	2.00	774	965.22	131.7
	1961	460.42	416.2	2.00	832.4	1292.82	150
	1975	339.22	438.2	2.00	876.4	1215.62	116.3
	1977	340.24	455.6	2.00	911.2	1251.44	107
	1979	371.42	572.3	2.00	1144.6	1516.02	101.2
	1980	483.38	511.6	2.00	1023.2	1506.58	96.3
Increase/Decrease in 1980 compared to 1959	Amount	292.16	124.6		249.2	541.36	
	%	152.8	32.2		32.2	56.1	
Increase/Decrease in 1980 compared to 1975	Amount	144.16	73.4		146.8	290.96	
	%	42.5	16.8		16.8	23.9	
Increase/Decrease in 1980 compared to 1979	Amount	111.96	-60.7		-121.4	-9.44	
	%	30.1	-10.6		-10.6	-0.6	

Item	Unit	Year						Increase/Decrease in 1980 compared to 1959		Increase/Decrease in 1980 compared to 1975		Increase/Decrease in 1980 compared to 1979	
		1959	1961	1975	1977	1979	1980	Amount	%	Amount	%	Amount	%
Net Output Value	Yuan	541.91	401.3	705.72	829.48	1126.57	1080.58	538.67	99.4	374.86	53.1	-45.99	-4.1
Net Profit after Tax	Yuan	-232.09	-431.1	-170.68	-81.72	-18.03	+57.38						
Production Cost (Per Dao)	Yuan	5.78	7.74	7.28	7.49	9.08	9.01						
Average Purchase Price (Per Dao)	Yuan	4.39	5.16	6.26	7.00	8.97	9.36	4.97	113.2	3.1	49.5	0.39	4.3
Standard Purchase Price (Per Dao)	Yuan	4.34	5.05	6.7	7.4	8.8	8.8	4.46	102.8	2.1	31.3	0	0
Net Output Value per Labor Day	Yuan	1.40	0.96	1.61	1.82	1.97	2.11	0.71	50.7	0.50	31.1	0.14	7.1

Source: *Comparison of Production Costs and Benefits of Yukou Paper* (April 3, 1981), preserved in Ninghua County Archives, Archive No. 35-30-6.

After the end of the Cultural Revolution, in 1978, the Zhiping Supply and Marketing Cooperative reflected on the handmade paper production over the past decade. They noted that "the interference and sabotage by the 'Gang of Four' had exacerbated the tendencies toward rural capitalism. Mismanagement of bamboo resources by some production teams had led to the depletion of nearby forests while distant hills lay fallow. Combined with climatic factors, the deterioration of bamboo species affected raw material preparation for paper, as it was manifested in irregular cycles of good and lean years in certain mountain areas, resulting in varying degrees of production decline."[337] Whether these explanations truly addressed the underlying causes of the decline remains a question that is worthy of deeper consideration. In 1981, Ninghua County compiled data regarding the costs and profits of Yukou paper from 1959 to 1980. Using the figures presented in Table 12, together with the previously cited data, we gain a richer understanding of the development of the Yukou paper industry in Ninghua over the first three decades of the People's Republic of China, as well as the actual production conditions and livelihoods of the paper farmers who participated in this historical process.

5.2.   Printing Mao Zedong's Works

Another source of pride for the Yukou paper-producing region was that its paper was once selected for the central government's printing of Mao Zedong's writings. The Volume I of *Ninghua Historical and Cultural Materials* (1982), in its section on "Specialties of Ninghua," mentioned Zhiping Yukou paper, noting that during Mao's lifetime he had sent a letter to the Fujian Provincial Party Committee, instructing them to procure Zhiping Yukou paper for his calligraphic works.[338] Later, the 1985 edition

---

337 *Report by the Zhiping Supply and Marketing Cooperative on This Year's Handmade Paper Production* (August 5, 1978), Ninghua County Archives, collected and provided by Lei Shaoqiu.
338 Qiu Hengkuan, "Specialties of Ninghua," *Ninghua Historical and Cultural Mate-*

of *Ninghua Local Chronicles Newsletter* reported that in 1974, when the central authorities planned to publish the thread-bound edition with vertical lines of the *Selected Works of Mao Zedong*, Fujian was asked to send samples of Yukou paper from across the province for selection. In the end, Zhiping Yukou paper was chosen as the best option. Officials from the Central Publishing Bureau and the State Publishing Bureau arrived in Ninghua on October 15, 1974, to place an order. To ensure the quality of paper used for printing the *Selected Works of Mao Zedong*, the county carefully selected premium sheets and sent a total of 640 tons over a period of three years, from 1974 to 1976, including special allocations from the provincial company. After the books were published, the Central Publishing Bureau also gifted thread-bound copies of the *Selected Works* to the county's Revolutionary Committee and other relevant units as encouragement and commemoration. [339] Accounts from within the supply-and-marketing system tell a slightly different story, claiming that "in 1974, Chairman Mao personally chose Fujian Yukou and Maobian paper for printing Marxist-Leninist works and the Twenty-Four Histories. That year, Ninghua supplied 59 tons of top-quality Yukou paper, and the State Publishing Bureau also presented thread-bound copies of the *Selected Works* to the Ninghua County Party Committee and county cooperative."[340] Later records vary further. The 1991 volume of *Ninghua Historical and Cultural Materials*, in its forestry chronicle, noted that on October 15, 1974, the Central Publishing Bureau and State Publishing Bureau sent officials to order Zhiping Yukou paper for the thread-bound edition of

---

rials, Vol. 1, 1982, p. 115.

339 Yu Zhaoting, "Yukou Paper," *Ninghua Local Chronicles Newsletter*, No. 2, 1985, p. 56.

340 Editorial Office of the Compilation Committee for the Chronicle of Supply and Marketing Cooperatives in Ninghua County, *Chronicle of Supply and Marketing Cooperatives in Ninghua County, Fujian Province (1931–1985)*, 1988, pp. 87–88.

the *Selected Works*, with a total of 640 tons sent.[341] In contrast, the 1992 edition of the *Chorography of Ninghua County* records in its "Major Events" section that "on October 15, 1974, officials from the State Publishing Bureau and other units came to order Zhiping Yukou paper for printing the *Selected Works of Mao Zedong*, with a total of 420 tons shipped."[342] These inconsistent accounts, though incomplete and inaccurate, circulated widely in society and had a lasting impact.

With the assistance of the Ninghua County Archives, the Zhiping She Ethnic Township government, and Gui Shuzhong[343], and confirmed by the recollections of Zeng Shaoteng[344], then head of the Zhiping Supply and Marketing Cooperative's handmade paper procurement station, we now have a clearer and more detailed picture. We can analyze how much Yukou paper was transported in 1974 for printing Mao's works, the specific procedures involved, and whether the copies returned to Ninghua were the *Selected Works of Mao Zedong* or *Chairman Mao's Poetry*. We also have more precise information on the versions of *Chairman Mao's Poetry* preserved in Zhiping She Township, allowing a more thorough assessment of these three historical sources.

5.2.1.　Central Procurement of Yukou Paper

Before 1974, when the Ninghua County Revolutionary Committee and the Zhiping Commune Revolutionary Committee issued documents on handmade paper production, they emphasized the importance of "preparing raw materials carefully, producing quality paper, increasing collec-

---

341 "Forestry Chronicle," *Ninghua Historical and Cultural Materials*, Vol. 12, 1991, p. 10.
342 Liu Shanqun (ed.), *Chorography of Ninghua County*, Fujian People's Publishing House, 1992, p. 53.
343 Gui Shuzhong had long harbored doubts about this issue, and the present follow-up investigation was carried out under his guidance. See Gui Shuzhong, *Visual Records of Local Customs in Western Fujian: From Yukou Paper to Old Clan Genealogies*, Minzu Press, 2019, p. 16.
344 See Appendix 2 of this book, "Self-Account by Zeng Shaoteng."

tive income, providing funds for agricultural production, supporting socialist construction in both urban and rural areas, and contributing to the global revolutionary cause. This is not only of great economic significance but also of profound political significance." The focus at the time was primarily on supplying exports and boosting the income of local cooperatives.[345] Even as late as March 8, 1974, when the Ninghua County Revolutionary Committee issued the notice regarding production and raw material preparation for that year, the emphasis remained on economic and social contributions: "Handmade paper is a crucial material for cultural life and foreign trade exports, and a major agricultural and local specialty in our county. This year is a good year for raw material preparation. Whether the production tasks are completed will directly affect our ability to support exports, aid socialist construction, meet urban and rural market demands, strengthen and consolidate the collective economy, increase cooperative income, and provide production funds for grain."[346] At that point, there was still no mention of requests from the central government for paper allocation. As noted previously, in late July 1974, the Ninghua County Planning Commission, the Bureau of Commerce, the Local Products Company, and the Zhiping Supply and Marketing Cooperative formed a joint team to investigate production costs of Zhiping Yukou paper.[347] That investigation made no reference to printing Mao Zedong's works.

The earliest official archival record we have found concerning the State Publishing Bureau's request to requisition Zhiping Yukou paper is

---

345 *Notice from the Production Command Group of the Zhiping Commune Revolutionary Committee on Assigning the 1972 Handmade Paper Production Task* (July 4, 1972), Ninghua County Archives, Archive No. 57–24–15.
346 *Notice from the Ninghua County Revolutionary Committee on Assigning the 1974 Handmade Paper Raw Material Preparation and Production Task* (March 8, 1974), Ninghua County Archives, Archive No. 57–24–15.
347 *Materials from the Zhiping Commune's Yukou Paper Production Cost Investigation* (July 30, 1974), Ninghua County Archives, Archive No. 57–24–15.

Document No. 34, Zhige [74], issued by the Zhiping Commune Revolutionary Committee. Its contents are valuable, and the full text is summarized below:

Notice on the 1974 Handmade Paper Production Task and
Quality Requirements

To all brigades, supply and marketing cooperatives, banks, and grain stations:

The 1974 handmade paper production task was originally issued on March 24 via document *Zhi Ge* (74) No. 015. Based on new instructions from higher authorities and the current status of raw material preparation, the tasks have now been readjusted (see attached table for brigade-specific assignments).

Recently, the State Publishing Bureau sent officials to Ninghua twice to request an additional 100 tons of top-quality Zhiping Yukou paper (Grades 1–3) in the fourth quarter of this year, for printing Chairman Mao's works and important articles for central leadership. Not long ago, the State Publishing Bureau gifted our cooperative two copies of *Chairman Mao's Poetry*, printed on Zhiping Yukou paper. This represents the greatest honor and encouragement for all people in the cooperative and serves as a powerful incentive. We must follow Chairman Mao's teaching that "all products must not only be produced in sufficient quantity, but also be of high quality, durable, and long-lasting." With a revolutionary spirit of "more, faster, better, and more economical," we must strive to complete this year's paper production tasks to repay the care and support of the Party and higher authorities.

1. Publicize widely the news of the State Publishing Bureau's gift and the central government's special requisition, so that cadres and workers as well clearly understand the significance of high-quality paper production for the revolution. Use the momentum of the "Criticize Lin, Criticize Confucius" campaign and maintain high political enthusiasm to fulfill this honorable task.

2. Each brigade should convene a meeting of vat managers to inspect preparations, confirm production assignments, and devise measures to ensure high-quality output. Brigades focused primarily on paper should begin full production by the end of August; mixed paper-agriculture brigades should start by early September. To concentrate efforts on paper production, key personnel should not be in charge of both agriculture and papermaking; instead, experienced poor and lower-middle peasants should take the lead, while young people and women should be trained as vat operators.

3. Quality control is paramount. This task carries both political and economic significance. This year, efforts should ensure that Grades 1–3 paper account for 25% of output, with an average production of Grade 4 across the cooperative, generating an additional 70,000 yuan in collective income. Political and ideological education should reinforce strengthen the implementation of tasks, measures, and policies. The tasks for Grades 1–3 paper must be allocated to the vats with the best production foundations, and the enthusiasm of all workers and cooperative members should be fully mobilized. Every stage of production must be carefully managed, and key measures must be carried out throughout. Currently, this includes promptly

washing *zhuma*, making full use of spring water, maintaining workshop hygiene, and implementing the principles of fixed workshop, fixed personnel, fixed task, fixed quality (grade), fixed remuneration, and fixed measures, so as to guarantee that tasks are completed with both quality and quantity.

4. Promote technological innovation and technical reform, pursue increased productivity and cost savings, protect collective property, and boost overall output and income.

5. Supply and related departments must ensure the provision of production and living materials, strengthen technical guidance, improve service attitudes and quality, and prepare for procurement to support task completion.

All units are required to study and implement this notice promptly.

Copied to: County Bureau of Commerce, Local Products Company, Grain Bureau, County Finance Office

August 3, 1974

Attached: 1974 Yukou and Coarse Paper Production Task Allocation Table

Brigade	Number of Vats	Unit	Yukou Paper Production Task Allocation								Production Task for Coarse Material Paper	Notes
			Total	Grades 1–3 For Printing Chairman Mao's Works				Grades 4–6 (dan)	Grades 7–10 (dan)		
				Sub-Total	October	November	December				
TianShe	21	dan	2250	600	200	200	200	1310	340	80	Coarse material paper refers to: wrapping *doufang* (斗方, typically 25–50 centimeters square) paper
Xiaping	31	dan	3300	800	270	270	260	2005	495	150	
Gaofeng	19	dan	2050	600	200	200	200	1150	300	100	
Gaodi	28	dan	3000	900	300	300	300	1650	450	100	
Guangliang	9	dan	1000	250	80	80	90	600	150	30	
Zhiping	18	dan	1700	200	65	65	70	1245	255	20	
Nikeng	9	dan	900	100	30	30	40	665	135	20	
Honghu	6	dan	600	60	20	20	20	450	90	80	
Pingfu	10	dan	950	100	30	30	40	710	140	10	
Pengfang	4	dan	380	50	15	15	20	280	50	3	
Dengwu	2	dan	180	50	15	15	20	120	10		
Shefu	7	dan	700	100	30	30	40	500	100	15	
Total	164	dan	17010	3810	1255	1255	1300	10685	2515	770	

In particular, Grades 1–3 were requisitioned by the central authorities for printing Chairman Mao's Poetry and other works. Both quality and quantity, as well as delivery deadlines, had to be strictly ensured.[348]

This document, distributed on August 3, 1974, was sent by the Zhiping Commune to all its brigades, the local supply and marketing cooperative, the bank, and the grain station. Since production targets for handmade paper had already been assigned that March, this new notice represented an urgent revision in response to the latest orders from higher authorities.

It records that "recently" the National Publishing Bureau had sent staff members twice, demanding an additional shipment of 100 tons of Zhiping Yukou paper of Grades 1–3. This paper was to be used for printing Mao Zedong's writings and other important articles for the reading of central leaders. The document also notes that "not long ago" the Bureau had presented the commune two copies of *Chairman Mao's Poetry*, printed on Zhiping Yukou paper. This clearly shows that earlier shipments of Yukou paper from Ninghua—most likely after the printing of the large-character edition of *Chairman Mao's Poetry* in March 1974 as detailed later—had already been sent to the central authorities. And because its quality was so highly regarded, the Bureau sent officials repeatedly to Ninghua to secure more. According to the recollections of Zeng Shaoteng, the Bureau dispatched a division chief in 1974 to handle this personally. The latest August order was a significant task: 100 tons—about 2,400 *dan* or 16,000 *dao*—of only the finest Grades 1–3 paper.

A few days before this document was issued, *Materials from the Zhiping Commune's Yukou Paper Production Cost Investigation* had

---

348 *Notice of the Revolutionary Committee of Zhiping Commune, Ninghua County, on Assigning the 1974 Native Paper Production Tasks and Quality Requirements* (August 3, 1974), Ninghua County Archives, Archive No. 57–24–16.

documented a general decline in the quality of Yukou paper. This August directive thus stressed the need to "firmly grasp paper quality" and to ensure that Grades 1–3 accounted for 25 percent of output. Between 1972 and 1974, Zhiping's annual output in an "average" year was roughly 600–700 tons (about 15,000 *dan*), yet the proportion of Grades 1–3 was low. The production task allocation table for 1974 gave a special line item for "Grades 1–3 For Printing Chairman Mao's Works", with a target of 3,810 *dan*—just 22 percent of the planned total of 17,010 *dan*—and with only three months left in the year. To achieve this, the commune ordered that the Grades 1–3 quota be assigned to the better-equipped vats, that workers' enthusiasm be mobilized, that all production stages be tightly managed, and that key measures be carried through to the end. It also used this moment to promote a six-point system: assigning specific factories, people, tasks, quality grades, pay, and implementation steps—so as to deliver both quality and quantity, especially for paper destined for the center for printing Mao's poems and writings.

In reality, such a goal was impossible to meet within 1974. Just one month later, on September 12, Zhiping's Supply and Marketing Cooperative submitted a report to the commune party committee about the difficulties facing paper production process. The report's first point was that production was lagging because labor was being diverted to agriculture in response to the new "Learn from Dazhai in Agriculture" campaign, as well as to building reservoirs, roads, and hydroelectric plants. Paper factories were unable to find enough workers. By September 11, the Zhiping paper purchasing station had collected only 2,688 *dao*, and the proportion of Grades 1–3 remained significantly below the 25 percent target; even Grade 4 paper was scarce. The cooperative recognized that such progress would gravely hinder the completion of production tasks, noting that "more importantly, selecting paper for printing Chairman's works and important documents for Beijing is a political task"—one that, at the current pace, "would not be completed." Zhiping's Supply and Marketing Cooperative proposed moving on two fronts: get the vats running and tighten quality control. The production of Grades 1–3 paper—needed for printing the Chairman's works and major central documents—must be treated as a political task to be fulfilled in both quality and quantity. To address the immediate situation, they recommended:

1. Emulating from the Gaodi, Xiaping, and Gaofeng brigades: they calculated work points for papermaking based on the graded quality of the paper submitted, thereby linking both vat keepers and workers' pay to the grade of paper they produced. This practice was intended to embody the principle of "more work, more pay," mobilize commune members' initiative, and strengthen their conscious commitment to quality.

2. Increasing the number of women workers and apprentices, adapting the workforce flexibly according to each brigade's conditions, and raising wages and grain subsidies for papermaking—since papermaking was heavier, longer work than farming, it deserved higher work points.

To summarize, the cooperative concluded, "only by setting work points in a way that motivated the commune members and rewarded higher quality could paper production be improved and the political task of supplying the finest Yukou paper be accomplished."[349]

On January 19, 1975, the Zhiping Supply and Marketing Cooperative released a report on the 1974 handmade paper production and raw material preparation. The year's production target had been set at 650 tons; the actual output reached 652 tons, of which 624.9 tons were purchased. In 1973, Grades 1–3 paper made up only 4.59% of the total purchased; in 1974,

---

349 *Report on Current Issues in Paper Production and Several Tentative Suggestions* (September 12, 1974), Ninghua County Archives, Archive No. 57-24-16.

that proportion raised to 9.6%. In other words, the cooperative purchased nearly 60 tons of high-grade paper—still 40 tons short of the 100-ton quota demanded by the central government. The report evaluated the year's work, noting that the Central Publishing Bureau and provincial and prefectural leaders had visited Zhiping Commune multiple times to inspect and guide production. The commune's Party committee had attached great importance to papermaking, introducing measures such as public commendations and dedicated bulletin boards to accelerate production and improve quality. Above all, it stressed the "glorious political task of supplying Beijing with paper for printing Chairman Mao's poetry." To meet this task, paper-making households across the commune "learned from Dazhai's spirit of working hard and enduring hardship." During the labor-intensive process of cutting *zhuma*, "men and women, old and young, all turned out—no idle hands in any home." The report cited vivid examples of such dedication: in Pingfu Brigade's Daji Production Team, "the entire family turned up for work, with husbands and wives side-by-side splitting *zhuma*"; in Nikeng's Yeliao Team, 53 of 97 members reported for duty, "even nine-year-old Red Guards carried *zhuma* down from the mountains"; and in Tianshe's Beikeng Team, a 74-year-old man was mobilized to split and peel bamboo in the rain-soaked forests.[350]

The cooperative also described a production meeting in Xiaping Brigade with brigade and team cadres and vat supervisors. There, it was decided to revert entirely to using axes for harvesting *zhuma*, while digging out root clusters, and to follow the principle of "cutting the old stalks first, harvesting the mid-growth at the right time, and finishing with the tender shoots." All *zhuma* split that day was to be soaked the same day. The meeting also set a ratio: of every 100 *dan* of raw material, at least 90%

---

350 *Report on the Preparation of Raw Materials and Production Work for Handmade Paper in 1974* (January 19, 1975), Ninghua County Archives, Archive No. 57-24-16.

must be turned into Yukou paper, with coarse paper not exceeding 10%. The slogan was: "Do everything possible to raise product quality—aim for Grade 1 or 2, never lower than Grade 3," for this was tied directly to the political mission of supplying paper to Beijing for Mao's works. To safeguard quality, the cooperative proposed several measures:

1. Strengthen vat supervisors' sense of responsibility. Candidates were to be recommended by poor and lower-middle peasants, chosen for their collective spirit, socialist orientation, and strong sense of duty.

2. Improve water sources. Since water quality directly affects paper quality, most workshops replaced irrigation-ditch water with filtered spring water, keeping it clean.

3. Pay by quality. Work points were to be determined by the grade of paper produced, to mobilize members' enthusiasm.

4. Tackle skill deficits. In 1974, there were 263 apprentices, including 152 workers who had been away from the workshops for many years and whose skills were rusty. Since papermaking involved many interdependent steps, a flaw in one could ruin the final product, the cooperative examined output promptly, worked with vat supervisors to identify causes of defects, and suggested solutions—sometimes by letter or word of mouth, sometimes by visiting the workshop to solve problems on the spot. At Dongfeng Team's central workshop, for example, good raw material was ruined by poor coordination between sheet-forming and screen-lifting, resulting in uneven thickness and torn sheets. After direct interventions, their product improved from Grade 4–5 to Grade 2–3.

By year's end, paper quality had generally improved. Gaodi Brigade's First, Second, and Third Teams produced 825 *dan* of paper, of which 462 *dan* were Grades 1–3—56% of output. Zhiping's Ge'ao Team and Xiaping's Rongzikeng Team, which had not produced Grade 1 paper since the Cultural Revolution began, finally succeeded in 1974, boosting local income while assisting national socialist construction.[351]

Still, the report made clear that Zhiping's high-grade output remained far from the targets set by higher authorities. The cooperative admitted that in 1974 it had failed to deliver the full 100 tons of Grades 1–3 Yukou paper to Beijing and urged the resolution of the concrete problems to complete this "glorious task." It also noted that the Central authorities had gifted the cooperative two copies of *Chairman Mao's Poetry* printed on Yukou paper—a detail matching the recollections of Zeng Shaoteng, who said both the commune and the cooperative had received such books.

The unmet 1974 quota was carried over into 1975. According to Zeng, Zhiping dispatched a total of 680 tons of Yukou paper to Beijing in 1974–75, including the required 100 tons of high-grade stock. This paper was sent to Beijing Printing Plant No. 1 for the production of thread-bound large-character editions.[352]

---

351 *Report on the Preparation of Raw Materials and Production Work for Handmade Paper in 1974* (January 19, 1975), Ninghua County Archives, Archive No. 57-24-16.
352 In Mao Zedong's later years, the large-character thread-bound editions he read were gradually enlarged from the usual Song typeface of sizes 5–6, all the way up to size 1 Chang Fangsong (long imitation Song), then to 36-point long Song, and eventually even specially designed fonts. This meant that font design, type engraving, typesetting, plate-making, mounting, proofing, proofreading, printing, and binding all had to be carried out in an entirely new production process. Few printing plants were capable of undertaking this task, and publishers commissioned to produce large-character thread-bound editions might have needed to establish a dedicated workshop for them. The Beijing No. 1 Printing Plant, for instance, set up such a workshop.
Gen Huo, "The Secret Printing of the Large-Character Editions in Shanghai," *Memories and Archives*, No. 4, 2015;

These records also reveal that some of the Yukou paper shipped to the National Publishing Bureau in 1974–1975 was deemed unsuitable for use. Zhiping Commune and the cooperative received this feedback directly. On September 24, 1975, the Ninghua County Native Products and Sundries Company relayed to them the Provincial Native Products Company's instructions—passed down from higher authorities—calling for urgent attention to the quality of Grades 1–3 Yukou paper. The following is a transcription of that document.

Jiangle and Ninghua County Native Products Companies:

In July of this year, we visited the Beijing First Printing Plant to hear their feedback on the Maobian and Yukou papers supplied from your counties. The plant reported that, among the Grades 1-3 delivered in 1975, as much as one-fifth could not be used for printing after inspection. The main defects were these: sheets uneven in surface; irregular thickness from one end of a sheet to the other; inconsistent color within the same *dao*; torn or patched sheets; and the presence of foreign matter such as dark root fibers, bamboo residue, grit, scorch marks, and *lan* leave waste. In the case of Jiangle County's supply, some even contained deliberately tampered with wet sheets, and certain sheets were narrower than the required standard. All of this has compromised printing quality and squandered state resources.

Supporting the National Publishing Bureau in completing the central government's assignment to print large-character thread-bound editions is an honorable political task. We urge you to intensify the political education of your paper workers,

Liu Wenzhong, "Tasks Assigned by the Central Authorities and the 'Large-Character Editions,'" *Historical Studies of Modern Literature*, No. 3, 2016;
Chen Yimin, "'Large-Character' Thread-Bound Books in Tianjin," *Research on the History of Publishing in China*, No. 1, 2022.

cultivate a stronger sense of responsibility, and produce more paper of high quality—thus contributing more to the fulfillment of this mission. At the same time, you must enhance inspection procedures and enforce quality control, ensuring that no sub-standard paper is dispatched for printing. Only by guaranteeing both quality and quantity can we meet this year's state allocation.

July 31, 1975

Copies sent to: Sanming Region Native Products Branch Company; Ninghua County Bureau of Commerce; Jiangle County Bureau of Commerce; Jiangle County Handicraft Management Section.

Issued by the Native Products Company, Bureau of Commerce, Fujian Provincial Revolutionary Committee (seal)[353]

---

353 *Notice of the Ninghua County Native Products and Sundries Company Regarding the Forwarding of Document No. 117 from the Provincial Native Products Company (Commercial-Native Products-Sundries-1975)* (July 31, 1975), Ninghua County Archives; collected and provided by Lei Shaoqiu

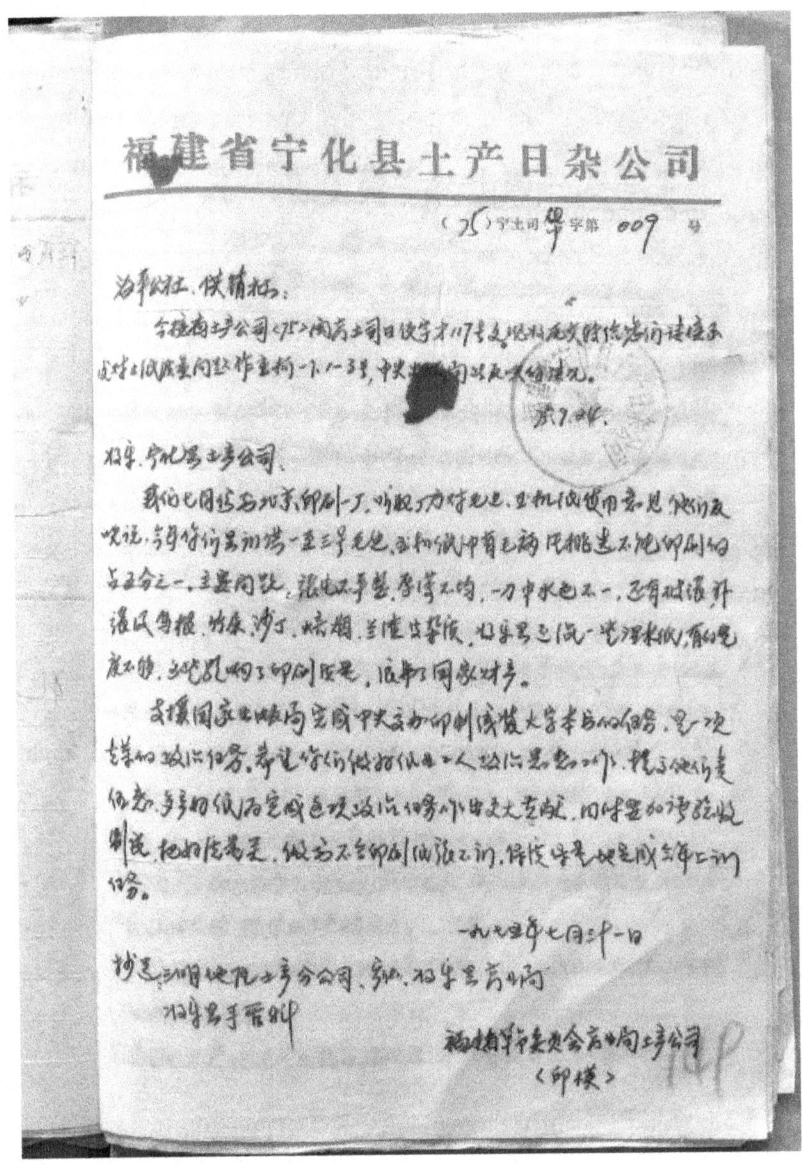

(Pic86 Notice of the Ninghua County Native Products and Sundries Company Regarding the Forwarding of Document No. 117 from the Provincial Native Products Company (Commercial-Native Products-Sundries-1975) (July 31, 1975), Ninghua County Archives; collected and provided by Lei Shaoqiu)

This document, issued by the Fujian Provincial Native Products Company to the native products companies of Jiangle and Ninghua counties, records a 1975 inspection trip to Beijing, where provincial represent-atives met with the Beijing First Printing Plant and received direct feed-back on paper quality. The meeting verified that the National Publishing Bureau had entrusted the Beijing plant with the printing of large-character thread-bound editions—such as *Chairman Mao's Poetry*. The plant's comments clarified that in 1975, fully 20 percent of the Grades 1–3 of Yukou and Maobian paper sent from these counties were unusable for printing, with defects ranging from warping and uneven thickness to in-consistent coloring, tears, patches, and assorted impurities. Jiangle Coun-ty's supply was additionally criticized for deliberately introducing defects. The document further emphasizes that this batch of Yukou paper was al-located specifically for the National Publishing Bureau's production of large-character thread-bound books. Combined with evidence from 1974 and 1975 on the central allocation and transport of Yukou paper, this rec-ord sheds new light on how we should understand the three versions of Mao Zedong's works held by institutions at different levels in Ninghua County.

5.2.2.   Mao Zedong's Poetry (Large-Character Edition)

Among the holdings of the Ninghua County Archives is a 1974 printed edition of *Chairman Mao's Poetry*, hereafter referred to as the "Large-Character Edition." The volume comes in an elegant blue six-panel case. On the case is a white patterned silk title slip reading "毛主席詩詞" (Mao Zhuxi Shici, Chairman Mao's Poetry). The book itself is also bound in blue, with a matching white patterned silk title slip. It is thread-bound, with the spine on the right and corners wrapped top and bottom. The printing and presentation are exquisitely refined and dignified. According to Zeng Shaoteng, this was precisely the version of *Chairman Mao's Po-etry* he saw in 1974, a gift from the central authorities.

Each page of the *Chairman Mao's Poetry* (Large-Character Edition) has a lining paper inside. The page edges bear a black fish-tail ornament. The text is in standard Song type, set vertically from top to bottom, right to left. The paper has now mellowed to a pale yellow. Zeng recalls that when first printed, the sheets were made from "immaculate" white Yukou paper, which over time naturally aged to its present hue.

According to its copyright page, this Large-Character Edition was based on the first edition published in Beijing in December 1963[354] and the second edition published in Beijing in March 1974.[355] It was first printed by the Beijing First Printing Plant in March 1974 and published by the People's Literature Publishing House. The book number is 10019·1765, and the price, printed on the page, states: "Thread-Bound Large-Character Edition, 11 Yuan." The mention of "Beijing First Printing Plant" here corroborates the earlier *Notice of the Ninghua County Native Products and Sundries Company Regarding the Forwarding of Document No. 117 from the Provincial Native Products Company (Commer-*

---

354 There is an innumerable variety of editions of *Chairman Mao's Poetry*. The version published in 1963 is referred to as the "63 Edition." It is the only edition personally proofread by Mao Zedong himself and contains 37 of his poems.
Li Zhi, "The Transcription, Publication, and Release of Mao Zedong's Poems," *Historical Studies of Modern Literature*, No. 3, 2006.
355 In March 1974, the People's Literature Publishing House issued *Chairman Mao's Poetry* in four different bindings: large-character thread-bound, small-character thread-bound, cloth-bound deluxe, and paperback. In terms of layout and design, the 1974 edition essentially restored the style of the 1963 edition—vertical typesetting in traditional Chinese characters—with the cloth-bound deluxe and paperback formats printed in "special 30 folio" size. The design differed from the 1963 edition in that the cloth binding of the deluxe edition was red, the title was stamped in gold, and Guo Moruo's calligraphy was not used; the title page, like that of *Quotations from Chairman Mao*, bore the slogan "Proletarians of the world, unite!" The poems included in the 1974 edition were identical to those in the 1963 edition, with only the wording and punctuation following the 1967 edition. Because the 1974 edition differed little from the 1963 edition, its copyright page identified it as the "second edition" of the 1963 version.
Li Xiaohang, "The Dissemination and Popularization of Mao Zedong's Poetry during the Cultural Revolution," *General Review of the Communist Party of China*, No. 6, 2013.

cial-Native Products-Sundries-1975). Both sources confirm that the Yukou paper requisitioned in 1975, and the Yukou paper used by the State Publishing Bureau in 1974, were sent to Beijing First Printing Plant for printing *Chairman Mao's Poetry.* The copy now in the Ninghua County Archives is, without doubt, one of the large-character thread-bound volumes gifted by the State Publishing Bureau to Ninghua County in 1974—printed entirely on Zhiping yukou paper.

5.2.3.   Selected Works of Mao Zedong (Four Volumes)

As noted earlier, both local historical documents and local chronicles in Ninghua County as well as the common sayings spread among the people generally agree on one point: that the consignments of Grades 1 to 3 Yukou paper sent to Beijing in 1974–1975 were used for printing the four-volume set of the *Selected Works of Mao Zedong.*

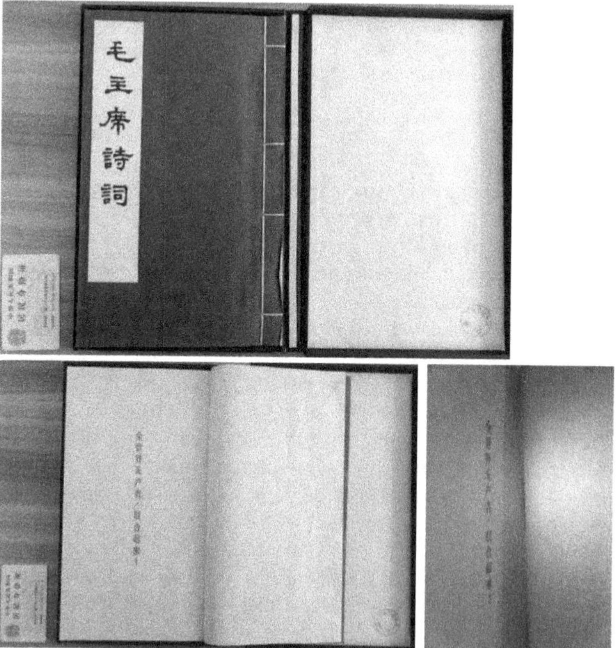

*(Pic 87-88 The Case and Cover of Chairman Mao's Poetry
[Large-Character Edition]; The Title Page of Chairman Mao's Poetry
[Large-Character Edition])*

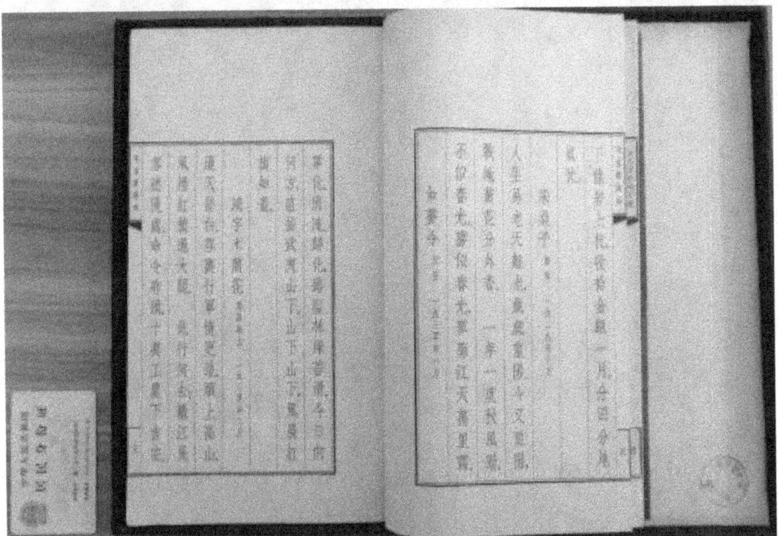

(Pic 89-90 The Lining Page of Chairman Mao's Poetry
[Large-Character Edition]; The Inner Page of Chairman Mao's Poetry
[Large-Character Edition])

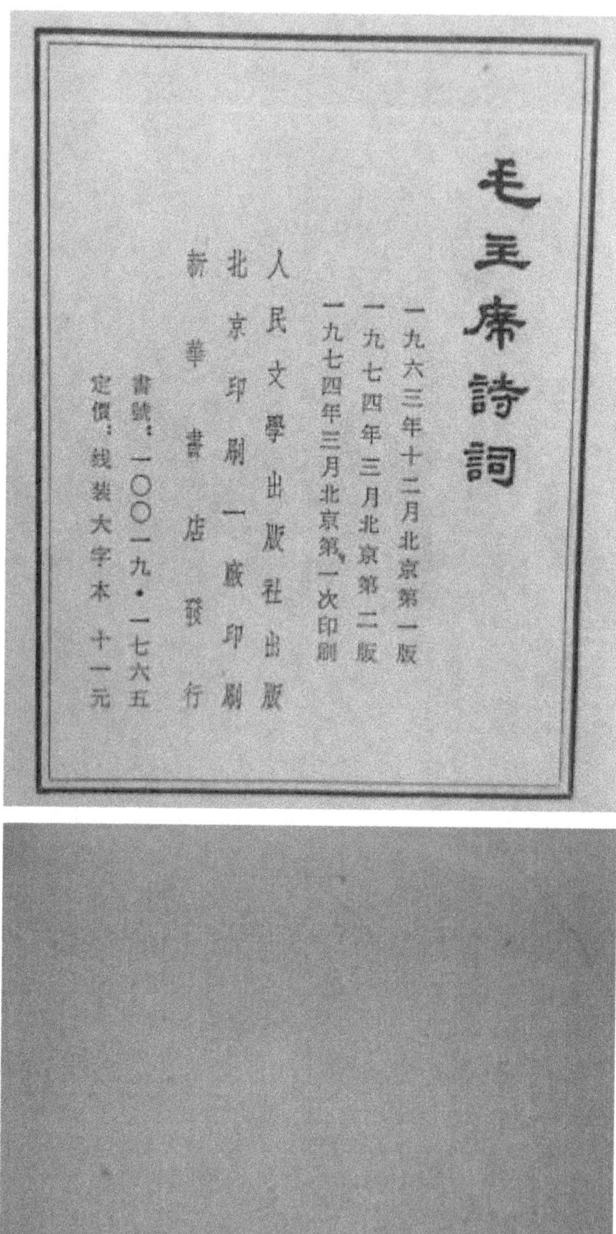

(Pic 91-92 The Copyright Page of Chairman Mao's Poetry [Large-Character Edition]; Paper Quality of the Inner Pages of Chairman Mao's Poetry [Large-Character Edition])

The Ninghua County Archives also preserves a complete four-volume set of the *Selected Works of Mao Zedong*, printed and published in 1965. Each volume is housed in a yellow slipcase, with the title label on the first volume reading *Selected Works of Mao Zedong (Volume I)* in white paper script. The covers themselves are also yellow, bearing the printed title *Selected Works of Mao Zedong (Volume I, Part 1)*. The books are thread-bound with the spine on the right, but without corner reinforcements. The printing is of high quality, though the page format is slightly smaller than that of the *Chairman Mao's Poetry* (Large-Character Edition). According to Zeng Shaoteng, he had never personally seen this particular edition.

The copyright page indicates that the set was published by the People's Publishing House and printed at the Shanghai Printing Plant of the Commercial Press in October 1965. It was based on the January 1964 thread-bound edition, reproduced in a reduced format,[356] with a unified book number of 1001·674 and a price of 11 yuan. From this publication data, it is clear that this set predates the *Chairman Mao's Poetry* and the 1974 central allocation of Yukou paper by over a decade. It was therefore not, as popular rumor has it, a product of Zhiping Yukou paper supplied to the State Publishing Bureau in 1974. That said, the 1965 edition of the *Selected Works* still holds significant cultural and historical value. Whether the paper used here was Zhiping type, and the exact story of its provenance, remain unanswered questions.

---

356 This edition of *Selected Works of Mao Zedong* should be the "Type C" version printed in 1965. The thread-bound large-character editions of Volumes 1–4, as well as the combined volume printed on dictionary paper, were published in the spring of 1964. The thread-bound large-character edition was issued in two versions—silk-bound and paper-bound (referred to as "Type A" and "Type B"), both in 16 folio format, boxed, with each volume divided into four fascicles, totaling four cases and 16 fascicles. In 1965, a reduced-size thread-bound edition (referred to as "Type C") was published based on the 1964 edition.
Fang Houshu, "Chronicle of the Publication of Mao Zedong's Works (1949–1982)," *Publication Archives*, No. 1 (2001).

5.2.4.   Chairman Mao's Poetry (Small-Character Edition)

Another mystery is a copy of the 1974 *Chairman Mao's Poetry*, preserved in the government offices of Zhiping She Ethnic Township, which we refer to as the Small-Character Edition. This copy lacks a slipcase, and the cover shows multiple creases. The cover is blue, with a white patterned silk title label reading *Chairman Mao's Poetry*, backed by a white paper backing. It is thread-bound with the spine on the right and no corner reinforcements. The page size is significantly smaller than that of the Large-Character Edition held in the Ninghua County Archives—contradicting Zeng Shaoteng's claim that all editions he had seen were of identical size. The inner pages bear multiple water stains and ink smudges. The title page, titled *Chairman Mao's Poetry*, carries a personal seal in raised script reading "Seal of Meng Haozhao."

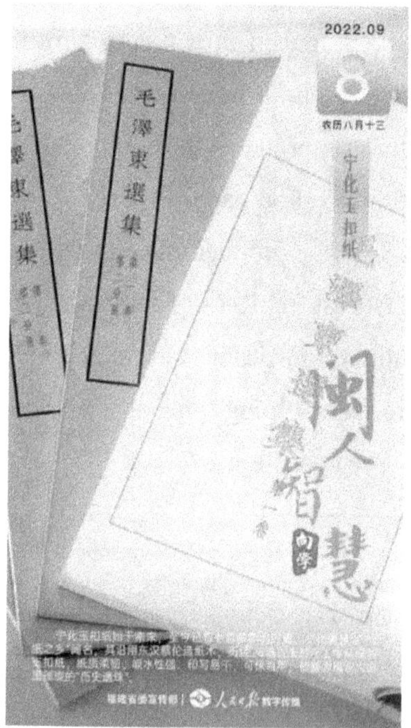

(Pic93 Promotional Image of Ninghua Yukou Paper by the Publicity Department of the CPC Fujian Provincial Committee and People's Daily Digital Communication Media, September 2022)

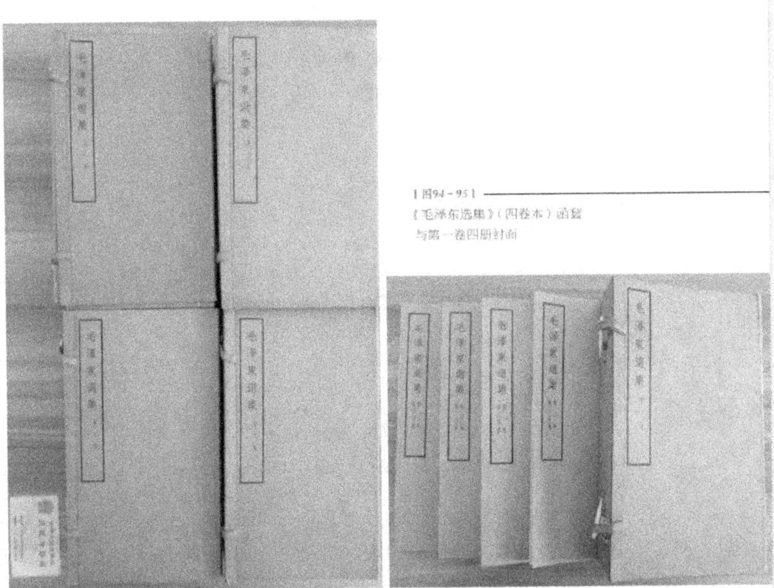

(Pic94-95 Slipcase and the Covers of Selected Works of Mao Zedong [Four-Volume Edition])

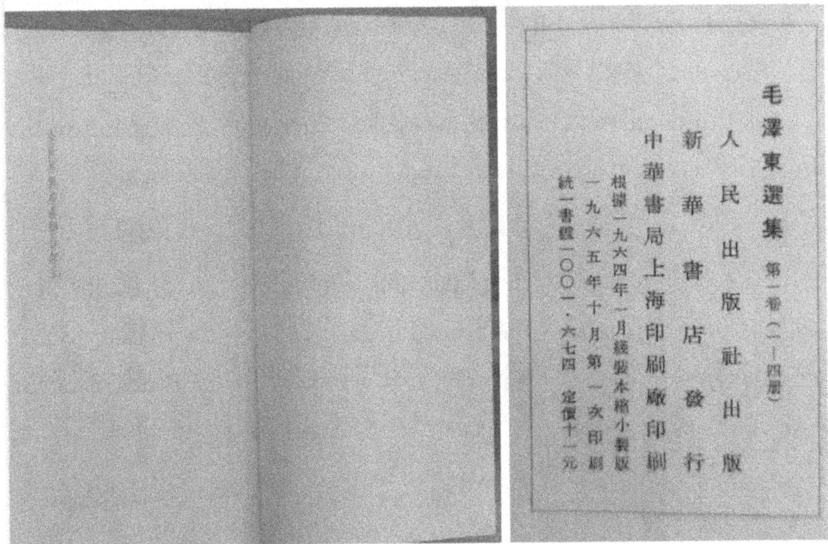

(Pic96-97 Title Page and Copyright Page of Selected Works of Mao Zedong [Four-Volume Edition])

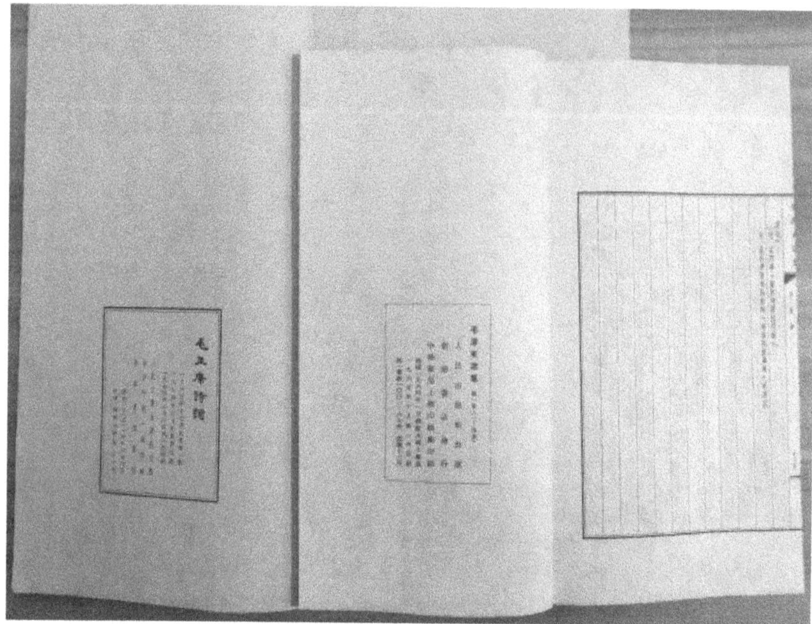

***(Pic98 Comparison between Chairman Mao's Poetry [Large-Character
Edition] and Selected Works of Mao Zedong [Four-Volume Edition])***

The inner pages lack lining papers. Each page edge is decorated with a black fish-tail mark; the text is in standard Song type, arranged vertically from top to bottom and read from right to left. The paper is a slightly yellowed white.

The copyright page states that this edition was based on the June 1974 Beijing Second Edition, printed in June 1974 by the Beijing Xinhua Printing Plant (Second Printing)[357], and published by the People's Literature Publishing House. It bears the same book number as the

---

357 The thread-bound small-character edition, the cloth-covered deluxe edition, and the paperback edition of the *Chairman Mao's Poetry* (1974 edition by People's Literature Publishing House) were printed for the second time in June 1974. In this reprint, the deluxe edition changed from a cloth cover to a paper cover.
Li Xiaohang, "The Dissemination and Popularization of Mao Zedong's Poetry during the Cultural Revolution," *General Review of the Communist Party of China*, No. 6, 2013.

340

Large-Character Edition—10019·1765—but is priced at "Thread-bound Small-Character Edition: 0.70." Several details raise concerns:

First, while the text is entirely in traditional Chinese characters, the copyright page alone uses simplified script.

Second, the personal seal "Seal of Meng Haozhao" suggests this book was once privately owned, and not continuously kept in the Zhiping Township offices.

Who was Meng Haozhao? Could such a valuable item have once circulated in the open market? And was it in fact one of the volumes gifted by the State Publishing Administration to the Zhiping People's Commune in 1974?

Third, earlier evidence shows the Large-Character Edition was printed at the Beijing First Printing Plant, and that in 1975 the Yukou paper was still being sent there. This Small-Character Edition, however, was printed by the Beijing Xinhua Printing Plant—a point that itself warrants scrutiny. Could the Xinhua Printing Plant undertake thread-bound book production? Did it have the right to use Yukou paper? These questions remain unanswered for further investigation.

By examining the Large-Character *Chairman Mao's Poetry* and the four-volume *Selected Works of Mao Zedong* from the Ninghua County Archives, alongside the Small-Character *Chairman Mao's Poetry* held in Zhiping She Township, we can be certain of one thing: among the Maoist works printed with Zhiping Yukou paper and sent back to Ninghua by the central authorities, one volume was indeed the Large-Character *Chairman Mao's Poetry* now preserved in the county archives. As late as 1977, the Zhiping Commune was still supplying high-quality paper for the State

Publishing Administration to print Mao's works.[358] By 1981, Zhiping was producing over 200 tons of Yukou paper annually, not only for central publishing needs but also for export.[359]

(Pic 99-100 The Cover and the Title Page of Chairman Mao's Poetry [Small-Character Edition])

---

358 Sanming Regional Supply and Marketing Cooperative, ed., *Supply and Marketing Cooperation Bulletin (No. 8)*, April 24, 1978. Ninghua County Archives, Archive Number: 57-28-20.

359 Ninghua County Committee of the Communist Party of China, *Investigation Report on Establishing the Zhiping Paper-Making Area*, April 3, 1981, Ninghua County Archives, archive number 57-31-7.

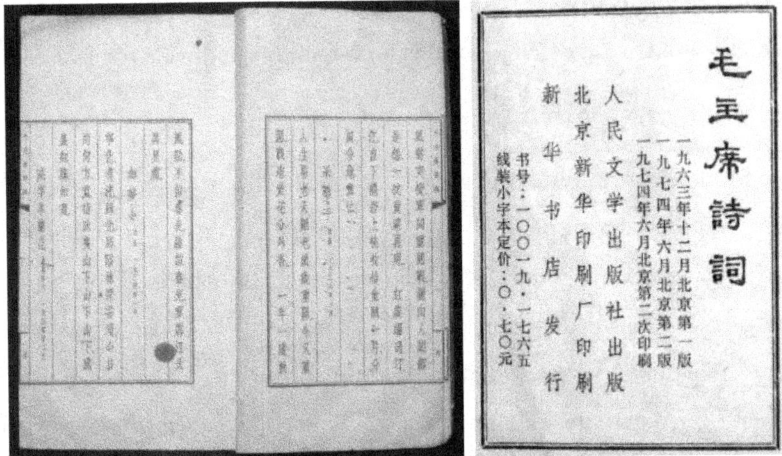

(Pic 101-102 Inner Pages and the Copyright Page of Chairman Mao's Poetry [Small-Character Edition])

5.3.　The Disappearance of Yukou Paper

During the Cultural Revolution, damaging policies such as "taking grain as the key link, cutting down everything, indiscriminately felling bamboo, digging up all the bamboo shoots, destroying forests for farmland—damaging both grain and paper" left "the hills near bare and the distant mountains barren." As a result, local handmade paper output fell year after year. In Zhiping, one of the most important papermaking areas, both per capita income and living standards steadily declined. After the reform and opening-up, Yukou paper was reclassified from a "Category II" state-controlled goods to "Category III," and in 1984 its trade was liberalized. This brought about more than a decade of high production and high profits. But after 2003, nearly all Zhiping's handmade paper workshops ceased operations. By 2008, only one small paper workshop, run by Hulanshan in Xikeng village, continued sporadic production—barely enough to survive. From 1978 to the early 2000s, What transformation in production, sales, and technological upgrading did Yukou paper undergo? The following section examines how, after market liberalization, the rise of market-driven distribution and the dominance of machine-made paper gradually eroded the demand for this high-quality handmade product.

5.3.1.   A Liberalized Market

In the early 1980s, Ninghua County repeatedly stressed, in its meetings and procurement plans for local handmade paper, the importance of adhering to state planning. Officials insisted that "handmade paper is a Category II good under state plan management. In accordance with the State Council's (approved minutes of the national meeting of supply and marketing cooperative directors) and Fujian Provincial Government Document No. 02 (1980), Category I and II goods cannot be subject to negotiated purchase or sale until state plans are fulfilled; nor can such negotiations proceed without higher-level approval." The county further required that handmade paper remain under the exclusive management of the supply and marketing system: "Procurement and allocation must be unified under the supply department. Multiple operators are not allowed, and any negotiated transactions must still be handled by the supply department. No other units or departments may interfere." Officials also stressed strict compliance with national pricing policies: "No unauthorized grade-based price hikes or cuts; no unauthorized cooperation or sales; operations must follow unified planning, unified pricing, unified allocation, and unified supply arrangements, to ensure all targets are met."[360]

---

360 *Speech by Comrade Wei Zongzhou at the Provincial Conference on Handmade Paper Production and Marketing* (March 29, 1980), Ninghua County Archives, collected and provided by Lei Shaoqiu;
Minutes of the County Conference on Handmade Paper Production (April 3, 1980), Ninghua County Archives, Archive No. 57-30-7;
Ninghua County Supply and Marketing Cooperative, *Decision on Issues Concerning Handmade Paper Production and Procurement in Fangtian Commune* (August 31, 1981), Ninghua County Archives, Archive No. 57-31-7;
Ninghua County Handmade Paper Procurement Plan in 1983 (September 26, 1983), Ninghua County Archives, Archive No. 57-33-14.

Up until about 1987, Ninghua County still enforced strict quotas for the purchase and allocation of handmade paper for export. In 1979, the county's export target was 200 tons.[361] In 1980, it procured 670 tons and exported 102.35 tons. The following years saw steady growth: procured 804.9 tons in 1981, 1,112.1 tons in 1982, 1,238.2 tons in 1983, 1,157 tons in 1984, 817.9 tons in 1985, 1,016.1 tons in 1986, and 1,139.2 tons in 1987, of which 254 tons were exported.[362] Zhiping alone produced about 750 tons of handmade paper annually. In 1979, it procured 817 tons (including 149 tons of top-grade paper allocated to the central government), exceeding the quota by 2.1%. The paper's total output value exceeded 1.1 million yuan—17.37% higher than in 1977—and accounted for over 60% of the commune's total income, more than double the agricultural income. Five production brigades—Gaodi, Xiaping, Gaofeng, Tianshe, and Guangliang—contributed between 70% and 95% of the total. Afterwards, much of the paper began leaking into private channels. In 1980, Zhiping's official procurement was 253 tons; by 1981 it had risen to 453 tons, by 1982 to 609 tons, and in 1983 it broke the thousand-ton mark. This trade brought significant economic returns to the local government and earned the country substantial amounts of foreign exchange.[363]

---

361 *Notice on Issues Regarding the Procurement and Allocation of Handmade Paper for Export* (September 25, 1979), Ninghua County Archives, collected and provided by Lei Shaoqiu.

362 Liu Shanqun (ed.), "Statistical Tables of the Main Agricultural and Special Local Products Purchased by the Commercial Departments of Ninghua County in Various Years," *Chorography of Ninghua County*, Fujian People's Publishing House, 1992, p. 385;

"Statistical Tables on External Sales of Several Major Export Products in Selected Years," *Chorography of Ninghua County*, Fujian People's Publishing House, 1992, p. 395.

363 Zhiping Commune Administrative Committee, *Produce More Handmade Paper for the Four Modernizations, Increase Income and Bring Joy to Thousands of Households* (March 12, 1980), Ninghua County Archives, Archive No. 57-30-7;

Zhiping Supply and Marketing Cooperative, *Supporting Handmade Paper Production and Revitalizing Purchase and Sales Operations* (February 1984), Ninghua County Archives, Archive No. 57-33-14.

In 1981, the Ninghua County Party Committee conducted a thorough investigation into Zhiping Commune's papermaking sector. On the basis of its findings, it proposed to the prefectural authorities that ten production brigades within Zhiping be officially designated as a "Papermaking Zone." The report revealed a fundamental problem: the quotas for state-supplied grain and incentive grain for papermakers were too low to meet the needs of workers' households. Paper farmers were selling their Yukou paper to the state at fixed official prices, yet had to buy part of their own staple grain from the market at much higher prices. The committee urged that—until Yukou paper prices could be raised—the supply and marketing cooperatives and the foreign trade department should allocate subsidies from production support funds and foreign trade management fees, offering 0.5 yuan for every *dao* of paper purchased. This, they argued, would support and expand papermaking at the team level. The report also called for an immediate correction of the "unreasonable" pricing structure. An attached document, *A Survey of Production Costs and Pricing for Yukou Paper in Zhiping Commune*, noted that prices had been raised in certain years, such as 1965 and 1979. But at that time, the disparity between state purchase prices and market prices had grown so wide that paper farmers' incomes suffered—making state procurement less attractive. For example, Zhiping's main producing teams—Gaofeng, Xiaping, and Tianshe—were only 15 to 25 *li* from Hengjiang Commune in Shicheng County, Jiangxi. Under the national plan, Jiangxi's Yukou paper was graded into eight quality levels, Ninghua's into 12. Each grade differed by 0.50 yuan per *dao*, and Ninghua's Grade 2 paper was equivalent in quality to Shicheng's Grade 1. Yet Ninghua's Grade 5 fetched only 8.8 yuan per *dao* in official procurement,[364] while in Hengjiang or Zhuji in Jiangxi, negotiated pur-

---

364 In 1978, the procurement price per *dao* of Grade 5 Yukou paper was 7.4 yuan; in 1980, 8.8 yuan; in 1981, 11 yuan; in 1984, 9.1 yuan; and in 1985, 11.3 yuan. Editorial Office of the Compilation Committee for the Chronicle of Supply and Mar-

chases brought 13.5–14 yuan—and in some Guangdong counties, merchants were paying 15 yuan. Faced with such disparities, Ninghua's 1980 plan to procure 750 tons in Zhiping yielded only 330 tons in reality.[365]

As the international market gradually loosened, Ninghua's state-controlled procurement and export system also began to soften. In 1979, for example, the county's export plan was handled by the County Sundry Company, which organized production and procurement and then transferred the paper directly to the foreign trade company—eliminating several layers of bureaucracy compared to earlier years.[366] Around 1981, outside merchants began arriving in Zhiping and other papermaking areas to buy Yukou paper directly from individuals. They were offering 14–15 yuan per *dao*—prices that quietly, but powerfully, reshaped the local market.[367]

In 1982, following the principles set out in the Central Committee's Document No. 1 of January 1983, Ninghua County and its supply and marketing system underwent structural reforms, introducing a responsibility system for bamboo forest management that assigned responsibilities to individual households.[368] By 1983, 82.6% of Zhiping's farming households had joined the cooperative. That year, the commune achieved 1.09 million yuan in commodity sales and 1.55 million yuan in procurement,

keting Cooperatives in Ninghua County, *Chronicle of Supply and Marketing Cooperatives in Ninghua County, Fujian Province (1931–1985)*, 1988, p. 207.

365 Ninghua County Committee of the Communist Party of China, *Investigation Report on Establishing the Zhiping Paper-Making Area*, April 3, 1981, Ninghua County Archives, archive number 57-31-7.

366 *Notice on Issues Regarding the Procurement and Allocation of Handmade Paper for Export* (September 25, 1979), Ninghua County Archives, collected and provided by Lei Shaoqiu.

367 *Decision on the Handling of Wu [Name Withheld] and Others for Jointly Trafficking in Yukou Paper* (1981), Ninghua County Archives, Archive No. 51-32-11; *Decision on the Handling of Yang [Name Withheld] for Engaging in Arbitrage of Yukou Paper* (1981), Ninghua County Archives, Archive No. 51-32-11.

368 Zhiping Commune Administrative Committee, *Prosperity Policies Reach the Bamboo Hills, Paper Industry Achieves Great Development* (February 1984), Ninghua County Archives, Archive No. 57-33-14.

surpassing profit targets and reaching the highest levels in turnover, cost control, and labor productivity since the commune's founding. Papermaking also entered a new stage. Responsibility contracts covered both bamboo management and papermaking itself, replacing the old "big pot" system of egalitarianism. Production, procurement, and sales changed dramatically: while reinforcing the papermakers' awareness of state plans, the system also opened the market to multiple trading channels.[369]

Zhiping's Commune Administration observed that after the Third Plenary Session of the Eleventh Central Committee, with the responsibility system steadily taking root, papermaking in Zhiping Commune began to flourish again. Output of Yukou paper increased year by year. Farmers took active steps to protect bamboo forests, improve their maintenance, and expand their area. Fine-tuned management became the standard practice, and "make more paper, make better paper" turned into a shared aspiration. With this revival, living standards in Zhiping improved markedly. A number of specialist households emerged as "first to prosper" through contracted papermaking. In Xiaping Brigade's Laijiashan production team, for instance, per capita net income reached 370 yuan—three times the 100-yuan average before the responsibility system.[370] In January 1985, Yukou paper was reclassified from a Category II to a Category III goods, with prices set according to market conditions and free negotiation—further accelerating the industry's growth.[371]

---

369 Zhiping Supply and Marketing Cooperative, *Supporting Handmade Paper Production and Revitalizing Purchase and Sales Operations* (February 1984), Ninghua County Archives, Archive No. 57-33-14.

370 Zhiping Commune Administrative Committee, *Investigation Report on Yukou Paper Production in Zhiping (The Past, Present, and Prospects of Yukou Paper)* (January 10, 1983), Ninghua County Archives, Archive No. 57-33-14.

371 Editorial Office of the Compilation Committee for the Chronicle of Supply and Marketing Cooperatives in Ninghua County, *Chronicle of Supply and Marketing Cooperatives in Ninghua County, Fujian Province (1931–1985)*, 1988, p. 88.

The new production system also brought new challenges. First, after bamboo forests were contracted to individual households, frictions began to emerge among papermakers—disputes over workshop space, ponds, production schedules, and even labor. To address these conflicts, the Zhiping Commune began signing agreements with paper-making households and dispatching staff to work alongside them and to villages to facilitate various forms of labor cooperation.[372] Second, the rise in paper prices did not translate into a substantial increase in per capita income. Take the Grade 4 Yukou paper as an example: in 1975, the cost per *dan* was around 45 yuan, the selling price 54 yuan, leaving a profit of 9 yuan. By 1982, the selling price had climbed to 80.50 yuan per *dan*, but production costs had also risen to 69 yuan, meaning the profit margin had grown by only 2.5 yuan in seven years. Third, even with an annual output of less than 800 tons, there were already issues of unsold stock, leaving papermakers worried about market demand for Yukou paper.[373]

From 1982 to 1983, the handmade paper market shifted dramatically. Buyers both within and outside Fujian felt that Yukou paper was overpriced and failed to meet quality standards; they were reluctant to place orders, resulting in piles of unsold stock.[374] The situation worsened after Guangdong reclassified handmade paper as a Category III commodity, opening its market to competition from all over the country. The seller's market quickly flipped into a buyer's market, sending prices and demand into sharp decline. International trade provided little relief. A global eco-

---

372 Zhiping Commune Administrative Committee, *Prosperity Policies Reach the Bamboo Hills, Paper Industry Achieves Great Development* (February 1984), Ninghua County Archives, Archive No. 57-33-14.
373 Zhiping Commune Administrative Committee, *Investigation Report on Yukou Paper Production in Zhiping (The Past, Present, and Prospects of Yukou Paper)* (January 10, 1983), Ninghua County Archives, Archive No. 57-33-14.
374 Ninghua County Supply and Marketing Cooperative Union, *Notice on Adjusting the Extra-Price Subsidy for Yukou Paper* (February 13, 1984), Ninghua County Archives, Archive No. 35–33–4.

nomic slump, combined with unfavorable exchange rates, sharply curtailed exports, further undermining the sales of Yukou paper.[375]

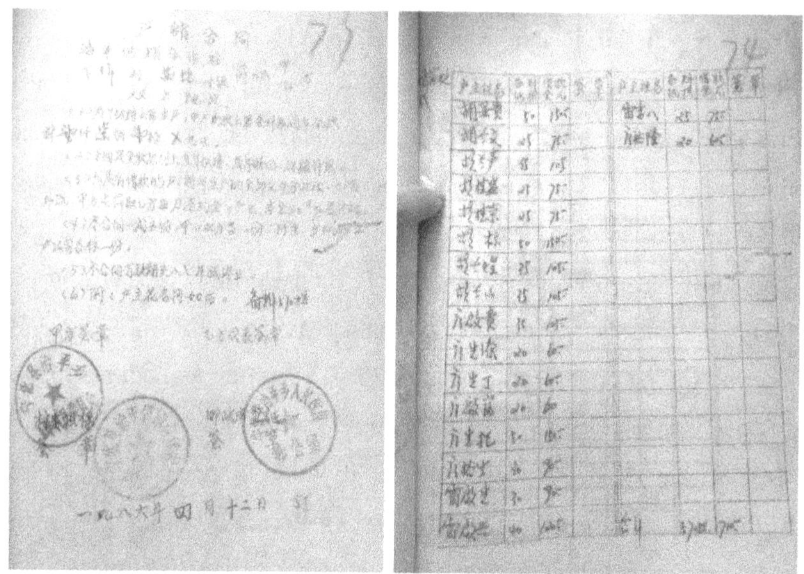

(Pic 103 Production and Sales Contract between the Xikeng Team of Xiaping Village and the Zhiping Supply and Marketing Cooperative, 1986 Ninghua County Archives, Archive No. 57-36-25)

In August 1989, Zhiping Township's handmade paper industry slid into an unprecedented crisis. Sales slowed to a crawl, and prices dropped repeatedly. A *dao* of Grade 4 paper sold for just 14.8 yuan—about 103 yuan per *dan*—representing a fall of over 56 yuan per *dan*, or 35%, compared with the same period the year before. This price collapse alone cut the earnings of township papermakers' earnings by over one million yuan, inflicting a heavy blow on both production and livelihoods. That year, the Zhiping Township government launched surveys in several villages—including Xiaping, Gaodi, and Niekeng—to tally the actual costs of handmade paper production as follows:

---

375 Ninghua County Supply and Marketing Cooperative Union, *Notice on Cancelling the Extra-Price Subsidy for Maobian Paper and Lowering the Extra-Price Subsidy for Yukou Paper* (May 15, 1984), Ninghua County Archives, Archive No. 35–33–6.

Detailed Breakdown of Costs and Workers' Wages for Producing One *Dan* of Handmade Paper in 1989

Lime: 80 *jin* (priced at 10 yuan per *jin*), 8 yuan

Cutting and peeling *zhuma* (including carrying it to the soaking pond): 4 days at 6 yuan per day, 24 yuan

Washing and bleaching *zhuma:* half a day, 3 yuan

Paper-making labor costs (11 workers in total):

Paper maker: 1 worker, paid 0.9 yuan per *dao* (7 *dao* per *dan*), 6.30 yuan

End lifter: 1 worker, 6.20 yuan

Drying and trampling *zhuma*: 4 workers at 6.1 yuan each, 24.4 yuan

Peeling *zhuma*: 2 workers at 6 yuan each, 12 yuan

Carrying raw fiber from pond to workshop: 1 worker, 6.1 yuan

Chopping firewood for drying: 1 worker, 6.3 yuan

Workshop caretaker: 1 worker, 6 yuan

Rice for workers:10 people, 20 *jin,* 13 yuan

Vegetables and cooking oil for workers: 3 yuan

Extra meals at start and completion of work: 2 yuan

Miscellaneous (pressing ropes, screens, *lan* leaves, oil, tool depreciation, etc.): 5.5 yuan

Workshop rent: 0.5 yuan

Total: 125.9 yuan

(Note: labor for replanting and restoring bamboo forests was not included in this calculation.)

This meant that producing one *dan* of paper cost roughly 126 yuan, while the market price was only around 103 yuan. In other words, every *dan* sold at a loss of about 23 yuan—the more paper produced, the greater the losses. That year, over 100 of the 220 paper workshops in Zhiping Township shut down almost overnight. Large quantities of processed *zhuma* rotted in the ponds or were sold off to outsiders at extremely low prices. The entire industry of paper makers suffered a severe economic blow. In response, the Zhiping Township Government proposed measures to protect paper farmers' livelihoods and alleviate their burdens. These included reducing taxes and fees (at the time, handmade paper sales were subject to 6.38% VAT, 1% business tax, 9% special product tax, plus 1% education surcharge, 1.5% resource management fee, and others), actively supporting technological upgrades and value-added processing of Yukou paper, and providing loans and subsidies to help producers survive the crisis.[376]

By 1991, the selling price of handmade Yukou paper in Southeast Asian markets had fallen year after year, inflicting further heavy losses on Zhiping's paper farmers. Based on market intelligence and field investigations, the Zhiping Enterprise Management Office concluded that using Yukou paper as a raw material to produce cigarette paper, ritual paper, improved writing paper, and similar products could be highly profitable. They proposed establishing the "Ninghua County Zhiping Yukou Paper Craft Factory," which would require only 30 tons of Yukou paper annually as raw material for further processing. The finished products could be sold

---

376 Zhiping Township Government, *Investigation Report on the Current Status of Handmade Paper Production in Zhiping Township* (1989), Ninghua County Archives, Archive No. 57-39-10.

to Guangzhou and beyond, even for export, with an estimated annual output value of 144,000 yuan. The township government approved the proposal.[377] Yet, behind this initiative lay an undeniable truth—high-quality Yukou paper had already lost much of its former market share.

5.3.2. The Trend Toward Mechanization

Plans to modernize handmade paper production in Zhiping—whether through full or partial mechanization—first emerged in the early 20th century, and the ambition to mechanize persisted well into its latter half. As early as 1959, in its work summary, Zhiping Commune declared the goal of a "major technological leap forward," aiming to "achieve three targets within the year: mechanized pulping, single-person screen-lifting in sheet formation, and steam-powered paper drying."[378] That same year, the commune also proposed the idea of building a machine-operated paper mill. Documents such as *Plan for Installing Machinery in Zhiping's Paper Mill* and *Report on the Commune-Run Paper Mill* reveal that chronic labor shortages—each good year requiring over 3,000 seasonal laborers hired from counties like Changting—were a key reason for pursuing a mechanized plant.[379]

Of the three goals, "single-person screen-lifting" was the first to materialize, since the limited water and electricity supply made mechanized pulping and steam drying difficult. By 1975 at the latest, experiments in producing coarse paper with suspended screens were already in progress

---

377 Zhiping Township Government, *Reply on Approving the Establishment of the "Ninghua County Zhiping Yukou Paper Craft Factory"* (April 13, 1991), Ninghua County Archives, Archive No. 57-41-7.
378 *Summary Report on the Current Situation of Handmade Paper Production by the CPC Zhiping Commune Committee* (May 24, 1959), Ninghua County Archives, Archive No. 26-5-30.
379 *Plan for Installing Machinery for a Paper Mill in Zhiping Commune* (February 24, 1959), Ninghua County Archives, Archive No. 26-5-30.

in Zhiping.[380] The dream of a machine paper mill, however, remained only a plan until September 1979, when the villagers and cadres of Xiaping Brigade—relying on "self-reliance supplemented by a small amount of state investment" and over 90,000 yuan raised locally—built their own facility. Without trained technicians, they sent people out to learn or brought in instructors. Once operational, the mill could produce half a ton of paper per day, yielding an annual output value of 72,000 yuan.[381]

In 1978, the Fujian Provincial Conference on Handmade Paper Production strongly endorsed mechanization. By then, the province already had 110 paper machines in use. In Shunchang, machines for making cultural paper had passed initial tests; in Jiangle's Lishan Paper Factory, machine-made Maobian paper reached near-handmade quality, with a daily output of half a ton. The meeting proposed establishing large-scale production bases, with the following plan: by 1980, six counties—including Shunchang, Nanping, Liancheng, Longyan, Youxi, and Yongding—were to mechanize or semi-mechanize over 85% of their paper mills; by 1985, Ninghua, Jiangle, Changting, Shanghang, and Wuping were to follow suit.[382]

Zhiping fell behind these counties. On one hand, the lack of water power and electricity made operating machinery difficult; on the other, Zhiping specialized in high-grade Yukou paper, unlike most regions that used machines to make coarse stock. After Ninghua was designated a na-

---

380 Ninghua County Revolutionary Committee Planning Commission, *Supplementary Notice on the Pricing of Screen-Hanging Coarse Paper* (January 6, 1975), Zhiping She Ethnic Township Archives.

381 Zhiping Commune Administrative Committee, "Produce More Handmade Paper for the Four Modernizations, Increase Income and Bring Joy to Thousands of Households" (March 12, 1980), Ninghua County Archives, Archive No. 57-30-7; *Speech Draft for the Zhiping Commune Handmade Paper Production Conference* (July 16, 1979), Ninghua County Archives, Archive No. 57-29-23.

382 *Minutes of the Provincial Handmade Paper Production Work Conference* (December 1978), Ninghua County Archives, collected and provided by Lei Shaoqiu.

tional handmade paper production base, both Xiaping's and Shuiqian's machine paper mills began producing coarse paper. The county encouraged trials of single-person screen-lifting and water-powered pulping, urging "experienced paper farmers and technicians to innovate without compromising the traditional character of Yukou paper." To support this, the county's hydropower department allocated 450,000 yuan to build the Zhaoguang Reservoir, whose dam could generate 750 watts—enough to power technical upgrades in the paper industry.[383]

Before Zhiping's machine mill, the commune discarded over 500 tons of bamboo bark annually—apart from small amounts used to make coarse paper, most simply rotted on the hillsides. From the 1960s onward, large quantities were sold cheaply to Fuyang, Zhejiang, for machine-made paper, or mixed with substitute fibers to produce toilet paper, with annual output around 200 tons. In 1974, the Chaoyang Paper Mill opened in Cuijiang Town, producing wrapping paper and roofing felt. In 1979, Anle Paper Cooperative built a machine mill with a 40-ton annual output of coarse paper.[384] By 1981, with energy constraints easing and vast amounts of unused bamboo bark available, Zhiping decided to build a second plant—half-machine, half-handcrafted—producing Yukou paper at half a ton per day, with funding from local trading companies and supply cooperatives.[385]

---

383 Ninghua County Revolutionary Committee, *Minutes of the County Handmade Paper Production Work Conference* (April 3, 1980), Ninghua County Archives, Archive No. 57-30-7;
Ninghua County Committee of the Communist Party of China, *Investigation Report on Establishing the Zhiping Paper-Making Area* (April 3, 1981), Ninghua County Archives, Archive No. 57-31-7.
384 Qiu Denong and Yi Juexun, "Overview of the Development of Paper Production," in *Ninghua Historical and Cultural Materials*, Vol. 4, 1984, p. 73.
385 Zhiping Commune, *Report Requesting Funding to Establish a Mechanized Yukou Paper Factory* (June 29, 1981), Ninghua County Archives, Archive No. 57-31-7.

By 1983, Zhiping's annual machine-made paper output, including coarse paper, exceeded 1,100 tons. That year, paper farmers' per capita income reached 180.74 yuan, up 22.71 yuan from 1982 and 57.70 yuan from 1981. [386] Technological reforms also brought cost savings—two-thirds of mills replaced hemp ropes with steel cables in pressing, saving over 10,000 yuan annually.[387] In 1983, Xiaping's machine mill was contracted by villager Lai Guangyao, who secured a 6,000-yuan loan to fix electrical and maintenance problems. With scientific and efficient management, both paper quality and economic benefits improved significantly: after deducting 20% for depreciation, 6,000 yuan in profits to the brigade, and production costs, the mill still generated 5,000 yuan in income that year, turning a loss-making, non-operational enterprise into a profitable one.[388]

Yet from 1983 onward, the widespread adoption of machine-made paper sharply reduced demand for Yukou paper, especially overseas. Export markets for this once-prized writing paper collapsed, forcing Zhiping to pivot toward making ritual gold and silver paper for burning for export.[389] Hu Lanshan, after adopting machine pulping with manual sheet formation, halted Yukou production entirely in 1989.[390] Luo Zhaotian, born in 1970 in Zhiping, entered the paper trade in the late 1980s and still makes ritual paper rolls for shipment to Guangzhou and Shantou for fur-

---

386 Zhiping Commune Administrative Committee, *Prosperity Policies Reach the Bamboo Hills, Paper Industry Achieves Great Development* (February 1984), Ninghua County Archives, Archive No. 57-33-14.
387 Zhiping Supply and Marketing Cooperative, *Supporting Handmade Paper Production and Revitalizing Purchase and Sales Operations* (February 1984), Ninghua County Archives, Archive No. 57-33-14.
388 Zhiping Commune Administrative Committee, *Prosperity Policies Reach the Bamboo Hills, Paper Industry Achieves Great Development* (February 1984), Ninghua County Archives, Archive No. 57-33-14.
389 Zhiping Commune Administrative Committee, *Investigation Report on Yukou Paper Production in Zhiping (The Past, Present, and Prospects of Yukou Paper)* (January 10, 1983), Ninghua County Archives, Archive No. 57-33-14.
390 See Appendix I of this book, "Hu Lanshan's Personal Account" (2022).

ther processing. He recalls that after 1988, virtually all Zhiping machine-made paper became raw material for ritual paper, with his purchases alone covering over 40% of the local market, shipping it all to Shantou, Guangzhou, and Hong Kong to be processed into gold and silver paper.[391] Zeng Shaoteng remembers that in Luo's era, mills didn't even peel bamboo bark—the focus was on output, not quality—because the paper was destined for burning, not writing. "That's no longer Yukou paper," he said. "Different times, different markets."[392]

By the close of the 20th century, large-scale Yukou production in Zhiping She Township had all but vanished. With the decline of the handmade paper market, the last generation of apprentices—those born in the 1960s and 1970s—trained by master papermakers left the trade entirely. Many left their hometowns, walking away from what was once celebrated as the "capital of Yukou paper."

---

391 Based on an interview with Luo Zhaotian conducted on September 3, 2022, at Luo Zhaotian's home in Zhiping.
392 See Appendix 2 of this book, "Self-Account by Zeng Shaoteng" (2022).

6. A Promising Future for Yukou Paper

When studying the history of book publishing in 18th-century Europe, Robert Darnton observed that the cost of paper could account for as much as 75 percent of a book's total production expenses. High-quality folio sheets—dense, heavy, and brilliantly white—were not only expensive but also notoriously difficult to obtain. In that era, the feel and appearance of paper often played a decisive role in whether a customer would purchase a book, giving rise to a distinctive paper consciousness. Paper, as the material backbone and foundation of the book economy, was indispensable—whether for movable type printing, woodblock engraving, or manuscript copying—amid the increasingly commercial rhythms of daily life. By the late 18th century, European publishers were already using paper quality as a marketing device to appeal to different audiences. Labels such as "Dutch paper" or "imitation vellum" signaled to buyers that the edition before them carried a certain value or prestige. The quality of paper—alongside its format and dimensions—became a key marker of social distinction. In the 19th century, the decline in paper quality and the rapid spread of machine-made paper paradoxically revealed another story: the rise of the modern mass readership.[393] The history of paper in European publishing reflects in minute detail, the commercial practices, technological capabilities, cultural tastes, and class consciousness of the societies that produced it. So, what will the paper of the future look like?

---

393 Robert Darnton, *The Business of Enlightenment: A Publishing History of the Encyclopédie, 1775–1800*, trans. Ye Tong and Gu Hang, SDX Joint Publishing Company, 2005, pp. 177, 509;
The Multigraph Collective, *Interacting with Print: Elements of Reading in the Era of Print Saturation*, translated by Fu Li, Beijing United Publishing Co., 2021, pp. 255–256.

6.1. Preserving an Intangible Cultural Heritage

The first person to notice the near extinction of Yukou paper-making skills and take action was Gui Shuzhong, whose real name was Ning Yuanguai, a native of Ninghua. Since 2008, Gui has been documenting local life and culture through film and photography, devoting years to collecting and preserving cultural information and local knowledge of Ninghua and the surrounding Hakka regions. His first full-length documentary, *Yukou Paper*, was born from the faint fragrance of a Yukou paper notebook in his childhood memory. When he realized that Ninghua's Yukou paper industry was in steep decline, he resolved to record the process faithfully through film. Shot in the old papermaking workshop of Hu Lanshan, the footage took years to collect, eventually woven into a complete record of the production process. With a visual language similar to poetry and oil painting, the film conveys his deep nostalgia for his homeland and its people.[394]

To better preserve and pass on the traditional craft, Ninghua County and Zhiping She Ethnic Township have stepped up efforts to protect Yukou paper-making—safeguarding its practitioners, production sites, tools, and the pristine waters of bamboo-covered mountains. They have gathered historical records, taken photographs and videos, interviewed inheritors, and worked to secure the craft's place on official intangible cultural heritage (ICH) lists. In July 2018, Yukou Paper-making Techniques was inscribed as a municipal-level intangible cultural heritage of Sanming City; in March 2019, it was included in the sixth batch of Fujian Province's intangible cultural heritage projects. Work is now underway to apply for national-level recognition.

---

394 Gui Shuzhong, *Visual Records of Local Customs in Western Fujian: From Yukou Paper to Old Clan Genealogies*, Minzu Press, 2019.

The nomination process involved detailed field surveys. Local governments and cultural historians examined the current inheritance methods and inheritor information, bamboo forest reserves, mountain water quality, the remains of paper workshops and ponds, and the protection of production equipment and tools. Based on these surveys, they formulated corresponding protection policies and conservation plans.

The craft is still passed on mainly through the traditional master–apprentice system. In Xikeng, a hamlet of Xiaping Village, Hu Lanshan (born 1951) and his son Hu Cheng (born 1975) continue their family tradition. In fact, this tradition mirrors other scattered inheritors of handcrafted Yukou paper: skills are taught by seasoned masters to apprentices, a traditional way of preserving the craft. Hu himself began learning papermaking at 16 under Xiao Chengjin (born 1922) in Tongfang, Changting, while also learning from his father Hu Xianfa. Over decades, Hu became especially skilled in paper drying.[395] Today, he trains his second son in managing vats and maintaining production standards, while Hu Cheng excels in the final screen-lifting stage and paper drying. Both were recognized in 2021 as provincial-level ICH inheritors of the craft. Currently, the key to preserving this traditional craft lies in protecting elderly masters skilled in ancient papermaking techniques, encouraging them to take on apprentices, and leveraging their dedication to train a new generation of Yukou paper makers and managers with traditional craftsmanship spirit.

In terms of bamboo forest reserves and mountain water quality, Zhiping She Ethnic Township provides both policy and financial support for conservation, while protecting its "green mountains and clear waters" through initiatives like the construction of the Tingjiang Source Scenic Area and ecological preservation. To ensure the quality of Yukou paper

---

395　For the history of papermaking in the Hu Lanshan family, see Appendix I of this book, "Hu Lanshan's Personal Account."

raw materials—*zhuma*, water, and lime—the township has standardized fertilizer and pesticide use in bamboo planting, addressed water pollution, and secured lime reserves. These measures guarantee an adequate, pollution-free, and sustainable supply of raw materials.

The Zhiping She Ethnic Township Government, with the help of village Party secretaries, village heads, and elderly villagers, collected geographical information regarding traditional paper workshops and ponds. It compiled and organized unified forms documenting details of historically existing workshops: names, owners, locations, area, bamboo forest coverage in the village, founding and shutdown dates, original annual output, inheritance status, current condition of buildings, altitude, and longitude/latitude, supplemented by photographs and video. Gui Shuzhong compiled these into an online "Ninghua Zhiping Papermaking Cultural Heritage Site Group" (https://yukoupaper.com), documenting over 270 former workshops. This "cultural map" of Zhiping's paper workshop forms a foundation for applying for national geographical indication status, establish a papermaking cultural heritage site group, secure national-level ICH project, and support future academic research.

The preservation of traditional equipment and tools is another focus. Special attention is paid to the production of clay drying wall and the supply of papermaking screens. The clay drying wall has largely disappeared since the 1980s, replaced by cheaper, longer-lasting steel structures, making its makers rare. Since the clay drying wall is essential in the traditional process, identifying and training artisans who can make them is urgent. Likewise, papermaking screens are consumable tools. Fortunately, villagers in Fuzhu, Longyan—such as Chi Canghai—and Zhong Jiusen in Ruijin, Jiangxi, still produce high-quality, custom-sized handmade screens for Yukou paper.

Cultural infrastructure has also been restored. The township has repaired the former site of the Minguang Paper Workers' Union in Zuokeng, Pingpu She Village, and established the Xikeng Yukou Paper Inheritance Center in Xiaping Village. It has integrated Yukou paper culture into local streetscapes and the Tingjiangyuan scenic area, and in 2023 opened the "Papermaking Capital—Zhiping" Museum (Yukou Paper ICH Inheritance and Experience Center) and Traditional Yukou Paper Workshop. These venues collect and organize information on Yukou paper-making techniques, build a database, and showcase the craft from multiple perspectives—strengthening protection and promotion efforts across the board.

In recent years, thanks to extensive promotion by local governments, cultural historians, and respected villagers, Yukou paper has attracted the attention of experts and scholars in specialized fields such as papermaking science and paper history. An increasing number of research teams have organized academic surveys of Yukou paper in Zhiping. Since 2019, over 20 experts and scholars from Peking University, Tsinghua University, the University of Science and Technology of China, and the National Museum of China conducted an academic survey on Yukou paper-making techniques and its historical culture in Zhiping, offering suggestions for the craft's protection and development. Since 2021, Xiamen University's history department has conducted repeated fieldwork and collected Yukou paper-related documents in Zhiping, Ninghua, Changting, and Shicheng. Experts agree that Yukou paper is the finest raw material paper and should strive to produce a top-tier Grade 1 paper, restoring its highest traditional quality and aiming for to be recognized as a representative of raw material paper in the national-level ICH list.

On the side of restoring production, the Zhiping Township Government commissioned Hu Lanshan to produce handmade Yukou paper in 2017, reviving the traditional process. In September 2022, with top-grade raw materials ready, Hu restarted full-scale hand papermaking. Influential local entrepreneurs with family ties to the craft see bright market prospects for reviving this heritage industry and are investing resources and networks to support the Yukou paper revival, preparing to play an active role in the new round of cultural industry development.

The *14th Five-Year Plan for Intangible Cultural Heritage Protection* (released in May 2021) emphasizes that the primary tasks for ICH protection include strengthening surveys, records, and research. This involves launching the second national ICH resource survey, engaging universities, research institutions, and society at large, and comprehensively documenting ICH items and inheritors through text, images, audio, and video. It also calls for improving the ICH documentation system and enhancing the development of ICH archives and databases. With the joint care and support of governments at all levels and all sectors of society, the future of Yukou paper is undoubtedly promising.

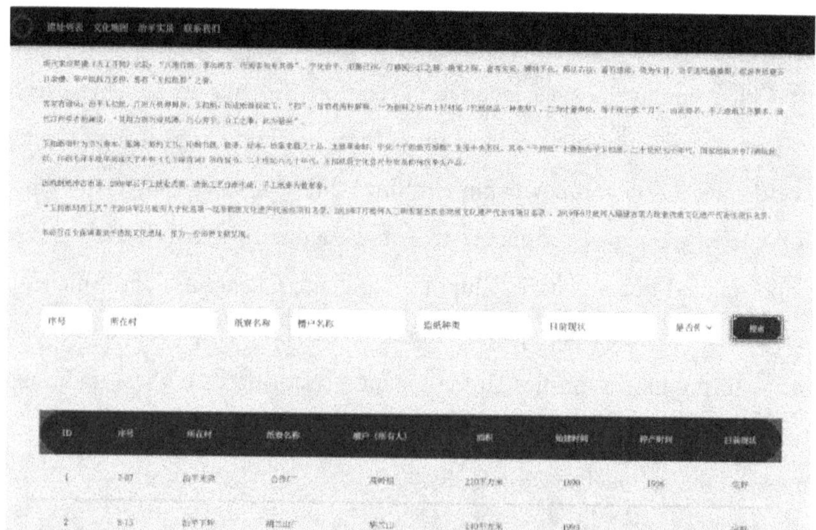

(Pic104 Homepage of the "Ninghua Zhiping Papermaking Heritage Cluster" Website)

(Pic105 Cultural Elements of Yukou Paper on the Streets of Zhiping She Ethnic Township)

6.2.　The Aesthetics of Yukou Paper

Yukou paper, as one of Fujian's celebrated regional papers, belongs to the broader family of bamboo papers common across southern China, as evidenced by its raw materials. Its distinctiveness lies in the method of production: it is made using the *shengliao* (raw material) technique. Through meticulous craftsmanship—careful selection of *zhuma*, scrupulous preparation of all the materials, and exacting control over each stage of papermaking—artisans manage to overcome bamboo's natural disadvantage of short, brittle fibers. In often harsh and difficult conditions, with the simplest of materials and the most basic processes, they produce paper of such refinement that it approaches the realm of art. The production of high-quality Yukou paper helps define its unique place in the global history of papermaking technology. Its freedom from chemical additives further broadens the potential uses for *shengliao* Yukou paper, offering versatile applications.

Particularly in the case of "Neishan Yukou paper," whose papermaking sites are deep in mountain forests, opportunities for outsiders to witness production directly have been rare. Since the late 19th century—when Japanese Inoue Nobumasa collected—until as late as the 1980s and 1990s, only a handful of people, mostly government investigators enforcing the PRC's state purchase and distribution system, were able to enter these remote paper workshops to observe Yukou paper production firsthand or communicate directly with workshop managers and workers. Even scholars from the Ming and Qing dynasties, such as Song Yingxing, Guo Bocang, and Yang Lan, never had such a chance. This isolation has been one reason why Yukou paper's renown has rarely spread beyond its production and consumption zones.

With the help of independent visual documentarians like Gui Shuzhong, local historians, and regional officials, I have had the rare privilege of traveling repeatedly into these mountains to observe papermaking on-site. Conversations with experienced papermakers such as Hu Lanshan—who grew up both making Yukou paper and managing paper mills—have yielded a wealth of historical records and oral histories of western Fujian's handmade paper industry. In Zhiping, nearly every man over 50 has participated in some stage of Yukou paper production or trade. Their life stories, interwoven with folk records and archival materials, vividly illustrate the impacts and hardships faced by the Yukou paper industry and its local communities amid modernization. The observant reader will have noticed my recurring concern with the earnings of papermakers and workshop owners. Even as I write this, simple yet lingering questions remain: Papermaking is backbreaking work with meager wages and even the risk of losses—so why keep doing it? And how, despite this, do they still produce Grade 1 Yukou paper?

I hope readers will see, in the rise and decline of this craft, the many ways in which handmade paper, paper products, and paper-based printed materials once enriched daily life. Papermakers' attachment to Yukou paper is not a shallow sentiment, but a deeply rooted pride in a local craft. Yet, paradoxically, I resist reducing this sentiment to the oft-repeated clichés of "craftsmanship spirit" or "master craftsmanship." This spirit is intangible and unsustainable. Like any craft, the making of Yukou paper—from learning the basic skills to honing true mastery—has always been shaped by the socioeconomic and cultural conditions in which the workers lived. It deserves to be told not as a romantic abstraction, but as part of a lived economy and culture.

The craft first took root in remote areas in Zhiping villages like Laijiashan, Tianshe, and Gaodi, later spreading to other villages in the area. Although the abundance of bamboo in the mountains made papermaking possible, the deeper reason lay in poverty. Local genealogies speak of families "with nothing but bare walls," where men and women endured a decade or more of backbreaking work to improve their lot until they achieved a comfortable life." For people born in these mountains, there were few ways to escape poverty beyond farming. Using local resources to engage in producing household handicrafts—like papermaking—became a way to supplement family income. In the paper market, workshop owners had little bargaining power. To break free from the high-interest loans and advance-purchase schemes of paper merchants, their only option was "frugality and the relentless pursuit of quality," which could win them some leverage in negotiating prices. Viewed through the lens of social history, what we call "craftsmanship spirit" in this context is nothing more than the mountain people's human qualities—the perseverance and frugality—combined with a pragmatic drive to improve their living standards via meeting market demand with superior products.[396]

Yet it is also true that, beyond these market forces and economic pressures, there emerged an inner drive—a devotion to preserving the craft's distinctiveness. This devotion is not confined to producers alone; it extends to distributors and consumers, forming a shared sentiment that I call the "Aesthetics of Yukou Paper."

Drawing on Robert Darnton's notion of "paper consciousness" in 18th-century Europe, it is a kind of collective knowledge and shared emotion surrounding a particular craft and product among producers, distributors, and consumers. The "Aesthetics of Yukou Paper" is about creating, cultivating, and preserving that sensibility. If there is still a chance to save this craft from fading, it begins with rekindling the "Yukou sensibility" in the last generation of traditional papermakers—those who work entirely by hand, without chemicals, perfecting each step of the process, and passing their exacting standards to apprentices. It continues with nurturing that sensibility in a new generation of papermakers, who will stubbornly strive to internalize traditional techniques and understand quality, proudly inheriting and promoting this unique craft—perfected by ancestors through

---

396 As early as the early 20th century, a series of international socialist women's movements had already raised the stirring slogan, "Bread for all, and roses too." It was a call for women's rightful claim to both the material essentials of life and the nourishment of the spirit. This rallying cry inspired the American poet James Oppenheim to compose his celebrated poem *Bread and Roses*. Over the decades, the poem has been translated into many languages and set to music in numerous versions, resonating across the world. A stanza of it reads: "Our days shall not be sweated from birth until life closes—/ Hearts starve as well as bodies: Give us Bread, but give us Roses./ As we come marching, marching, unnumbered women dead/ Go crying through our singing their ancient song of Bread;/ Small art and love and beauty their trudging spirits knew—/ Yes, it is Bread we fight for—but we fight for Roses, too." The papermakers of Yukou Paper, as this book relates, were much the same. They did not merely produce the paper that served daily needs—the bread of ordinary life. They also offered the world works of beauty, as precious and enduring as roses.

long years of labor—and developing their own appreciation for its beauty. It must also reach users—those who love the paper's warm hue and faint bamboo scent, who explore its potential in ancient book restoration and book printing, or use it for specialized calligraphy and painting. When makers and users together exercise this "Yukou sensibility," they ensure that this beautiful paper remains in the world, to accompany the next generation's cultivation of aesthetic taste, and to offer diverse, distinctive experiences.

Ultimately, the "Aesthetics of Yukou" is not confined to Yukou paper. It can be applied to any traditional craft. An artisan who dedicates themselves to perfecting a unique skill can find joy in reaching the pinnacle of their art; a connoisseur who cherishes a particular object can take pleasure in its singular beauty. Each can love what they love, and beauty can meet beauty—until together they form a shared realm where "the beauty of each enriches the beauty of all."

Appendix
1. Hu Lanshan's Own Account[397] (2022)

My name is Hu Lanshan. I was born in 1951 in Xikeng, a small natural hamlet in Xiaping Administrative Village in Zhiping Township, Ninghua County, Fujian Province. When I was three, I was sent to live with my grandmother in Changting, and I stayed there all through my childhood, even finishing junior high at Changting No. 1 Middle School. In the countryside, there's an old saying: "Grandparents treasure the first grandson most." I was the eldest grandson in the family, and my grandmother really spoiled me. Back then, there was no TV, no mobile phones. On summer nights during the school holidays, we'd sit outside in the cool air, and my grandmother would tell me stories from the past. I remembered quite a few of them.

I started learning papermaking from my father, Hu Xianfa, when I was around 10. My father, in turn, had learned the craft from his uncle—my great-uncle. His name was Hu Liangbao. He belonged to the Liang generation of our family, the generation before my father's. I never met him, and I don't know when he was born. From what I've heard, Hu Liangbao was the first of our clan to come to Xikeng to make Yukou paper. He bought bamboo hills, set up paper mills, and got the Hu family's business started here. Life in his time was hard. He had been born in Shifu Village, Changting—with too many mouths to feed, too little land to cultivate. This was before hybrid rice or multiple harvests a year; famine was

---

397 This account is based on interviews with Hu Lanshan conducted on 21 July 2022 and 3 September 2022 at his home in Xikeng Natural Village, Xiaping Village, Zhiping She Ethnic Township, Ninghua County, Sanming City, Fujian Province. The transcripts were reviewed and approved by Hu himself. The July 21 interview was carried out by Chen Yao, Gui Shuzhong, Hong Yulin, Wang Mukun, Jia Yi, Huang Yazhen, and Zhuo Yingping; the September 3 interview by Chen Yao and Gui Shuzhong. On both occasions, the research team was also received by Hu's wife Lai Yongdimei, his second son Hu Cheng, Cheng's wife Liu Qingxiangzi, and their son Hu Shenghai.

common. Like many others, he had to leave home to make a living. Liangbao first went to Gaodi in Zhiping, collecting *zhuma* bark—the outer layer shaved from bamboo during papermaking, or leftover bark from other people's Yukou paper production. At that time, no one else in Gaodi was using it. He used the bark to make wrapping paper. Making wrapping paper was profitable—it wasn't as complicated to make, and it sold really well. Why? Because wrapping paper was used for making "two-kick" firecrackers—the big Gaosheng firecracker. The fibers in the wrapping paper were strong enough to make firecrackers fly high. In the countryside, every year during the first lunar month—when families opened their doors for the new year, or at weddings, or any happy occasion—people would set off those firecrackers. So making wrapping paper was a good money-maker, and Hu Liangbao made a small fortune from it.

With some savings in hand, he moved to Xikeng to start making paper. At first, he worked for others; later, with more money, he bought a small mountain and began his own Yukou paper production. Every time he earned more, he bought more bamboo hills. Soon, Xikeng had several paper workshops under his ownership. There was Shiqiangbei—if you walked five *li* in from there, you'd reach Paizi Paper Mill, and a bit further in, the Shapingli Paper Mill. He owned multiple bamboo hills for Yukou paper production, accumulated his capital, and expanded his business. Liangbao became a well-known figure in the area. My grandmother said that at that time, our family had about 40 or 50 people living together and eating from the same kitchen—we hadn't split into smaller households yet.

In Liangbao's day, our family would come to Xikeng to make paper, earn money in Zhiping's mountains, and then return to live in Changting. Back then, Zhiping was known as the "economic district." Changting was purely agricultural, so if you wanted to earn real money, you came here.

Even into the 1980s, about 90% of Zhiping's people relied on the paper industry. They called the township the "paper capital," and the profits from papermaking were considerable. It wasn't like today—now it's the other way around: the outside world is developed, and this place is remote.

When Liangbao first came to develop the area, his five brothers came too, including my grandfather. My father Hu Xianfa, and his brothers Hu Xiangui and Hu Xianrong also came to build their lives here. Our clan had over a dozen households here. By the early years after the founding of the People's Republic of China, Liangbao had become one of the wealthier men in Xiapin—though really he was just a paper workshop owner, not some great landlord. He was somewhat wealthier than others. I heard when the "suppress the local tyrants" campaign started, he fled. He didn't take much money with him, and he left all his stock of paper unsold. On his way out, he fell ill and died somewhere on the road. His son met a tragic fate too—during the War of Resistance against Japanese Aggression, he was playing in the streets of Changting City when a Japanese bomb fell, killing him. The later generations of his family had a hard life.

My grandmother used to tell me the story of how my father first began making paper, which has stayed vivid in my mind. My grandfather's name was Hu Liangji. He passed away when my father was only three years old. My father, Hu Xianfa, was born in 1923. The family was poor, so by the age of 14, he was already sent to learn papermaking. His master lived in Zhoukeng Village, Tiechang Township, Changting. In those days, apprenticeships worked like this: the master took in a pupil, and the pupil worked for free for one or two years—payment in the form of labor instead of money. My grandmother said that when my father went off to learn the craft at 14, he worked a full year. At the year's end, the master gave him three Guangyang silver dollars, bought him 15 *jin* of tea oil, and added some other New Year goods, then personally walked him back to our old home in Changting. That master was a good man. My Grandma told me—my dad would lie in bed at night, under the mosquito net, holding a lamp and staring at those silver dollars one by one. He just kept smiling, so happy. He thought, "I can make money now! This hard life will finally get better!" I get really touched every time I think about that story.

From 14 to 16, my father worked as a kangwei—the man who carried the wet paper sheets to be pressed. He was good at it. By the time he was 18, our family split into separate households, and he received a patch of bamboo hill as his share. Making paper required both skill and capital. Once my father had his own bamboo hill and knew the craft well enough, he decided to start his own operation. But my grandmother told me, at the time, we were still poor, and starting a paper workshop meant buying equipment and hiring workers. So my grandmother went to the Tai'an Paper Firm in Changting to get what, back then, they called *Tian Hang*. It was a Nationalist-era term—today we'd call it a loan. You'd borrow money from the firm, but you were obliged to sell them your paper, with the debt repaid from the sales. When she first approached the firm, the manager hesitated: "A loan? Not sure you can handle it." My grandmother was a formidable woman. Her maiden name was Zeng, from a respected family in Changting's East Street. She had powerful relatives who looked out for her. Just then, her relative Zeng Yunshan—who had a good reputation—spoke up to the firm owner: "Lend her the money. I'll guarantee it for her." With his word, the deal went through without another question. *Tian Hang* worked like this: you filled in the amount yourself—100 *dan* of paper, 50, 70—and they lent you the equivalent amount of cash. It was enough to start production. Thanks to that, our family business began—managing bamboo hills and producing Yukou paper. My grandmother was an extraordinary woman. She never went to school, but her way with people, her social sense, and her diplomacy were unmatched. She passed away in August 1987 in Changting, at the age of 97, and is buried there. We still go to her grave twice a year, in spring and autumn, to pay our respects.

My father's very first batch of paper on his own was a success—he always said, "The first shot must hit the mark." Back then, paper was sent to the Tai'an Paper Firm in Changting, then shipped by boat to Guangzhou. They'd tie 7 *dao* of paper together, pack them into bamboo baskets, wrap the baskets with bamboo leaves, and then ship everything to Guangzhou to sell. In those days, there was an industry rule: out of the seven *dao* in a basket, one could be a *Pi Ba*—it could have quite a few torn or damaged sheets. Because when paper is dried, it might tear, crack, or split a little—you'd cut off the bad parts, but some damaged bits were still okay to use. But my father refused to cut corners. He removed any imperfect sheet, no matter how small the flaw. Every *dao* in every basket was pristine. That first shipment—well-made and high quality—arrived in Guangzhou and made a name for him instantly. After that, telegrams would arrive at Tai'an saying, "We want paper with Hu Xianfa's stamp!" His paper could charge two extra silver *jiao* per *dao*. Back then, one silver dollar (Guangyang) was worth 10 silver *jiao*—so an extra two *jiao* per *dao*? That was a big deal!

Since then, my father kept on making paper here. Before 1950, whenever it was papermaking season, he would hire workers to come here, make the paper, and once the work was done, they'd go back to Changting. Our family owned a "paper mountain" of about 100 *dan* worth of stock. My father had two brothers. All three of them lived in Changting farming the land, but when the papermaking season came, my father would head up to Xikeng to make paper. That entire 100 *dan* "paper mountain" was run under his management, and it brought in the main income for the family. He was the backbone of the household—not only making paper for our own workshop, but also working for others when his own work was done. He was paid well for it, too. If our bamboo stock ran short, we could lease more resources by *Pi Shan* (批山, renting a mountain) for a term. My family once leased bamboo forest in Chaigougu, in Tiechang Township, Changting. The bamboo from that mountain supplied our mill. And a mill itself could also be rented—because not every household owned one. Leasing a mountain or renting a mill required a written contract. Without one, you could get into all kinds of trouble. Even with a contract, trouble could still find you. Like the time we rented a mill in Chaigougu—my older sister happened to be born there. Local superstition said that "blood must not touch the ground." The mill owner tried to squeeze us for money, insisting on holding a *jiao* ritual to "calm the gods." Those old contracts are all gone now. Usually, leasing a mountain ran on what was called a *Dan Ban* (单班, a term)—two years—because bamboo grows in cycles, with good years and lean years. The specific term was set privately between the two parties. When time was up, the contracts became no more than scrap paper. No one thought to keep them. To be honest, I never actually saw one myself. We didn't think they were anything valuable. Who could have known back then that these old papers would be as precious as cultural relics now, if we'd kept them as historical records?

Most of the paper workers were skilled masters from Changting. It wasn't like today—back then, every household in Changting had its own craftspersons. It was easy to find good masters, almost like picking talent from a labor market. Every paper mill kept a ledger called the *Daoxia Bu* (刀下簿, Under-the-Knife Book). My father explained the name—paper was cut to size with a knife, so the records were literally "under the knife book." Every mill had one hanging on the wall for everyone to see. It was a two-sided account book. On one side—the Under-the-Knife records:

how many vats were working, how many sheets were made each day—"On the first lunar month, so many *dao*; on the second lunar month, so many *dao*," and so on. On the other side—the workers' spending ledger: which day a worker took as an advance on their wages, what food they bought, how much meat, and other small purchases—all were recorded in writing. When it came time to settle wages, each worker received their own page of their records. The worker calculated how much paper he had made, how much he had earned, then subtracted whatever he had already drawn or spent. That's how his final wages were figured. The boss kept a separate ledger for himself—tracking costs like lime purchases, labor costs, and other expenses. The Under-the-Knife Book was part of the paper mill itself. If you made paper, you had one. It wasn't just bookkeeping—it was tradition, a rule we followed.

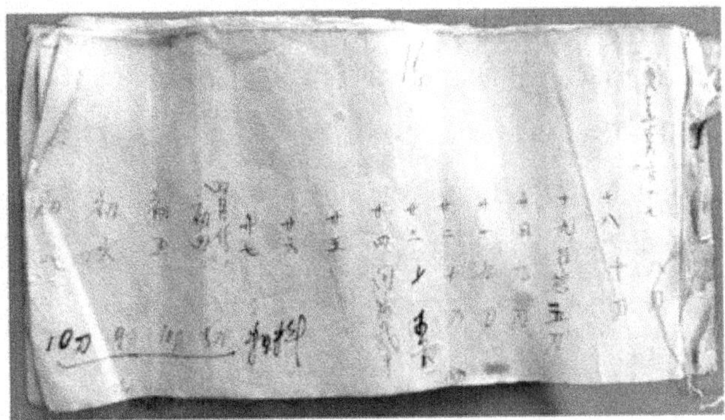

(Pic 47   Steel-Structured Paper-Drying Wall; Clay-Structured Paper-Drying Wall)

The finished paper had to be carried over mountain paths to the market in Changting. My father used to say that before the founding of the

People's Republic of China, the real danger was on the way back. Bandits were clever—they knew the papermakers would sell their goods in Changting and then return with cash to start the next round of production. In those days, you had to carry all your cash with you. So people came up with all sorts of tricks to bring it home safely. One time, my father sewed silver dollars inside huge taros he brought back from Changting—bandits never bothered to rob taros. But he wasn't always lucky. Once, he was robbed and left with nothing but his shorts, left with nothing but his shorts as he walked home. Another time, in the freezing winter, they even took his padded coat, and he had to run back shivering.

In my grandfather Hu Liangbao's generation, and even my father's, the family still lived mainly in Changting—birth, death, and burial all took place there. After 1949, when land reform came to Zhiping, they seized landlords' property and redistributed the land, so our family settled here and received our own bamboo mountains. Descendants of Hu Liangbao's five brothers also got land here. Back then, we were just scattered households, not an organized village. My father recalled that in the early years after 1949, the entire Xikeng area had barely 40 people, including children and the elderly. When I first came up here, the population had grown to 97; at its peak, around 115 to 120. During bamboo harvest season in April and May, the place suddenly filled with people. From my own village alone, 100 or so would be working, joined by outsiders—hauling bamboo, splitting it, carting lime, doing odd jobs. It was a constant stream of people coming and going. In the 1950s, both my parents were making paper here, and even my grandmother would lend a hand during the hardest work, like cutting and stripping *zhuma*.

Unlike Jiangxi Province or Jiangle, Zhiping never formed a handicraft cooperative. Around 1953 or 1954, though, it did set up a primary cooperative, then a bigger collective under public ownership. That was when my parents settled here permanently, and so I grew up as a native of Xiaping village, Zhiping township, Ninghua county. At first, we lived in an old house in Shiqiangbei—bought long ago by Hu Liangbao—that was said to have belonged to Shiliao Village in Jiangxi. The current house in Xikeng was built around 1971 or 1972. Travel used to be a nightmare: the old narrow mountain paths made it hard to get to work in the collective era. Moving closer was the only solution. From Changting, the walk from the production team back home took all day—from dawn until dark. I first came to live here at age three, and didn't return again until I was in third grade, about eight or nine years old. During the production team era, all Yukou paper had to be sold through the state's unified purchase system. It was destined for export to Southeast Asia and Singapore. Making paper cost money, so the production team—since we were a collective economic unit—would have the cashier or team leader go borrow money from the handmade paper purchasing station (a unit sent down by Ninghua County Foreign Trade Company). To borrow, they had to file a production plan—say, how many *dan* of paper you planned to make—and would then receive a matching loan, interest-free, called a "advance payment." When the team delivered its paper to the station, an official grader would judge its quality against provincial samples, record the purchase, and issue a check. The advance payment was deducted, and whatever remained became the team's actual income. That purchasing station was created during collective era. We could only sell our paper to it, because Yukou paper was classified as a Category II commodity—state-controlled, no private trade allowed. Making paper and selling it on your own was illegal. Only in 1983 or 1984 did the state abolish the monopoly system, downgrading Yukou paper to a Category III commodity, which allowed private sales. Before then, Yukou paper from our Zhiping township was considered a foreign-exchange earner—a highly valued export. In the 1980s and earlier, its status was remarkably high. Ninghua county would buy it at a very low price, but once exported abroad, it fetched far more, bringing in significant foreign currency. It was too valuable for the state to ignore.

Back then, in Xikeng, people used to say life here was "half farmland, half mountains." That meant you had to farm and make paper simultaneously. It was exhausting. Our village leaned more toward paper—we had more bamboo hills and less farmland. But in places like Gaofeng or Laijiashan in Xiaping, where families had no farmland at all, they lived off paper-making alone. Compared with us, their lives were actually easier. Villages like Shangping, Xiaping, Rongzikeng, and our own Xikeng were stuck in the middle—half farming, half papermaking—and that made things very hard. The paper season always had to fit around the farming cycle. Usually, by June the *zhuma* had been soaked and washed, and by August or September it was softened and ready for papermaking. That way, the busy season for paper didn't clash too much with the peak of farm work. But springtime was the hardest: you had to sow rice, cut bamboo, and also start the paper process. By the solar term *Xiaoman* (late May), the *zhuma* was already in the ponds soaking, and right after that, it was time to transplant rice seedlings. Families that had both land and bamboo to manage carried the heaviest burden.

The collective management system was complicated and tiring. For example, our Xikeng production team ran three paper mills. Paizi Mill at Shiqiangbei, Yonglian Mill at Shapingli, and Yongsheng Mill at Gongqiaozi Liaoxia. Each year, the team tried to fairly divide us up based on how much paper we needed to make and how many people there were. They grouped several households into a single vat and then drew lots, because some bamboo hills were better than others. That was the only way to avoid quarrels. There weren't wages then, only "work points," and these work points were calculated with extraordinary precision for every specific task. For instance, carrying one *dan* of *zhuma* earned a certain number of points; hauling 100 *jin* of lime from Xinqiao Shirenxia to here earned another set of points. Washing bamboo fiber, bleaching, stripping, smoothing—it was all carefully counted. Even making tools like bamboo sieves or carrying baskets was assigned points. Locals were paid in work points, while hired outsiders received cash wages. Once the paper was finished, it was graded—Grade 1, Grade 2, or Grade 3—and the quality affected both points and wages. The managers kept detailed records. For each vat of paper, they wrote down who did what, how much was produced, and of what grade. All that was sent to the team's accountant. Every family had its own ledger too—how many points from papermaking, how many from farming—and at the end of the year your household income was calculated from the total. It was a huge bureaucratic machine, endlessly complicated.

My father started out as the team cashier but he never stopped making paper—he was in charge of the vats the whole time, 'cause he had experience managing them.. He never went back to farm work—his whole life was in papermaking. He managed Paizi Mill, which always produced the best paper in the area. Most of it was Grades 1, 2 or 3. People said it was partly because he managed things extremely carefully, knew the craft inside out, and kept an eye on every single step, and partly because the water source was so pure. The mill drew water from mountain springs that were clear and free of impurities. Buyers could tell just by looking: "The water color of this paper is excellent," the graders would say. But keeping the water clean was a constant battle. My father would lead spring water down from the mountains, then filter it through buckets stuffed with palm fiber to remove impurities. For soaking bamboo, the water quality didn't matter much, but for bleaching it was critical. If rain muddied the flow, it could ruin an entire pond of fiber. He would never risk that. Even in a downpour, he'd put on a rain cape and straw hat, and rush out to cut off the water supply before dirty runoff could reach the vats. So he had to stay on top of it, make sure no impurities got in. He always said: "The first secret to good paper is good raw material. No matter how skilled you are, if the fiber is full of impurities, you'll never make fine sheets."

Because of his expertise, he trained several apprentices in Changting. There were strict rules for that. Under the collective system, a master who took on an apprentice got extra pay. Usually it was "half share"—the apprentice's wage was split 50-50 with the master. If, after a year, the apprentice still wasn't skilled, the split might drop to 30–70 or even 40–60, depending on ability.When teaching an apprentice to make paper, you'd start them with *Kang Wei* (lifting bamboo screens). You'd get someone from another vat to help out, and once in a while, let the apprentice make a *dao* on their own until he was skilled enough to take charge. When he finally "took the vat" on his own, it was called *Deng Cao*—"officially take over a vat." That's the whole process for a *Kang Wei* apprentice. After *Deng Cao*, tradition required him to host a banquet, treating all the workers in the mill. We called it *Deng Cao Jiu* (the vat-taking feast). Only then could he work alongside the master officially. That was the rule. Other jobs had their own apprenticeships. Learning to tread the fiber was less formal—if you found a skilled master willing to teach, you would simply followed along. But drying paper was a more delicate craft. Beginners had to start with the basics: taking the wet paper off the screen, holding the corners, flipping it, then the master would teach you to paste each sheet onto the drying wall one by one. The wet sheets tore easily, so you had to move slowly, gently. Some masters would often paste one end of the sheet first, then let the apprentice brush the rest into place. Day after day, the apprentice's hands learned the rhythm, until the motion was smooth and sure.

My father kept making paper until he was 54 or 55. By then, the work was simply too heavy. Papermaking demanded tremendous physical strength, and he could no longer manage it. After that, the most he did was help out during the bamboo-cutting season—keeping an eye on the ponds, lending a hand where he could. He passed away in 2007 at the age of 87, just a year after my mother, who died at the age of 86.

I moved back to Xikeng in 1966, right after graduating from Changting No.1 Middle School. That was the year the Cultural Revolution broke out. Classes were suspended and teachers were being criticized and struggled against. It was terrifying, and I came here to live. In the early seventh lunar month of 1967, the production team leader from Tongfang in Changting, Xiao Chengjin, came to work at our Paizi Mill at Shiqiangbei. He was a skilled dryer, and I apprenticed under him for six months to learn the technique of drying paper. The following year, I studied under another master in Changting, Wu Yutong, for another half year. Paper drying isn't just one skill; it involves many tasks, including taking care of the drying walls. Back then we used clay drying walls, not the steel ones used today. Every two weeks the drying master had to go inside the hollow walls to sweep out the dust that had accumulated over half a month. It was filthy work, but if you didn't do it, the flues would clog, the temperature would drop, and the paper wouldn't dry. You also had to know how to fight fires if one broke out. The hardest skill of all was oiling the walls. A newly built clay drying wall had to be coated with tung oil three times, and afterward it had to be re-oiled every month. If the oil was too thin, the paper wouldn't stick; if it was too heavy, the sheets dried blotchy, what we called "Buddha's face." Every master had his own tricks, and they never revealed them all at once. That was how my apprenticeship went. Steel dryers didn't need oiling—only a protective coat of fireproof paint when first installed.

Because I had a middle-school education, the village relied on me for paperwork. Over the years I served as production team leader in my group, then as brigade head in Xiaping, which was like being the village chief. Later, when the workload became overwhelming, I took on roles like deputy secretary, accountant, or cashier. The paperwork was endless. Every year we had to do population movement reports—births, deaths, people moving in or out. Then there were township's distribution plans. What kind of distribution? Like, every year the village and village groups had to make end-of-year reports: how much money each production team could get from their work points, how much they had to hand over to the village, how much to deduct for public funds. We compiled the numbers at the village level, and passed them to the township, where the chief accountant would review and approve them. Only then could the money be distributed. It was exhausting work. I held various posts—brigade head, deputy secretary, cashier, accountant, even party secretary—until I was in my fifties.

In the 1960s, our household was small: my parents, my two brothers, my adopted younger sister-in-law, and myself—five people. When I returned to Xikeng at 16 or 17, my work was mostly preparing materials and felling *zhuma*. After I married, my wife added another pair of hands, and by 1973, when my eldest son was born, our family began to grow. By the 1970s, there were nine of us at home. My eldest son, Hu En, was born in 1973; the second, Hu Cheng, in 1975; and the youngest, Hu Ming, in 1982. Today, the family numbers 14.

Back in the 1970s, a family would earn two to three thousand work points in a year. In our production team, people used to joke: "Go loaf around, you'll still get eight points." A normal day's work meant about eight points. Ten points translated to roughly one yuan at best. But here in Xikeng, because our paper was good, ten points could fetch one yuan, sometimes even 1.1 or 1.2 yuan—quite high. In Laijiashan, where there was no farmland and people did nothing but papermaking, they could get as much as 1.4 or 1.5 yuan, the highest around. In Xiaping, by contrast, poor management meant both farming and papermaking suffered, so they earned only fifty to seventy cents for the same points. The difference between making paper and not making paper was significant. Paper work was far harder than farming, but it paid better. In our village, the system of work points was also different. Papermakers could earn up to 16 points a day. Workers treading pulp or drying sheets got 14. Same pay for treading and drying was an old rule. It had always been that way: papermakers and *Kang Wei* (screen lifter) were first-tier, pulp treaders and dryers second-tier, and bamboo strippers third-tier. Therefore those who strip fiber earned two points less, 12 a day. It was three tiers, with 2 points between each. In farming, by comparison, seven or eight points were standard. But we got 16 for papermaking—and that was fair, 'cause a day of papermaking was harder than two days of farming. Papermaking days started before dawn. If the weather was cold, snowing, or icy, the hardship doubled. And once you began, there was no stopping. Even meals were snatched quickly, like soldiers charging into battle. You had to keep going till you were done 'cause there was a daily quota: seven *dao* of paper a day. Only then could you rest. Life was brutally harsh in those years.

Life here was actually pretty decent—people even called it "Little Hong Kong"—because at least we had enough food to fill our bellies and could afford some daily necessities. For papermakers like us, the state provided a grain subsidy. This was rationed grain, cheap grain, about 0.13 yuan a *jin*, though anything beyond the allowance had to be bought at the higher market price, more than 0.20 yuan a *jin*. Since papermaking villages couldn't grow their own rice, the government allocated this "paper industry grain" based on how much paper you produced. For example, the men who made paper or trampled pulp got two *jin* of rice a day; those who dried sheets or stripped bamboo got one and a half *jin*. If you produced extra or high-quality paper, you might even be rewarded with bonus grain at the subsidized price. There was a fixed amount of subsidy grain for a certain amount of paper, and good quality earned you that bonus grain. Still, pork was a rarity—we might have meat once a month, and that was already a luxury. My mother was hard-working, though; she always kept two or three pigs at home. But eating pork every two weeks? That was unthinkable back then.

For 30 years, Yukou paper was classified as a Category II commodity under strict state control. That meant the government monopolized both its purchase and sale. The price the state paid us was extremely low, yet every sheet was precious foreign exchange. Grades one through four were all exported; grades five through 12 stayed in domestic markets. When China's industry was still backward, Yukou paper quietly earned the country huge amounts of hard currency. Then, in 1982 or 1983, policy changed: Yukou paper was downgraded to a Category III good, meaning it could be freely traded. That was a turning point. Before that, local procurement stations bought it for just over 8 yuan a *dao*. But if you carried the same paper over the hills into neighboring Jiangxi, buyers in Zhují brigade were paying 16 yuan. Consider the significant difference! Looking back, Ninghua County's papermakers generated massive profits for the nation during those decades. And yet today people tell us, "You never paid into social security." Meanwhile, places like Jiangxi province and Bailian in Jiangle organized real paper-making cooperatives. Their papermakers, once too old to work, could still enjoy retirement benefits. We got nothing like that here.

When the household responsibility system came in after the Third Plenary Session of the Eleventh Party Congress, each family began working on their own. That's when I could finally run my papermaking business freely. In the 1980s, when Yukou paper switched from Category II to III, things changed a lot, and we started having more money too. As soon as the policy implemented, small machine-pulping plants sprang up everywhere in Zhiping Township making *Pi Zhi* (皮纸, a type of thick paper). Before the policy, not a single family owned a machine paper workshop; afterward, they flourished for about 20 golden years. My two brothers could load 200 or 300 *dao* of paper in a cart each month and sell them in Zhuji across the Jiangxi border. Back then, we'd organize people to carry it over. We'd leave at 4 or 5 in the morning, walk all the way to Shangping, go up Jiangjuncha from Nanfengduan, then head downhill, and reach Zhuji by noon. We could make a round trip in a day. Later, Jiangxi traders came directly to the Fujian-Jiangxi border to collect by vehicle. Every household in our production team had people carrying paper to sell—I carried it myself, usually six to eight *dao* at a time.

When my family finally bought our own papermaking machine, efficiency soared. The pulping was mechanical, but sheet-forming was still by hand. We could earn 100 or even 200 yuan a day. Compare that to the collective era, when a family's annual income rarely exceeded 1000 yuan, sometimes only a few hundred after expenses. By the 1980s, though, a papermaker's wage was about two yuan a day, plus two *jin* of rice. Workers were thrilled—60 yuan a month was more than what the county Party secretary made, and people were proud. We also made wrapping paper and small sheets, and they sold like hotcakes. I could finish a *dan* in two days, and my wife helped me strip the bamboo bark. One *dan* sold for 24 yuan, sometimes 26 yuan, and traders from Jiangxi would come collect it. Sometimes I'd barter with them—our paper in exchange for oil or pig heads. Back then, a *jin* of pig head in Jiangxi was only 0.15 yuan, while rice cost 0.20 yuan. Wrapping paper was in such demand that I kept at it until about 1988 or 1989, making 10 yuan or more a day. I was young, strong, and motivated—it felt good.

After 1989, I stopped making Yukou paper altogether. But in 2008, a businessman from Fuzhou placed a special order, and I took it up again—over 100 yuan a *dao* that time. That was when Gui Shuzhong came filming; it was the first time I'd restarted production, and I made 200 or 300 *dao* for that order. Later, in 2013, 2015, 2018, and 2019, I also made paper. This year, 2022, I prepared materials the year before—200 or 300 *dao*'s worth. We were supposed to start a month earlier, but it's so hard to hire papermakers now that we didn't get going until the fifth day of the eighth lunar month. After just one day of operation, we realized the drying wall was leaking water. That steel wall had been in use for over 30 years. We had to pour water into it to fix it temporarily, just to finish the paper, which will probably take more than 20 days. The cost now is enormous—300 to 400 yuan per *dao*. First, lime alone is expensive. Each *dan* of *zhuma* needs eight *jin* of lime, and I used 200 *dan* of *zhuma*, so we bought 2,000 *jin* from Yanxia Mountain in Ruijin, Jiangxi, at 0.4 yuan per *jin*, plus transport, totaling 1,500 yuan. Then a new papermaking screen cost 2,500. Labor is another big chunk. My son and I handled pulping and drying, while his wife stripped bamboo bark and still cooked meals with her mother-in-law. But we had to hire five outside workers: two master papermakers at 30 yuan per *dao*, making at least seven *dao* a day, two dryers at 25, and one pulp treader at 25. And that's not even counting all the other costs: mountain rent for *zhuma*, cutting and stripping bamboo, picking and extracting *lan* leaves, fixing tools, repairing the pond, daily meals for workers, extra food for festivals… If you add all those in, it's even more. So yeah, each *dao* costs 300 to 400 yuan.

Looking ahead, I want to make smaller Yukou paper and adjust the technique—I won't make the kind that needs two people anymore. Large sheets require two workers in perfect coordination, which is too difficult now. Smaller sheets allow finer craftsmanship, and I can manage the process myself. It's easier to manage alone, especially since it's so hard to hire workers now. Finding two people who work well together? Even harder. The sad truth is that the old skills are nearly lost. Young people aren't learning. The older generation is aging fast, losing strength. If we want papermaking to survive, we must go back to the old way: masters teaching apprentices. Pick a few, give them a small stipend each year, and make sure they learn well. It wouldn't even cost much.

2. Zeng Shaoteng's Own Account[398] (2022)

My name is Zeng Shaoteng. I was born in 1954 in Guangliang Village, Zhiping Township. I am a descendant of the Tian She branch of the Zeng lineage, tracing back to the ancestor Qilanggong. Our family moved to Tian She in the 60th generation, and later relocated again to Budiling Production Team in Guangliang Brigade. I went to school until 1967, but with ten mouths to feed at home, my parents struggled to provide for us. So I left school and started working. I did jobs in paper mills—stripping and trampling *zhuma*, and even worked for a month or two at a paper factory in Pingshang, Caofang Township. In 1971, when I was 17 years old (18 by traditional reckoning), I joined the local handmade-paper purchasing station. 13 years later, in 1984, I was promoted to deputy director and then director of the Zhiping Township Supply and Marketing Cooperative—where I was also responsible for overseeing the paper trade. Originally, the cooperative office was located in Zhiping Village. In 1979, I personally oversaw the construction of a new cooperative building on

---

398 This account is based on interviews with Zeng Shaoteng on September 3–4, 2022. The content was reviewed and approved by Zeng himself. The conversations took place en route to, and later at, the home of Hu Lanshan in Xikeng Natural Village, Xiaping Village, Zhiping She Ethnic Township, Ninghua County, Sanming City, Fujian Province (September 3), as well as at the residence of Zhang Jian in Ninghua County (September 4). Interviewers: Chen Yao and Gui Shuzhong.

Zhiping Street, which still stands today. At that time, the cooperative ran two paper purchasing sites: the main one at Mabeiling in Zhiping Village, and another at the Li ancestral hall in Xiaping Village. In 1990, I was transferred to serve as director of the Caofang Supply and Marketing Co-operative. The following year, I was formally reclassified from worker to cadre. Then, on January 5, 1993, I was moved to the Ninghua County Supply and Marketing Cooperative, assigned to the County Native Products Company, which was located on South Avenue. From the moment I first entered the paper purchasing station in 1971, I have spent my entire career within the supply and marketing system.

The county supply and marketing cooperative and its Zhiping paper purchasing station were both established around 1953. The station operated as a branch under the cooperative, and the Native Products Company was likewise an enterprise under the County Supply and Marketing Coop-erative Union. Before the Socialist Education Movement, the Zhiping paper station was managed by a few men from Liancheng. During the campaign, however, they were relieved of their duties due to "historical prob-lems." At that point, Zhiping Township petitioned the county to appoint one or two capable locals as paper graders for the station. Since there were no schools that trained such specialists, candidates had to pass both a lit-eracy test and a practical exam. The literacy part was simple—just writing a short essay. The key part was the hands-on test: they would hand you samples of paper and ask you to rank their quality. You had to spot all the flaws in the paper, explain what caused each flaw, and make sense of it all. That was the real test.

Once I began working at the native paper purchasing station, I ap-prenticed under Master Zeng Qinquan, learning the delicate craft of grad-ing paper. Zeng was already in his fifties or sixties at the time. He was originally from Tianshe, though later he moved to live in Zhiping. In his youth, he had worked in a paper trading firm in Changting, and even before the founding of the PRC he was known for managing paper mills with skill and authority. Around 1966, during the Social Education campaign, when the several men from Liancheng who had been running the station were dismissed due to political issues, Zeng was brought in as a paper grader. When I entered the station in 1971, there was still another grader from Fuzhou, surnamed Zou, who had also worked in a paper firm before. Another was Li Yinxiang, an old hand from the paper trade firm as well—if he is still alive today, he must be over 100 years old. Normally it took two or three years to fully master the skills of grading, but because I had already labored in paper workshops, I managed to learn the craft well enough to operate independently in less than a year.

At that time, our station had four graders, two men checking defective sheets, and more than 20 workers assigned to wrapping and packing the paper. The staff never really grew; a few new hires were employed briefly, but none stayed long. The station itself was at Mabeiling in Zhiping. Today only remnants of the old brick walls remain where the buildings and warehouses once stood. Back then, there was also an agricultural by-products station nearby. Our paper station, however, dealt exclusively with handmade paper. For the Zhiping Supply and Marketing Cooperative, handmade paper was the backbone of its business. It managed farm products, fertilizers, and pesticides, but more than 70 percent of its revenue came from handmade paper. The paper we bought had to be repackaged for shipment. We would weave baskets out of bamboo strips, line them with bamboo leaves to keep moisture out, and repack the paper in bundles. When we bought it, it was 7 *dao* per *dan*, but for repackaging, we did 6 *dao* per basket. We'd load them up basket by basket, send them to Changting for final inspection, before dispatch them to Xiamen, Shantou, and

Guangzhou. Later, once a road reached Zhiping, the paper was first trucked to Ninghua, then sent by train from Sanming.

In the 1970s, Ninghua County produced roughly 1,100 tons of handmade paper annually. Zhiping was the undisputed center, contributing about 80 percent of that. Anle came second with about 10 percent. Paper producers from every production team in Zhiping carried their bundles of Yukou paper to our station. Neighboring Caofang and Fangtian had no stations of their own, so their output was purchased through us as well. Other producing townships in the county, like Anle, Quanshang, Hucun, and Jicun, had much smaller outputs; their paper was purchased by the county's sundry goods or native products companies. The way it worked was simple: the Supply and Marketing Cooperative charged a three percent handling fee, which was then turned over to the county company. The actual transport and export was managed by the Ninghua and Sanming native products companies, while overseas trade was handled through the provincial company. All the way up until the late 1980s, our county's handmade paper was classified as a state-controlled Category II commodity. Everything was distributed through central planning, and our role at the station was limited to purchase and packaging. Only around 1990, when private trade was finally allowed, did we gain a small measure of freedom in transporting and selling paper ourselves.

Grading paper was no easy job. Every year, Zhiping township held a meeting where a red notice board was posted for all to see. It listed how much of each grade of paper each production team had delivered. Once the numbers were made public, it wasn't just about money anymore—it became a matter of face. Back then, us graders and the people managing the paper workshops in each production team were all really professional. If you handed us a *dao* of paper, we could tell its weight almost exactly—error no more than half a *liang* (approximately 25 g in total). The production team managers would even test us sometimes to see if we were right, testing our skill against theirs. So the grader's job was tough: you had to be professional, and you had to be fair. If you weren't, people would complain, and you couldn't keep the job.

To be a grader, you needed deep knowledge. First you judged color—see what "water color" it has. Then you looked at each stage of production—was it coarse or fine, thick or thin, strong or weak? Did the fibers show through too much? Were there blemishes or broken sheets? Every flaw had to be identified, and you had to explain which stage of production caused it. We were given an official handbook issued by the provincial company, a volume known as *Fujian Handmade Paper*. Fujian had different kinds of handmade paper: Yukou paper, Maobian paper, and others. Each page in *Fujian Handmade Paper* featured a specimen of one type of paper, accompanied by notes detailing its grade, weight, thickness, size, and required qualities. All the samples were bound into a book. For example, Maobian paper, weighing about eight *jin* per *dao*, was categorized as "light paper." Yukou paper weighed 12 *jin* per *dao* and was called "heavy paper." Each of these types was divided into 12 grades. Unfortunately, a few years ago, I carelessly burned my copy, and it was lost forever.

The processes of making Yukou paper and Maobian paper were essentially the same—same steps, same methods. What set them apart was weight and thickness. When the pulp mixture was denser during sheet forming, the result was Yukou paper. Each sheet of Yukou paper measured about 138 centimeters long and 62 centimeters wide. For the highest grades—Grade 1 and Grade 2—the weight had to reach precisely 12 *jin* and 2.5 *liang* (approximately 6.125 kg in total). Grade 1 sheets were required to have a clean bluish hue. Grade 2 sheets, on the other hand, came in two types: one ranged from white to pale blue, while the other carried a faint pinkish hue—a slight red tint was acceptable. Grade 3 sheets could be bluish, pinkish, or slightly yellowish. From Grade 4 downward, the colors varied more widely. Most of the paper produced fell into the Grades 3 to 5; the top grades, Grade 1 and Grade 2, were relatively rare. By calculation, 24 *dan* made a ton, and with our packing standard of six *dao* to a basket, that worked out to roughly 167 or 168 *dao* per ton.

In 1974 and 1975, Beijing's National Publishing Bureau ordered more than 800 tons of handmade paper from Fujian to print *Chairman Mao's Poetry*. Zhiping alone supplied over 600 tons, and I was the one responsible for inspecting every bale. I still recall: in 1974, a section chief from the National Publishing Bureau flew into Fuzhou, then came down to Ninghua under the escort of the Provincial Local Products and Sundries Company. County leaders directed him straight to our Zhiping Supply and Marketing Cooperative. At the time, I was both station head and chief grader, officially under the sundry goods company. We didn't dare ask his name, but everyone understood he was from the National Publishing Bureau. Before 1974, Yukou paper was still under state unified purchase and sale. Since it was allocated by the province, we never knew how much was sent to the central government. But when we shipped the paper, we'd clearly mark on the packages that it was Zhiping Yukou paper. The National Publishing Bureau must have used our paper before and known where it came from—otherwise, why would they come all the way to this remote mountain area of Zhiping? The 1974 paper allocation from the central government must have gone through official channels. It started at the central government, then was passed down to the provincial native products company, followed by the Sanming Local Products and Sundries Company, the county government, the county's supply and marketing system, and the county Local Products and Sundries Company, before finally reaching Zhiping Commune and our Supply and Marketing Cooperative.

I personally supervised the testing of that batch. They required two rounds of grading: an initial evaluation and a re-check. The reasoning was practical—under strong sunlight, every flaw and shade of color was much easier to judge than on a cloudy day, so they wanted confirmation. I also handled the allocation personally. In the end, 680 tons went out from our Zhiping station alone, while other counties like Jiangle supplied only a hundred tons or so. The *Chorography of Ninghua County* records in its "Major Events" section that 420 tons shipped in 1974, but it omits the 260 tons from 1975. Zhiping didn't have enough paper in 1974, so we made up the difference the following year, adding up to 680 tons total. We were in charge of purchasing, and the Local Products Company sent trucks to load the paper directly at Jingxi Railway Station in Sanming, then ship it to Beijing by train. Since I started working at the station in 1971, Zhiping's paper was sent up to the central government every year. But usually, we were just a purchasing agent—we had no idea how much was allocated to the central government or other regions in other years. That was the job of the provincial Local Products Company and Sundries Company. But in 1974, since the National Publishing Bureau needed 800 tons at once to print *Chairman Mao's Poetry*—a huge amount—they must have sent documents directly down to the township level.

It was for *Chairman Mao's Poetry*, not the *Selected Works of Mao Zedong*. I remember it clearly, because I handled the paper allocation. The Bureau sent us a specimen illustrating the exact quality they required: which grades were suitable for printing and which were not. From our stock, I carefully selected high-quality Grades 1, 2, and 3 sheets for the job. I've seen those copies of *Chairman Mao's Poetry*. Back then, the Bureau presented two complete sets of the printed *Chairman Mao's Poetry*: one to Zhiping Commune, and one to our cooperative. Each set contained four volumes, all the same size, in blue covers, housed in a neat slipcase.

The paper inside was excellent—mostly Grade 2 and 3. Grade 1 sheets were simply too rare for bulk use, which is why those gift copies weren't Grade 1. I never saw the *Selected Works of Mao Zedong*—only *Chairman Mao's Poetry*. Today, one copy should still be kept in Zhiping Township's offices, another in the county cooperative, and a third in the county archives. I've held them all in my hands. The *Poetry* were the only edition I saw printed with our paper—I never saw the *Selected Works*. The copy in Ninghua County Archives is exactly the same one I remember. The printing method was also distinctive: because Yukou paper was relatively light and thin, ink tended to bleed through. So they had to use two layers.

A few of us from the cooperative drafted the document for that 1974 allocation together,[399] then issued it in the name of the Zhiping Commune Revolutionary Committee. Back then, the cooperative didn't have the authority to assign tasks, nor did the Local Products Company—only the township government could issue such orders. I remember that detail well, because it was my colleague Zeng Qinshun, known for his fine handwriting, who copied the document by hand, then cut the stencil and printed it with ink on wax paper.

There was a 1975 document[400] that claimed the National Publishing Bureau had raised concerns about the quality of Yukou paper from Zhiping. Honestly, I had no idea about this at the time. Judging from the handwriting, the text was copied by a clerk named Zeng Shaoqiu from the Native Products Company. On paper, the complaint didn't quite make sense to me. When we bought the paper, the grades were top-notch. How could those problems have slipped through? Still, the document bore the official

---

399 *Notice on the 1974 Handmade Paper Production Task and Quality Requirements* (Document No. 34, Zhige [74]), 1974. Ninghua County Archives.
400 See Pic86: *Notice of the Ninghua County Native Products and Sundries Company Regarding the Forwarding of Document No. 117 from the Provincial Native Products Company (Commercial-Native Products-Sundries-1975)*

red seal of the Ninghua Native Products and Sundries Company, and it was circulated to both the Zhiping commune and the supply and marketing cooperative. So it was very much a formal notice. We sent 420 tons in 1974, and this document came out in 1975—meaning the National Publishing Bureau must have run into issues while using the paper, so they sent back feedback. They said some sheets varied in thickness—likely because the papermaker made one side thinner when he first lifted the bamboo screen our of the pulp vat, while *Kang Wei* working the other side left the other side thicker since the other side was lifted later. They mentioned uneven color within a batch, which usually happened when paper from two different soaking pits was used back-to-back. They also cited dark root fibers caused by bamboo left too long before soaking, bamboo residue that were nodes hadn't been cleaned out, grit from earthen soaking ponds where *zhuma* was soaked in lime and a little sand would get in, smoke stains from cracked clay drying walls because smoke would seep through the cracks and leave marks on the paper, and even *lan* leave residue left when *lan* extract wasn't properly filtered. Most of the document was actually about Jiangle County, which had extra issues: damp paper and insufficient width. Damp paper was a trick—they'd leave paper in humid places to absorb moisture and boost its weight (since it was underweight). Insufficient width happened when torn paper wasn't put back into the pulp trough; instead, they made small sheets from it and cut them even smaller. That same year, 1975, the province organized a massive inspection of handmade paper across Fujian. I was assigned as a quality inspector, traveling to places like Changting, Qingliu, Nanping, and Shunchang. Compared with Zhiping's paper, theirs was generally worse. Sheets we would have graded as Grade 4 were being rated Grade 3, even Grade 2, in other places. So, the National Publishing Bureau's complaints weren't baseless. Once, almost all cultural paper (for archives, etc.) was handmade. But by the late years of the planned economy, almost all cultural paper had shifted to machine-made, and the old craft was sliding in quality. Most handmade sheets ended up being used for ritual purposes instead of books.

When I worked at the Zhiping paper station, I was in charge of keeping records for 173 paper mills. Every delivery from every production team went into my ledgers. Additionally, I issued advance purchase deposits and invoices. Unfortunately, those documents didn't survive. When the Zhiping cooperative was dissolved, the accounting records were transferred to the Caofang cooperative, and I don't know if they still exist. Since our cooperative gave production teams advance deposits and reward grain, and the paper station was the cooperative's dedicated spot for buying handmade paper, I knew every detail about Zhiping's paper mills.

Our work went far beyond just buying paper and grading it. We had to visit mills, evaluate their operations, and then decide how much of an advance purchase deposit they could receive. Each year, us buyers and cooperative staff would spend a month or two traveling on foot to the villages. There were four of us, splitting into two teams. A trip to Xiaping could take five or six days, and to Gaofeng even longer because there were more mills to check. We lodged in village homes and got to know the factory heads well. Only after verifying these production teams—how much raw material they had prepared, how each mill was doing—would we issue advance purchase funds. Mills without stockpiles got nothing. For example, the Xikeng production team, where Hu Lanshan belonged, operated four mills.[401] Each year, they'd draw up a plan for how much bamboo they would prepare and how much paper they intended to make, then apply to us for loans. I even spent three months in 1972 living in the Li clan ancestral hall in Xiaping, which we rented as a storage site for the

---

401 Paizi Mill (Shiqiangbei), Datong Mill (Shiqiangbei, operated at Shifu village from Changting), Yonglian Mill (Shapingli), and Yongsheng Mill (Gongqiaozi, Xialiao).

handmade paper procurement center. That's why we knew everyone so well.

Food was another key issue. Grain for papermakers—especially those in mountainous production teams—was arranged by the state. In full "paper villages" like Gaofeng and Xiaping, there was almost no farmland—sometimes not even one *mu* per household. Guangliang had a little farmland, so it was "half-farm, half-paper." Any production team who sold handmade paper to the cooperative received ration tickets, which could be exchanged at the grain stations for rice at subsidized prices: 9.8 yuan per hundred *jin* for late rice, 9.5 yuan for early rice. Without these rations, they simply couldn't survive. Take Xiaping Brigade as an example: they only had 50 *mu* of farmland, but hundreds of people. We calculated how much grain they needed, subtracted what the 50 *mu* could produce, and the state covered the shortage with low-price grain. We kept lists, which were submitted to the township government, so that grain could be allocated to brigades like Xiaping. Teams that excelled in paper production also received "bonus grain" in addition to their quotas. Farming villages like Pengfang and Dengwu didn't qualify for ration grain since they could feed themselves, but if they sold paper, they too could earn bonus grain at the same subsidized price. You still had to buy it, but at the same low price as the subsidized grain. Families with too many mouths to feed often fell back on sweet potatoes. Until about 1990, grain was still rationed at those prices.

At the time, handmade paper was classified as a Category II commodity. The purchase prices were set by the provincial price bureau: Grade 4 paper sold for 7.4 yuan per *dao*, Grade 3 for 7.7, Grade 2 for 8, and Grade 1 for a little over 8 yuan. The price difference between grades was just 0.3 yuan. The cooperative, Local Products Company, and paper station were just business units—we had nothing to do with setting prices.

After 1990, prices climbed above 10 yuan per *dao*. Production teams sold their paper, utilized the money to cover costs—fertilizer, pesticide, lime, outside labor—determined how much each work point was worth, and then distributed the remainder to each person or household according to their work points.

Work points weren't standardized. Papermaking points differed from farming points, and even within papermaking, the value varied by task. Rules also differed between teams. For example, the rule in Xiaping wasn't the same as in Xikeng. As a result, yearly incomes varied widely. On average, one *dan* (7 *dao*) equaled about 10 points. However, a skilled worker making 8 or 9 *dao* could earn extra. Higher-grade paper also earned more points: Grade 3 and Grade 7 had different prices, so different points too. I remember in 1966 my father managed a paper mill near Xianghuo Hall in Budiling Brigade. They administered it really well and got the highest dividends that year. Some teams earned as little as 0.08 yuan per 10 points, others 0.24 yuan. But we managed 1.73 yuan—an extraordinary difference. Papermaking was considered more technical than farming, so it carried higher point values. Officially, the policy didn't allow "more work, more pay," but in reality, we were flexible. Naturally, this created complaints. People from other teams often raised objections, even reported it to our cooperative.

Another thing: Zhiping never had enough local workers. More than half of the papermaking labor force had to be hired in from outside—workers from Changting, from Jiangxi province, or from nearby townships. The production team paid them by the piece: for each *dao* of paper, a fixed wage. Take our Budiling production team, for example. We recruited outside workers to process *zhuma*. One man was expected to strip more than 20 *dan* of bamboo per day, but if he managed more, he earned more. Outsiders received their wages in cash. Locals, on the other hand, had to deduct various charges, and only after a whole year were they paid in work points—so naturally, some felt it was unfair. In the 1970s, a township cadre made barely over 20 yuan a month, whereas some papermakers, by contrast, could earn more than 40. Of course, cadres and supply-and-marketing staff had guaranteed income, while paper earnings rose and fell with the market.

Until 1988, handmade paper was still a Category II commodity, meaning it could not be traded freely. People did sneak batches across the border to sell in Hengjiang, Jiangxi, but if caught, they faced punishment or even prison. Usually it didn't come to prison, since the quantities were small and fell short of sentencing standards. After 1988, the state lifted the ban and ended compulsory purchase. There must have been an official directive, but those documents only circulated to township offices (county-level and above)—we never saw them. I was still in Zhiping then. Overnight, everyone could do business, and things changed completely. During the unified purchase and sale era, even the lower-grade papers from our station—often used for ritual burning—were still considered part of the cultural paper market. Handmade paper was the main medium for archives, for painting, for writing. Demand was strong, and good sheets earned high work points, so people strove for quality. After reform and opening-up, though, merchants like Luo Zhaotian in Zhiping were in it for quantity, not quality. They omitted steps like stripping the bamboo bark and sent coarse paper straight to Guangdong, where it served as ritual paper, so no one cared if it was good. That was no longer Yukou paper anymore. Times changes, and the market demand changes with them. Now, with cheap 70- or 80-gram machine-made sheets everywhere, handmade paper was unable to compete. Costs were too high, and one by one, the workshops closed.

Today, if we want to revive Yukou paper in the true sense, we must bring back the version made for painting and calligraphy. In the old days, the best Grade 1 sheets collected by the paper stations weighed about 35 grams. For painting, people now expect at least 40 grams. Technically, it can be done. But making Grade 1 Yukou paper has always required the right timing, the right place, and the right people. First comes the *zhuma*, which depends on soil quality. The same species grows everywhere in Zhiping, but bamboo from rocky hills is denser, tougher, more resilient. Bamboo from heavy clay soils, by contrast, is brittle and makes weak paper that tears too easily. Then there's the lime. After stripping the bark, the bamboo must be treated with lime to remove the lignin. Only fine, bright, high-alkaline lime will whiten the fibers—you need enough of it too. In the old days, the lime from Anjie in Changting was prized. Poor lime left the pulp yellow, and the sheets would never reach Grade 1 or even Grade 2. Water, too, was crucial. Our mountain springs in Zhiping were pure and clean; we used bamboo bark filters in bamboo tubes to channel the water down. With that, good paper could be made. Finally, everything depended on technique—on how each step was handled. Villages like Tianshe, Guangliang, Xiaping, and Gaodi all produced Grade 1 sheets. But even then, they were rare. In the best years, all of Zhiping might turn out only a few hundred *dao*. What made Grade 1 paper distinctive? First, its color:white—not the bright white of A4 paper, but something closer to "clear as ice, pure as jade." Second, its weight: traditionally, a *dao* of Grade 1 or 2 had to reach 12 *jin* and 2.5 *liang* (around 6.125 kilogram). To push the weight higher, toward 40 grams a sheet, the pulp had to be thickened and stirred evenly. The papermaker dipped deeper into the vat, lifting up more fiber with each pull, producing denser, sturdier sheets. Third, uniform thickness. That depended both on the skill and the number of workers. In the 1970s, Zhiping experimented with single-person suspension screens, and the results were strikingly even. We can adjust these steps now. If Yukou paper is to return as a true art paper, the price must reflect its worth. At 600 yuan per *dao*, it simply cannot survive. At a minimum, it needs to sell for 1400—a fair equivalent of the eight yuan a *dao* that it achieved in the 1970s.

3. Hu Lanshan: A Brief Introduction to the Yukou Paper-Making Process (2022)[402]

At the end of the Southern Song dynasty, when Jurchen forces swept southward and the two emperors were held captive, the Central Plains were descended into chaos. A group of refugees via Xiushui county of Jiangxi province escaped to Fujian. With them, they carried the papermaking techniques of Yukou Paper, which had developed in the Northern Song dynasty.

The making of Yukou Paper involves many step-by-step processes—labor-intensive and time-consuming. In historical periods with low productivity, ownership of a paper workshop was comparable to middle-class wealth, and for nearly a thousand years, Yukou Paper experienced unparalleled prosperity, once accounting for 80% of the economy of Zhiping She Ethnic Township. From the 1950s through the early 1980s, it was designated a Category II commodity: Grades 1–4 were exported to Southeast Asia for foreign exchange, while Grades 5–12 served domestic needs. By the late 1980s, machine-made paper took over, and Yukou Paper—constrained by high labor intensity, low output, and declining market demand—gradually faded away. What follows is a step-by-step description of the traditional production process, recorded here for reference.

(1) Mountain Maintenance

In lean years (years with low bamboo yield), mountains must be maintained: shrubs, inferior bamboo and old bamboo are cleared to pro-

---

402 This text has been reviewed and approved by Hu Lanshan.

mote the growth of young bamboo shoots. Meanwhile, certain shrubs, known locally as *Ying Shan Chai* (firewood left for mountain protection), must be preserved, a practice locally referred to as *Xiu Qiu* (mountain tending).

(2) Pond Maintenance

Around Qingming, repair the ponds used for soaking bamboo fibers. Based on the pond's condition from the previous year, major leakage require full reconstruction, minor leaks partial repair, and even ponds that do not leak must be reinforced. The key challenge lies in identifying the causes of leaks in the pond walls and base. *Zhuma* soaked in a leaking pond cannot produce quality paper; in severe cases, the entire batch of *zhuma* may rot.

(3) Pond Drying Acceleration

Newly repaired ponds must be compacted daily with wooden boards to dry evenly without cracking. If water is introduced before full drying, leaks will form, and the repair effort will be wasted.

(4) Water Diversion

Using bamboo conduits with nodes removed, water is guided from the source into the pond. Each bamboo conduit is joined end-to-end to create a continuous channel.

(5) Water Testing

After pond maintenance, leak testing is mandatory to verify water retention. First, processed yellow clay is used to seal cracks in the pond. Fill the pond with water; once full, remove the clay seals and mark the water-line. Observe after 24 hours: a 3–5 cm drop indicates no leak; a *chi* (approximately 33 cm) or more indicates a small leak; a major drop signifies a large leak. Large leaks must be carefully repaired until the pond is completely leak-proof.

(6) Harvesting *Zhuma*

After *Guyu* (Grain Rain, late April), bamboo shoots are harvested, though timing slightly varies with temperature and altitude. Due to variations in bamboo shoot growth cycles, harvesting requires four rounds of careful collection. To ensure uniformity, only tender shoots, about the size of a small wine cup at the tip, are acceptable. Shoots must not be "crooked at the top" or have branches. Harvesting, stripping, and soaking in the pond must be completed before *Xiaoman*, for, as papermakers say: "*Zhuma* shouldn't drink the *Xiaoman* waters."

(7) Piling *Zhuma*

The cut shoots are transported down the mountain based on the valley terrain and stripping direction. A flat area for stripping is reserved, and shoots are piled neatly.

(8) Peeling *Zhuma*

Workers use a bamboo "horse" to peel the bamboo shoots. It has two legs, one "mouth", and one "waist"—shaped like an inverted "V." The tops of the two legs cross to hold the bamboo shoot. The technique requires skill: "white at the base, green at the middle, egg-green at the tip." Top artisans produce curled strips of green peel.

(9) Stripping *Zhuma*

Zhuma have two kinds: *Qing Tong* (green stalks, unpeeled) and *Bai Tong* (white stalks, peeled). Two bundles of peeled *zhuma* make one *dan*, each weighing over 90 *jin* (approximately 45 kg). Requirements for stripped *zhuma*: all nodes removed, uniform thickness, consistent weight per *dan*.

(10) Transporting *Zhuma*

The peeled stalks are quickly transported to the pond. Delay is not permitted, as overnight stalks deteriorate. Transporting shoots is the most difficult job to hire for, as it is extremely laborious and exhausting.

(11) Sealing the Pond Drain

Commonly known as "Making Pond Drain Outlet." Beat sticky yellow clay with lime until it mixed well, and then spread a small amount of lime in the drain hole of the pond to prevent snakes from entering. The hole is layered with stones, sealed with the yellow clay mixed with lime, and sprinkled with water and lime on the clay surface to ensure absolute impermeability.

(12) Pond Loading

Bamboo stalks are laid in rows in the pond with water added to just cover them. Bamboo strips are removed, and stalks are pressed flat. For every load of stalks, 8 *jin* of powdered lime per *dan* of bamboo are evenly sprinkled. Layers of bamboo and lime are added until the pond is full.

(13) Pond Pressing

Bamboo is pressed under split long bamboo strips and stones, then sprinkled again with lime, with water covering the surface.

(14) Lime Renewal

After two weeks, the lime on the pond surface fades and its alkalinity decreases, necessitating additional lime. To prevent bamboo rot, procedures must be taken. On sunny days, remove bamboo strips and stones pressing on the surface, and stir the pond with feet or sticks. Then put the bamboo strips and stones back, add fresh lime on sunny days until the water turns the color of tea oil—considered ideal.

(15) Washing and Piling

After three months of soaking, the bamboo fibers soften and are ready to be washed. Next, manually lift bamboo stalks and pile them around the pond. Open the pond outlet to drain lime water. Place wooden beams (support beams) at the pond bottom, long bamboo strips on top, and "pond edges" (side supports) along the pond walls. Then pile the washed shoots on the supports.

(16) Leaching

After piling *zhuma*, block the pond outlet, and then the fibers are repeatedly soaked and drained with fresh water to wash away lime. After four rounds, they are left to steep for about half a month, which is called "leaching." After 20 days, until the water turns black, drain it. Maintain water in the pond thereafter, draining every more than 10 days or so. As papermakers say: "The first soak turns yellow, the second turns black."

Vat water for papermaking is critical to paper quality—experts refer to it as "water color." Spring water from caves is preferred, as it is pure and free of sand; stream water is not allowed. Bamboo conduits joined end-to-end with nodes removed are used to divert water from the source to the workshop.

(17) Drying Wall Construction

From the start of Yukou paper production until the 1980s, paper drying walls were made of yellow clay. Due to their complex production process, clay drying walls have been replaced by steel ones. To help future generations understand its production, the process is recorded below:

1. High-quality yellow clay is sifted three times (through grain sieves, rice sieves, and chaff sieves). The clay is soaked, drained, and mixed with *Pi Si* (shredded old bark) in proportion. The mixture is repeatedly stirred

with rakes for several days, then lime is added and stirred again. Finally, the clay is trodden (called "treading the clay") until it becomes smooth and creamy—this process requires over 100 workdays.

2. The master constructs the wall's structure (supports, beams, small frames, bamboo strips), applies the clay mixture, and baked the wall to set it. Copper tools are used to accelerate drying, with 3–4 workers polishing the wall all day. The wall is complete when it is dry, seamless, and smooth as a mirror.

(18) Workshop Preparation

A specific date is chosen to start production, with all craftsmen in attendance. Papermakers and screen lifters prepare screens (installing edges on new screens and weaving edges), assemble paper presses, and sharpen cutting knives. Pulp treaders need to lean the paper vats. Paper dryers must oil the drying walls. Workshop owners transport bamboo presses, while bamboo cutters clean the kitchen. Once preparations are complete, the workshop awaits the arrival of bamboo pulp.

(19) Final Peeling of *Zhuma*

Remaining impurities—outer skins, nodes, dark spots, red spots, bamboo joints—are removed, leaving only pure white fiber.

(20) Pressing *Zhuma*

The *zhuma* is pressed in wooden presses to squeeze out water, then transported to the workshop.

(21) Treading *Zhuma*

Zhuma is trampled in four rounds—dry, wet, splashed, and final treading. The first round is dry treading to break down fiber roots, while the second round is wet treading to dissolve fibers. The third and fourth rounds needs to add large amount of water to turn fibers into pulp.

(22) Beating in Vat

The pulp is placed into the vat, stirred with bamboo rakes, and strained through bamboo sieves to remove coarse fibers, leaving only fine pulp suitable for papermaking.

(23) *Lan* leaves Extract

Place leaves of downy holly (*Ilex pubescens*) in a wooden vat, seal it, and steam over high heat for about an hour (adjust based on quantity). Remove and rinse with cold water, then return to the vat and tread to extract juice. Add water to leach the liquid—this serves as a sizing agent and lubricant for papermaking.

(24) Sheet Formation

Two artisans work in tandem with bamboo screens: dipping, shaking, lifting and transferring sheets in rhythm. The papermaker stands at the front, the screen lifter at the back. They transfer the formed paper to the press board, with the papermaker taking 2.5 steps forward and the screen lifter 2.5 steps back—coordination (called harmonious hands) is essential; uncoordinated craftsmen cannot produce paper. Skilled teams achieve seamless production, producing even sheets without tears and forming neat paper stacks. A local saying notes: "A papermaker's skill is judged by the neatness of the paper stack."

(25) Pressing Sheets

Sheet pressing is done twice a month, with three stacks of paper per pressing. Place paper sheets on the press stack, add drainage bamboo mats, and cover with press boards. Place short and long iron weights on the boards. Start pressing gently; increase pressure only after most water has drained to avoid paper stack breakage, the breakage called *Bao Zhu Tuo*. After pressing, release the press, use a carrying pole to move the paper to the table, align the three stacks, and trim the edges. The screen lifter uses clips to stack 15 sheets together; the papermaker arranges the stacks neatly and hands them to the dryer for drying.

(26) Drying Sheets

The dryer carries wet paper to the drying room. Sheets are brushed onto drying walls one by one using pine-needle brushes. Skilled dryers use a shoulder strap (called *Dai Zhi*) and swing their bodies to assist brushing—this technique is called *Jian Feng* (shoulder momentum). Paper dried with *Jian Feng* is firm, flat, and has slightly drooping corners. A local saying summarizes this: "Papermaking requires agility; drying requires swinging."

(27) Trimming and Bundling

Pulp treaders prepare bamboo strips for wrapping paper, while papermakers "sharpen the knife" (a specific knife-sharpening method), oil the knife, and prepare paper fibers bundles (a tool used to prevent paper sticking and align paper stacks during cutting).

The screen lifter fetches dried paper from the drying room, places it flat on the workshop table, and press a pole onto the paper. With slightly bent hands, he press firmly along the outer edge of the pole to secure the paper. The pulp treader holds the other end of the paper stack to stabilize the paper. The papermaker cuts the paper edges with a knife in his right hand, following length and width marks on the table. After trimming all four edges, the treader assist the papermaker in bundling the paper into *dao*. The peeler and the treader then stack the finished paper for the day.

Appendix:

Nomenclature for Paper Corners: Presser's corner, Tip corner, *Zhuma* edge corner, End corner.

Nomenclature for Paper Edges: Head edge, Ridgepole edge, *Zhuma* edge, Knife edge (cut edge).

4. Zhang Fapeng: The Production of Yukou Paper and Explanation of Related Terminology (2022)[403]

1. Production of Yukou Paper

1.1. Harvesting Bamboo Shoots

After rainfall or storm, bamboo shoots can grow as much as five to six *chi* (approximately 1.67–2 meters) in a single day. Timing is therefore crucial. Harvest should take place when the shoot has elongated, its tip bent like a fishing rod, and is about to break through the sheath and sprout branches. At this stage, it must be cut down.

1.2. Trimming and Stripping *Zhuma*

Once *zhuma* (bamboo shoots) has been harvested, trimming can begin. The shoots felled in the mountains are slid down to the foothill and stacked. They are cut to a standardized length (generally around 1.5 meters) with a chopping knife. Using a curved trimming knife, the outer green rind is shaved off. The whitened culm is then split into uniform strips. These strips are bound tightly with bamboo splints into bundles and carried to the pond for further processing. (Two bundles constitute one *dan*, weighing approximately 90 *jin* [45 kg].)

---

403 Zhang Fapeng, born in 1947 in Zhiping, studied at high school but did not complete his degree. Afterward, he apprenticed in papermaking at the Nanshan Paper Mill in Pingpu Village and worked in papermaking for more than ten years. In 1977, he became a local-funded teacher at Zhiping School. In 1981, he enrolled at Ninghua Normal School, and upon graduation taught Chinese language and art at the junior middle division of Zhiping School as well as at primary schools in villages including Shefu. He retired in 2007. The content of this article has been reviewed and approved by Zhang Fapeng.

1.3. Soaking *Zhuma*

The trimmed bamboo bundles are then transported to the pond and "submerged into the pond." First, the outlet of the pond must be securely sealed. Bundles of *zhuma* are layered evenly, with lime sprinkled over each layer at a ratio of 10:1 (bamboo to lime by weight). The pond is then filled with clear water until the water level stands one *chi* (approximately 33 cm) above the bamboo surface. Finally, long bamboo strips and stones are placed atop the bundles to prevent them from floating.

1.4. Washing and Leaching of *Zhuma*

After soaking for about three months, the bamboo is ready for washing and leaching. This is physically demanding work. Workers, nearly unclothed, must stand waist-deep in caustic lime water, because wearing clothes would increase the area of skin irritated by the lime water. Once half the bundles have been washed and laid along the pond's edge, the outlet at one corner of the pond is gradually unsealed to release the lime water. In later practice, long water pipes were used: one end submerged in the pond, the other placed outside at a lower level, allowing the lime water to siphon out naturally. When all bundles are washed and the lime water discharged, the outlet is resealed and the pond is refilled with fresh water. The washed bamboo is then restacked neatly in the pond, covered with layers of Miscanthus or banana leaves, and kept submerged under water about one *chi* above the bundles. Since lime particles often remain adhered to the *zhuma*, water replacement must be repeated two or three times—a process known as "bleaching the bamboo." Workers trample repeatedly on the bamboo to dislodge residual lime particles.

1.5. Flow-Line Processing of Matured *Zhuma*

Because the position of the *zhuma* soaking ponds determines the amount of sunlight they receive, the time required for *zhuma* to reach full maturity varies. In general, two months after washing and bleaching, the bamboo fiber is ready for processing, and paper production can begin.

1.5.1. Stripping *Zhuma*

Two workers bend over carefully to clear a working spot (their own standing place) and begin sorting the raw material: removing the inner bamboo residue (impurities) from the fiber slices, peeling off the green skins that could not be shaved away from the young *zhuma* tubes, and piling these green skins in one corner. *Dou Tong*, the tougher reddish fibers at the base of the shoots, is also separated and gathered; these later serve as raw material for *Chibei* paper. Once all fiber from a pond has been stripped, this green-skin material is processed into coarse wrapping paper, also known as *Baopi* paper. The separated white bamboo fiber becomes the prime raw material for Yukou paper. The quantity of white fiber stripped in half a day is called one *fang*. A bamboo-fiber press is installed at the pondside: the fiber is loaded into square compartments inside the press, and the water is squeezed out. Operating twice a day in the pond yields two *fang* of stripped fiber.

A bamboo-fiber press

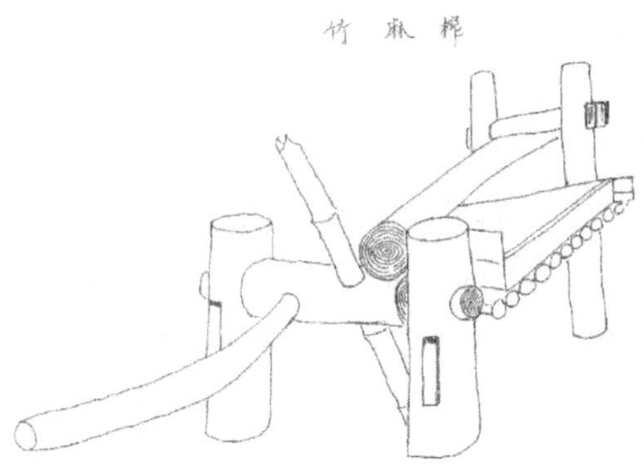

1.5.2.   Carrying *Zhuma*

This stage involves no technical skill. Workers simply carry the pressed, partially dried fiber back from the pond to the paper workshop. However, the number of workers needed (one or two) depends on the distance of the transport route.

1.5.3.   Treading *Zhuma*

Once carried into the workshop, the fiber is dumped into a *Cuo Gu* (a trough-like container) next to the main vat. Two workers begin the process. *Cuo Gu* is shaped like a long dustpan, its bottom woven of coarse bamboo strips. The workers tread the fiber with their feet until it is pulped. Each worker holds onto a rope tied overhead to a bamboo pole with one hand, swinging the other in rhythm, producing a steady "thump—clunk—thump—clunk" sound—an almost dance-like motion.

The pulped fiber is shoveled into the side compartment, ready for beating in vat. From there it is transferred into the main vat. Clear water is added while the front-side worker stirs with a bamboo rake to disperse the fiber evenly. When all fiber has been transferred, the "beating" begins: two workers, one at the front and one at the back of the vat, grip their rakes firmly and thrust them straight across to the opposite wall, pulling back in rhythm, left to right, then right to left, repeating continuously. The sound of beating is steady and resonant—"whoosh—whoosh—whoosh." Next comes vat-pulling: with a split bamboo tool called a *Na Zi*, the worker reaches to the bottom, stirring in circles, lifting out the coarse, long fibers. This produces a rhythmic "rustle—rustle—rustle" sound, almost musical.

Through repeated cycles, the fibers are processed until the long, coarse ones are fully removed. Finally, install a vat partition and a small bamboo sieve (for pulp filtering) about one meter from the main vat in the direction of the front vat. Another screen is placed at the front vat, weighed down with three flat stones (left, center, right). As the screen slowly sinks, thick pulp seeps upward through the bamboo weave, ready for the next stage of papermaking.

1.5.4.   Paper Formation

After the treading master completes beating, the screen lifting master sets the vat poles in place, arranges the screen bed, and lays the paper screen. The stone weights on the front vat screen are removed, and the surface pulp is leveled with a bamboo rake. At this point, the sheet-forming master enters. Two operators stand outside the front vat: the sheet-forming master on the left, the screen lifting master on the right. The first sheet is made as follows: both operators pick up the wooden clamps that secure the screen to the screen bed, fixing the screen and the screen bed together. They then align the screen bed, plunge it vertically into the pulp, and draw it back in one decisive motion. The sheet-former's left-front corner rises first, slowly lifting the pulp onto the bamboo screen, the pulp flowing gradually toward the screen-lifter's end. Finally, the entire sheet is lifted from the vat, as illustrated.

Rises first   Position of the Sheet-Forming Master   Position of the Screen Lifting Master

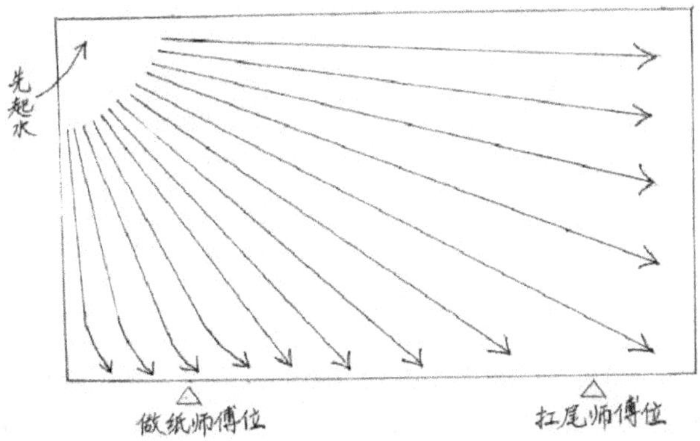

With perfect coordination, the two masters repeat this action, one sheet after another. Each wet sheet is transferred onto the pressing board, placed at two and a half steps away and at a 90-degree turn. As more sheets are laid, the pile of wet paper gradually rises. To ensure even sheet thickness, the sheet-forming master frequently smooths the pulp surface—ideally, after ten or so sheets the pulp must be leveled again. The concentration of pulp in the vat must be carefully monitored by the sheet-forming master. Leveling the pulp surface means, if a wet sheet comes out too thin, it represents the pulp concentration in the front vat is too low. In this case, the front vat screen needs to be gently pressed down with the bamboo rake, allowing thicker pulp from below to seep upward. If necessary, pulp is also drawn carefully from the rear vat into the front vat to restore proper concentration.

In practice, two sets of paper are produced daily, each consisting of 700–800 sheets. These are stacked into three piles: the bottom pile (≈300 sheets), the middle pile (≈300 sheets), and the top pile (≈100–200 sheets). During stacking, dry paper edges and prepared cedar bark strips are inserted to aid later separation. A cross-section is shown in the picture.

Corner   Cedar bark strip   Cedar bark strip   Cedar bark strip
Cedar bark strip   Each piece of bark is laid crosswise in staggered layers

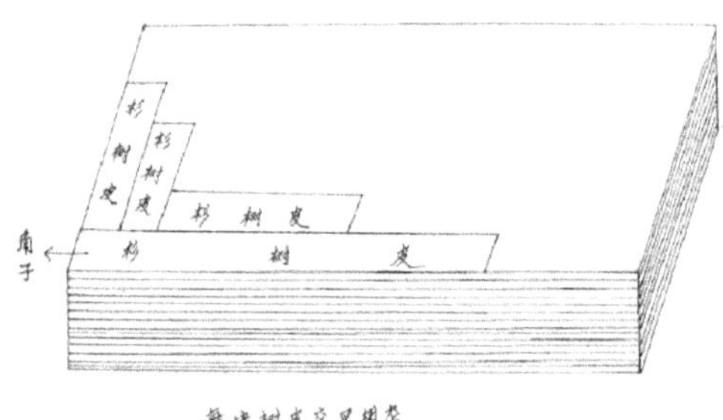

To protect the wet sheets from tearing, each piece of cedar bark is carefully padded with paper edges underneath at the pile corners, which are compressed the hardest, resulting in the driest area of the pressed stack. The screen lifting master begins separation at these corners.

Once all three piles are arranged, the lower pressing board is placed carefully on the top pile. The pile is then shifted along the pressing bridge, with "pads" and "pillows" placed in sequence. The press beam is lowered into place, the rope secured, and pressing begins. First, a hollow bamboo tube is used to gently drain water. When this can no longer be pressed, a thick bent lever is fitted into the "wheel" hole. The sheet-forming master joins in and presses further, first by hand, then—when resistance grows—by standing together on the lever, gripping the support rope, and applying synchronized downward force. At peak load, even the treading master joins in. After a short pause about ten minutes, the three return to the beam and press again until the pile is fully dewatered, typically within half an hour. When pressing is complete, the rope is loosened, the beam lifted, "pads", "pillows" and the lower pressing board removed, and the pile returned to its place. Using a carrying board, the pile is moved onto the paper table. The sheet-forming master trims three pile edges (*Maxian, Aotou, Dongzi*) with a curved knife, then scrapes the trimmed edges of *Dongzi* and *Aotou* upward with a scraper, forming a rolled ridge. Special care is given to the junction of *Dongzi* and *Aotou*, enabling the screen-lifting master to perform his task. Seated on a small bench, the screen-lifting master holds a clip in his right hand, and uses his left hand to lift sheets one by one from the "pigeon's beak" corner (the corner of first lift from the vat), arranging them neatly into neat stacks shaped like "<<<", usually 14 sheets per *bei* (bundle). The sheet-forming master, bending over the rear of *Maxian*, receives each bundle and carefully separates the wet sheets with both hands.

Because cedar bark was laid at the *Aotou* and *Dongzi* edges during stacking, those areas remain drier. At this stage, the sheet-forming master calls out "Pile surface!" (*Tuo Pi Ya!*) to alert the drying master to carry away the wet sheets. This surface requires additional sprinkling of water; otherwise, it cannot be properly brushed onto the drying wall.

See diagram: Schematic of "separating paper" into individual sheets

Schematic of "separating paper" into individual sheets　　Position of the sheet-forming master　　*Maxian*　　*Aotou*　　Pigeon's beak　　Position of the screen-lifting master　　*Dongzi*

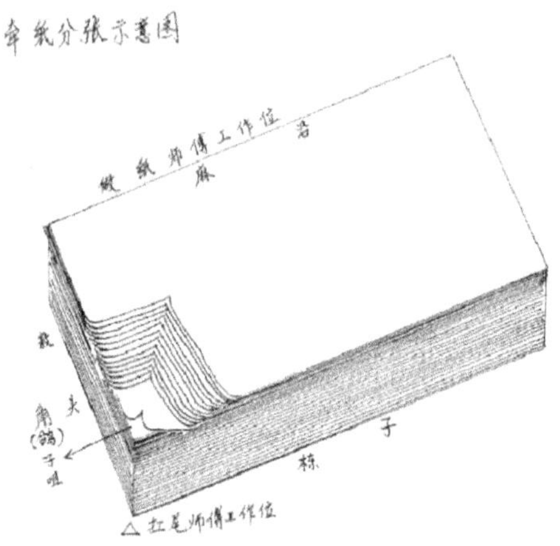

1.5.5.　Drying the Paper

After the wet sheets are carried into the drying room, the drying master arranges them into *bei*—each *bei* usually consisting of 14 sheets—which are then dried. The most challenging part is the handling of the paper piles's surface, namely *Tuo Pi* (坨皮, the top sheet of the pile) and *Tuo Da* (坨笪, the bottom sheet of the pile). The *Tuo Pi* is especially difficult because both its *Aotou* (敖头, sheet edge) and *Dongzi* (栋子, sheet edge) tend to be drier, a result of compression from the cedar bark used during the papermaking process.

Drying masters bear the heaviest workload. Every 15 days the drying wall must be swept of dust, and once a month the drying walls must be oiled. On these days, the entire workshop stops production, yet the two drying masters continue working—without any additional pay.

Sweeping the drying wall is done as follows: after the last sheets are dried in the evening, the firewood in the hollow wall is extinguished. By dawn, when the wall has cooled to ambient temperature, the drying master opens the door and, stripped to the waist, crawls inside. The space is cramped, making it difficult for tall or robust workers to turn around. The dust swept from the walls is carried outside the factory for disposal. This task must be completed within half a day.

Oiling the wall is a different process. Why must the wall be oiled? Because after one month of use, the walls become dry and porous. On the morning of oiling, the wall is first swept clean of dust, then the hearth is fired to heat the walls. Once sufficiently hot, tung oil is brushed over the walls. As the oil begins to dry, a coating of soybean milk is brushed over the surface—this is called "sealing the oil." A wall that has been properly oiled responds more readily to drying, and the finished paper comes out flat and firm.

However, after drying each sheet of paper, an invisible layer of paper fiber adheres to the walls. Over time this buildup causes sheets to peel away from the wall surface, disrupting the process. For this reason, the wall must be washed frequently.

1.5.6.   Trimming the Paper

As soon as the wet sheets have been dried and arranged in order within the drying room, the screen-lifting master removes them in bundles of 200 sheets, known as one *dao*. The sheets are placed on the cutting table, where the sheet-forming master wields a large hooked knife. The treading master steps in to assist, and each *dao* is cut and immediately packed. On average, producing seven *dao* of paper in a day is considered meeting the work quota. Some masters may produce an additional one or two *dao*; in such cases, compensation is calculated by piecework—more labor earns more pay.

2.   Glossary Related to the Production of Yukou Paper

2.1.   Facilities

2.1.1.   Hutang (湖塘, soaking pond).

A pond used for soaking and fermenting *zhuma*. It must be capable of retaining water, and is usually located where water sources are abundant and clean. A Hutang may vary in size and depth.

2.1.2.   Shihui Liao (石灰寮, lime shed).

Since large amounts of lime are needed for soaking *zhuma*, sufficient lime must be stockpiled in a lean year to prepare for use in a good year. Typically, a simple shed is built near the Hutang for lime storage. Some are made with earth walls and tiles; others use fir wood, bamboo strips, and thatched grass. The key requirement is protection from rain.

2.1.3.   Caohuang (槽楻, pulp vat).

Located in the paper workshop, this vat holds the *zhuma* pulp. Traditionally built with thick fir planks joined together, typically 1 m in height and 2.5 m along each side, with a square base. Later, reinforced concrete vats were also used.

2.1.4.   Chuogu (踔股/蹉鼓, trampling vat).

A long, trough-shaped structure where workers trample the *zhuma* with their feet to break it down. The ends and walls are made from thick wooden planks, while the base is woven from bamboo strips. See diagram:

Caohuang   Chuogu

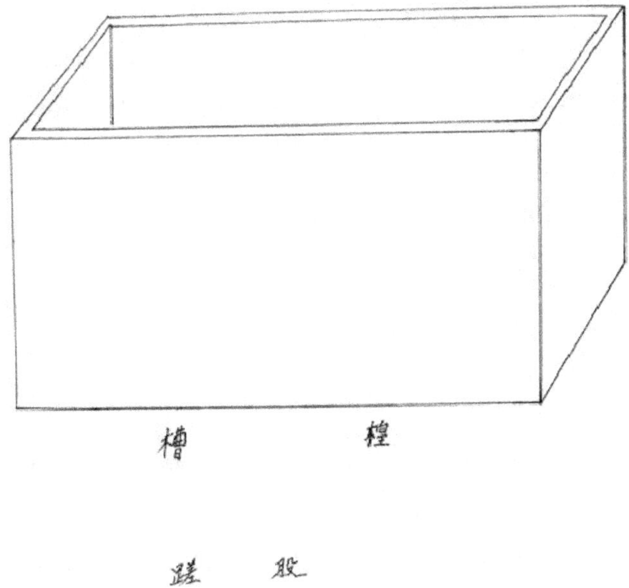

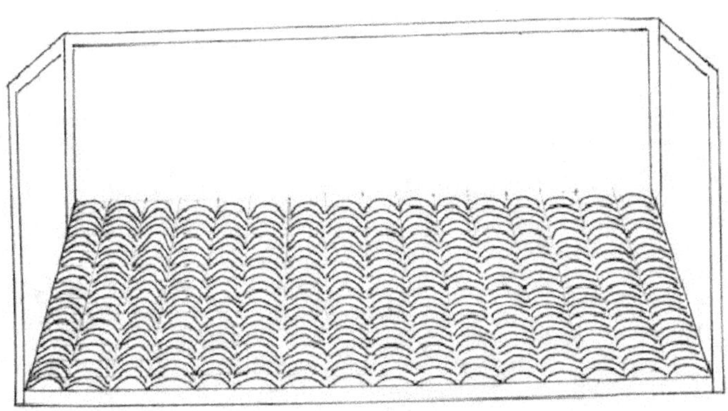

2.1.5.　Bian Huang, Natou Huang, Lan Huang, Dengshui Huang (边榱、
纳头榱、蓝榱、等水榱, auxiliary vats).

Bian Huang: Holds trampled *zhuma* and scraps from trimming three
edges (*Dongzi, Aotou,* and *Maxian*) of wet paper before separating the
paper from the half-day production batch, as well as torn wet sheets.

Natou Huang: Holds long fibers skimmed repeatedly with a *Na Zi* during beating over 4–5 days of work.

Lan Huang: A vat for holding *Lan Shui* (lan water). Equipped with a small bamboo basket for filtering and separating *lan* leaves from the water, and a small ladle bucket for scooping *Lan Shui*.

Dengshui Huang: A reserve water vat, maintained in case of sudden water supply interruptions.

All these vats are cylindrical in shape.

2.1.6.　Na Zi (纳子, bamboo skimmer).

A tool made from thick bamboo strips. During the beating process, treading masters repeatedly skim long fibers from the pulp vat with the Na Zi, accumulating them as Na Tou (coarse fibers). Once a Natou Huang is filled (after 4–5 days), these fibers can be used for making Natou paper. See diagram:

Na Zi

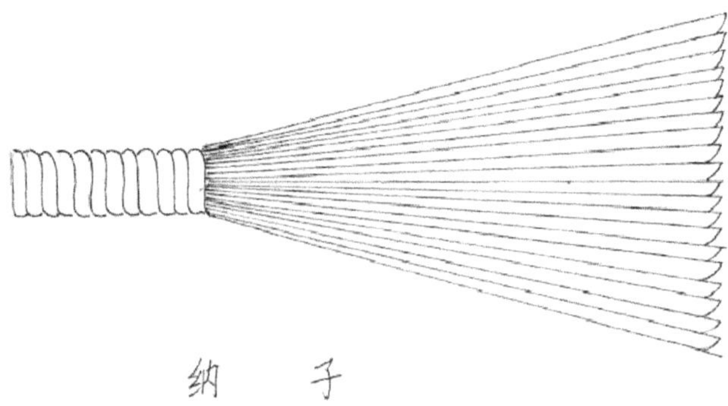

2.1.7. Jiangjun Ding & Meizi Ding (将军顶, 妹子顶, bamboo supports).

Crosswise bamboo poles set on the pulp vat, used to temporarily hold the papermaking screen bed. They are equipped with two small bamboo poles. See diagram:

Jiangjun Ding   Meizi Ding

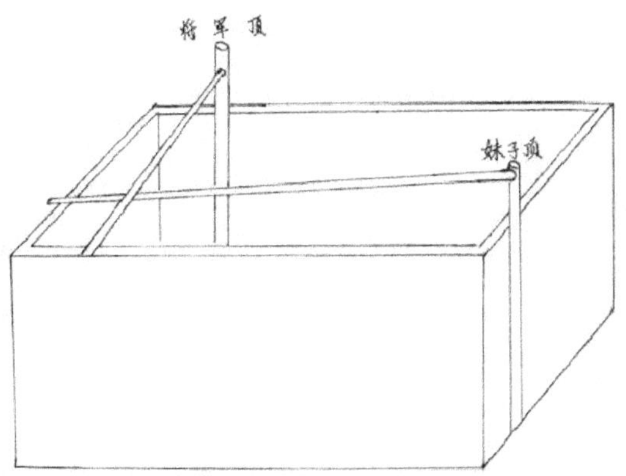

2.1.8. Zha (榨, press).

A device for pressing water out of wet sheets. See diagram:

Press pole   High supporting pole   Press board   Short supporting pole   "wheel" device

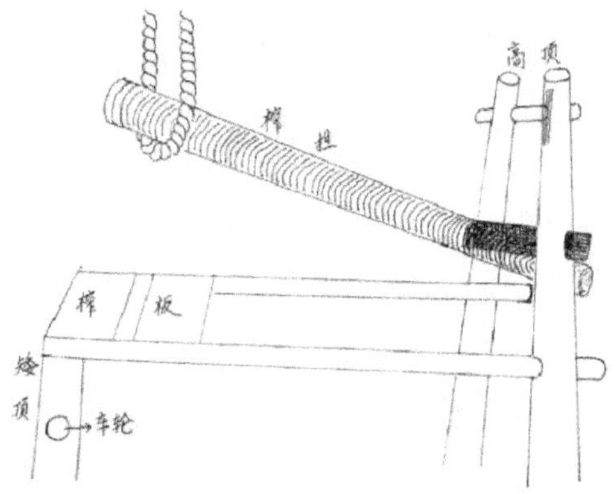

2.1.9. Paper Table (纸桌).

Used both for separating wet sheets and as the dining table for workers. See the diagram for seating arrangements during meals:

Flexible seats for other masters   Close to the drying room   Seats for two drying masters   Seats for the sheet-forming master   Flexible seats   Seats for the screen-lifting master   Additional note on the seating arrangement diagram for paper separating

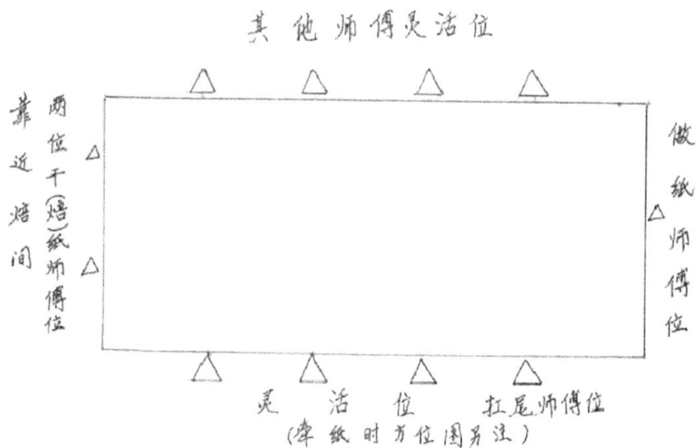

2.1.10. Beijian (焙间, drying room).

A room for drying sheets, divided into inner and outer sections. Traditionally the drying walls in the middle were constructed from bamboo, wood, clay, and lime, with very smooth surfaces. Heat from the central trench passes through to the drying walls. Firewood is placed at the trench mouth and must be fed consistently to maintain steady and even heat, requiring constant monitoring and refueling. See front-view diagram:

Inner drying section (rear)   Outer drying section (front)

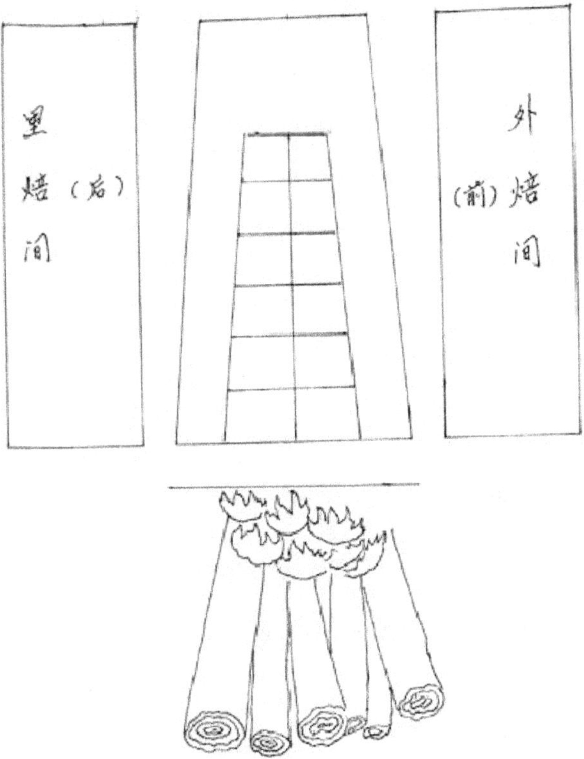

Over time, soot accumulates on the inside of drying walls, reducing heat conduction. Therefore, every 15 days the fire is extinguished and workers enter the walls to clean the drying walls of both sides and remove accumulated dust. Every month, production is halted for a day for oiling. As the drying walls gradually lose their stickiness for wet paper, oiling involves rebrushing the walls with tung oil while heat is applied at an appropriate temperature, followed by soybean milk brushing to seal the oil. This restores wall adhesion and ensures smooth drying. Notably, extinguishing and cleaning must be done first before oiling. The cycle is as follows:

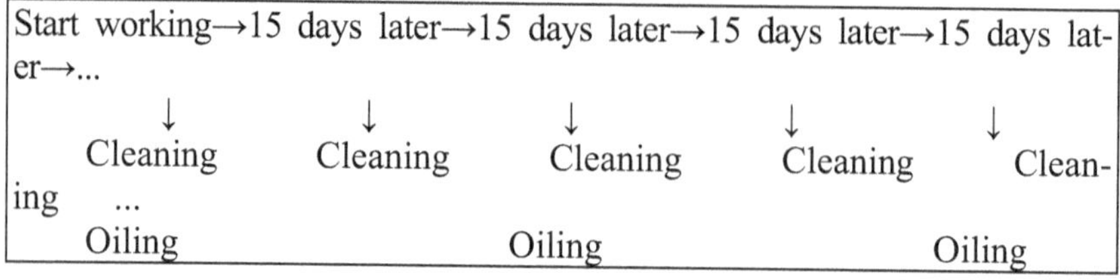

2.1.11. Grasping Rope (抓手绳).

Above the trampling vat, a bamboo pole 3–4 m long is suspended with two thick ropes, allowing two trampling masters to hold on while exerting force safely. During pressing, the sheet-forming master, the screen-lifting master and the trampling master in charge of the front vat must climb onto a steep press lever; they hold onto overhead ropes for stability and leverage.

2.1.12. Pu Tuo Table (铺坨桌, staging table).

A long narrow table set parallel to the main paper table, 80–90 cm apart. Used to temporarily stack wet sheets after they are separated.

2.1.13. Che Lun (车轮, "wheel" device).

Not a vehicle wheel. A mechanism used in pressing: the press lever cycles through three circular holes, with the rope tightening step by step, gradually expelling water. Both ends of the "wheel" rest on two short supports. See diagram:

"wheel" device

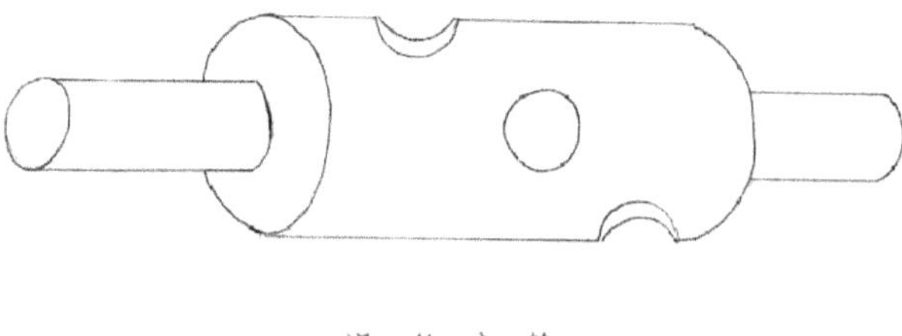

2.1.14. Yashui Gun (压水棍, water-pressing pole).

When the wet paper pile is positioned on the press, "pads", "pillows", and press pole are set in place and the cables are fastened. A 2 m bamboo pole is then inserted into the "wheel" to begin pressing gradually. This pole is called the Yashui Gun.

2.1.15. Zha Gun (榨棍, press lever).

When the Yashui Gun can no longer press further, it is replaced with a bent lever inserted into the "wheel" holes. This stronger bar is called Zha Gun. See diagram:

Press lever

2.1.16. Gecao Ban (隔槽板, partition board).

After the treading master completes pulp beating, a long plank (as long as the pulp vat's side) is installed at the water surface inside the pulp vat. It divides the vat into two parts: the "front vat" and "rear vat."

2.1.17. Xiao Da (小笪, small bamboo mat).

A bamboo-woven mat hung behind the partition board to prevent pulp in the rear vat from seeping forward. Typically as long as the vat side and 50 cm wide.

2.1.18. Da Cao Da (大槽笪, large bamboo mat).

A bamboo mat lightly placed on the pulp surface of the front vat after the treading master completes pulp beating and installs the partition board and small bamboo mat, used to regulate pulp concentration in   the front vat and ensure even sheet thickness.

2.1.19. Kang Tuo Ban (扛坨板, transfer board).

A long wooden plank used to move pressed wet piles to the paper table. Slightly longer than the table, approximately 8 cm thick and 10 cm wide. Also used in the final step of trimming. See diagram:

Transfer board

2.1.20. Cai Dao (裁刀, trimming knife).

A curved, hook-shaped knife used for trimming wet piles and dried sheets. See diagram:

Trimming knife

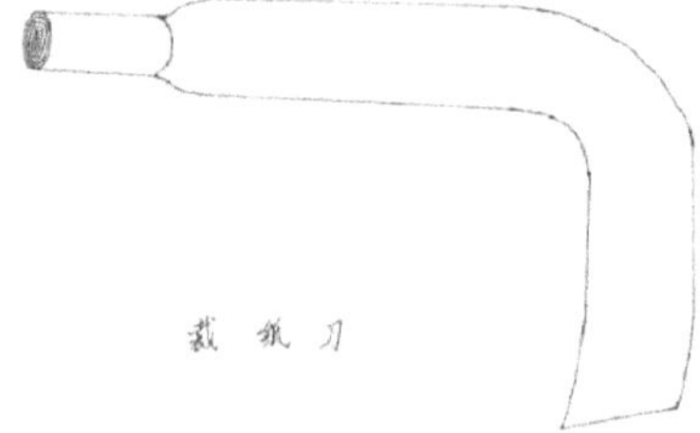

2.2.   Tools

Craftsmen of different roles uses different tools, and these tools must be provided by the craftsmen themselves.

2.2.1.   Sheet-forming master's Ge Zi (割子, cutter):

A short bamboo tube, without a node, about 12 cm in length. It is split lengthwise, and one half is taken for use. The edge is processed to make it as sharp as a blunt knife. During the separation of wet sheets, this tool is used to trim the Aotou and Dongzi of the paper, producing a neat side ridge that facilitates sheet separation and clamping the corners (also known as "shaping the stack"). See diagram:

Sheet-forming master's cutter used in sheet separation

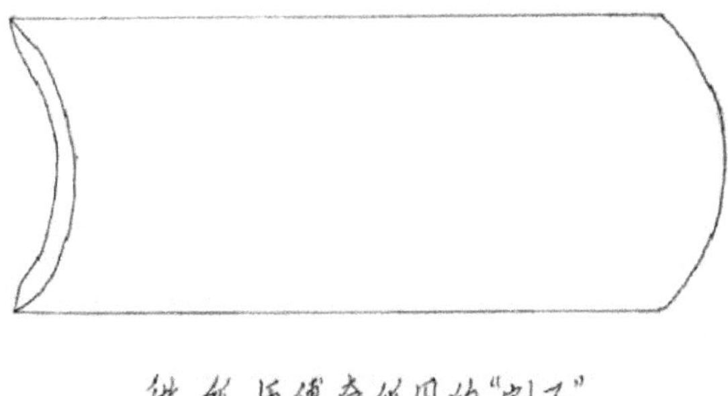

2.2.2.   Screen-lifting master's Jia Zi (夹子, clip):

Most craftsmen use a self-made bamboo clip, while some commission a blacksmith to forge an iron one. This tool is used during sheet separation to clamp the corners. See diagram:

Screen-lifting master's clip used in sheet separation   Bamboo clip Iron clip

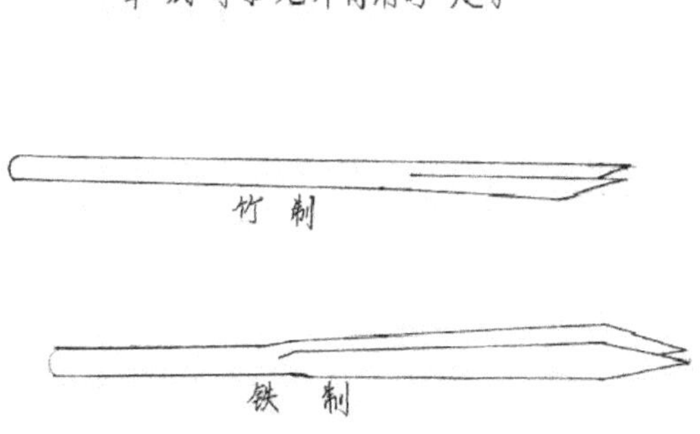

2.2.3.   Treading master's Na Zi (纳子, bamboo skimmer):

As described earlier.

2.2.4.   Drying master's Shua Ba(刷把, brush):

Made of bundled pine needles, this brush is used to press the wet sheets firmly against the drying-wall surface. See diagram:

Brush

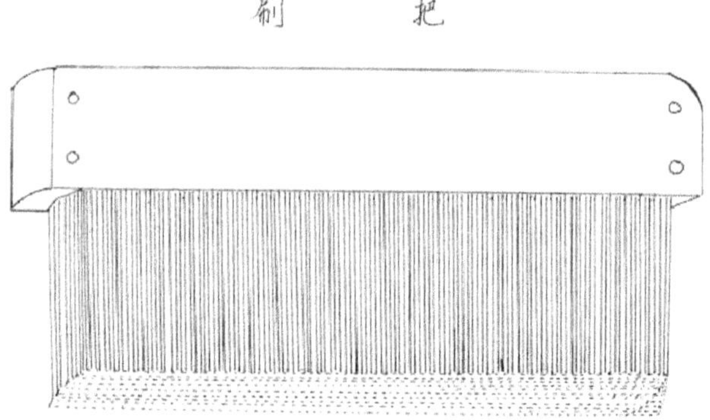

In addition, the drying room is equipped with two auxiliary items: a water basin and a water-sprinkling brush, both of which must be provided by the workshop owner.

Water basin and water-sprinkling brush

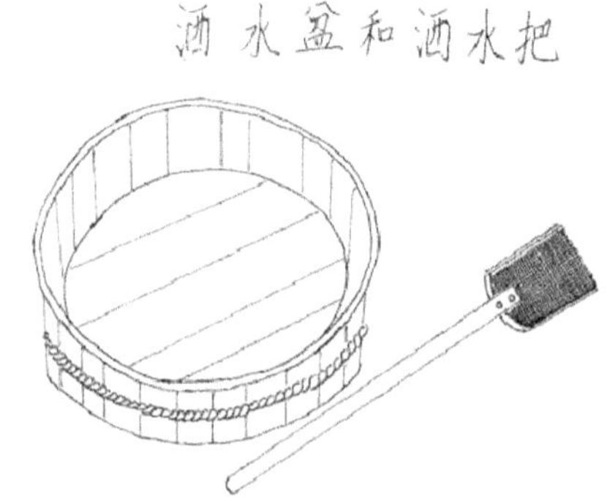

Afterword

On September 4, 2021, I had the chance to conduct field study in the papermaking regions of Liancheng and Ninghua, together with five undergraduate students from the Department of History at Xiamen University—Wang Siheng, Jiang Yunlin, Yu Yue, Dong Aijia, and Pan Yini (all from the 2020 cohort)—and with the guidance of our mentor, Gui Shuzhong. What began as a modest field trip turned into an extraordinary harvest. We received generous support from Secretary Lei Haiming and Township Head Lei Huaping of Zhiping She Township, who encouraged our gathering of materials and research. In the months that followed, I returned multiple times with different groups of students. Each trip was enriched by the patient guidance of local historians—Gui Shuzhong, Lei Shaoqiu, Deng Xuanjiu, Zeng Youchun, Zhang Fapeng, and Ma Huajun. We were also warmly welcomed by the intangible cultural heritage inheritors of Yukou paper-making—Hu Lanshan, Hu Cheng, Lei Yusheng, and Lei Changtian. Lei Changtian, a new-generation bearer of the craft, together with his friend Zhang Jianxiong, frequently coordinated and assisted our fieldwork, making significant contributions to the project. Zhiping Township officials Liu Jiao, Zeng Xianshou, as well as village party secretaries and directors Lei Rongqing, Zeng Younan, Zeng Nianfu, Zeng Shaoqun, Chi Tingcheng, and Fan Renning solved countless practical difficulties for us along the way.

The Ninghua County Archives provided the solid documentary foundation upon which this book rests, supporting our research and working tirelessly to facilitate access to their collections. In Shicheng, we were assisted by Director Liu Shanyong of the County Archives, Director Liu Min of the County Library, collector Zhao Lidong, and the Hengjiang Township Government. Their help made our investigations and archival work possible. In Gutian Township, Liancheng County, Mr. Deng

Jinkun—an inheritor of the intangible cultural heritage of Lianshi paper-making—welcomed us on multiple occasions, generously opening his family's trove of contracts, paper-industry records, and rare documents and artifacts he had collected over the years. In Changting, we were aided by historians Wang Ying, Huang Majin, Hu Shiya, and by the County Archives, who all helped us trace valuable sources. On the consumer side of Yukou paper, in Penang, Malaysia, Datuk Lee Yong Kwang, chairman of the Penang Shunde Association, warmly recounted how Yukou paper once entered Penang—a story that echoes with the archival record of the production region. Hearing such memories, we were deeply touched.

The Department of History at Xiamen University has long cherished a tradition of social investigation and historical research in northwest Fujian. Since Professor Fu Yiling's discovery of a collection of contracts in Huangli Township, Yong'an, in 1939, and launched research on them, more than eighty years have passed. In the early 1980s, many faculty members and students of the department—including Yang Guozhen, Kong Yongsong, Chen Zhiping, Zheng Zhenman, Xu Xiaowang, Zeng Ling, and Lin Renchuan—carried this legacy forward, organizing fieldwork and document collection in Longyan and Sibao, Liancheng.[404] By the 1990s, a new generation—Liu Yonghua, Zhang Kan, Rao Weixin, Zhou Xuexiang, among others—continued this work, guiding undergraduate students (including me and my cohort, which enrolled in 2001) into Sibo and Peitian for field practice. I myself, since first entering Xiamen University, have often gone to western Fujian to study traditional villages and clan societies. I still recall Professor Liu Yonghua's passionate words: that the materials in Ninghua alone were rich enough to sustain several doctoral theses, which sparked my fascination.

---

404 See Yang Guozhen, *Between the Hoklo and the Hakka*, Fujian People's Publishing House, 2023.

Later, while pursuing doctoral studies at the Department of History at Chinese University of Hong Kong, I was fortunate to have supervisors such as Professors Choi Chi cheung and Ma Muk chi, along with Professors Liu Tik-sang, Cheung Siu-woo, and Ma Jianxiong at the Hong Kong University of Science and Technology. They often led students to Tai O the fishing town to observe the "Dragon Boat Water Parade" during the Dragon Boat Festival, to Tai Hang for the "Fire Dragon Dance" during the Mid-Autumn Festival, and to Cheung Chau for the "Cheung Chau Bun Festival" folk belief activities—all recognized as national intangible cultural heritage. They shared their own experiences of participating in the application, evaluation, and approval of these ICH projects. Looking back, those experiences planted in me the seeds of a lifelong concern for intangible cultural heritage. Today, as ICH projects gain new prominence from government departments at all levels, local traditions are rediscovered and revitalized, offering fresh opportunities for research in history, cultural heritage studies, anthropology, and sociology.

Throughout our investigation of Yukou paper, many students contributed in meaningful ways. Undergraduate Yu Yue compiled an essay titled "The Papermaking Economy and Social Changes in Western Fujian Amidst the KMT-CPC Struggle, 1920–1940," presented at the 5th "Future Stars" Undergraduate-Graduate Academic Forum of the Faculty of History, Nankai University; parts of her research are incorporated into Chapter Four of this book. Pan Yini carefully verified several of the notes. Doctoral student Jia Yi secured funding for a social practice project titled "Modern Western Fujian Papermaking and Soviet Revolutionary Research" from the Longyan Industry-Education Integration Research Institute of Xiamen University, which supported our research trip in July 2022—I would like to express my gratitude for this support. Other students—Fu Huiling, Zhang Fengying, Lin Yun, Jia Yi, Huang Yazhen, Zhuo Yingping,

Wang Mukun, Hong Yulin, and Peng Xing—joined our expeditions in different batches, witnessing the fragile persistence of papermaking and assisting in the collection of materials. I am also grateful to the Office of Social Sciences Research Administration of Xiamen University for their recommendation, to the China Construction Bank for funding, and to our editors for their tireless work. This book, completed under pressure of time, is but a preliminary collection of archival records and oral histories. It aspires only to provide a foundation for deeper, more mature studies in the future—and to spark wider interest in the history of papermaking technology and the paper industry in China.

Finally, I owe a profound gratitude to Mr. Gui Shuzhong, who began filming Yukou paper-related materials at Hu Lanshan's home in the early 2000s. When I first saw his documentary *Yukou Paper*, I was stunned by the ingenuity of traditional papermaking. Thanks to his constant support, this book could come into being. In my encounters with him, with Hu Lanshan, and with other masters of the craft, I have seen what it means to work with patience, perseverance, and precision; to strive for excellence while honoring continuity. Perhaps this is the deeper meaning of artisanship: to spend a lifetime refining a skill, fashioning an object, savoring beauty in the process. In this way, the Dao reveals itself—and the world is given a glimpse.

Chen Yao

Gaolin, Xiamen

November 24, 2022

Bibliography

1. Historical Sources

(1) Archival Materials

"Report on the Date of Re-election and Request for Officials to Attend and Supervise" (September 22, 1941), preserved in the Changting County Archives, Archives of the Changting Paper Industry Trade Guild, Archive No. 81-6-704.

"Report on the Results of This Re-election and Request for Verification of the Oath-taking Date of the Executive and Supervisory Committee Members" (October 7, 1941), preserved in the Changting County Archives, Archives of the Changting Paper Industry Trade Guild, Archive No. 81-6-704.

"Report on Changes in the Registration Number of the Original License, the Name of the Party-appointed Supervisor, the Revised Charter after the Election, and Submission of Membership Rosters (four copies each)" (October 19, 1941), preserved in the Changting County Archives, Archives of the Changting Paper Industry Trade Guild, Archive No. 81-6-704.

"Report Requesting Action Against Paper Merchants Who Have Persistently Refused to Join the Guild Despite Repeated Notices, in Order to Uphold Regulations", preserved in the Changting County Archives, Archives of the Changting Paper Industry Trade Guild, Archive No. 81-6-704.

"The Articles of Association of the Changting County Paper Industry Trade Guild, Fujian Province" (October 19, 1941), preserved in the Changting County Archives, Archives of the Changting Paper Industry Trade Guild, Archive No. 81-6-704.

"Supply and Marketing Cooperative of Zhiping Township, Seventh District, Ninghua County" (1952). preserved in Ninghua County Archives, collected and provided by Lei Shaoqiu..

Yong'an Special District Cooperative General Association: "Adjusting the Purchase Prices for Handmade Paper" (March 24, 1953), preserved in the Ninghua County Archives, Archive No. 35-2-8.

"Summary Report on Old Revolutionary Area Work in the Seventh District of Ninghua County" (April 2, 1953), preserved in the Ninghua County Archives, Archive No. 0057-003-0031-0001.

Ninghua County Cooperative General Association: "Request for Prompt Readjustment of the Purchase Prices for Maobian Paper and for Setting

Prices for Yukou Paper Produced in Zhiping" (April 2, 1953), preserved in the Ninghua County Archives, collected and provided by Lei Shaoqiu.

China Native Products Company, Yong'an Branch, and Fujian Province Yong'an Special District Supply and Marketing Cooperative: "On Arranging the Task of Maobian Paper Export and Hoping for Firm Implementation" (February 15, 1955), preserved in the Ninghua County Archives, collected and provided by Lei Shaoqiu.

"Survey Report on Neishan Yukou Paper in Zhiping District, Ninghua County" (June 8, 1955), preserved in the Ninghua County Archives, collected and provided by Lei Shaoqiu.

"Yukou Paper Supply and Marketing Contract" (10 August 1955), preserved in the Ninghua County Archives, collected and provided by Lei Shaoqiu.

Ninghua County Government: "Mobilize Laborers to Rush the Transport of Native Paper for Export within September" (September 6, 1955), preserved in Ninghua County Archives, collected and provided by Lei Shaoqiu.

"Request for Review of Constructive Opinions on Issues Concerning the Circulation of Ninghua Zhiping Yukou Paper" (November 1, 1955), preserved in Ninghua County Archives, collected and providedby Lei Shaoqiu.

"Survey on the Situation of Veteran Cadres During the Land Revolution in Zhiping District, Ninghua County" (December 22, 1956), preserved in Ninghua County Archives, Archive No. 6-9-19-148.

"Equipment Installation Plan for the Machine-Powered Paper Mill in Zhiping Commune" (February 24, 1959), preserved in Ninghua County Archives, Archive No. 26-5-30.

"Summary Report on the Current Situation of Handmade Paper Production by the CPC Zhiping Commune Committee" (May 24, 1959), preserved in Ninghua County Archives, Archive No. 26-5-30.

"Paper Industry Production Plan of Zhiping People's Commune" (June 10, 1959), preserved in Ninghua County Archives, collected and providedby Lei Shaoqiu.

Commercial Bureau of Qingning County: "The Indigenous Paper Purchasing Station Active in the 'Paper Capital' Zhiping" (September 23, 1959), preserved in Ninghua County Archives, collected and providedby Lei Shaoqiu.

Zhiping Handmade Paper Procurement Station, Agricultural Products Division, Ninghua County Supply and Marketing Cooperative: "How the

Zhiping Handmade Paper Purchasing Station Participates in Production, Improves Quality, and Enhances Business Management" (May 6, 1964), preserved in Ninghua County Archives, collected and providedby Lei Shaoqiu.

Communist Party Committee of Zhiping Commune: "Work Summary Report on the Handmade Paper Raw Material Preparation Phase in 1964" (June 4, 1964), preserved in Ninghua County Archives, collected and providedby Lei Shaoqiu.

Ninghua County Planning Committee, "Notice on Implementing the 1964 Handmade Paper Export Plan" (November 4, 1964), preserved in Ninghua County Archives, collected and providedby Lei Shaoqiu.

"Specifications and Quality Standards for Fujian Handmade Paper" (December 1964), preserved in Ninghua County Archives, collected and providedby Lei Shaoqiu.

"Zhiping Commune's Opinions on the Management of Handmade Paper Production and Operations in 1966" (February 8, 1966), preserved in Ninghua County Archives, collected and providedby Lei Shaoqiu.

"Notice on Several Issues in Current Handmade Paper Production" (November 13, 1966), preserved in Ninghua County Archives, collected and providedby Lei Shaoqiu.

"Notice from the Production Command Group of the Zhiping Commune Revolutionary Committee on Assigning the 1972 Handmade Paper Production Task" (July 4, 1972), preserved in Ninghua County Archives, Archive No. 57-24-15.

"Notice from the Ninghua County Revolutionary Committee on Assigning the 1974 Handmade Paper Raw Material Preparation and Production Task" (March 8, 1974), preserved in Ninghua County Archives, Archive No. 57-24-15.

"Materials from the Zhiping Commune's Yukou Paper Production Cost Investigation" (July 30, 1974), preserved in Ninghua County Archives, Archive No. 57-24-15.

"Notice on Issuing Handmade Paper Production Tasks and Quality Requirements for 1974 by the Revolutionary Committee of Zhiping Commune, Ninghua County" (August 3, 1974), preserved in Ninghua County Archives, Archive No. 57-24-16.

"Report on Current Issues in Paper Production and Several Tentative Suggestions" (September 12, 1974), preserved in Ninghua County Archives, Archive No. 57-24-16.

Ninghua County Revolutionary Committee Planning Commission, "Supplementary Notice on the Pricing of Screen-Hanging Coarse Paper" (January 6, 1975), preserved in the Archive of Zhiping She Ethnic Township.

"Report on the Preparation of Raw Materials and Production Work for Handmade Paper in 1974" (January 19, 1975), preserved in Ninghua County Archives, Archive No. 57-24-16.

"Notice of the Ninghua County Native Products and Sundries Company Regarding the Forwarding of Document No. 117 from the Provincial Native Products Company (Commercial-Native Products-Sundries-1975)" (July 31, 1975), preserved in Ninghua County Archives, collected and providedby Lei Shaoqiu.

Sanming Regional Supply and Marketing Cooperative, ed., *Supply and Marketing Cooperation Bulletin (No. 8)* (April 24, 1978), preserved in Ninghua County Archives, Archive No. 57-28-20.

"Report by the Zhiping Supply and Marketing Cooperative on This Year's Handmade Paper Production" (August 5, 1978), preserved in Ninghua County Archives, collected and providedby Lei Shaoqiu.

"Minutes of the Provincial Handmade Paper Production Work Conference" (December 1978), preserved in Ninghua County Archives, collected and providedby Lei Shaoqiu.

"Speech Draft for the Zhiping Commune Handmade Paper Production Conference" (July 16, 1979), preserved in Ninghua County Archives, Archive No. 57-29-23.

"Notice on Issues Regarding the Procurement and Allocation of Handmade Paper for Export" (September 25, 1979), preserved in Ninghua County Archives, collected and providedby Lei Shaoqiu.

Management Committee of Zhiping Commune, Ninghua County: "Produce More Handmade Paper for the Four Modernizations, Increase Income to Benefit Thousands of Households" (March 12, 1980), preserved in Ninghua County Archives, Archive No. 57-30-7.

"Speech by Comrade Wei Zongzhou at the Provincial Conference on Handmade Paper Production and Marketing" (March 29, 1980), preserved in Ninghua County Archives, collected and providedby Lei Shaoqiu.

Revolutionary Committee of Ninghua County: "Minutes of the County Conference on Handmade Paper Production" (April 3, 1980), preserved in Ninghua County Archives, Archive No. 57-30-7.

Ninghua County Committee of the Communist Party of China, "Investigation Report on Establishing the Zhiping Paper-Making Area" (April 3, 1981), preserved in Ninghua County Archives, Archive No. 57-31-7.

Zhiping Commune: "Report Requesting Funding to Establish a Mechanized Yukou Paper Factory" (June 29, 1981), preserved in Ninghua County Archives, Archive No. 57-31-7.

Ninghua County Supply and Marketing Cooperative, "Decision on Issues Concerning Handmade Paper Production and Procurement in Fangtian Commune" (August 31, 1981), preserved in Ninghua County Archives, Archive No. 57-31-7.

"Decision on the Handling of Wu [Name Withheld] and Others for Jointly Trafficking in Yukou Paper" (1981), preserved in Ninghua County Archives, Archive No. 51-32-11.

"Decision on the Handling of Yang [Name Withheld] for Engaging in Arbitrage of Yukou Paper" (1981), preserved in Ninghua County Archives, Archive No. 51-32-11.

Zhiping Commune Administrative Committee, "Investigation Report on Yukou Paper Production in Zhiping (The Past, Present, and Prospects of Yukou Paper)" (January 10, 1983), preserved in Ninghua County Archives, Archive No. 57-33-14.

"Ninghua County Handmade Paper Procurement Plan in 1983" (September 26, 1983), preserved in Ninghua County Archives, Archive No. 57-33-14.

Zhiping Supply and Marketing Cooperative: "Supporting Handmade Paper Production and Revitalizing Purchase and Sales Operations" (February 1984), preserved in Ninghua County Archives, Archive No. 57-33-14.

Zhiping Commune Administrative Committee, "Prosperity Policies Reach the Bamboo Hills, Paper Industry Achieves Great Development" (February 1984), preserved in Ninghua County Archives, Archive No. 57-33-14.

Ninghua County Supply and Marketing Cooperatives Union: "Notice on Adjusting the Extra-Price Subsidy for Yukou Paper" (February 13, 1984), preserved in Ninghua County Archives, Archive No. 35-33-4.

Ninghua County Supply and Marketing Cooperatives Union: "Notice on Cancelling the Extra-Price Subsidy for Maobian Paper and Lowering the Extra-Price Subsidy for Yukou Paper" (May 15, 1984), preserved in Ninghua County Archives, Archive No. 35-33-6.

Zhiping Township Government, "Investigation Report on the Current Status of Handmade Paper Production in Zhiping Township" (1989), preserved in Ninghua County Archives, Archive No. 57-39-10.

Zhiping Township Government, "Reply on Approving the Establishment of the 'Ninghua County Zhiping Yukou Paper Craft Factory'" (April 13, 1991), preserved in Ninghua County Archives, Archive No. 57-41-7.

Communist Party Committee of Zhiping She Ethnic Township & People's Government of Zhiping She Ethnic Township, "Research Report on the Development of the Yukou Paper Industry in Zhiping She Ethnic Township, Ninghua County" (December 2021)

(2) Local Chronicles and Historical Materials

Hu Taichu (Compiler), Zhao Yumu (Calligrapher of Inscriptions) (Song Dynasty): *The Chorography of Linting*, Fujian People's Publishing House, 1990.

Chorography of Renhua County (compiled during the Tongzhi era of the Qing dynasty), Block-printed Edition of the 9th Year of Guangxu era.

Chorography of Ninghua County (compiled during the Kangxi era of the Qing dynasty), Chengwen Publishing House, 1967.

Chorography of Ninghua County (Republic of China Period), Shanghai Bookstore Publishing House, 2000.

Revised Chorography of Dapu County (Republic of China Period), Shanghai Bookstore Publishing House, 2003.

Chorography of Changting County (Republic of China Period), Shanghai Bookstore Publishing House, 2000.

Compiled by the CPC Ninghua County Committee Party History Office, *Collected Historical Materials on the Revolutionary Struggle in Ninghua County* (Vol. 2), 1962.

Compiled by the Foreign Trade Station of Longyan Prefecture, Fujian Province: *Handbook of Export Handmade Paper*, July 1976.

Rewi Alley: "An Account of the Gonghe Movement," in *Selected Historical and Cultural Materials*, Vol. 71, 1980.

Compiled by the Ninghua County Toponymy Leading Group Office: *Toponymic Directory of Ninghua County*, 1981.

Qiu Hengkuan: Specialty Products of Ninghua, *Ninghua Historical and Cultural Materials* (Vol. 1), 1982.

Qiu Denong and Yi Juexun: "Overview of the Development of Paper Production", *Ninghua Historical and Cultural Materials* (Vol. 4), 1984.

Yu Zhaoting: "Yukou Paper", *Ninghua Local Chronicles Newsletter* (No. 2), 1985.

All-China Federation of Trade Unions, "Survey of the Paper Workers' Union in Changning District," *Ninghua Historical and Cultural Materials* (Vol. 5), 1985.

Compiled by the Party History Working Committee of the Ninghua County CPC Committee: *Ninghua Party History Materials* (Vol. 9), 1988.

Compiled by the Editorial Office of the Compilation Committee for the Chronicle of Supply and Marketing Cooperatives in Ninghua County: *Chronicle of Supply and Marketing Cooperatives in Ninghua County, Fujian Province* (1931–1985), 1988.

Mao Xing: "The Historical Origins of the Paper Industry in Ninghua and Tingzhou", *Ninghua Historical and Cultural Materials (Special Volume on Industry and Commerce)*, compiled by the Committee for the Study of Historical Materials, CPPCC Ninghua County, 1990.

Ninghua Historical and Cultural Materials (Vol. 12): "Forestry Chronicles", 1991.

Liu Shanqun (Chief Editor): *Chorography of Ninghua County*, Fujian People's Publishing House, 1992.

Compiled by the Fujian Provincial Local Chorography Compilation Committee: *Fujian Provincial Chorography: Light Industry Records*, Fangzhi Publishing House, 2000.

"Investigation Report on the Old Revolutionary Base Area of Zhiping Township", provided by Lei Nianfu.

Li Wensheng and Fu Huochang: "Some Historical Aspects of Industrial and Commercial Construction in Changting During the Second Revolutionary Civil War Period", *Changting Historical and Cultural Materials* (Vol. 2), 1982.

Narrated by Huang Yushu, compiled by Weng Wei: "Memories of the General Trade Union of Tingzhou City During the Second Revolutionary Civil War Period", *Changting Historical and Cultural Materials* (Vol. 4), 1983.

Zou Zibin: "'Skilled Papermakers in Tingzhou Prefecture'—Interviews with Veteran Papermakers and Industry Elders on the Overview of Tingzhou's Handmade Paper Industry", *Changting Historical and Cultural Materials* (Vol. 5), 1983.

Fu Rutong: "Overview of Commerce in Tingzhou in the Soviet Areas", *Changting Historical and Cultural Materials* (Vol. 10), 1986.

Mao Xing: "Ten Years of the Gonghe in Changting: 1939–1949", *Changting Historical and Cultural Materials* (Vol. 10), 1986.

Mao Xing: "Fragments of Commerce and Trade in Changting before the Founding of the PRC", *Changting Historical and Cultural Materials* (Vol. 12), 1987.

Zhong Min: "A Brief History of the Electric Power Industry in Changting", *Changting Historical and Cultural Materials* (Vol. 12), 1987.

Mao Xing: "Several Works and Writings of the Gonghe in Changting", *Changting Historical and Cultural Materials* (Vol. 13), 1987.

Qiu Renyuan: "Overview of Commercial Organizations (Guilds) in Changting County during the Republican Era", *Changting Historical and Cultural Materials* (Vol. 14), 1988.

Mao Xing: "The 'Changting Chaos-Suppression Committee' on the Eve of Liberation", *Changting Historical and Cultural Materials* (Vol. 15), 1989.

Wang Qisen: "A Brief Discussion on Foreign Trade in the Central Soviet Area", *Changting Historical and Cultural Materials* (Vol. 15), 1989.

Lai Luan: "Summary of Industry and Commerce Administration in Changting during the Central Soviet Period, Changting", *Historical and Cultural Materials* (Vol. 18), 1990.

Liang Xinbin: "Mr. Li Hongdong: A Devoted Supporter of Local Education", *Changting Historical and Cultural Materials* (Vol. 18), 1990.

Mao Xing: "Random Notes on Improved Paper in Changting", *Changting Historical and Cultural Materials* (Vol. 18), 1990.

Geng Sheng: "Work and Works of the Chinese Industrial Cooperatives in Changting During the War of Resistance Against Japanese Aggression, Changting Historical and Cultural Materials (Vol. 26), 1995.

Li Yangmin: Industry and Handicrafts in Changting During the War of Resistance Against Japanese Aggression", *Changting Historical and Cultural Materials* (Vol. 26), 1995.

Wang Qisen and Zhang Hongxiang: "Peng Shengbiao: From Papermaker to General", *Changting Historical and Cultural Materials* (Vol. 39), 2006.

Lin Sixian: "My Recollections as Administrative Inspector of Changting", *Selected Historical and Cultural Materials* (Vol. 4, "Political and Military" Series, Book 5), compiled by the Committee on Historical and Cultural Materials of the CPPCC Fujian Provincial Committee, 2006.

(3) Newspapers and Magazines

Agriculture and Commerce Bulletin

Monthly Bulletin of the British-American Tobacco Company

Nanyang Commercial News

Red China

Shen Bao (Shanghai)

Women and Domestic Products

China Construction (Shanghai)

Monthly Bulletin of the Ministry of Industry and Commerce

China Farmers' Bank Monthly: Investigations

Statistical Record of Political Achievements Under the Guidance of the Kuomintang

Fujian County Administration

Industrial Center

Weili

Journal of Economic and Commercial Studies (Xiamen)

Construction Weekly

(4)   Genealogies

Deng Clan Genealogy of the Nanyang Commandery (Front House, Dengwu Village), 1946.

Compiled by Descendants of the Siyilang Gong of Zhiping, Ninghua County, Fujian Province: *Liao Clan Genealogy of the Xikeng, Wuwei Commandery (Yuankeng, Shaoguang)*, 2019.

Lei Clan Genealogy of the Fengyi Commandery (Lianliping), 1926.

Chi Clan Genealogy of Baixi (Gaodi), the Sixth Revision in 1917, supplemented in the Seventh Revision in 1989.

The Concise Genealogy of the Hu Clan, Transcribed by Hu Youtao, 1988.

Compiled by the Compilation Council of the *Lan Clan Genealogy*, Descendants of Nianqi of the Jiaoli Branch, Lineage of Ancestor Rishan: *Lan Clan Genealogy*, 2016.

The Third Revised Genealogy of the Li Clan of Longxi Commandery, 1879.

The Sixth Revised Genealogy of the Fan Clan (Pengfang), 1993.

Peng Clan Genealogy of the Longxi Commandery (Pengfang), 1995.

Lai Clan Genealogy of the Songyang Commandery (Pengfang), 1995.

Lian Clan Genealogy of Shangdang Commandery (Pingpu), 1993.

The Genealogy of the Chen Clan of the Sanshisilang Gong in Shanhu, Shanghang, 1997.

The Fifth Revised Genealogy of the Lai Clan of Shangping, 1993.

Qiu Clan Genealogy of the Tianshui Commandery, 1993.

Zeng Clan Genealogy of Yunzhuang (Upper House—Line of Qilang, Tianshe), 1879.

The Sixth Revised Genealogy of the Lan Clan of Runan Commandery (Chushuling), 1993.

Xie Clan Genealogy of Dongjiafang (6th Revision, Nikeng), 1834.

Xie Clan Genealogy of Dongjiafang (7th Revision, Wubai Keng, Nikeng), 1866.

(5)   Collected Works and Notes

Qin Guan (Song Dynasty): *Huai Hai Ji* (Collected Works of Qin Guan), National Library of China Publishing House, 2018.

Su Yijian (Compiler, Song Dynasty), Zhu Xuebo (Collator and Annotator): *Book of Four Treasures of the Study*, Shanghai Bookstore Publishing House, 2015.

He Qiaoyuan (Ming Dynasty): *Min Shu (Book of Fujian)*, Fujian People's Publishing House, 1994.

Shen Bang (Ming Dynasty): *Wanshu Zaji* (Miscellaneous Records of the Wanping County), Beijing Publishing House, 1962.

Shen Bang (Ming Dynasty): *Taichang Xukao* (Further Studies of the Court of Ceremonies), Shanghai Ancient Books Publishing House, 2003.

Song Yingxing (Author, Ming Dynasty), Pan Jixing (Translator and Annotator): *Annotated Translation of Tiangong Kaiwu* (The Exploitation of the Works of Nature), Shanghai Ancient Books Publishing House, 2008.

Guo Bocang (Author, Qing Dynasty), Hu Fengze (Collator and Annotator): *Min Chan Lu Yi* (Record on Specialties of Natural Products of Fujian Province), Yuelu Publishing House, 1986.

Ye Changchi (Qing Dynasty): *Yuandulu Riji Chao* (Excerpts from the Diary of the Yuandu Studio), Shanghai Ancient Books Publishing House, 1995.

Yang Lan (Qing Dynasty): *Linting Huikao* (General Survey of Linting), Block-printed Edition of the 4th Year of Guangxu era, collected in the Library of Fujian Normal University.

Yuzhi Zengding Qingwenjian (Imperial Revised Manchu-Chinese Lexicon), Shanghai Ancient Books Publishing House, 2003.

(6)   Japanese Survey Materials

Masamuro Yukinori: "Inspection Record of the Papermaking Industry in the Qing Empire", Civil Affairs Department of the Governor-General of Taiwan, *Investigative Report on the Papermaking Industry of Taiwan*, with the "Inspection Record of the Papermaking Industry in the Qing Empire", 1909.

Compiled by the East Asia Common Culture Society: *Comprehensive Chorography of Chinese Provinces*, Volume 14: "Fujian Province", 1917.

Seki Takeshi (Compiler): *Papermaking Industry in China*, Tokyo: Seishindō, 1934.

(7) Compilations of Various Materials

Mo Guli: *The Native Papermaking Industry in Guangdong*, Lingnan Journal Press, Lingnan University, 1929.

Compiled by the Zhejiang Provincial Planning Council: *The Paper Industry in Zhejiang*, 1930.

Selected Historical Materials on the Economy of Revolutionary Base Areas, Vol. 1, Jiangxi People's Publishing House, 1986.

Compiled by the Jiangxi Provincial Department of Construction: *Paper*, 1939.

Compiled and Mimeographed by the Statistics Office of the Secretariat of Fujian Provincial Government: *The Paper Industry of Fujian* (Statistical Bulletin on the Fujian Investigation, No. 1), Mimeographed Edition, 1939.

Compiled by Lin Cunhe: *Papers of Fujian* (Fujian Survey and Statistics Series No. 4), Issued by the Statistics Office of Fujian Provincial Government, 1941.

Zhang Renjia: "The Paper of Hunan", in *Selected Historical Materials on the Economy of Republican-Era Hunan (Vol. 3)*, compiled by Zeng Saifeng and Cao Youpeng, Hunan People's Publishing House, 2009.

Compiled by the Southeast Changting Office of the Chinese Industrial Cooperatives Association: *Survey of Papermaking in Changting, Fujian* (1946), collected in Changting County Archives.

Compiled by the Central Archives and Fujian Provincial Archives: *Collected Revolutionary Historical Documents of Fujian: Soviet Documents* (1930), 1985.

(8) Others

Record Book of the Reconstruction of Lingguan Dadi, 1981, currently preserved in Shangjie of Zhiping, provided by Deng Xuanjiu of Dengwu.

Wutong Wuxian Lingguan Dadi Council of Zhiping She Ethnic Township: "Application for Religious Activity Venue Certification for 'Wutong Temple' and 'Fengtian Temple'", May 4, 2017, provided by Deng Xuanjiu of Dengwu.

Ten-Village Council: "Meeting Minutes", September 28, 2020, provided by Deng Xuanjiu of Dengwu.

Deng Xuanjiu: *The Origins of the Lan and Lei Surnames* (unpublished handwritten manuscrip).

2. Recent Scholarly Works

(1) Chinese Monographs

Ai Junchuan: *New Studies on the History of Chinese Printing*, Zhonghua Book Company, 2022.

Chen Xiejun (Chief Editor): *Zhi* (Paper), Peking University Press, 2012.

Deng Jinkun: *Liancheng Xuan Paper*, Economic Science Press, 2008.

Dai Jiazhang (Chief Editor): *A Concise History of Chinese Papermaking Technology*, China Light Industry Press, 1994.

Fang Houshu and Wei Yushan: *A General History of Publishing in China: Volume on the People's Republic of China*, China Book Publishing House, 2008.

Fang Xing (Chief Editor): *General History of Chinese Economy: Qing Dynasty Volume I*, Economic Daily Press, 2000.

Institute of Historical Geography, Fudan University: *Dictionary of Chinese Historical Place Names*, Jiangxi Education Press, 1986.

Fu Yiling: *Collected Essays on the Social and Economic History of the Ming and Qing Dynasties*, Zhonghua Book Company, 2008.

Gui Shuzhong: *Yukou Paper and Visual Records of Local Customs in Western Fujian: From Yukou Paper to Old Clan Genealogies*, Ethnic Publishing House, 2019.

Guo Tiemin and Lin Shanlang: *A History of the Development of China's Cooperative Economy*, Contemporary Economic Press, 1998.

Hong Guang and Huang Tianyou: *A Brief History of the Development of Papermaking in China*, China Light Industry Press, 1957.

Huang Majin (Chief Editor): *A History of Papermaking in Changting*, China Light Industry Press, 1992.

Kong Yongsong and Qiu Songqing: *Economic Construction in the Western Fujian Revolutionary Base Area*, Fujian People's Publishing House, 1981.

Lin Renfang (Chief Editor): *Guarding and Exploring: Selected Works of Directors of the Fourth Hakka Association in Western Fujian*, China Yanshi Press, 2017.

Liu Renqing: *A Historical Narrative of Ancient Chinese Papermaking*, China Light Industry Press, 1978.

Liu Renqing: *A Manual of Ancient Chinese Paper*, Intellectual Property Press, 2009.

Liu Renqing: *The Traditional Craft of Chinese Handmade Paper*, Intellectual Property Press, 2019.

Li Shuhua: "The Spread of Papermaking and the Discovery of Ancient Papers" (2nd Revised Edition, 1985), included in *Collected Essays on Historical Artifacts, vol. 1*, compiled and printed by the Chinese Series Editorial Committee of Taiwan Compilation and Translation Bureau.

Li Shaoqiang and Xu Jianqing: *General History of Chinese Handicraft Economy: The Ming and Qing Dynasties*, Fujian People's Publishing House, 2004.

Liu Shanyong: *Walking through Tingzhou*, Jiangxi Science and Technology Press, 2019.

Lai Yang'en: *Research on the Structure and Driving Forces of Rural Chinese Society*, Huazhong University of Science and Technology Press, 2014.

Liang Zhiping: *Saving the Nation and Saving the People: Industrial Wastewater Pollution and Social Responses in the Republic of China Period — A Study Based on the "Wastewater Incident" of Jiaxing Hefeng (Minfeng) Paper Mill*, Hefei University of Technology Press, 2017.

Pan Jixing: *A Draft History of Chinese Papermaking Technology*, Cultural Relics Press, 1979.

Pan Jixing: *History of Science and Technology in China*: Papermaking and Printing Volume, Science Press, 1998.

Pan Jixing: *A History of Papermaking in China*, Shanghai People's Publishing House, 2009.

Peng Nansheng et al.: *Perseverance and Change: A Study on the Rural Handicraft Economy in the Middle and Lower Reaches of the Yangtze River in the Republic of China Period*, Hubei People's Publishing House, 2014.

Tsuen-Hsuin Tsien (Author), Liu Zuwei (Translator): *History of Science and Technology in China: Paper and Printing*, Shanghai Ancient Books Publishing House, 1990.

Tsuen-Hsuin Tsien: *Ancient Chinese Books, Paper, Ink and Printing Technology*, National Library of China Press, 2002.

Sun Ji: *Material Culture in Ancient China*, Zhonghua Book Company, 2014.

Compilation Group of *A Brief History of the She People*: *A Brief History of the She People*, Fujian People's Publishing House, 1980.

Tang Shukun et al.: *Library of Chinese Handmade Paper*, University of Science and Technology of China Press, 2020.

Wang Juhua: *A Technological History of Ancient Chinese Papermaking Engineering*, Shanxi Education Press, 2006.

Wang Xi, Yang Xiaofo (Chief Editors): *Collected Works of Chen Hansheng*, Fudan University Press, 1985.

Wang Yuquan (Chief Editor): *General History of Chinese Economy: Ming Dynasty Volume*, Economic Daily Press, 2000.

Wu Jialing: *The Cultural Industry and Experiencing Aesthetics of Paper: Taking Chih-liao-wo, Guang Shin Jr Lyau, and the Suho Memorial Paper Culture Foundation As Examples*, Liwen Culture Publishing, 2015.

Xu Dixin and Wu Chengming (Chief Editors): *History of Chinese Capitalism, Volume 1: The Germination of Chinese Capitalism*, People's Publishing House, 2005.

Xu Mingqi: *A Study on the Origins of Ancient Chinese Papermaking Technology*, Shanghai Jiao Tong University Press, 1991.

Xu Xiaowang: *Socioeconomic Transformation in the Southeastern Mountain Regions during the Ming and Qing—Focusing on the Fujian-Zhejiang-Jiangxi Border*, Zhejiang and Jiangxi, China Literature and History Press, 2014.

Yang Yanjie: *Into the Hakka Historical Field: Local Society and Cultural Traditions*, Guangdong People's Publishing House, 2018.

Yu Ruxian: *A Study of Rural Informal Lending in Western Fujian from the Qing to the Republican Era*, Tianjin Ancient Books Press, 2010.

Compiled by the Institute of Economics, Shanghai Academy of Social Sciences and the Research Center for Light Industry Development Strategy: *History of Modern Chinese Papermaking Industry*, Shanghai Academy of Social Sciences Press, 1989.

The Party History Materials Collection and Research Committee of the CPC Longyan Prefectural Committee: *History of the Revolutionary Base Areas in Western Fujian*, Huaxia Publishing House, 1987.

Zhou Xuexiang: *Socioeconomic Changes in Hakka Border Areas of Fujian and Guangdong during the Ming and Qing Dynasties*, Fujian People's Publishing House, 2007.

(2) Chinese Translations of Foreign Monographs

Jacob Eyferth (Author), Han Wei (Translator): *Eating Rice from Bamboo Roots: The Social History of a Community of Handicraft Papermakers in Rural Sichuan, 1920-2000*, Jiangsu People's Publishing House, 2016.

Robert Darnton (Author), Ye Tong, Gu Hang (Translators): *The Business of Enlightenment: A Publishing History of the Encyclopédie, 1775–1800*, Joint Publishing Company, 2005.

Lothar Müller (Author), He Xiaoyi, Song Qiong (Translators): *White Magic: The Age of Paper*, Guangdong People's Publishing House, 2022.

Tsuen-Hsuin Tsien (Author), Xia Zukui (Translator): *Chinese Paper and Printing: A Cultural History*, Guangxi Normal University Press, 2004.

The Multigraph Collective (Author), Fu Li (Translator): *Interacting with Print: Elements of Reading in the Era of Print Saturation*, Beijing United Publishing Co., Ltd., 2021.

Alexander Monro (Author), Liao Yanbo (Translator): *The Paper Trail: An Unexpected History of a Revolutionary Invention*, Linking Publishing Co., Ltd., 2017.

Alexander Monro (Author), Shi Xiantao (Translator): *The Paper Trail: An Unexpected History of a Revolutionary Invention*, Joint Publishing Company, 2018.

Oodaira Kazue (Author), Kobayashi Kiyu (Photographer), Yang Ling (Translator): *The God of Paper*, Shanghai People's Publishing House, 2020.

(3) Theses & Journal Articles

Chen Gang: "Inoue Nobumasa and *The Papermaking Methods of the Qing Empire*," Historical Review, No. 3, 2012.

Chen Ling: "The Craft of Lianshi Paper and Its Scientific Significance", Journal of Dialectics of Nature, No. 3, 2021.

Chen Pan: "On Papermaking Derived from Ancient Technique of Flocculating Silk—With a Refutation of the Theory That 'Paper Before Cai Lun Referenced Silk Cloth", *Bulletin of the Academia Sinica*, Vol. 1, 1954.

Reprinted in Chen Pan's *Collected Essays on Traditional Learning and History (Volume 1)*, Shanghai Ancient Books Publishing House, 2010.

Chen Yimin: "Thread-Bound 'Large-Character Editions' in Tianjin", *Research on the History of Chinese Publishing*, No. 1, 2022.

Chen Zhiping and Zhuang Linlin: "Analysis of Misuses of Historical Materials in the Study of Chinese Paper History", *Researches in Chinese Economic History*, No. 3, 2021.

Fang Houshu: "Chronicle of the Publication of Mao Zedong's Works (1949–1982)", *Publishing Historical Materials*, No. 1, 2001.

Fu Kui: "Records of 'Paper' (Zhi) and 'Hun' in the Eastern Han Bamboo Slips Unearthed in Changsha and Related Issues", *Journal of Chinese Historical Studies*, No. 2, 2019.

Fu Qiankun: "The Flow of the White Paper: the Market, Power and Society of Heshui Area during the Period of Republic of China", Master's Thesis, Southwest University, 2017.

Gen Huo: "The Secret Printing of 'Large-Character Editions' in Shanghai", *Memories and Archives*, No. 4, 2015.

Guan Ming: "A Preliminary Study on the History of Papermaking Technology in Changting", Fujian, in Zhou Ji (ed.), *Studies on the History of Science and Technology in Fujian*, Xiamen University Press, 1990.

Han Haijiao: "Product Levels and Technological Evolution: The Development of Paper Industry in Modern China (1884–1937)", Master's Thesis, Central China Normal University, 2015.

Huang Shengzhang: "On the Time and Route of Chinese Paper and Papermaking Technology Spreading to the Indian Subcontinent", *Historical Research*, No. 1, 1980.

Jiang Boying: "An Investigation into the Land Revolution in the Western Fujian Soviet Area", *Fujian Party History Newsletter*, No. 11, 1985.

Ji Xianlin: "On the Time and Location of Chinese Paper and Papermaking Technology Introduced into India", *Historical Research*, No. 4, 1954.

Lao Gan: "On the Origin of Chinese Papermaking Technology", *Bulletin of the Institute of History and Philology, Academia Sinica*, Vol. 19, 1948.

Liao Han: "Small Commodity Economy in the Papermaking Industry of the Qing Dynasty—Centered on Yanshan County, Jiangxi Province", *Anhui History Studies*, No. 6, 2020.

Liao Han: "Social Mobility of Shed People in Jiangxi Province during the Qing Dynasty—Centered on Huangbi Village, Yanshan County", *The Qing History Journal*, No. 3, 2021.

Lin Renchuan: "Production and Distribution of Paper in Fujian During the Republic of China Period", *The Journal of Chinese Social and Economic History*, No. 1, 1989.

Liu Renqing: "On Lianshi Paper", *Paper and Paper Making*, No. 4, 2012.

Li Wei: "Distribution and Changes of the Papermaking Industry in China Throughout History", *Geographical Research*, No. 4, 1983.

Li Xiaocen: "The Route of Chinese Paper and Papermaking Technology Spreading to the Indian Subcontinent", *Historical Research*, No. 2, 1992.

Li Xiaocen: "Paper Pouring Method and Paper Dipping Method: Two Different Papermaking Technology Systems Preserved in Mainland China", *Journal of Dialectics of Nature*, No. 5, 2011.

Li Xiaocen and Wang Shan: "The Application of Ethnic Surveys in Archaeology—A Case Study of Handmade Papermaking by Ethnic Minorities", *Journal of Guangxi University for Nationalities (Philosophy and Social Sciences Edition)*, No. 2, 2018.

Li Xiaohang: "The Dissemination and Popularization of Mao Zedong's Poems during the 'Cultural Revolution'", *General Review of the Communist Party of China*, No. 6, 2013.

Li Zhi: "The Private Copying, Publication and Issuance of Mao Zedong's Poems", *Historical Studies of Modern Literature*, No. 3, 2006.

Lu Xuming: "Paper and War: Paper Shortage in Sichuan during the Full-Scale War of Resistance Against Japanese Aggression and Social Responses", *The Journal of Studies of China's Resistance War Against Japan*, No. 4, 2019.

Li Zhihui and Yu Shulan: "The Spread of Revolution in the Soviet Area and the Rise and Fall of the Paper Industry in Jiangxi and Fujian Provinces", *Journal of Jiangxi Normal University (Philosophy and Social Sciences Edition)*, No. 3, 2015.

Liu Wenzhong: "Tasks Assigned by the Central Government and the 'Large-Character Editions'", *Historical Studies of Modern Literature*, No. 3, 2016.

Pan Jixing: "On the Origin of Papermaking Technology—A Thematic Study on the History of Ancient Chinese Papermaking Technology", *Cultural Relics*, No. 9, 1973.

Pan Jixing: "A Perspective on the Origin of Papermaking Technology from New Archaeological Discoveries", *China Pulp & Paper*, No. 2, 1985.

Pan Jixing: "The Origin of Papermaking Based on Archaeological Discoveries and Laboratory Analysis of Unearthed Ancient Paper", *Chemistry*, No. 1, 1999.

Tsien Tsuen-hsuin: "New Evidence for the Origin of Paper: A Discussion on the Character 'Zhi' (Paper) in the Qin Bamboo Slips of the Warring States Period", *Documents*, No. 1, 2002.

Song Muwen: "The Evolution of National Press, Publication and Copyright Administration Institutions (Part 1)", *China Publishing Journal*, No. 10, 2005.

Su Junjie: "A Study on the Protection of the Making Craft of Lianshi Paper", Master's Thesis, Fudan University, 2008.

Tang Jiaqing: "The Revolutionary Struggle in Western Fujian Before and After the Long March of the Red Army and Its Historical Contributions", CPC History Research and Teaching, No. 6, 1986.

Tang Shukun and Zhu Yun: "Field Research on Handmade Papermaking in Southern China and the Construction of Its Industrial Ecosystem", *Southeast Culture*, No. 4, 2017.

Wang Anchun: "The Papermaking Industry in Guangxin Prefecture, Jiangxi Province during the Ming Dynasty", *Journal of Shangrao Normal University*, No. 4, 2001.

Wang Shiwen: "A Historical Review of Traditional Chinese Bamboo Paper and   an Exploration of Its Production Technical Characteristics", *Paper History Research*, No. 15, 1996.

Wen Xiaoxing: "The Changes and Protection of Traditional Handmade Papermaking Craftsmanship of the Hakka People—A Case Study of 'Hengjiang Heavy Paper' in Shicheng County", *Journal of Gannan Normal University*, No. 4, 2016.

Wen Xiaoxing: " 'Sacred Consumption' and Productive Protection of Intangible Cultural Heritage of Traditional Craftsmanship—A Case Study of 'Hengjiang Heavy Paper' Production in Shicheng County, Jiangxi Province", *Journal of Northwest Minzu University (Philosophy and Social Sciences Edition)*, No. 4, 2017.

Xu Jianqing: "The Papermaking Industry in the Qing Dynasty", *Journal of Chinese Historical Studies*, No. 3, 1997.

Xu Jing: "A Study on Handmade Papermaking and Hakka Ethnic Culture—Taking 'Liancheng Xuan Paper' as an Example", *Journal of Yunnan Minzu University*, No. 7, 2010.

Xiao Kunbing: "Paper Travels Across the World: A Social and Historical Narrative of Papermaking in Jiajiang (1644–1949)", Master's Thesis, Southwest Minzu University, 2007.

Yan Junru: "The Evolution of Traditional Papermaking Industry in Modern China—A Case Study of Jiajiang County, Sichuan Province", Master's Thesis, Sichuan University, 2005.

Yang Yong: "A Discussion on the Papermaking Industry in Jiangxi Province During the Republic of China Period", *Journal of Jiangxi Normal University (Philosophy and Social Sciences Edition)*, No. 3, 2001.

Zou Chunwen: "A Study on Lianshi Paper in Liancheng County", Master's Thesis, Fujian Normal University, 2016.

Zhu Xia and Li Xiaocen: "Investigation and Research on Papermaking Technology of Ethnic Minorities in Yunnan Province", *Ethno-National Studies*, No. 1, 1999.

Glossary

CN	EN
《柏溪池氏家谱》	*Chi Clan Genealogy of Baixi*
《陈留郡闽赣楚建宁谢氏宗谱》	*Xie Clan Genealogy of Chenliu Commandery (Fujian, Jiangxi, Hubei, Jianning)*
《陈氏三十四郎公一脉宗谱》	*The Genealogy of the Chen Clan Descended from the Sanshisilang Gong*
《出版史料》	Publication Archives
《出口土纸手册》	*Handbook for Export Handmade Paper*
《党史博览》	General Review of the Communist Party of China
《党史资料与研究》	*Party History Data and Research*
《档案春秋》	Memories and Archives
《董家坊谢氏宗谱》	*Xie Clan Genealogy of Dongjiafang*
《董家坊谢氏宗谱》	*Xie Clan Genealogy of Dongjiafang*
《范氏六修族谱》	*The Sixth Revised Genealogy of the Fan Clan*
《冯翊郡雷氏族谱》	*Lei Clan Genealogy of the Fengyi Commandery*
《扶风郡马氏九修族谱》	*The Ninth Revised Genealogy of the Ma Clan of Fufeng Commandery*
《福建党史通讯》	*Fujian Party History Newsletter*
《福建科学技术史研究》	*Research on the History of Science and Technology in Fujian*

CN	EN
《福建省宁化县土产日杂公司关于转发省土产公司（75）闽商土司日使字第 117 号文的通知》	Notice of the Ninghua County Native Products and Sundries Company Regarding the Forwarding of Document No. 117 from the Provincial Native Products Company (Commercial-Native Products-Sundries-1975)
《福建省土纸规格质量标准》	Standards for the Specifications and Quality of Handmade Paper in Fujian Province
《福建省长汀县纸商业同业公会会员名册》	The Membership List of Paper Industry Trade Guild, Changting County, Fujian Province
《福建省长汀县纸商业同业公会章程》	*The Articles of Association of the Changting County Paper Industry Trade Guild, Fujian Province*
《福建长汀造纸调查》	*Survey of Papermaking in Changting, Fujian*
《福建长汀造纸调查》	*Survey of Papermaking in Changting, Fujian*
《福建之纸》	*Papers of Fujian*
《福建之纸业》	*The Paper Industry of Fujian*
《高平郡范氏族谱》	*Fan Clan Genealogy of the Gaoping Commandery*
《革命根据地经济史料选编》	*Selected Historical Materials on the Economy of Revolutionary Base Areas*
《合作社讲授大纲》	*A Teaching Outline on Cooperatives*
《合作社条例》	*the Cooperative Regulations*
《胡氏简易族谱》	*The Concise Genealogy of the Hu Clan*
《淮海集》	Huai Hai Ji, (淮海集, Collected Works of Qin Guan)

CN	EN
《赖氏敦伦堂九修谱》	*The Ninth Revision of the Lai Clan Genealogy, Hall of Respecting Ethics*
《蓝氏族谱》	*Lan Clan Genealogy*
《临汀汇考》	Linting Huikao (临汀汇考, General Survey of Linting)
《临汀志》	*The Chorography of Linting*
《陇西郡李氏族谱》	*Li Clan Genealogy of the Longxi Commandery*
《陇西郡彭氏家谱》	*Peng Clan Genealogy of the Longxi Commandery*
《陇西李氏三修族谱》	*The Third Revised Genealogy of the Li Clan of Longxi Commandery*
《鲁国曾氏族谱》	*Zeng Clan Genealogy of the State of Lu*
《毛泽东选集》	*Selected Works of Mao Zedong*
《毛主席诗词》	Chairman Mao's Poetry
《闽产录异》	Min Chan Lu Yi (闽产录异, Record on Specialties of Natural Products of Fujian Province)
《闽书》	*Min Shu* (闽书, Book of Fujian)
《闽西革命根据地史》	History of the Revolutionary Base Areas in Western Fujian
《闽西苏区土地革命之考察》	An Investigation into the Land Revolution in the Soviet Areas of Western Fujian
《南阳郡邓氏族谱》	*Deng Clan Genealogy of the Nanyang Commandery*
《南洋商报》	*Nanyang Commercial Daily*
《宁化方志通讯》	*Ninghua Local Chronicles Newsletter*
《宁化文史资料》	*Ninghua Historical and Cultural Materials*
《宁化县地名录》	*Toponymic Directory of Ninghua County*

CN	EN
《宁化县志》	*Chorography of Ninghua County*
《彭城刘氏族谱》	*Liu Clan Genealogy of Pengcheng*
《清國製纸業地視察録》	Inspection Record of the Papermaking Industry in the Qing Empire
《清河郡张氏十四修族谱》	*The Fourteenth Revised Genealogy of the Zhang Clan of Qinghe Commandery*
《清至民国闽西乡村民间借贷研究》	*A Study of Rural Informal Lending in Western Fujian from the Qing to the Republican Era*
《仁化县志》	*Chorography of Renhua County*
《汝南蓝氏六修族谱》	*The Sixth Revised Genealogy of the Lan Clan of Runan Commandery*
《山湖六地记》	Record of the Six Lands by the Mountain and Lake
《上党郡连氏族谱》	*Lian Clan Genealogy of Shangdang Commandery*
《上杭珊瑚陈氏三十四郎公宗谱》	*The Genealogy of the Chen Clan of the Sanshisilang Gong in Shanhu, Shanghang*
《上坪赖氏五修族谱》	*The Fifth Revised Genealogy of the Lai Clan of Shangping*
《畲族简史》	*A Brief History of the She People*
《申报》	Shen Bao
《实业部月刊》	*Monthly Bulletin of the Ministry of Industry and Commerce*
《四库全书》	Siku Quanshu (四库全书, Complete Library of the Four Treasuries)
《松阳赖氏族谱》	*Lai Clan Genealogy of the Songyang Commandery*
《太常续考》	*Taichang Xukao* (太常续考, Further Studies of the Court of Ceremonies)
《太平寰宇记》	*Taiping Huanyu Ji* (太平寰宇记, Universal Geography of the Taiping Era)

CN	EN
《天工开物》	*Tiangong Kaiwu* (天工开物, The Exploitation of the Works of Nature)
《天工开物译注》	*Annotated Translation of Tiangong Kaiwu*
《天水郡丘氏族谱》	*Qiu Clan Genealogy of the Tianshui Commandery*
《宛署杂记》	*Wanshu Zaji* (宛署杂记, Miscellaneous Records of the Wanping County)
《文房四谱》	*Book of Four Treasures of the Study*
《文史资料选辑》	*Selected Historical and Cultural Materials*
《武威郡茜坑廖氏族谱（圆坑、绍光）》	*Liao Clan Genealogy of the Xikeng, Wuwei Commandery (Yuankeng, Shaoguang)*
《新文学史料》	Historical Studies of Modern Literature
《新修大埔县志》	Revised Chorography of Dapu County
《以竹为生：一个四川手工造纸村的20世纪社会史》	*Eating Rice from Bamboo Roots: The Social History of a Community of Handicraft Papermakers in Rural Sichuan, 1920-2000*
《御制增订清文鉴》	*Imperial Revised Manchu–Chinese Lexicon*
《缘督庐日记钞》	*Yuandulu Riji Chao* (缘督庐日记钞, Excerpts from the Diary of the Yuandu Studio)
《云庄曾氏族谱》	*Zeng Clan Genealogy of Yunzhuang*
《长汀文史资料》	Changting Historical and Cultural Materials
《长汀县志》	*Chorography of Changting County*
《长汀造纸概况》	Overview of Papermaking in Changting
《长汀纸史》	*A History of Papermaking in Changting*
《支那省别全誌》	*Comprehensive Chorography of Chinese Provinces*

CN	EN
《纸的大历史》	*The Paper Trail: An Unexpected History of a Revolutionary Invention*
《纸的文化产业与体验价值——以纸寮窝、广兴纸寮、树火纸文化基金会为例》	*The Cultural Industry and Experiencing Aesthetics of Paper: Taking Chih-liao-wo, Guang Shin Jr Lyau, and the Suho Memorial Paper Culture Foundation As Examples*
《纸的文化史》	*White Magic: The Age of Paper*
《纸史研究》	*Research on the History of Paper*
《纸影寻踪：旷世发明的传奇之旅》	*The Paper Trail: An Unexpected History of a Revolutionary Invention*
《治平公社玉扣纸生产成本调查材料》	*Materials from the Zhiping Commune's Yukou Paper Production Cost Investigation*
《治平公社玉扣纸生产成本价格的情况调查及调价意见》	A Survey of Production Costs and Pricing for Yukou Paper in Zhiping Commune
《中国出版史研究》	Research on the History of Publishing in China
《中国古代造纸工程技术史》	*A Technological History of Ancient Chinese Papermaking Engineering*
《中国古纸谱》	*A Manual of Ancient Chinese Paper*
《中国历史地名词典》	*Dictionary of Chinese Historical Place Names*
《中国农村社会的结构与原动力研究》	*Research on the Structure and Driving Forces of Rural Chinese Society*
《中国造纸技术简史》	*A Concise History of Chinese Papermaking Technology*

CN	EN
《中国造纸技术史稿》	*A Draft History of Chinese Papermaking Technology*
《中国造纸史》	*A History of Papermaking in China*
《重建灵官大帝序记簿》	Record Book of the Reconstruction of Lingguan Dadi
熬蓝	Extracting the lan liquid
北京印刷一厂	Beijing First Printing Plant
衬纸	lining page
祠堂	ancestral hall
粗料纸（草纸）	coarse straw paper
打醮	jiao ritual
东亚同文会	East Asia Common Culture Society (東亜同文会)
非遗传承人	intangible cultural heritage inheritors
副号纸	Second Class (fuhao), fuhao paper
赣江	Gan River
割据势力	regional separatist forces
工业合作社	industrial cooperatives
供销社	supply and marketing cooperatives
関彪 関彪	Seki Takeshi
红色政权的宣传教育	revolutionary education in political philosophy of the Red political power
黄麻	jute
会馆	Guild Hall
火墙	heated walls
井上陈政 井上陳政	Inoue Nobumasa
扛尾	end lifter
扛尾	lifting bamboo screens
抗日战争	the War of Resistance against Japanese Aggression
刻本	block-printed
客家	Hakka people

CN	EN
里屋	Rear House
连史纸	lianshi paper (refined durable paper)未定
灵官大帝理事会	Lingguan Dadi Council
罗墩	ancient-tree-protecting Luodun earthen mounds
麻纸	hemp paper
毛边纸	maobian paper (thin paper)未定
内阁中书	Neige Zhongshu (Secretary in the Grand Secretariat)
宁化县供销合作社联合社	Ninghua County Supply and Marketing Cooperative Union
宁化治平造纸文化遗址群	Ninghua Zhiping Papermaking Cultural Heritage Site Group
农合	Rural Cooperative
农合委	Rural Cooperative Committee
农会	Peasants' Association
皮纸	bast paper
茜坑	Xikeng
汝南	Runan Commandery
三宝佛	the Sakyamuni Buddha, the Bhaisajyaguru Buddha and the Amitabha Buddha
三号纸	Third Class
社会主义改造	socialist remolding
神主牌	ancestral spirit tablet
生产大队	production brigades
生料法	raw material method
生料制浆法	raw material pulping method
省计委/计划委员会	Provincial Planning Commission
十乡轮祀灵官大帝仪式	Ten-Village Rotating Worship of Lingguan Dadi
实业部统计处	Statistical Office of the Ministry of Industry and Commerce
书脊	spine

CN	EN
熟料法	cooked material method
苏区	Soviet area
藤纸	rattan paper
汀江	Ting River
同业公会（民国时期称法，更规范）	Trade Guild
同业组织（统称）	Trade association
统购统销	state monopoly for purchasing and marketing
外屋	Front House
文物出版社	Cultural Relics Press
五口通商	opening of five treaty ports for foreign trade
锡纸冥边	tinfoil spirit money
洗焙把	Xibeiba (ash-cleaning brush)
线装	thread-bound
行会（古代到近代）	Guild
行佣	brokerage fee
宣纸	xuan paper (rice paper)
一担	one dan
一刀	one dao
一挑	one load
玉扣纸	Yukou paper
玉扣纸副号	The Second Grade Yukou paper
玉扣纸正三号	Prime Third Grade Yukou paper
预付款	advance payment
长汀县工业生产合作社联合社	the Changting Industrial Cooperative Federation
长汀县纸商业同业公会	Changting Paper Industry Trade Guild
长汀纸业工合	the Industrial Cooperatives of Changting Paper Industry

CN	EN
真室幸教 真室幸教	Masamuro Yukinori 未定
正号纸	First Class (zhenghao), zhenghao paper
纸槽户	paper workshop owners
纸浆	pulp
纸史	the history of paper
纸行	paper firms
纸药	sizing agents
纸业工会	Paper Workers' Union
纸业史	the history of papermaking indusctry
中共龙岩地委党史资料征集研究委员会	The Party History Materials Collection and Research Committee of the CPC Longyan Prefectural Committee
中共治平公社委员会	Communist Party Committee of Zhiping Commune
中国工业合作协会	Chinese Industrial Cooperatives
中国工业合作协会东南区长汀办事处	Southeast Changting Office of the Chinese Industrial Cooperatives Association
中国工业合作协会汀东南区办事处	Southeast Changting Office of the Chinese Industrial Cooperatives Association
中国土产公司	China Native Products Company
重松义则 重松義則	Shigematsu Yoshinori
竹簧	inner bamboo membrane
竹片木简	bamboo and wood slips
竹穰	bamboo stalks
竹纸	bamboo paper
主事	zhushi (Section Chief)
奏折	memorials to the throne